W9-BYP-108

STREET SMARTS, BOOK SMARTS

Personal Finance through Facts, Fiction, and Conversation

FOURTH EDITION

Sugato Chakravarty

Copley Custom Textbooks

An imprint of XanEdu Custom Publishing

Copyright © 2009 by FinTech Training, LLC. All rights reserved
Printed in the United States of America

ISBN 13: 978-1-58152-667-7
ISBN 10: 1-58152-667-9

No part of this book may be reproduced in any manner without permission in writing from the publisher.

Copley Custom Textbooks
An imprint of XanEdu Custom Publishing
138 Great Road
Acton, Massachusetts 01720
800.562.2147

Contents

Section A: Investments

Section C: Insurance

Section D: Retirement

A Guide to Understanding Time Value of Money

Specific Applications of Annuities in the Various Areas of Personal Finance   343

Foreword

Recent world events have combined to give a new urgency to financial literacy in general and personal finance in particular. The sub-prime mortgage market collapsed and brought down with it the mortgage market as a whole. Banks went into their holes, much like Punxsutawney Phil seeing his shadow, and refused to lend money to anyone. It was then we realized that credit is the glue that holds the world's financial markets together. The largest financial services companies started falling like dominoes because they had bet the firm on a little understood derivative product called credit default swaps to protect their interests but which had little regulation, and when it came time to collect on these investments there was no one on the other side to honor them. In short, it was a big mess! That said, it is what it is and we are stuck in a big mess holding the bag and many trillions of dollars of national debt. And there is no end in sight. No one really knows how long or how deep we will be in this financial morass and it is in our collective interest to know as much as possible about personal finance issues so we can make reasonably educated decisions and even know what questions to ask of a financial professional. This book is an attempt to reach that goal with as little math as possible.

As the Internet becomes ever more accessible and to an increasingly younger generation of users, the question becomes how we can optimally use this tool for education and to improve the quality of our lives and of those we love. Commercials peddling financial products of all stripes are increasingly sophisticated requiring a certain degree of skepticism and knowledge to be able to separate the wheat from the chaff. The world is full of hucksters who come in all stripes and family backgrounds who are able to separate investors from their money by using simple and time tested schemes like those invented by Charles Ponzi in the first part of the twentieth century. We are left scratching our collective heads trying to figure out how to make sense of it all. This book is a humble attempt to accomplish just that—to provide some simple and easy to apply tools to cut through the clutter of information that buffets every waking moment of our lives.

I've been asked why I wrote this book. When I started teaching Personal Finance over ten years ago, I was disappointed with the textbooks that were available. There was a lot of information but the presentation made students (and me) tune out very quickly. While the books were great cures for insomnia, I was not sure if much Personal Finance learning was taking place. Also, being a researcher myself, I wanted to see a textbook bring cutting-edge research findings to students so they could see the practical relevance of such research to their lives. None of the textbooks I used had such material. The authors were still using the eighties model to write their books and they were all about practice without the appropriate theoretical background. There was a lot of support material for professors teaching from those books which made my life easier but I felt the students were being short-changed by the information they were getting—or, more importantly, what they were not getting. I then decided to try and write one myself.

My goal was to write a nontraditional textbook in the spirit of a self-help manual and the entertainment value of a storybook. A cross between a traditional textbook and Wayne Dyer or Tony Robbins with a dash of Harry Potter (I hoped!). It was going to be a sedan with the spirit of a mustang! Initially I put some notes together, mixed it up with some hard Personal Finance material, and flavored the material with some stories and anecdotes I had heard growing up. That was the beginning about ten years ago.

Those early experiments had mixed success and I learned what worked and what bombed. And just because I thought something was funny or entertaining did not necessarily make it so. Through numerous revisions and rearrangement of the material and infusion of new material, the current form of the book slowly took shape. Through all the iterations and the rewrites the original spirit of the book— that of a combined textbook/self-help manual with attitude that is designed to entertain and educate—lives on. Along the way, many colleagues, friends, and students were kind enough to read the manuscript and share their opinions with me— the good, the bad, and the ugly. Professor Christine Jiang from the University of Memphis, and Professor Amber Anand from Syracuse University deserve special thanks in that regard.

Over the years, many generations of undergraduate and graduate students have also been reading and sharing their thoughts with me and the book is better as a result. Among them, Adam Hagen and Rob Scherer have provided important feedback that has improved the exposition. Kent Brewster was instrumental in the book's current structure. Lucy Miskin and her team at Copley Custom Textbooks have done a wonderful job of bringing the manuscript to life. In particular, Sandy Hayes, the copy editor, and Susan Myrick, who handled the formatting of the book. Special thanks go to Atul Todi for his wonderful cover design.

At the end of the day, this is a labor of love. There is no professional benefit for me other than the childlike delight in communicating material I love in a way that people of all ages can understand easily. The goal, through all these years, is still to educate and entertain all ages regardless of educational background. If some of you get pleasure out of reading the book and learn something from it, I will have considered my experiment a success.

Go forth and prosper!

Sugato Chakravarty
West Lafayette, Indiana

Acknowledgments

To my father, Ardhendu, who taught me to dream big; to my mother, Chua, who gave me my pragmatism; to my dogs, Matthew and Baby, who have taught me unconditional love; and to my wife, Ajita, who completes me.

Pre-course Questionnaire

Pre-course Questionnaire

Name: _____

Age: _____ Gender: M / F

Major: _____

School/College: _____

Class: _____

Home State: _____

General Questions

1. Which describes you best?
   a. Laid back
   b. Accommodating
   c. Goal-oriented
   d. Driven
   e. Get out of my way!

2. I believe I am a risk taker.
   a. Strongly disagree
   b. Disagree
   c. Could go either way
   d. Agree
   e. Strongly agree

3. I am very comfortable allowing others to run my life.
   a. Strongly disagree
   b. Disagree
   c. Could go either way
   d. Agree
   e. Strongly agree

4. Which of the following activities gives you most pleasure?
   a. Working on your tan
   b. Working on your wardrobe
   c. Working on your mind by solving puzzles and brain teasers
   d. Working on your body in the gym
   e. Sleeping

5. What type of books do you read for pleasure?
   a. Romance novels
   b. Strictly nonfiction
   c. Suspense/thriller
   d. Science fiction/comics
   e. "Get rich quick" books
   f. Reading is for the birds.

6. I love the uncertainty of jumping into any new experience.
   a. Strongly disagree
   b. Disagree
   c. Could go either way
   d. Agree
   e. Strongly agree

7. I hate uncertainties with any aspect of my life. I love for everything to be pre-dictable.
   a. Strongly disagree
   b. Disagree
   c. Could go either way
   d. Agree
   e. Strongly agree

8. I get less pleasure from winning $100 relative to the pain I feel when I lose $100.
   a. Strongly disagree
   b. Disagree
   c. Could go either way
   d. Agree
   e. Strongly agree

Course Specific Questions

9. I believe investing is only for those with lots of money.
   a. Strongly disagree
   b. Disagree
   c. Could go either way
   d. Agree
   e. Strongly agree

10. Time-value-of-money (TVM) concepts are a total waste of my time. I know I will never use them in my life.
    a. Strongly disagree
    b. Disagree
    c. Could go either way
    d. Agree
    e. Strongly agree

11. I know how to pick stocks/mutual funds.
    a. Strongly disagree
    b. Disagree
    c. Could go either way
    d. Agree
    e. Strongly agree

12. I believe that mutual funds are the only way to invest—individual stocks are for the professional investors only.
    a. Strongly disagree
    b. Disagree
    c. Could go either way
    d. Agree
    e. Strongly agree

13. I know what an ETF is.
    a. Strongly disagree
    b. Disagree
    c. Could go either way
    d. Agree
    e. Strongly agree

14. I am not in favor of making investment decisions myself. In the future, I plan to hire professional financial planners to make those decisions on my behalf.
    a. Strongly disagree
    b. Disagree
    c. Could go either way
    d. Agree
    e. Strongly agree

15. Only qualified professionals should be making investing decisions—not individuals like me.
    a. Strongly disagree
    b. Disagree
    c. Could go either way
    d. Agree
    e. Strongly agree

16. Credit cards are wonderful things. I wish I had more of them.
    a. Strongly disagree
    b. Disagree
    c. Could go either way
    d. Agree
    e. Strongly agree

17. Checking my credit report is a waste of my time.
    a. Strongly disagree
    b. Disagree
    c. Could go either way
    d. Agree
    e. Strongly agree

18. I know all there is to know about insurance. This class cannot teach me anything new.
    a. Strongly disagree
    b. Disagree
    c. Could go either way
    d. Agree
    e. Strongly agree

19. I know what a Roth IRA is.
    a. Strongly disagree
    b. Disagree
    c. could go either way
    d. Agree
    e. Strongly agree

20. I believe that I am too young to think about planning for retirement. I will consider it when I am older and have money to spare.
    a. Strongly disagree
    b. Disagree
    c. Could go either way
    d. Agree
    e. Strongly agree

Section A: Investments

1

Why Study Personal Finance?

Success is where preparation and opportunity meet.
—Bobby Unser

There are scholars who argue that studying personal finance or anything related to financial literacy is a waste of time. Their arguments are based on variations of the following refrain: The difference between the knowledge, comprehension, and the skills of most American adults and those needed to understand the sophisticated markets cannot be bridged by financial literacy education. For instance, a reading assessment of credit card holder agreements found that information regarding grace periods, balance computation methods, and payment allocation methods was written at a fifteenth grade or higher level while about half of the adults in the U.S. cannot read beyond the eighth grade level. A 2006 survey found that over 80 percent of the Baby Boomers approaching retirement could not correctly answer the following question: "You have $200 in a savings account that earns 10 percent interest per year. How much would you have in the account at the end of two years?"

The critics of financial literacy education further argue that evaluating financial courses of action often requires multiplication, division, and compounding and amortization calculations involving annuity type cash flows. Consumers need to understand these operations in order to understand which calculations to perform. And most adults have no idea about future value calculations involving either single sums or annuities. At the end of the day, the financial services industry will always be one step ahead of the customers it serves and the deck will always be stacked in their favor. Like gambling in a Las Vegas casino, the odds are always in favor of the House. In the long run you will give back your money and probably more. Furthermore, the critics say that the very fact that financial services companies pay for and finance a lot of this push to educate consumers is, in itself, proof of the fact that they don't work. After all, if we all became educated consumers then these companies would lose money. Credit card companies wouldn't be able gouge consumers for the late fees and outrageous fines because we will know how to avoid those charges to begin with.

You see the cynical logic at work here? Picture this: In some boardroom in New York City, some senior bank executives are plotting away in the dead of night. Pizza boxes are everywhere as are empty Coke cans. Some are smoking away at their Marlboro Lights. The purpose: to come up with innovative strategies to ensure profits while simultaneously appearing to be sympathetic and helpful to the masses.

The night has been long and hundreds of balled up sheets of paper are strewn around the conference room floor. Finally, Bill pipes up: "I think I have it!" He seems excited as he rubs his tired, slightly red and sleep-deprived eyes. "Here's how we approach this: We start to fund various financial literacy initiatives across the country. I will have a chat with legal tomorrow and we might be able to write some of this expenditure off. But the purpose of this initiative will be to educate consumers and thereby we will create a lot of goodwill. Our customers will love us because they will see us as the good guys . . . except . . . ," and here Bill's voice drops. He is going to deliver the punch line. "Except we know that these initiatives don't work. They are useless. So, our customers will not really learn anything and we will continue to make money off them while creating a good buzz around our initiatives!" Bill stops and looked around. "What do you think about that, huh?" The rest of the room is hushed. Finally, Megan breaks the silence. "It's absolutely brilliant, Bill! We pretend we care except we don't and we continue to clear our profit margins and the American public has no clue what it is we are unleashing on them!" The rest of the room goes crazy and the great financial literacy program funded by the financial services industry is born. I just have one question. Does this seem like a realistic scenario to you? Not to me.

So, let's get back to the question. We should study personal finance not for everyone to become geniuses overnight and outwit the juggernaut of the financial services industry. That is not realistic. What is realistic, however, is the goal of knowing enough to know when someone is feeding us a line and to know enough to ask the hard questions. It's not like we have to do the work ourselves. We have to ask the right questions so the industry itself has to work hard to provide answers we can all understand and appreciate. We don't always have to rise up to their level. We have to drag them down and meet them halfway. We have to understand the basics of discounting, compounding, valuations and interest rate calculations. We have to understand the rudiments of stocks, bonds and mutual funds. We have to understand the basics of risk and insurance pricing so we can be aware of how the premiums we are paying are being calculated. We have to understand the basics of risk and return and how to invest our hard-earned dollars in ways that will generate maximum wealth for us in our golden years. I don't know about the cynics who are sure all this is a waste of time and we should really do nothing. This is the same argument we are now hearing regarding the huge stimulus package that was passed in Congress. Doing nothing is never an option. We have to try to do something, including educating ourselves and attempting to meet the brains of the industry half way. It seems to me that is the least we can do as a nation.

The worst financial crisis to hit us since the Great Depression of the 1930s is right here and we cannot sit still and be steamrolled. Nowhere in our history in the last seventy-five years has it been more important for us to understand the basics of the financial products we deal with either directly or indirectly than it is today. In some sense it is even more important than in the thirties because of the complexity of the whole picture. While the cynics say: Give up, I say: Let's educate ourselves in the ways of finance so we can ask the right questions. But before we start with financial literacy, let's take a moment and examine the evolution of the first global financial crisis of the twenty-first century. Examining why we are where we are today is important because there are lessons to be learned in all this. Examining how disparate pieces came together in such a devastating manner to create the perfect financial storm is a lesson in itself; one that will be debated for centuries to come. We are fortunate, in a sense, to be living through history in the making. Long after we are gone, these times will be analyzed by future historians, policy makers, and economists. We might as well get a head start.

Evolution of the Financial Crisis

Philosophically, it is important to examine how the current financial crisis evolved and what the root circumstances were before addressing the problem and what effect various actions on the part of the government might or might not have. It is indeed ironic that some of the same mechanisms that fuel an economy's growth at one point in time turn out to be the very same mechanisms that contribute to its decline at a different point in time, which is essentially where we are today. Over the last decade we saw a few things happen, which when considered in isolation, would be considered innocuous and even hugely beneficial to the economy. Much like individual medications that are so beneficial in fighting diseases, in combination they may interact to quietly create the perfect storm—and the financial catastrophe that we are experiencing is the result of an interaction of circumstances in the financial sector.

Over the last decade, the world saw tremendous strides taken to ensure that the smallest of investors had essentially the same tools that the largest Wall Street bankers had. This empowerment and the democratization of the investment landscape meant that millions of people were now able to freely jump in and out of markets at the drop of a hat. With this whole new client pool, Wall Street saw a huge opportunity and went looking at the nation's top business schools, hiring hundreds of PhDs in mathematics and business who could combine finance with high speed computing and create increasingly complex financial derivative products that not a lot of people understood. Once the products were created with an incomplete understanding of the risks involved, the marketing machinery went to work, convincing millions of new investors, who were flush with newfound power and itching to jump in the market, what wonderful investment opportunities these products represented. It was the classic case of the "blind leading the blind."

While Wall Street's marketing machinery was roping in thousands of new investors into their esoteric investment products, their lobbyists were hard at work in Washington convincing the nation's lawmakers to ease up on the regulations so the U.S. investment companies could compete on the global stage and U.S.'s international image could improve. The lawmakers did not see any problem with this line of thinking and started tinkering with policies that had been in place for many decades, in order to further empower these Wall Street giants.

So it happened that at the end of the twentieth century and the beginning of the twenty-first, certain policy shifts occurred at the federal level that are important contributors to today's events. The Gramm-Leach-Bliley Act and the Commodities and Modernization Act were passed in 1999 and 2001, respectively. What this legislations accomplished was essentially to rescind the same banking regulations that were put in place by the Glass Steagall Act (and subsequently by the Bank Holding Company Act of 1956). These Acts established the Federal Deposit Insurance Corporation and also placed barriers between commercial banks and investment banks. This legislation came in the wake of the 1929 stock market crash and was instituted in 1933. The Gramm-Leach-Bliley Act of 1999 essentially removed the barriers and allowed commercial banks to operate as investment banks. The justification for this was to place U.S. banks in a stronger position to compete internationally with banks from other countries that were not so constrained.

With the new administration in 2000, the Federal National Mortgage Association (also known as Fannie May) and the Federal Home Loan Mortgage Corporation (also known as Freddie Mac) were given the mission to increase home ownership in the U.S. At some point, this mandate to increase home ownership was interpreted to mean that the goal should be reached regardless of whether home buyers could afford to sustain home ownership. Such unwise lending required a mechanism to insure against default and the so-called Credit Default Swap (CDS) was born. Initially, the CDS contracts were meant to apply to municipal bonds, corporate debt, and mortgage securities and were sold by banks, hedge funds, and other institutions. However, in the past decade these CDS contracts expanded into structured finance contracts containing pools of mortgages and, more importantly, these pools contained subprime borrowers who were increasingly getting loans through the Freddie Mac and Fannie May programs. In isolation, CDS is an insurance contract

Credit Default Swaps

These insurance-like contracts exploded on the world stage around the middle of 2008 when it was revealed for the first time to a largely unsuspecting world that these little known products were behind much of the global meltdown. At its height in the middle of 2007, the CDS market was worth almost $50 trillion—many times the worth of the U.S. stock markets. CDS contracts are insurance contracts that promise to cover the losses of the underlying financial products in the event of a default. So far so good, and that is precisely what any insurance product—like homeowners' insurance, for example—would do. CDS contracts were designed to insure municipal bonds, corporate bonds, and mortgage securities and were sold by banks and hedge funds. The buyer of a CDS contract would pay premiums with the knowledge that if something bad happened to his financial product the seller of the CDS would reimburse him his losses—still sounding exactly like any standard insurance product that you and I deal with in our daily lives.

The problem, however, was that while standard banks and standard insurance companies (you know the ones that ask us if we are in good hands or the banks that ask us to open savings and checking accounts) are heavily regulated, the CDS market was not. Consequently, CDS contracts could be traded or swapped in secondary markets just like one would with stocks and bonds. Since the market was not regulated there was no one at the controls to ensure that the buyers of these contracts had the financial capability to honor them in the event of default of the underlying security that the particular CDS was meant to insure.

taken out by banks to protect their loans against default, much like an individual or family would secure a homeowner's insurance policy to protect their investment in a home. However, by referring to them as swaps (and not insurance) they became classified as investment products rather than insurance products. This allowed the CDS industry to avoid the regulation and scrutiny that applies to the insurance industry and rendered CDS totally outside the purview of any regulatory mechanism.

The ingredients for an explosion of classic proportions were all in place by early 2005. All that was needed now was a spark to set it off. That spark came in the form of a downturn of the housing market and the resulting wave of defaults among subprime borrowers that caused the holders (all major banks) of trillions of dollars in CDS contracts to exercise their option to trigger the insurance policies. Unfortunately, there was no one on the other side of the relationship to honor them because, thanks to deregulation, the CDS had been sold, resold again many times over by banks to investors across the globe who had no interest in the original contracts and had simply bet on them much like a gambler might bet on the outcome of a sports competition. To these speculators, the CDS was purely a speculative position of high risk. Defaults in the CDS market led very quickly to the great uncertainty concerning the financial positions of major banks that held these mortgage backed securities. It was difficult for the banks themselves to determine the exact value of their CDS portfolio, not to mention the difficulty faced by potential creditors in evaluating the ability of these banks to repay loans.

Thus, the great risk to the economy was that this uncertainty reduced and threatened to halt the willingness of banks to lend to one another, creating a liquidity crisis in financial markets. In such a situation, there is great potential that businesses will find it impossible to secure operating capital and will be forced to shut down. We have seen the first signs of borrowing limits, and if this kind of a crisis were to truly take hold, the result would be an economy that would come to a screeching halt and create a panic in the banking sector. The economy would unquestionably be careening toward a very severe recession or even depression. Recent Congressional action was targeted toward loosening the lending between banks and providing liquidity to capital markets. What has not happened to date is a re-evaluation of regulations such as the Glass Steagall Act and the Gramm-Leach-Bliley Act to close loopholes in the regulation of banking and investment activities.

The Japanese experience of the nineties provides one final note of caution. When Japan went through its economic crisis in the early 1990s, the central bank of Japan employed a similar approach to that which the Federal Reserve and the Treasury are now taking. The Japanese were not successful in stemming an economy-wide recession that lasted over a decade. What is not known at this point is how severe the U.S. recession will be and how long will it last. Granted, the American economy is more resilient than the Japanese economy ever was. The ability of our economy to stand a macro shock such as this and still be a dominant force is exponentially better than that of any other country. That is precisely what gives us hope that at the end of the day we will come out stronger than ever before with some fundamental structural changes in how we do business and how we interact with the rest of the world. The question is, when?

Thought Questions

1. Do you believe studying personal finance is a waste of your time?

2. It is clear that every action has a benefit and a cost even if some of the costs are not immediately obvious and reveal themselves to us over time. Can you think of other examples in your life or in the world around you where an action intended to be a benefit turned out to be a nightmare?

3. Should Congress repeal the Gramm-Leach-Bliley Act and go back to the way banks could operate over the past seventy years following the Glass Steagall Act?

4. Does every American deserve to own a home? Why or why not?

2

Time Value of Money

Take a chance! All life is a chance. The man who goes
the furthest is generally the one who is willing to do and dare.
The "sure thing" boat never gets far from shore.
　　　　　　　　　　　　　　　　　　　—Dale Carnegie

Stocks were not a part of my vocabulary as a teenager. Neither were they in the vocabulary of anyone I knew. Moreover, my parents were very educated people. You would think that if anyone knew about stocks it would be my parents. Yet, they had no clue. My parents had a bank account, and they invested some of their money in a "chit fund," which involved depositing a given sum of money and receiving periodic interest. In hindsight, it is shocking that they would invest their hard-earned money this way when they knew nothing about the credit worthiness of such institutions or how the company was investing the money. These seemed like minor technicalities no one cared about. Everybody trusted these funds, but were ignorant of how they worked, why they were (or were not) smart investments, or whether they could do better. Why no one worried about such things, I don't know. Maybe we are just trusting people.

　　Upon thinking back on these chit funds, it is clear they were nothing more than Ponzi schemes designed to lure new investors with promises of whopping interest payments, needing a constant influx of new investors whose monies fed the astronomical interest payments made to the older investors. As long as the influx of new investors outweighed the interest payments, the Ponzi scheme kept going. The trick in these rackets was to be first in the line. I say "racket" because it was an exploitative scheme designed to separate unsuspecting investors from their money. The funds never got invested anywhere—they were just used to pay off one group of investors to keep them happy while new investors came in looking to make a quick buck. In such setups, the relative newcomers to the party were the ones who were the biggest losers because the scheme unraveled before they could recover their money. There was no government regulation of such shady schemes. Bribery was rampant (as it is today), and all it took for these shysters to work their magic was a selective greasing of the palms of senior government and police officials for them to look the other way. But I digress.

　　Back to the chit fund my parents invested in. It had an astronomical interest pay-out of 48 percent. One of my uncles had opened an account and was raking in money hand-over-fist. He came over to tell my father about all the interest he was earning on his investment.

My father was a physics professor, and about as worldly a man as the next professor. What did not occur to him, or to anybody else around us, was that the interest rates paid out seemed absurdly high and, in a rational and reasonable world, such astronomical rates would almost certainly mean that there was something fishy afoot. Clearly, my father did not have "rational expectations." Remember the old cliché, if it is too good to be true, it probably is? Obviously, he had not yet taken this maxim to heart. Nobody ever asked questions like how the interest rate could be so high, how the money was being invested so that returns could be so good, or even what the average return on investment was under the circumstances? Everybody simply trusted the system. It is no wonder we were ruled by the British for 400 years! Instead, my parents simply invested in the incredible money pot where you just had to reach in and pull money out. It was there for everybody. Or, so they thought.

For a while, things went very well. My parents received those incredibly high interest rates. Then they, God bless them, made the cardinal mistake that people, even those well educated in the ways of finance, make today when trying to make a killing in the markets: They got greedy. They invested more of their money in this scheme.

My parents had no idea what Ponzi schemes were, so it is hardly surprising that they—along with a million others dreaming of riches—lost a bundle when the scheme finally came crashing down. The police busted the brains behind this particular Ponzi scheme, and one of the directors of the firm committed suicide by throwing himself from the balcony of his high-rise luxury apartment. It made the local media headlines and was the subject of society gossip for a while afterwards. In case you are still scratching your head wondering what exactly was wrong with this scheme, the organizers of the scheme and their friends and family (who were the early entrants) made fabulous amounts of money and recovered their initial investments many times over. The rest of the unsuspecting investors lost their entire investment capital.

My parents never spoke of it again. The embarrassment was too much to bear, so denial was their remedy. In fact, I never heard them consider any form of investing

Charles Ponzi

Ponzi schemes are a type of illegal pyramid scheme named after Charles Ponzi, who duped thousands of New England residents into investing in a postage stamp speculation scheme back in the 1920s. His idea was to take advantage of differences between U.S. and foreign currencies used to buy and sell international mail coupons. Ponzi promised his investors he could provide them with a 40 percent return in just 90 days compared to the 5 percent offered by bank savings accounts in those days.

Not surprisingly, Ponzi was deluged with funds from investors, taking in $1 million during one three-hour period—this was 1921! Though a few early investors were paid off to make the scheme look legitimate, an investigation later discovered that Ponzi had, in fact, only purchased about $30 worth of the international mail coupons. Over time, the term *Ponzi scheme* has come to denote the concept of "rob-Peter-to-pay-Paul." And, to do so, the money from new investors is used to pay off the earlier investors. The scheme continues as long as enough new investors come in. As soon as the stream of new investors and, by extension, new money starts drying up, the scheme unravels.

again. Their sole investment activity after that was restricted to the measly returns they received from their savings account at the bank.

Bernard Madoff

Bernie Madoff was a genial, outgoing person that everyone liked and looked up to. He was a Wall Street legend who got started in the sixties by trading in penny stocks that were considered risky by most investors of the time. He earned his profits by pocketing the bid ask spread which we will discuss later in the

> ## Ask the Right Questions
> You should ask questions of any investment opportunity you come across . And do it BEFORE you invest. Such timely soul searching will save you a lot of headaches, and maybe even heartaches, later.

book. He would promise his customers a penny a share discount for trading with him. This was a legal practice used to generate business. In the nineties, as the stock market heated up, he began courting the regulators in Washington. A smart move since he had counted on not being regulated too closely if he was considered one of the regulators. And was he right! The Securities and Exchange Commission (SEC) used to consult with Madoff about a variety of issues related to the stock markets.

As Madoff's reputation grew, investors from the world over flocked to him to invest their money. They were dazzled by his ability to deliver steady returns year in, year out, regardless of market conditions. How he was doing this was something nobody seemed too concerned about. Unlike most other shysters, Bernie was not out there selling his stuff. They were flocking to him. By cultivating this exclusive image of himself for the better part of forty years, he was the one everyone came to, begging him to take them on as clients. And as long as these new investors came to him, all he had to do was to take their money and pay off the older investors. No one was any wiser. It was the good old Ponzi scheme all over again. And as the internet bubble took hold in the mid nineties, so did Madoff's fortunes. More people had more money than they knew what to do with and who better to turn to in order to invest it than the reliable Madoff?

This scheme continued unabated until the very end of 2008 when the slowing economy finally caught up to Madoff. He realized that there were no longer enough new entrants to his investment company to provide enough money to pay off his remaining investment clients. At this point, he decided to come clean and confess his scheme to his sons who immediately notified the authorities. Interestingly, Madoff has been compared to modern-day psychopaths like Ted Bundy who also had an engaging personality and was extremely intelligent. The difference: Bundy took people's lives; Madoff killed people in their wallets!

> ## BIG PICTURE
> Unfortunately, this same scenario, although not on such a large scale, gets repeated over and over again all over the world. People get into investments they have little understanding of, get burnt and subsequently develop a fear of investments. Hopefully, after you have read this book you will no longer be afraid of diving into the investment pool.

A Bubble

Bubble is the term applied to an environment where prices appreciate in ways that defy common sense, for as long as enough people buy into the euphoria, sending prices upward. It's like a big old Ponzi scheme.

As long as enough new investors come into the market the bubble continues to grow. But sooner or later, the market runs out of new investors. And the astronomically high prices might induce some investors to start selling, take their profits, and run. This act usually starts an avalanche of selling; the house of cards comes crashing down and the bubble bursts.

The first financial bubble in the modern world is the famous tulip bulb mania in Holland that started in November 1636. The bubble burst in February 1637, with prices falling to insignificant levels bringing defaults on many outstanding contracts.

The case of Madoff goes on to show that there are con artists living right in our midst. They can be our friends, relatives or loved ones. Our problem is that sometimes the proximity makes us blind to the red flags that are usually there. In Madoff's case, the red flag was the fact that he could deliver the same returns year after year, good market or bad, and no one thought it unusual. We have a tendency to not ask the hard questions if things appear to be going right, and sometimes that is exactly the wrong thing to do. If the Madoff lesson does not teach us to question a good thing, nothing else will.

I Believe I Too Was a Ponzi Trader

Upon reflecting back to my childhood I realized that I once briefly ran my own little Ponzi scheme. Only thing is, I had no clue of who Charles Ponzi was and I was just about ten years old. Every day my father walked me to the corner of our street where the school bus would pick me up. On the way to the corner there was the local candy store where he would buy me my favorite soft malted candies. I absolutely loved those candies and could never get enough.

One day, however, my father was busy and could not take me to the bus stop, so the responsibility of taking me to the bus fell on one of our servants. The problem with that was that the servant did not have the money to buy me my malted candies. I was desperate! Like a true addict, I needed my candy fix. I had to think fast on my feet. I told the servant we had to make a slight detour to the store.

I then managed to talk the store owner into giving me my malted candies by convincing him that my father would for sure pay him back extra for this small favor he was doing for me today. Somehow he bought my arguments.

The next day my father happened to be busy again, so I pulled the same trick on the candy store owner and once again told him that he would get his due plus something extra from my father for giving me my candy. This went on for a week or so. I was getting my regular candy fix and my dad, unknowingly, was piling up debt to the store owner. At my tender age I had clearly not understood the trade-offs between short term gains and long term pains!

Famous Clients of Bernard Madoff

Since the arrest of Bernard Madoff, the famous financier who could deliver incredible returns to his clients year after year, details of some of his famous clients have emerged. They include such diverse personalities as Steven Spielberg, Mort Zuckerman, John Malkovich, Henry Kissinger, Barbara Bach, Sandy Koufax, and John Denver Enterprises; banks such as HSBC; many charitable organizations; a foundation run by holocaust survivor Elie Wiesel; Austria's Bank Medici; as well as Madoff's personal lawyer, Ira Sorkin. That is ironic!

I understood that trade-off in a real way about a week later when the store owner happened to run into my father on the streets and mentioned all the money (including the extras) that my father owed him. I believe my father settled the dues with him and then came home to take up the matter with me. Let it just be said that I was thrashed within an inch of my life for making up this story for candy. Like all schemes, this too unraveled real quickly and I was candyless for quite a while after that. I have not tried to pull a financial scam like that since.

A Theory of Investment Decision Making

The theory of investment decision making is embodied in the well-known Modern Portfolio Theory (MPT). The basis of MPT rests in reducing all investments to two important numbers: The mean return and the fluctuation of returns around the mean (also known as variance or volatility). This second measure captures the risk of the investment. The higher the volatility, the greater the risk of the investment. Investors should always seek combinations of investment assets that provide the highest mean return for a given level of risk. The academic term for this is being at the "efficient frontier." We, as individual investors, are presumed to be risk-hating. That is, we like certainties and hate uncertainties. We are even ready to give up some potential gains at the expense of a lower certain value. It's the "bird-in-hand-is-worth-two-in-the-bush" syndrome. Hence, we will demand additional return on our investments for holding additional risk. We may not get it all the time but we will be actively seeking it all the same.

And not only that: As the underlying risk of our investment increases, we will demand greater compensation for taking on this added risk. This relationship between risk and return is an important one and one that you will have to be cognizant of all the time. An important financial formula illustrates this relationship between risk and return: It is call the Capital Asset Pricing Model (CAPM).

Expected Return = risk-free return + sensitivity x expected market risk premium

This formula captures the intuition that the expected risk premium (return we would expect over and above that from a risk-free investment) is directly proportional to the risk sensitivity term above, known as beta, which we will revisit in future chapters. CAPM is an important formula for everybody including corporate managers when they are attempting to determine if a new investment is worth making or an individual investor trying to decide if a stock is worth purchasing.

The risk-free rate is assumed to be the rate paid on short term Treasury bills of the U.S. Government. The expected market risk premium is usually computed from the historical average on the market portfolio which is widely accepted to be the S&P 500 Index. We will discuss the indexes later in the book.

And CAPM is simple which makes it easily accessible.

One important prediction flowing out of the MPT is that investors should not expect to be appropriately compensated for the risks of investing in individual securities, like individual stocks. Rather, investors should only expect to be compensated for the aggregate market risk they take on. Note that an interesting offshoot of the latter prescription is that individual investors are taking a disproportionately higher risk (relative to the returns) to invest in individual stocks and bonds in the markets. According to MPT, they should all be in index mutual funds—a class of investments we will be discussing later in the book.

Another implication of the venerable MPT is that the closer you are to the point where you are going to break into the bank to start spending your accumulated wealth, the less risky your portfolio should be. This latter implication is behind the famous "Life-Cycle" hypothesis considered to be the Holy Grail of financial planners.

The Reality of the Beta

As the discussion on the CAPM shows, knowing, or being able to estimate, a company's or a project's beta is essential to getting a good handle on the company or the project's discount rate. It is important because if the discount rate is too high, you could estimate a project's Net Present Value (NPV) to be negative when it was positive. Hence you could lose out on a valuable investment opportunity.

Unfortunately, estimating the beta is more of an art than science. According to a recent paper by Pablo Fernandez, calculated betas appear to change considerably from one day to the next—which is not normal. A company's beta is estimated by taking five years of monthly return data of the company in question and regressing it against a value-weighted market index. The problem is that using this approach provides beta estimates that are significantly different from day to day. The article provides an example of the estimated betas of three well-known companies, Coca Cola, Walt Disney and Wal-Mart, using the method outlined above during the month of April 2009. In the empirical estimation, the beta of Coca Cola varies from 0.06 to

Life-Cycle Hypothesis

The Life-Cycle Hypothesis of consumption enunciated by three economists, Franco Modigliani, Richard Brumberg, and Albert Ando, in a series of articles in the 1950s and 1960s, provides an economic explanation for why people save. People save because they generally live longer than they earn income—that is, people usually retire. And if they are to keep spending after they no longer earn income, they must have accumulated assets while they were earning so that they can spend from their accumulated wealth. Consequently, the closer they are to retirement, the more critical it is to not take unnecessary risks with their portfolio (i.e., scale down portfolio risk) because there is less time to recover from a downturn in their net worth.

0.57, the beta of Walt Disney from 0.66 to 1.07 and the beta of Wal-Mart varies from -0.05 to 0.5. Thus, betas estimated from historical data of a company appear to not be a good estimation of the underlying risk of the company. Another problem is that the betas will change depending on the time period over which it is estimated (five years versus ten years and so on) as well as the market index chosen (value weighted versus equally weighted, etc.).

To overcome these problems with estimating individual company betas, some recommend using the industry average beta that a given company belongs to. An industry average beta is considered to be more reliable since the individual company errors tend to wash out in aggregate. Another suggested approach is to calculate a qualitative beta associated with a company or a capital project. In this approach, we use the following scale to estimate the beta.

		Risk Classification (on a scale of 1–5) Where 1 is Low and 5 is Very High				
Weight		**Low**	**Average**	**Substantial**	**High**	**Very High**
10%	Management					
25%	Assets					
3%	Strategy					
15%	Country Risk					
10%	Operating Leverage					
15%	Financial Leverage					
5%	Liquidity of Investment					
5%	Access to Funds					
2%	Partners					
5%	Exposure to Other Risks (e.g., Currency Risks)					
5%	Cash Flow Stability					
Total =100%						

Keep in mind there are other potential scales as well. The criticism with a qualitative approach is that they are somewhat ad hoc and different institutions can use different scales or weight them differently to arrive at their own beta estimates. The recommendation is to use these beta estimates prudently and cross check with other measures. The particular beta used in order to evaluate a company or project should best reflect its risk—however estimated.

In sum, while different approaches lead to different beta estimates, the discount rate that is used to convert cash flows to the present using the Time Value of Money approach should be the same for everybody. Almost everyone understands the drawbacks associated with the estimation of beta.*

---

*Fernandez, Pablo, 2009, Betas used by professors: A survey with 2,500 answers, working paper, IESE Business School, Madrid, Spain.

Cost of Equity in Emerging Markets

CAPM works well in developed markets; not so well in underdeveloped emerging markets. The reasons are as follows:

- Genuine risk-free rates do not exist in emerging markets
- Emerging markets display thin trading and illiquidity, so beta is difficult to estimate
- Calculating market returns is problematic since emerging markets have limited market histories.

Therefore, adjustments have to be made to the standard CAPM to make it applicable to emerging market projects.

Various models (tweaks of the basic CAPM model) that have been used to deal with projects in developing countries are: (1) the Lessard Approach, (2) the Godfrey Espinosa Approach, (3) the Goldman Sachs Approach, (4) the Salomon Smith Barney Approach. These approaches are all somewhat ad hoc and are based on adjusting the basic CAPM framework for an added risk factor that incorporates the risk of operating in a specific country and the specific industry within that country.

Reference: Estrada, J., Discount rates in emerging markets: Four models and an application. *Journal of Applied Corporate Finance*, 19, Spring 2007.

Trading versus Investing

Discount brokers would rather have you trade more often than less because they make money off you in commissions when you do. That is why they give you free trades when you sign up, and force you to use them within 30 to 45 days. They want you to get in the habit of trading frequently. So if you buy and sell ten times in a month (say), they get to make about $100 in commissions (after your free trades are used up) regardless of whether you make any money. That is the beauty of being an intermediary—whether the economy is booming or in the dumps, they get to make their commissions. If you prefer to trade frequently, you are most likely concerned about costs related to trading, including commissions. Later, we will have a full description of what those costs are.

By contrast, if you happen to be an investor who trades once every so often and you buy a stock in order to hold it for a while (you buy-and-hold) then the daily vagaries of the stock market, including trading related volatilities and how much you are paying to have your trades executed, are of less concern to you. You are an investor more than you are a trader. You care about the financial soundness of the companies you invest in.

In sum, if you are a day-trader (someone who buys and sells several times a day) you probably don't care two-hoots about the underlying companies you are buying and selling. You only care about the trading characteristics of these companies. At the other end of the spectrum, if you trade about once a year you are a pure investor and you care solely about the underlying characteristics of the company. You don't give a flying

Investors versus Traders

Traders trade frequently and care about trade-related characteristics including the commissions they pay. Investors trade infrequently and care about the underlying company fundamentals and not about the implicit and explicit trading costs.

tomato (didn't he win a gold medal in the winter Olympics?) about trading characteristics, commissions, and the like. Most of us are probably somewhere in the middle with both characteristics in our trading/investing activities.

Discounting and Compounding

Which would you rather have? A thousand dollars today or a case of bananas? For a monkey, the choice is obvious but what about people? For non-primates, the appropriate question is Do you want $100 dollars given to you today or $100 given to you a year from now? Conversely, what if you had a choice between paying someone $100 today versus $100 a year from now? When should you pay your bill? Right now or wait until the last minute? Before you answer, let me also add that there is no risk of nonpayment and that there will be no inflation in one year. That is, buying power will remain the same over this period.

When I was a young boy (arguably a little monkey), I had little knowledge of a bank. I knew all about wolves and monkeys but not banks. I may have occasionally chased a monkey or two into buildings that may have been banks but that is neither here nor there. However, I did understand the concept of storing my money under my pillow. I did that on a regular basis. Whenever my grandmother gave me any money, it would go straight under my pillow. The pillows in my day were large goose-feather-filled substantial pillows with lots of real estate under them. So storage was a breeze. Of course, whenever I got new shoes, I would try and sleep with them under my pillow too. The smell of new leather was like perfume. There would be little lumps at various sections of the pillow and my neck would hurt but it was a small price to pay to have all my favorite possessions under the pillow with me. It was comforting. But, sadly, my pillow did not pay any interest (nor, for that matter, did any other pillows in my acquaintance). So I would be totally indifferent to either of those two options. When I received money or when I paid it out simply would not matter. It would go under the interest-free pillow anyway. Luckily, there is nothing under my pillow these days except an occasional book. I use the bank for all my money deposits. It pays me interest. Oh, and I leave my new shoes in the closet.

That was me. For the rest of you, with access to banks with interest-bearing accounts, which option would you choose? What if you deposited about $95 in a bank today and it became $100 a year from now? Which option would be better for you? A little thinking should convince you that you would prefer to get the $100 today rather than wait for it. Why? You could deposit the $100 in a bank immediately and have about $104 in a year which would certainly beat getting $100 a year from now. Likewise, if you had to pay out, you could deposit $95 right now and have about $100 in your account in one year which you could use to pay off your debt. So don't pay out now—wait till the last second to pay out. In sum, your mantra should be "money in now; money out later."

If you can really understand the above concept, you are well on your way to understanding discounting and compounding. Formally, discounting is the method used to calculate the present value of a given sum of money received in the future.

Compounding is the technique used to calculate the future value of a given sum of money received today.

Let's start with discounting first. If you are a student and cash is hard to come by, you will understand what I'm about to say now. Suppose you want a better car than the clunker you drive currently. But working and saving for it is not an option. You have to have the car now. Let's call you a spender. You can get the money you need now from a bank. But this money comes at a cost. The money is a loan and you have to pay interest to the lender on top of paying back the loan amount. On the other hand, if you are a saver by nature, you can deposit the money in a bank and get paid interest on your money. The bank can take your money and loan it out to a spender and earn interest on the money. They keep some of it and pay the rest to the saver as interest. That is how banks operate. They stand as intermediaries between the savers and spenders of the world.

Compounding is best illustrated with the following example. Let's say you want to go to Maui for Spring Break in a year or so. You cannot wait to feel the taste of salt water in your mouth, the smell of the ocean. You have done your research and calculated it will cost you about two thousand dollars after plane tickets, hotel expenses and all those drinks at the beach. You have about twelve months to get this money together and you would like to know how much you need to deposit in your savings account per month in order to have the required sum in a year.

Discounting and compounding, collectively referred to as time-value-of-money (TVM), are everywhere—both within the sphere of Personal Finance as well as outside it. We will be using TVM concepts either directly or indirectly throughout the book. In the investment-related chapters, TVM concepts are used to understand how to value financial assets. The price of any financial asset, for example, is the discounted present value of all its future cash flows. This is true for any asset, whether it is stocks, bonds, mutual funds, or anything else you can think of. Credit card companies charge you interest on unpaid balances at the end of each month. Computing the present value of such obligations will give you a good idea of what those credit obligations are worth to you today and help you budget accordingly. Insurance companies calculate the premiums of policies based on present value calculations. For instance, if you are a 25-year-old, buying a whole-life policy, your premium is based on the present value of the expected cost to the insurance company depending on your risk category, defined by your lifestyle choices, assuming you can live up to a maximum of 100 years. Remember, all else being equal (also called *ceteris paribus*), the longer you live, the less costly it is for the insurance company to insure you because most of the policy payout is coming from your pockets. We will see this in more detail later in the book. Finally, retirement is all about investments again and we are back to our starting point in the circle of this book.

Even outside of Personal Finance, make it a habit to spot TVM concepts when you are reading a newspaper or a magazine. In fact, I challenge myself to find at least one TVM concept no matter what I am reading—yes, even the phone book. For instance, one word that will often crop up is "amortization." What is it? It is simply the process of paying off a loan—principal and interest. The longer the process, the less is the drain on your budget which makes you feel relatively cash rich. So, for example, if you had a choice between a 15-year mortgage and a 30-year mortgage (both for the same dollar amount), the monthly payments (interest + principal repayment) will be smaller with the latter than with the former (even adjusting for the fact that the 30-year mortgage rate will usually be higher than the 15-year rate).

Here is an excerpt from an article I came by a while ago in a magazine I was reading in an airport while waiting for a connecting flight:

> . . . The new wave of professional-team ownership has taken cues from the leveraged buyouts of the 1980s. Though these owners often have accumulated substantial holdings in real estate development and other areas, they typically only put up 10 to 20 percent of these assets as collateral when buying their teams.
>
> The team's purchase price may be amortized as long as 40 years, lessening its drain as an expense and thus making the franchise look far more profitable than it actually is.
>
> Also, franchises sometimes amortize players' signing bonuses and contracts far beyond their actual lengths. This has a huge impact on reported profitability. Many accountants in the field use this rule of thumb: Amortize franchises no longer than 15 years and player contracts no longer than the period for which services are being rendered.

Let us examine the above excerpt. It is talking about how the new sports team owners are increasingly raising the exorbitant purchase prices through creative financing and by borrowing a page from the leveraged buyout of companies in the 1980s which involved selling bonds and raising the required funds. If you happen to have real estate holdings for 10–20 percent of the purchase price of the team, say, then you go to a bank, use these holdings as collateral and simply borrow the rest using the team's current assets as further collateral for the 80 percent or so of the purchase price (hence, the leveraged buyout analogy).

The loans taken out to purchase the team can be amortized over a very long period (i.e., 40 years or more) thereby making the monthly loan payments more affordable since the payments are spread out over a longer period. This is true for any loan, including your mortgage payments as I discussed above. Moreover, doing so

What Determines Bank Interest Rates?

Banks operate on a very simple principle: taking money in and loaning money out. Specifically, there are depositors who park their monies in banks and borrowers who loan monies from these banks. Banks then take the parked monies and loan out a fraction of it to lenders and earn interest on the loans. As long as the bank earns more from its lending activities than what it pays to its depositors, everyone is happy.

At various times in the economy you have more savers than spenders (recession) or more spenders than savers (inflation). When savers outnumber spenders the bank has a lot of money in its reserve and so it lowers the interest rate in order to encourage more spenders to come out and borrow money. Likewise when spenders outnumber savers, the bank has to come up with its own funds to meet the excess demand and it increases interest rates to discourage (or cool off) the borrowing frenzy.

also makes the organization look more cash healthy than it actually is. Another way to think about a longer time horizon of amortization is to think of it as using a relatively lower discount rate. Doing so increases the present value of a project for any given cash flow stream.

Teams will also amortize those hefty contracts given to star players over far greater periods than the contract is valid for—with the blessing of their accountants of course. This again has the effect of making the organization look healthier than it actually may be. It is sort of like accounting magic—the kind that got Enron into loads of trouble and made the big accounting firm Arthur Andersen almost disappear from the face of the earth.

TVM concepts are not restricted to the print media either. Here is a brief excerpt from a recent CBS Sunday Morning news show from one of the networks. The backdrop of the segment was Sprint employees on strike in Hickory, North Carolina, over their declining health benefits from the company.

> (Network Reporter) "The people are just fed up with their benefits being cut," one employee remarks. Instead, it's "hands off my benefits."
>
> From health care to disability to pensions, across many industries, workers today are realizing with dismay that company-provided benefits are costing them more and providing them less.
>
> "Every benefit cut that you have is a cut in your wages," says the local president of the Communication Workers of America union. "It's a cut in your ability to provide for your family."
>
> The union president says his members walked, much of their anger fueled by Sprint's proposal to eliminate the caps on how much they pay for health insurance; a bitter pill for members who remember once paying nothing at all.
>
> "From going from paying nothing in 1996, we now have some members who are paying as much as $2,400 a year in premiums."

Where are the TVM concepts in the vignette above? When benefits are cut, the future value of the cash stream is reduced and that, in turn, reduces the present value of the future cash flow stream of benefits. And employees are trying to preserve the promised cash flow of benefits and thereby keep the present value of this annuity stream of benefits high. The company wants the exact opposite for its own long-term survival. Hence, the struggle between the two sides. The economic term for this struggle is a "zero sum game." One side's benefit is exactly equal to the other side's loss. It sums to zero. That is exactly how both sides are viewing this for better or for worse. It does not have to be a zero sum game, of course, but there we have it.

The union president implies that benefits are like additional wages and every dollar cut in future benefits is like a less-than-a-dollar cut in your present value of all wages. The employees' collective anger sparked after Sprint decided to eliminate the cap on how much employees would have to pay for their health benefits. The obvious understanding here was that the employees' health benefit costs would go up and the company's cost of funding these benefits would stay down or, at least, not increase. Sprint is looking at this as one way of increasing the present value of the company by cutting the present value of its expenditures. In a strictly dollars and cents kind of world, the argument does have some merit although one can argue that unhappy employees translate into less productive employees and thereby contribute less dollars in company revenue which ultimately affects the present value of the revenue stream. The company, by trying to curtail the present value of its expenditure stream may, at the end of the day, be curtailing the present value of its revenue stream—an unintended (and certainly economically foolish) consequence.

And just when you may be saying to yourself that maybe time value of money concepts are only associated with sports- or finance-related articles, let me show you another example totally unrelated to either of these areas.

> As the third season of Fox's hugely popular talent search gears up for its finale, millions of fans wonder who will emerge as the next "American Idol" and receive a recording contract.
>
> But winning isn't everything. Some of the show's past contestants have signed record deals and released chart-topping albums without winning the competition. Clay Aiken, who finished a controversial second to Ruben Studdard in season two, has sold more than 2.5 million copies of his debut album, Measure of a Man.

Think of the winner of the Idol contest as one whose present value (of all future earnings) is considered to be the highest by the judges (one in particular) and the voting body. Remember that the winner will get a record contract from a label owned by one of the Idol judges. That is not to say that those who do not win do not have as high a present value. So far, a lot of near winners have managed to release successful CDs and received significant publicity after their Idol days (i.e., Clay Aiken). They can be thought of as undervalued commodities who since have emerged as shining stars and taken their "stock" upward. Then there are Idol stars whose stars have since dimmed. Recall Justin Guarini who started with a bang but has since fizzled out. His present value has declined considerably.

At the other extreme is the 21-year-old engineering student, William Hung, famous for his off-key singing and comic performance of Ricky Martin's "She Bangs" during the first round of auditions for Idol's third season that won him a record contract with Koch Entertainment. His first album, "Inspiration," debuted on the Billboard Top 200 charts at number 34, selling almost 38,000 copies during its first week. Talk about an undervalued commodity! Here is someone whose present value was initially considered almost zero in the entertainment field and who since then has capitalized on his notoriety and silliness to propel his present value of future cash flows sky-high.

And you thought TVM was boring?

Thought Questions

1. Can you think of other Ponzi-like schemes that are prevalent today? Are chain letters Ponzi schemes?

2. Who loses the most in Ponzi schemes? Why?

3. When stock markets are not viable, what other ways can you invest your money?

4. What is a bubble? What are some of the historical bubbles you can think of?

5. What are the similarities and differences between a bubble and a Ponzi scheme?

6. What factors came to collide at the same time to create the dot-com bubble?

7. Why did the Internet bubble burst?

8. What can you extrapolate from the MPT about your "ideal" investing behavior?

9. What does the Life-Cycle Hypothesis imply about your investment portfolio over time?

10. Why are trading commissions competitive in the United States?

11. What are some of the trade-related costs a trader could be worried about?

12. What are some differences between full-service brokers and discount brokers?

13. Why are there so many brokerage houses in existence? Are they all doing the same thing?

14. Can you think of other areas in your everyday life where you could have been using TVM concepts without realizing it? If so, try to describe them in detail in order to tease out the concepts as clearly as you can.

15. In TVM terms, was William Hung initially an undervalued or an overvalued commodity? Why?

16. Why is it optimal from a TVM standpoint to wait until the last minute to pay a bill but to take any payments at the earliest opportunity?

3

What Are Stocks?

Risk—If one has to jump a stream and knows how wide it is,
he will not jump. If he doesn't know how wide it is,
he'll jump and six times out of ten he'll make it.

—Persian Proverb

Let us say you have lived in your house for a while and your family has grown steadily over the years. The same house that looked so much bigger a few years ago is not looking as large. You and your wife are thinking of adding a wing to the house in order to have some privacy to do fun things. So what do you do? You probably walk over to the neighborhood bank to see if they will loan you some money for the renovations.

Well, that is exactly why companies sell shares: They need money to build more factories, hire more people, or develop new products. And, like you, a company could get a loan from a bank or it could get a loan from the capital markets (by selling bonds on themselves as we will see later). The problem with loans is that the creditors, whether it is a bank or outside investors, would be looking constantly over the company's shoulders. Every time you felt like going outside for a latté you would feel like your creditors are following you. It would be most annoying. The company would also have to pay regular interest on the money borrowed, which can become a nuisance since companies have most of their cash tied up in the business.

Unlike you and me, however, a company has other options. It could sell shares. A company does not, however, make any money from the daily buying and selling of its shares in the stock exchanges (or, through secondary market transactions). Those transactions just result in monies moving between investors buying and selling the company's shares. The company itself makes money one time only. And

> ## The Kabuliwallahs
>
> In India, there is a wandering group of money lenders from Afghanistan known as Kabuliwallahs. They are big men with beards and turbans, wearing long, flowing robes, who lend money at exhorbitantly high interest rates. Only people who cannot get loans anywhere else resort to taking money from the Kabuliwallahs. One salient feature of these money lenders is that they do not badger you for their money. They simply find out whre you work and come and stand across the street quietly watching your every move. It is apparently a very effective monitoring device since the default rates are reportedly very low.

that one time is when it sells its shares for the first time (in what is called a primary market) through what is known as an Initial Public Offering (IPO). Keep in mind that an already public company can further sell shares to the investing public in the form of a Seasoned Equity Offering (SEO).

Private and Public Companies

You can broadly divide corporations into two types: private and public. Private companies (as the name implies) are privately held. Being private means there are fewer shareholders and very little information about the company has to be disclosed by the owners. Anybody can go out and incorporate a company; all you have to do is put in some money, file the right legal documents, and follow the reporting rules of your local jurisdiction. Most small businesses are privately held. But don't think of only small companies as private. There are many large private companies such as IKEA, Domino's Pizza, and Hallmark Cards. It isn't usually possible to buy shares in a private company. Technically, you could approach the owners about investing, but they don't have to sell you anything.

Types of Businesses

A business owned by one person (a proprietorship) or a few people (a partnership) cannot issue stock. Only a business corporation can issue stock. A corporation has a special legal status. Its existence does not depend on the people who run it. By law, it is separate from the people associated with it, and has special legal rights and responsibilities as well as its own unique name.

Public companies are those that have sold at least a portion of itself to the public and that trade on a stock exchange. This is why an IPO process is also referred to as "going public." Public companies have thousands of shareholders and are subject to strict rules and regulations. They must have a board of directors and report financial information every quarter. In the United States, public companies report information to the Securities Exchange Commission (SEC). All countries that oversee public companies have governing bodies similar to the SEC. From an investor's standpoint, the most exciting thing about a public company is that if you have the cash, you can invest. Nobody can keep you away. It's a totally democratic process and everyone has free access. The stock is traded in the open market like any other commodity.

Research on IPOs

Research has shown that when an initial public offering of a company hits the market, it is typically underpriced. Underpricing means that it is sold for less than what a similar share would normally trade for in the secondary markets. Frequently the underwriter will buy some of the shares to prop up the price and attract investors during the first few days of trading. While this practice is often regarded as a way of ensuring liquidity of new issues, little is known about what types of IPOs get bolstered and whether this really affects liquidity. Is this kind of price support of any economic consequence? Are supported IPOs merely small offerings from fringe underwriters who are buttressing stocks at artificially high prices? Until recently the data has not

Underwriters

Underwriters are investment firms like Merrill Lynch, Shearson-Lehman, Morgan Stanley, and others of that ilk, who are actively responsible for doing a risk assessment of a private company trying to go public and for bringing its stock to the investing public for the first time through the IPO process.

been available to fully answer these questions. There is now evidence through research showing that supported IPOs are typically larger, have lower underwriter commissions, offer higher prices than unsupported stocks, and are likely to be underwritten by well-known investment banks. So the lemons of the world are not supported—rather it is the big companies (and, by extension, the big issues) that are. And price support seems to have an important role in determining aftermarket liquidity. And, as we have already seen, liquidity is very important.

For about sixty years, Securities and Exchange Commission (think of the SEC as the stock market cops) rules have exempted price supports from anti-manipulative measures on the grounds that they improve liquidity—the reason bankers often laud the practice. Yet until now there has been little proof that liquidity justifies price support. In fact, research finds that investment banks sometimes support newly issued stocks to help institutional customers out of bad issues.[1] If a stock price flounders, the issuing investment bank simply buys back the issue.

In fact, the data show that once price supports are withdrawn, the unsupported stocks actually drift down in price more than the ones that had been supported, demonstrating that bankers had not propped up lemons. Finally, the research findings refute accusations that banks participate in underwriter reimbursement. (That is, they require a larger gross spread—the difference between the price at which the underwriter buys stock from the corporate issuer and the price at which it sells the stock—which is effectively the underwriter's commission in exchange for promising to buy back some of the stock after the offering.)

In sum, the research finds that IPOs are underpriced, even after accounting for price supports. What does this finding mean for us, the investors? It means that we can expect an IPO to shoot up in price as soon as it hits the secondary market. In fact, that is what we observe. So if you cannot get in on a new issue at the IPO price, do not touch it right away because once it starts trading in the secondary market, chances are you will lose money!

Importance of the Stock Price

If the company does not make any money directly from the daily buying and selling of its shares, why does it care about its stock price after the IPO is over and done with?

As a company makes money selling its products and services, the value of its stock goes up. For instance, pretend you bought some shares of stock for $10 each. If it does well, the shares might later be worth $15 each. You could then sell your stocks and make a profit of $5 on each share. Of course, if the company loses money, you incur a loss on your holdings. But let us focus on the good news. As a company's stock price rises, so does its prestige and reputation in the market. Experts start talking about the stock, word spreads, and more investors line up to buy into the company, which further drives up the price, and so on. The company can also attract talented people to leave their existing companies in order to come and work for them. Most importantly, the company's shareholders are happy and that makes for happy shareholders' meetings. Google (the Internet search company) is a good example of a company that has done well over the last few years and to which all the above can be ascribed. In sum, even though a company does not make direct profits from the secondary market transactions, it stands to gain a lot indirectly when its stock price rises.

What Does Stock Ownership Provide?

Owning stock in a company means owning part of that company. Each part is known as a share. If a company has issued one hundred shares of stock, and you bought one, you own 1 percent of that company. People who own stock are called stockholders, shareholders, or equity holders.

Have you seen those commercials by Ameritrade that show a mother and daughter having lunch and the daughter casually mentions that she now "owns" EMI? A waiter hovering nearby, who is also an aspiring singer, hears the conversation, takes the word "owns" literally and breaks out into a song-and-dance routine to impress the "owner" of EMI. Then we see written on the bottom of the screen that she owns something like 0.00000017 percent of EMI. Cute! Well, that's stock ownership for you.

Stockholders (yes, even if you are a 0.0000017 percent owner) hope the company will earn money as it grows. If a company earns money, the stockholders share in the profits. Over time, people usually earn more from owning stock than from leaving money in the bank or under their pillows.

Stockholders in a company usually have voting rights. They vote on such issues as who will be elected to the board of directors—the group of people who oversee company decisions—and whether to buy other companies. Stockholders typically have one vote for each share they own.

However, companies have a way of selling shares of the company without distributing the voting rights proportionately. A common way to accomplish this is to issue a different class of shares, say Class B. When you buy a Class B share of a company, you do so with the understanding that while your shares are almost equivalent to the company's Class A shares in every way, your Class B shares may have fewer votes than are enjoyed by Class A shareholders. A good example of this is with Warren Buffet's company, Berkshire Hathaway. Each Class A share trades in the neighborhood of about $90,000. This is because Buffet does not believe in stock splits and is not particularly concerned if you, the small individual investor, ever hold any of his shares. But, every Class B share of Berkshire Hathaway (which is valued at around 1/30 of the Class A shares and trades at around $3,000 a share) has 1/30 the voting rights of each Class A share. This is one way a company can maintain control. So, a stockholder with 1,000 BRK-A shares will have a greater say in Berkshire than a shareholder with 1,000 BRK-B shares. Large shareholders are courted aggressively by companies. They have a big voice in everything. Unfortunately, you need more than a 0.0000017 percent ownership in the company for that to happen.

Most companies have annual meetings, where stockholders cast votes and ask questions of the company's leaders. If they cannot attend, stockholders may use an absentee ballot to vote. Shareholders also receive quarterly and annual reports that inform them how the company is performing.

What to Look for When Buying Stocks

There are different approaches to stock investing. Some investors prefer one, while others rely on no particular method or employ a mix of all of them—just like the amazing choice of cereals in the cereal aisle of your neighborhood grocery store. There are also different types of investors—each preferring a particular type of stock.

Growth investors focus on companies whose earnings are expected to grow faster than both inflation and the economy over time. These companies usually have not only several years of consecutive earnings growth well above that of the average Standard & Poor's 500 corporations but also prospects for continued rapid growth. Therefore, growth stocks normally carry higher price to earnings ratios (P/E) than the general stock market. We discuss P/Es more thoroughly later in this chapter. Growth companies reinvest much of their earnings back into their businesses and do not pay out large dividends.

Remember, however, that growth stocks are quite risky and they may not turn out to be what you expected. Sometimes there is a "fad" factor to consider. Also, keep in mind that you may have to be patient with growth stocks as nothing may happen to them for quite a while. It took a better part of ten years after Microsoft's founding for it to become a household name. And, within the gestation period of a growth company's evolution, separating facts from the hype can sometimes be a daunting process especially in this day and age when we are constantly bombarded with information.

In contrast, value investors look for stocks that are temporarily out of favor with investors, who have sold them down to prices sometimes below their intrinsic value. Value stocks ordinarily pay relatively high dividends, and the combination of low P/Es and high dividend yields makes them attractive to investors looking for income and eventual appreciation. A good example of this would be the oil sector stocks like Exxon Mobil, Shell, etc., which went down in the wake of hurricane Katrina's wreaking havoc on the Gulf Coast and destroying off-shore oil rigs. The prices came back up subsequently when it became clear that the damage to the oil companies was not as severe as initially estimated. And, for a while, the entire sector represented a great buying opportunity for the opportunistic buyer. [The following website lists all the oil and gas companies in the USA: http://www.subsea. org/company/allbycountry. asp?qcountry=USA.]

Both growth and value stocks take turns in leading the market. Growth stocks are usually more popular when the economy is slowing, since their high earnings growth makes them more alluring. Value stocks tend to come into their own when the economy is booming, then fade when a recession looks imminent.

In reality, investors have been notoriously unsuccessful at predicting changes in market conditions. For that reason, they are better off owning both types of stocks—growth for long-term appreciation, and value for both appreciation and dividends (a significant component of total return over time).

Blue-chip stocks represent the opposite end of the spectrum from growth stocks and are the most venerable companies. These are household names like AT&T, McDonald's, IBM, Microsoft, and Starbucks. Blue chips have a long record of accomplishment and a great reputation. They usually have heavy trading volume. Starbucks' average daily trading volume is about 6 million shares a day. They are usually considered "safe" investments especially when markets are falling. However, nothing is guaranteed. Eastman Kodak, for example, another venerable name, has performed quite poorly over the last few years and has lost a significant portion of its market value.

Last, but certainly not least, for the speculative readers, there are the penny stocks. These are stocks trading under $5. The really bad ones trade under $1. Penny stocks represent newer companies with little or no operating history or older companies that have fallen on hard times. Either way, these are speculative to the max. They have very low trading volume. For example, Royal Laser Corporation (ticker: T.RLC), a penny stock trading around $0.89 a share, has a daily trading volume of about 10,000 shares. This site, http://www.allpennystocks.com/apsc/us/index.htm., provides information on penny stocks if you are interested.

In general, investors prefer a variety of the above in their portfolios. You can also add foreign stocks (including emerging market stocks), and cyclical stocks to the mix. Cyclicals are stocks that rise and fall with the business cycle. An example of a cyclical stock is GM. People buy new cars when interest rates are low (i.e., when the economy is coming out of a recession and moving towards inflation). By contrast, Coca Cola is a non-cyclical stock because people drink Coke come hell or high water, in summer and in winter, in good times and bad. The same can be said for Anheuser-Busch (ticker: BUD). The ultimate mix of stocks in your portfolio is a function of your risk tolerance and your time horizon.

Are All Stocks Equally Risky?

Not all stocks carry the same degree of risk. Before the NFL draft every year, a host of college players make themselves eligible to be drafted by one of the professional football teams. These players go through a series of drills and other workouts (like the 40-meter dash) under the watchful eyes of talent scouts of the various teams and, accordingly, the stock of some of the players rises while others fall. It is like a beauty pageant without the evening dress and the serenading by ex-American Idol contestants. However, in spite of all the scrutiny, the teams take a big risk when they draft players—sometimes for millions of dollars in salaries and signing bonuses. These players are essentially unproven talent at the topmost level of the game and on many occasions such players fall flat on their faces. (Remember Ryan Leaf and the San Diego Chargers who drafted him?) Then the team has essentially wasted millions of dollars in explicit and implicit costs.

Compare that to football players who have played for a few years in the NFL and have a record of accomplishment on which to lean. When teams sign on these proven talents, they are taking less of a risk. While there is no such thing as a sure shot, not in football and certainly not in stocks, pros who have been in the league for a few years are more of a proven commodity than rank newcomers who are just entering the league. On the risk scale, the proven talents are less risky than the rookies. (Of course, in another sense, the risk with proven players is how many more games they still have in them. Additionally, newer players are relatively cheaper to sign than the established stars who will demand astronomical contracts). Stocks can be thought of in a similar way.

Blue-chip companies, ones that have been around for a while, are proven commodities, for example, and provide a greater margin of safety (i.e., less risk) than do small start-up companies who are the rookies entering the market. Blue-chip corporations often occupy leading market positions that are expected to be maintained, or enhanced.

Large-cap companies with market capitalizations above four or five billion dollars are considered less risky than mid-cap (market capitalization between one and five billion dollars), or small-cap (market capitalization below one billion dollars) stocks which are considered quite risky. Further down the ladder are micro-cap stocks with market values below $500 million. Large caps are considered least risky because there is a large, liquid market for their shares, and normally a longer history of earnings and dividend growth.

Emerging growth stocks can be among the riskiest of all since they are shares of fledgling companies still in their developing stages, with hopes of superior earnings growth over time. Some of these companies will make it, but others will fall by the wayside.

Value stocks are generally less risky than growth stocks, since their higher dividend yields and lower P/Es offer some protection if the market declines. These are stocks that have been so beaten down by the markets that they have actually become good buys.

Foreign stocks carry the additional risk of currency fluctuation. If U.S. investors put money in European stocks and those currencies decline in relation to the dollar, the falling foreign currencies can reduce an investor's profits or add to losses. In the case of emerging markets, there are also the risks of political instability; extreme volatility, as previously state-run economies convert to free markets; illiquidity, which could exaggerate price swings; and other risks associated with particular regions.

In any event, with stocks, as with professional football players, it is probably not a good idea to become too attached. Keep your eyes open for other good prospects and don't forget to sell quickly when you hit your pre-established selling rules (when to sell is discussed later). The NFL is in fact very good at that—sometimes to the frustration of the fans. There should be no mercy on that front! Trade the talent who are past their primes but have bloated contracts (i.e., overvalued stocks) in favor of younger players at cheaper prices (i.e., undervalued stocks). Some team presidents, like Bill Polian of the Indianapolis Colts, have taken this value-based recruitment to an art form.

Tracking Stocks

Tracking stocks are a class of shares of the parent company that is linked to the performance of a particular business—usually the fastest-growing one. Tracking stocks can be issued when company management feels that parts of their company are worth more than the whole. The advantage of tracking stocks is that by focusing attention on one, usually profitable, division of the company, it is better able to obtain the appropriate market value of the business. This is because tracking stocks often result in greater analyst coverage because they can value a part of the company easier than a complex corporate behemoth.

Creating a tracking stock is like carving a corporate spinoff with one important difference: Management retains control with the issuance of a tracking stock. Additionally, there is a lot less corporate red tape involved in terms of approvals needed to issue a tracking stock than there is to carve out a spinoff. Once issued, tracking stocks trade as any other equity security on the U.S. stock exchanges, and you buy them as you would any other stock. General Motors (GM) issued the first such shares in 1984 and 1985 for its Electronic Data Systems (EDS) and Hughes Electronics (GMH) subsidiaries. Other issuers of tracking stocks include AT&T (T); Donaldson, Lufkin & Jenrette (DLJ); and Ziff-Davis (ZD).

Critics of tracking stocks have alleged that interlocking board members between the parent company and its tracking subsidiary can create serious problems in terms of resource allocation (read conflict of interest). Another way to look at this is one head football coach coaching two different NFL teams simultaneously. The inherent conflict of interest emerges clearly in the following quote from a Donaldson, Lufkin & Jenrette (DLJ) prospectus for DLJdirect (a tracking stock for the parent company, DLJ):

> The board of directors may make decisions that favor DLJ at the expense of DLJdirect. Due to the extensive relationships between DLJ and DLJdirect, there will be inherent conflicts of interest.

Further along, the prospectus gets more explicit.

> There can be no assurance that DLJ will not expand its operations to compete with DLJdirect.

According to the above, the directors of one entity were not ruling out the possibility of competing with the other. Do you smell lawsuits down the road?

Since their birth over twenty years ago, tracking stocks became wildly popular on Wall Street in the late nineties coinciding with the dot-com boom (to be discussed later). All the new entrants in the market were trading at fantastic multiples and the remaining companies got jealous. They looked at each other and said, "If these newbies with no track record (read pets.com and ivillage.com) are trading at these super-high prices, what can we, the established companies, do to cash in on this financial bonanza? We have to find a way to shake the money tree so we can get some of the fruits too." Okay, so they didn't say exactly that but you get the idea. And the answer was . . . issue tracking stocks, of course.

After the collapse of the dot-com boom, however, the stars of tracking stocks fell and they went the same way as dinosaurs and woolly mammoths. According to a 2004 article in *USA Today*, there has not been a tracking stock issued since 2002. Worse, only about 5 of the 38 tracking stocks issued since 1984 are still around. The same article reports that, on average, the performance of the 28 tracking stocks issued prior to 1999 lagged behind their appropriate benchmarks.

A research article that examined the determinants and consequences of a company's decision to create spinoffs versus issuing tracking stocks reports that a key determinant is market-timing. Management decides on one versus the other in order to cash in on investor euphoria. The study also finds no new clients enter the shareholder pool as a result of such corporate restructurings. Finally, the research finds that tracking stocks are more likely to be issued when the underlying division of the corporation generates tax benefits and if the management is entrenched with no fear of being unseated by shareholders.

In sum, given the few remaining tracking stocks in the market, the topic itself has more historical relevance than investment value. If you do come across one you would like to invest in, please read the above and perform diligent research before investing.

Setting of Stock Prices

How are stock prices set? Surprisingly, it is not a simple question to answer. From a rational expectations standpoint, the price of a stock is the present discounted value of all future cash flows associated with the asset. Although the rational expectations hypothesis forms the underpinnings of most contemporary financial asset pricing models, its empirical validation has been weak. For example, economist Robert Shiller has shown that the price volatility shown in the stock markets is too large to be justified by rational expectations models. Confronted by this apparent failure of the rational expectations framework as a way to price stocks (and other financial assets), many economists have argued that some other "irregularities" may be at work here to explain the excess volatility puzzle. Behavioral finance, for example, deals with these supposed irregularities and provides its own twists to explain the excess volatility shown in the market (we discuss behavioral finance later). And, lately, experts have suggested another potential "non-fundamental" factor to better explain

> The price of a stock is the present discounted value of all future cash flows associated with the asset.

stock pricing. To understand this, we have to go back to 1936, and a British economist named John Maynard Keynes, who argued that in order to form their demand for a stock, investors not only forecast its future payoff (consistent with rational expectations) but (and here is the important point) also try to guess other market participants' forecasts of the same stock and others' forecasts of other forecasts, and so on. So, the price of a stock is not what you think it is worth, but your estimate of what others think it's worth. Sort of like a beauty contest where the winner is not who the judges personally think is the most beautiful but who each think others will find most beautiful. This concept is known as having "higher order beliefs."

There has been some preliminary theoretical research showing that, when you factor in higher order beliefs in stock pricing, the volatility displayed by the stocks is significantly higher than those displayed by pricing without including higher order beliefs. While such esoteric research may be satisfying to academics in their proverbial ivory towers (I personally have never known an academic who could afford an ivory tower, let alone live in one), it provides scant comfort to Joe Investor deciding what is the "right" price for a stock he is interested in buying. But Joe should not worry because he is interested only in "relative" pricing as opposed to the economists puzzling about the "absolute" pricing of a stock.

In simple terms, Joe's problem is that he wants to buy stocks and make some money doing so through price appreciation and occasional dividends. So, if he wants to buy stock of a given company, he wants to know if it is currently over-priced or underpriced. To do so, he needs to examine his stock's price on a daily basis and understand that, on a given day, the price represents the consensus value created as if by an "invisible hand." The fact that this price may be inaccurate in an absolute sense is less of a concern for Joe as long as everyone (or, almost everyone) is playing by the same rules. To paraphrase Keynes: If you find a stock that seems like a good stock to you but everyone else out there thinks it's bad, then the weight of the belief works against you (and a few others who hold your view), and it becomes a bad stock.

But, things happen on a day-by-day basis that make prices jump around its "true" unobservable value. That is, the market value of the stock is the true value plus some slack to account for market imperfections (or, market frictions, as the academics would say). And the market value of any stock—the price people are willing to buy and sell it for—is, among other things, a function of the marketplace and things like fads and trends, corporate earnings, and the level of dividends paid to shareholders. Stocks are just like any other commodity: Buyers and sellers come together in a competitive marketplace and transact business at mutually agreeable prices. Of course, the agreed upon prices should seldom deviate too far from their "true" value in a well-functioning market. Institutional forces, such as demand from mutual funds and a host of psychological factors can also either boost or depress stock prices. At times, investor demand drives prices beyond reasonable valuations, while at other times, investor disinterest pushes stock prices lower. Finally, the political climate is also a major influence on stock prices, as is the general state of the economy, the level of interest rates, and the attractiveness of competing investments. For these and other reasons, investors may be willing to pay $25 today for a stock that seems fairly valued at $20, and six months later pass up the opportunity to buy it for $15.

Valuation of Stocks: The Dividend Growth Model

In the last section, we discussed stock valuation in somewhat general terms. We discussed, for example, how supply and demand for a particular stock will determine its value at any given point in time. Also, as indicated above, a direct consequence of the rational expectations principle is that the value of any financial asset (be it a stock, bond, or an elephant) is the current discounted value of all future cash flows accruing from this asset. That's it. Case closed!! But, wait a minute! How do I obtain all future cash flows of an asset and what the heck do I use for a discount rate?

The answer to these questions depends on the kind of asset we are discussing. For stocks, the future cash flow is very hard to determine accurately. For starters, stocks don't have a finite maturity date. As long as the company exists, its stock exists. That is a problem from a valuation standpoint. The other problem is that stock dividends are unpredictable. It depends on the discretion of the company's board of directors. For other kinds of financial assets, such as bonds, the problem of determining future cash flows is much more simple. For one, bonds have a finite life. Also, bond coupon payments are fixed and occur at predetermined intervals as long as the company is financially healthy. Coupon payments occur with clock-work-like regularity until the bond matures and then you get the face value back (more on this in the Bond section later). So, this underlying predictability with bond cash flows makes it easier to price them.

Let us return to how we can use the dividend growth model for pricing stocks. Let's start with a simple one period model where we have the current period (time 0) and the future (time 1). We now have to figure out what the dividend for the stock is going to be at time 1, given that we know what it is currently. Let's assume that the dividend at time 1 is denoted by D1. Also, let's assume that our required rate of return for investing in this particular stock is given by another number, K. Intuitively, K can be thought of as the sum of the risk free rate and a premium for holding a risky stock. One final point. Assume that the dividend growth rate for the stock is given by g. Given the above assumptions, the current value of the stock (at time 0) in this two-period world would be given by D1/(K-g). A fair amount of non-trivial math is involved in obtaining this formula and we will not go into it here. If you are interested, you will find it in any standard MBA-level investment book.

Of course, in real life, we have to consider a complicated multi-period model, but the underlying intuition outlined above stays the same. We might then have to worry about the process by which the dividend itself would grow: Linearly (i.e., constant growth rate)? Exponentially? And so on and so forth! Also notice that if the growth rate of the firm exceeds the firm's required rate of return (i.e., g>K), we would be left scratching our heads and not be able to calculate the value of the stock. Finally, the above model does not take into account the series of intangibles that can realistically impact the value of a stock—things like good will, trends, image, and so forth. So, a model like this can, at best, provide a bottom line value of the stock. The actual value of the stock will then have to be marked up appropriately over this base value.

In the final analysis, ascribing the true value of a financial asset is more an art and less a science.

Practical Ways to Tell If a Stock Price Is Too High or Too Low

We can calculate some important ratios based on publicly available information in order to determine if a stock at any given point in time may be undervalued or over-valued. Some of the major ratios are

Price/Earnings

A stock's price/earnings multiple (P/E) provides some idea of whether a stock is overvalued or undervalued. To find the P/E, you divide the current stock price by its earnings per share. For example, let's say that pharmaceutical stocks are currently trading at an average P/E of 14. If Help-to-die (HTD) Pharmaceutical's current stock price is $25 and the company earns $2.50 per share, the P/E is 10, less than the industry average. The stock appears undervalued based on this measure, but before you get too excited, other data must be considered to be sure that it is a good buy.

Be aware of the kind of earnings number you use to compute the P/ E ratio: It makes a difference. For example, the Yahoo! Finance Web site reports P/E ratios

Equating Stock Picking with Bride Picking

We have looked at a variety of issues related to stocks and stock trading. Buying stocks responsibly is clearly not an easy task. Picking what stock to buy in a way reminds me of the way men have traditionally picked their brides in India and in a lot of ancient civilizations around the world.

It is the girl's family who makes the first move in the game of "Who Wants to Marry Your Daughter?" Unfortunately, girls with rich dads have a head start in landing a "quality" guy. Potential grooms come with different price tags determined by where he went to college and how many letters there are after his name and, most importantly, the socioeconomic background of the groom's parents. As a result, many parents of girls of marriageable age can, and do, go into significant debt in order to find suitable matches for their daughters. The concept of dowry is alive and well, especially in the villages, and takes the form of cattle, land, jewelry, household furniture, and cold hard cash.

An arranged marriage is a contract between two families, coming together through marriage, and completed either discreetly, in the case of upper-class educated families, or more openly, in the case of lower income families. Such contractual arrangements can get so oppressive and unbearable that the groom's parents have been known to sometimes set their daughters-in-law on fire if their parents were unable to deliver on the promised dowry. Certainly gives new meaning to "heated negotiations."

In spite of occasional fireworks (and, in truth, they are few in number), the search for the perfect match goes on—primarily through advertising in the daily newspapers and through word of mouth. While dating is significantly more common with the younger crowd, arranged marriages are still the popular choice in ultraconservative families and for the socially challenged.Typically, Indians will defend the practice by arguing that the process is similar to when you want to buy a car in the U.S.; you want the best and shop around until you get it. After all, one cannot pick out a wife or husband in the name of love while ignoring the equally important qualities of intellectual, cultural, and social compatibility. The wisdom of an ancient land that goes back before time!

The institution of arranged marriages in India has, however, evolved over time. Prospective grooms at one point were not even allowed to see a photograph of their prospective brides so as to preserve an unmarried woman's purity, her most valuable asset. By the 1930s, during my grandmother's wedding, the couple exchanged photographs to decide if they liked each other. By the 1960s, when my parents got married the arranged way, they were actually allowed to talk to one another prior to the wedding—with a roomful of gawking people, of course.

Today, potential couples, depending on how progressive their parents are, meet for coffee or a meal either at home or in a restaurant, before deciding to commit. Some are even allowed to go out on a "date" one-on-one. Middle-class women are even allowed to reject suitors favored by their parents. Engagements can last six months or longer. A far cry from even a decade ago!

based on a stock's prior 52-week earnings. However, many market professionals I know use a stock's projected next year earnings in order to compute the P/E ratio of the stock. While the latter is a forward-looking P/E ratio, the former is a backward-looking measure. Make sure you understand this the next time you have reason to look up a firm's P/E ratio. That is, make sure you know how the P/E is computed before you take the number and make your investment decision.

Dividend Yield

This measure gives you the percentage of a company's income that is returned on your investment. You can calculate the dividend yield by dividing the stock's dividend per share by the current stock price. We'll assume that the current average dividend yield in the utility sector is 5 percent. If Lights Out (LO) Electric pays a dividend of $1.60 and its stock is selling for $40 per share, the 4 percent yield is below the industry average. The stock may be overvalued according to this measure, since the yield is low, but once again investors should look at other factors to see if this is indeed the case.

Price/Book Value

This refers to the relationship between a stock's current price and its intrinsic worth or book value, which is based on a company's assets minus its liabilities. By dividing the stock price by the book value per share, you come up with the price/ book value ratio. A lower P/B ratio might imply that a stock is undervalued. It could also imply that there is something fundamentally wrong with the firm. A higher P/B ratio might imply an overvalued stock. As with other key measures, you will need to check the company's numbers, with those of its main competitors, as well as with the industry group (that the company belongs to) as a whole.

Finding Winning Companies

Let's face it, sometimes finding winning companies can result from merely being in the right place at the right time. Like just attending Harvard around the same time as Bill Gates, choosing the same major as Gates, and happening to strike up a friendship with him; or attending Oxford with Bill Clinton and becoming his party buddy; or even attending Hravard Law with Barrack Obama. It is like winning the jackpot of life except you don't really know it's the jackpot when it occurs. Only years later do you recognize the jackpot and the size of it. Don't tell me Robert Reich knew what Clinton was going to become when he was throwing one down with him in the pubs of Oxford way back in the sixties. The rest of us need to work hard and have a lot of luck.

It's the same with finding winning investments: Hard work and a bit of luck. They say Peyton Manning of the Indianapolis Colts is a fanatic about preparation. He reviews hours of tapes on his opponents to find that little edge he can exploit on game day. Your approach to investing should be like Manning's for football. While you cannot control luck, you can certainly control research (or, your own preparation). Do your research and the investment gods are likely to smile upon you.

The key is to find trends before they become major trends. Find that one small company with a killer product and do your research. For example, if you are interested in the biotech sector, read medical journals or attend pharmaceutical trade shows. Or, read *Consumer Electronics* if you are into technology and gaming. You can get a sense of who is manufacturing what and what its likely potential is. You may also want to read journals like *Nature* and medical journals like JAMA (*Journal of the American Medical Association*) in order to become knowledgeable about ongoing drug trials by pharmaceutical companies for currently incurable diseases like AIDS and cancer. For example, when a drug company completes a successful testing phase for any of its drugs under the auspices of the Food and Drug Administration (FDA) and gets approved for the next phase of tests (a successful drug has to go through many testing phases before being formally approved by the FDA to release the product in the market), its stock price goes up. Failure at any stage will almost certainly lower stock prices, the exact magnitude of decline being determined by the importance of that drug to the company as a whole. Later on, in the chapter on insider trading, you will read about how one drug company, IMCLONE, gambling on a critical drug it had spent many years and millions of dollars in developing and nursing through the FDA trials, was rejected by the same agency after successfully navigating through the early rounds. And how Martha Stewart, who was friends with the CEO and a large shareholder herself, may have gotten advance word (read insider information) on the FDA rejection privately before the information became

Learning by Analogy:
The Exploits of Chippy the Squirrel

When my grandfather was young and living in his country home in India almost a hundred years ago, he would have his evening tea in his beautiful flower garden. One day a squirrel (we will call him Chippy) happened to climb down from the huge oak standing over his deck chair, and drank the little tea left at the bottom of the cup.

The caffeine in the tea must have done its trick because Chippy was hooked. From then on, little Chippy would wait in one of the low-lying branches of the tree for grandpa to show up with his teacup. Then, Chippy would wait patiently for him to finish his tea and go back into the house before climbing down and drinking the rest of the tea from the bottom of the cup. Pretty soon, the little guy became bolder and bolder (maybe it was the caffeine speaking). He would sit right next to grandpa's chair chirping impatiently for his evening fix. It got so bad that on those days grandpa could not make it to the garden with his tea cup, Chippy would come inside the house through one of the open French windows and impatiently demand his tea. Soon after, my grandmother, being the angel she was, started fixing tea separately for the regular evening house guest. Time passed and, after a while my grandparents noticed another squirrel trailing Chippy during his evening visits to the house. This newcomer was shy, and not given to the Chipster's boisterous behavior. It was assumed she was Chippy's significant other. So a second cup of tea was fixed for the new guest and pretty soon both Chippy and his girlfriend became permanent fixtures of the house—both addicted to caffeine and needing their daily fix.

The point of this little anecdote (it is a true story, by the way) is that Chippy accidentally found a good thing and stayed with it. He even got his girlfriend in on it. But you can't always be so lucky. Sometimes you have to do the hard work in order to get lucky.

public and then tried to sell all of her stocks in the company and spent time in prison as a punishment for her efforts. In sum, reading about drug trials and then trying to project how these trials will go and accordingly buying stock in the parent company might be a lucrative investment strategy.

Another example in a different area is the technology behind the RFID (Radio Frequency Identification) tags. Imagine the barcode on the retail products of today being replaced with something that has a whole host of information on it. So when you go to Abercrombie and Fitch and buy a sweater, they will know that you bought a red sweater a couple of months ago. And maybe you bought a green sweater last year. And every time a box passes through a warehouse door, RFID tags on the boxes will allow it to record all the information contained in it. Have you seen the IBM commercial about a truck headed the wrong way being pulled over by a lady sitting in the middle of the road and telling the truck driver that the boxes in the truck had sent out warnings that they were headed the wrong direction? That is what I am talking about. Do you think the technology will take off? If you are right, you will make a tidy pile of cash. If you are wrong, as you will be in many cases, you will lose money. Like I said, it's all about preparation but nobody said it was going to be fun.

The Top-Down Approach

One specific way to find winning stocks is to follow what is known as the Top-Down approach. Identify winning industry groups that are likely to perform well in the coming years and then eventually burrow down from there to identify specific companies within these industry groups. What are the possible industry groups, you ask? They can be anything from Basic Materials to Energy, Cyclicals to Noncyclicals, Health Care, Technology, Financial, Utilities, Media and Leisure, Retailers and Wholesalers, and others. Each of these industry groups is, in turn, divided into a number of sectors, so once you have identified an industry group that you think is a winner, you have to unravel it down to its various sectors. Do not break out that wine quite yet. We still have work to do.

For instance, if it's the technology sector that you identify, you have a variety of sectors within this industry group such as semiconductors, hardware, software, and telecommunications. Just because the tech boom is over does not mean that the prospects of all tech sub-sectors are grim. Semiconductors could easily come back in the next few years behind an ultra-powerful, ultra-small, chip!

Random Thoughts on Specific Stocks

Another approach is to find individual stocks showing market dominance potential, i.e., possessing a strong business model. These companies should have sustainable, competitive advantages, and a track record of consistent growth. And if the company has had a poor performance record in the past, has there been some kind of major turning point that makes it look better moving forward? Ask yourself, what is the financial strength of the company in terms of debt and cash flows, and cash on the balance sheet? Too much debt on the books is bad and too much surplus cash on the balance sheet could be both good news and bad. For example, too much cash can attract the attention of other companies to identify it as a potential takeover target (good news). It could also signify inefficient management unable to put its cash to good use (bad news).

Take a company like Intel—a giant in the semi-conductor universe. They are the world's largest provider of chips. These chips go inside every personal computer. They have a very strong balance sheet with a healthy cash position. They own very strong intellectual property in terms of the designs, manufacturing processes, and so on, that go into making chips.

And consider the personal computers (PCs) themselves. If you think growth in the PC market is slowing down you could be dead wrong. Maybe the growth has slowed a bit but the role of the PC is also changing—slowly but surely. Ten years from now, PCs may play a very important role, like the set top cable box in our living rooms today, only it is going to direct our digital content, whether that is pictures, home videos, what have you, and allow you to take it with you wherever you go. That technology is in existence today, but it's a little clunky and a little pricey. That will change over time. This means storage will become important as will the software to ensure that the storage is used and directed efficiently. Companies like Microsoft, Red Hat and Oracle are likely to be major players in the future. And how about companies like Cisco Systems (CSCO) within the communications sector? CSCO is a leading provider of communications equipment. Why is this important? Because, in the old world, we made phone calls over plain old telephone systems of copper wires, which carried voice signals only. In today's world, we want it to be able to carry voice and video content in a common language that is in bits and bytes, or in digital ones and zeros. If you want to invest in any of the above stocks, you should check to see where it is trading. Is it overvalued? A standard measure used by professionals in evaluating tech companies is to use a P/E ratio (based on one-year forward earnings) of about 20–25. If the current stock price puts the P/E ratio of the stock below this number, it is an undervalued stock. Another trend to watch for is the seasonal one, which hits most retail stocks in the fourth quarter—the Christmas season. Try to guess which companies are likely to have hit products that consumers must have. Does XBOX 360 ring a bell?

Now consider a company like Apple (ticker: AAPL). It is based mostly around the personality and the vision of its founder Steve Jobs. It is arguable that the company would be nearly as phenomenal as it has been should something happen to him. Recently there have been rumors of Job's failing health and recurrence of his cancer. The company typically has been tight-lipped about him. A reasonable question to ask for investors and potential investors alike is: Is it worth hanging on to the shares of the company or even invest in the company in the first place? If you believe that Jobs is not the main driver of the company, and that the company will do just fine without him, then your choice is clear.

Beware of E-mail Scams

If you are like me, you have a plethora of e-mails from all kinds of stock-picking experts extolling the virtues of their stock-picking ability and how they had correctly identified some little-known stocks trading in pennies that, since their selection, had gained astronomically in value, all in the space of about eighteen months. If you had only invested your money with the company, you too would be the recipient of huge gains.

An e-mail I received recently, brought to my attention a small company based in Reston, Virginia, called Global Exploration (ticker: GXXL), that operates Web sites aimed at Americans from South Asia. The day after I received the e-mail, the stock was trading for as much as twice its typical price, on twice the average volume of the prior two weeks. Before too long, investors had paid anywhere from 5 cents to 7 cents to snap up nearly 1.2 million shares of the company. Before the e-mail was sent out, the stock had typically traded for 3.4 cents to 4 cents per share. Sadly, for anyone who bought in that rally hoping to make a quick buck, the stock has since fallen to about 3 cents per share. Try not to fall into these traps! They are designed to get you excited about a stock and to get you to buy its shares, thereby pushing its price up, when the people who sent you the e-mail cash in on their holdings at the elevated prices you have helped create. It is the old "pump and dump" scheme we will see again later in the book.

The Saga of the Beardstown Ladies: Crooks or Just Naïve?

This is the saga of the Beardstown Ladies—a rag-tag gaggle of stock-picking grandmas who made national news by popularizing the mee-maw way of investing. They would gather around the kitchen table over milk and cookies and pick their moneymaking stocks. At least, that's the fairy-tale version.

Specifically, the fifteen women who now comprise the Beardstown, Illinois, Ladies' Investment Club—of book, video and television fame—boast an average return of 23.4 percent on their investments, out-performing mutual funds and professionals. The women formed their club in 1983, each investing $100. Subsequently, each member contributes $25 a month. They meet the first Thursday of every month, usually in the basement of First Lutheran Church in Beardstown.

Unfortunately, a few years ago, the lovable grannies were unmasked as frauds—unintentional, mind you—but frauds nonetheless. Five books, hundreds of speeches and dozens of national-TV appearances later, *Chicago Magazine* challenged their claim of earning compound annual average returns of 23.4 percent in the ten years ending in 1993.

Feeling the heat but undaunted, the ladies went to Price Waterhouse for an audit and discovered that their actual return was an unimpressive 9.1 percent—far less than the Standard & Poor's 500 average annual return of 14.9 percent or even the average general-stock-fund return of 12.6 percent during that same period. Updated in 1997, the audit shows that the ladies have picked up some of the slack, earning an average annual return of 15.3 percent. But that still lags behind the comparable S&P 500 figure of 17.2 percent, although it's better than the average stock-fund gain of 13.8 percent. It should be noted, however, that beating the average stock fund is no harder than beating the Arizona Cardinals or the Cincinnati Bengals. Translation, not that difficult!

The ladies, who for a while thought they might have been counting annual club dues as investment gains (they weren't), evidently were making incorrect entries in their computer. Nobody double-checked the math. So there goes their mystique, along with the potentially lucrative cottage industry they had developed. Their first book, which combined down-home recipes with investment tips, had that Warren-Buffett-like 23.4 percent emblazoned across the cover. It sold eight hundred thousand copies.

Investor Sentiment and Overconfidence

We often hear the term "investor sentiment" being bandied around. Have you ever wondered what it means? Investor sentiment happens to be trading based on "stuff" that is not fully rational—or something that defies common sense. The tulip bulb fiasco in 17th century Holland is a classic example of this kind of behavior. Tulip bulbs were trading at fantastically elevated prices and those who bought them rationally believed that they could sell them at even higher prices.

Another term that is related to the above is the notion of investor overconfidence. I mentioned investor overconfidence earlier when we were talking about investing only in stocks or companies you know, remember? Overconfidence reflects a very basic human instinct to overestimate our skills, our prospects of success, or the accuracy of our information. Overconfidence can also manifest itself in thinking we are somehow smarter than "them." Such an attitude can lead to entrepreneurs or investors seriously overestimating their chances of success. It's the same as when you may want to invest only in companies in your backyard that you think you know. When a lot of entrepreneurs rushed in to capitalize on the Internet bubble by taking companies with half-baked ideas public, you know what happened next! Silly companies, with even sillier ideas, were selling at fantastically high prices because of market and investor overconfidence. Remember crybaby.com? (Well, okay, I made that up!)

But overconfidence prevails not only with investors. It has been shown that almost 70 percent of negotiators believe that the arbitrator will rule in their favor. Over 80 percent of the drivers on the road believe that they rank among the best 30 percent. So how does such overconfidence translate into trading strategies and trading profits?

Research has found that investor overconfidence generally leads to higher trading volume, higher price volatility (more choppiness in prices) and more informed stock prices. All of these are good things except the price choppiness part. And overconfidence usually begets more confidence and prices get choppier (or, more volatile) as a result.

Women Are No More Risk Averse than Men

A recent paper measures the gender difference in risk aversion using a sample that controls for bias in the level of education and finance knowledge. The authors survey approximately 1400 Finance and English professors from universities across the United States and compare their actual portfolio allocations to that of respondents in the Federal Reserve's Survey of Consumer Finances (SCF). Their findings suggest that when individuals have the same level of education, irrespective of their knowledge of finance, women are no more risk averse than men.

Reference: A. M. Hibbert, E. Lawrence, A. Prakash, 2008, Are Women More Risk Averse than Men? Working paper, Florida International University

The theoretical underpinnings of how traders might become overconfident might go as follows. Let's say that the trader in question does not initially know his own ability. As he goes along in life, he infers his ability from observing his own successes and failures. But in assessing his ability, he assigns too much weight to his successes and little weight to his failures such that, in expectation, it is his successes that stand out and the failures fade into insignificance. He becomes an overconfident investor. And we know that in our society we are conditioned to never take blame for any of our shortcomings. It's always someone else's fault. We have enough daytime talk shows that are only too ready to substantiate this feeling. So it is not surprising that, as a society, we create more overconfident people than in other parts of the world.

Some say that the questioning of modern finance began with the seminal paradigm known as Prospect Theory put forward by two economists, Dan Kahneman and Amos Tversky, in the 1970s. Prospect Theory, based on several experimental studies conducted by these gentlemen, could be thought of as an alternative to the utility maximization idea on which modern finance, including EMH (we will talk about the Efficient Market Hypothesis on the next page), is based.

The utility maximization idea simply states that individuals, through all their decisions in everyday life, are trying to maximize some unobservable utility function. Prospect Theory, too, is a description of how individuals evaluate losses and gains. In its original formulation, the term *prospect* was used to refer to a lottery. And so the theory was a way to understand how the winnings and losses from a lottery will be evaluated (and internally processed) by individuals.

An important difference between the Utility Maximization Theory and Prospect Theory is that, with the latter, the way in which an individual subjectively "frames" an outcome or transaction in his mind will affect the utility he expects to receive. Thus, if an investor loses a lot of money in the stock market, but frames the loss as a learning experience, he may gain positive utility from the loss—a notion that is unthinkable in the Utility Maximization Theory, where losing money is a bad thing relative to making money and the concept of framing has no place at the table.

Of course, just like the battle for dominance between cable and satellite, behavioral finance has its critics too. These critics argue that everything behavioral researchers claim as death blows to the standard finance paradigms can, in fact, be explained rationally. To understand this more clearly, we need a bit of perspective.

In 1970, a Chicago economist, Eugene Fama, put forward the Efficient Market Hypothesis (EMH). The basic idea behind it was very simple. EMH argued that, in an effcient market, the price of an asset should reflect all of the available information n that asset. Fama further conceived of three different types of markets: A weak form efficient market, a semi-strong form efficient market and a strong form efficient market. If markets were weak form efficient, an investor could not make systematic profits by simply trading based on the past sequence of prices.

A practical implication of the EMH is that if the U.S. markets were merely weak form efficient, then all the technical traders, chartists, and day traders, who claim to make their living looking for price patterns, would be out of work very quickly. The fact that they are able to make a living looking for, and trading on, price patterns indicates that the markets are better than weak form efficient. If, by contrast, markets are semi-strong form efficient, then an investor could not make systematic profits by trading simply on publicly available information—because all public information would already be in the stock prices!

How could an investor make profits in a semi-strong form efficient market? Only by coming up with new information not already in the price through research and other means.

Finally, a strong form efficient market implies that stock prices contain all information—public and private. Put differently, if our markets were strong form efficient, there would be absolutely no legal way to make profits on a consistent basis.

So what kind of markets do we have in the United States? Common sense suggests that they are probably closer to a semi-strong form efficient market. By contrast, markets in emerging countries are probably closer to weak form efficient.

The EMH, however, changed how we viewed markets overall—not just the financial markets. From a regulatory standpoint, the EMH perhaps argued for governments to back off from interfering with its day-to-day operations.

The other foundation of modern finance was constructed by three economists in the late 1960s and early 1970s. It is known as the Capital Asset Pricing Model (CAPM) and shows a linear relationship between market returns and an individual firm's returns. The slope of this relationship, also known as " beta," is the sole determinant of risk. And investors should be expected to earn a premium for being willing to hold beta risk. The interesting thing is that the CAPM and the EMH are connected. The validity of the CAPM implies the existence of EMH.

For the next twenty-five years or so, Fama and company basked in the afterglow of the EMH and went on to fame and personal fortune. EMH and CAPM continued to be the cornerstones of modern finance. But then dark clouds started gathering on the horizon. Researchers, analyzing actual market data, started getting results that seemed to challenge the established doctrine.

Thus, for example, researchers in the 1990s reported significantly higher returns for NYSE-listed firms than for firms listed in the NASDAQ. And another economist found that smaller NASDAQ stocks were more "liquid" than comparable NYSE stocks. To make matters worse, researchers also started coming up with findings that suggested end-of-the-month effects with stocks and end-of-the-year effects, January effects, weekend effects, Yom Kippur effects, Hanukkah effects, Festivus effects (Seinfeld), and so on. Simply put, these researchers were reporting that the simple act of buying, holding, and then selling stocks across the periods mentioned above provided systematically abnormal stock returns. The problem was that if the EMH was true, such abnormalities should not be observed. What was going on here?

Interestingly, rather than accepting the possibility that something may be going on here to challenge the status quo, these reported effects were given the moniker "anomalies" to classify them as an aberration that blunted a possible challenge to the establishment.

So what did the fathers of the EMH do? They did what anybody whose life's work was being challenged would do. They went on a rampage and attacked the new body of literature with scorn and disdain. Their argument in defending the EMH was that we should stick with EMH because there is no other viable alternative; that it has worked in the past and that it is now firmly ingrained in the professional psyche. They also attacked the empirical evidence itself arguing that since the evidence is random (i.e., not systematic), it actually proves the existence of EMH rather than the demise of it. They called the new evidence incapable of independent existence and that it is not a methodology in its own right.

So there you have it. Whether or not behavioral finance will become viable and eventually be able to displace EMH remains to be seen. As the weight of the evidence builds, the conventional framework of the EMH will have to be adjusted to accommodate the new entrants—whether the EMH founding fathers like it or not.

In some sense, we are at a crossroads of economic thought. Or, put more dramatically, at something akin to the burning out of a star with another being created at the same time. The behavioral finance researchers are like academic terrorists (or, freedom fighters, depending on your outlook) challenging conventional thinking!

At this point, I am almost tempted to say that we in academia publish the results we have and not the results we would like to obtain. It's similar to former Defense Secretary Donald Rumsfeld's now infamous comment about going to war with the army one has and not with the army one would like to have. So even if the founding fathers of the EMH get indignant, the weight of the evidence will eventually force a consensus decision, whatever that may be. We will just have to wait and see.

How Does Behavioral Finance Help (or Hurt) Individual Investors?

Contributed by Avanidhar Subrahmanyam
Goldyne and Irwin Hearsh Chair in Money and Banking
University of California, Los Angeles

Traditional finance has focused on explaining asset prices, while trading activity itself has generally been ignored. Yet, the NYSE website indicates that the annual share turnover rate in 2003 on the NYSE was almost 100 percent of all shares outstanding. Simple math reveals that the investing public is voluntarily paying several billion dollars in commissions to brokers every year. Therefore, it seems reasonable to want to analyze the extreme levels of trading volume and provide an intuitive explanation of where such volume comes from.

It has been shown that there is a disposition effect prevalent among individual investors which can be described as a tendency to sell winners too soon and hold on to losers too long.[2] The disposition effect is consistent with the notion that realizing profits allows one to maintain self-esteem but realizing losses causes one to implicitly admit an erroneous investment decision, and hence is avoided. In a comprehensive study of trading activity in the Finnish markets, two economists confirm the disposition effect. They also show that there are reference price effects, in that individuals are more likely to sell if the stock price attains a past month high.[3] Furthermore, there is also a significant increase in volume if the stock achieves new maximum and minimum prices, again suggesting evidence of reference price effects. Such studies have added to our understanding of why people trade, but a calibration of a specific model that would deliver the magnitudes of volume observed in reality would be desirable in order to build a complete understanding of trading activity.

Interestingly, past winners do better than losers following the date of sale of stock by an individual investor, suggesting a perverse outcome to trades by individual investors. A particular study finds that individuals who trade the most are the worst performers.[4] A related study reports that women outperform men in individual stock investments. The researchers attribute their findings to the fact that men are generally more overconfident than women.[5] The intuition is based on an evolutionary rationale where men, as hunter-gatherers, are required to be overconfident to take risks for the purpose of hunting to acquire food, an essential ingredient for survival. Others have found that investors who choose to make investments online are better performers than those who did not go online before the switch to online

Skewness

In order to understand what skewness is, let's first understand what skewness isn't. First, skewness is related to a probability distribution. What is a probability distribution? It is simply a range of various outcomes that are plotted against the frequency that those outcomes occur. The skewness of a probability distribution simply refers to the "tails" of the distribution and how they slope at each end. For comparison purposes, consider the normal distribution, which has the familiar bell shape and no skew. This means that each tail of this distribution is of equal shape and length. Put differently, the normal distribution is symmetric around its mean. The implication of a symmetric distribution with no skew is that the probability of occurrence of an outcome below the mean is equally likely as an outcome above the mean.

An asymmetric probability distribution, on the other hand, has one tail that is longer than the other tail. Specifically, a positively skewed distribution has a longer left hand side tail. At this point, you may be wondering how all of this is related to Personal Finance. The skewness of a probability distribution can determine the relative likelihood for extraordinary gains versus extraordinary losses. Thus, for example, if I told you that the prices of small cap stocks are positively skewed, it should immediately suggest to you that investing in such stocks might reward you with significant price gains (more so than incurring significant losses). Similarly, bond prices and, in particular, investment grade bonds, have been shown to demonstrate a negative skewness which should suggest that the chances of abnormal losses outweigh the chances of abnormal gains.

investing but became worse performers after the switch. Apparently, overconfidence induces them to switch but then excessive trading after the switch dissipates their profits.[6] Another study shows that individuals appear to particularly prefer stocks with lottery-like characteristics (i.e., high volatility and skewness).[7]

Recently, it has been shown that small traders, on net, buy losers and subsequently become net sellers in these stocks suggesting that, by under reacting to negative information, they may create momentum.[8] An earlier related study reveals that the trade imbalances of small investors are negatively related to future stock returns. These findings are consistent with the notion that small investors overreact to information, and the reversal of their sentiment may cause stock return predictability.

A small but growing line of literature also provides evidence from derivative markets that investors do not seem to incorporate information properly. For example, individual investors appear to exercise their stock options when it would clerly be more profitable to sell them. Additionally, investors in the options market do not react properly to volatility information about the stock market.

Do behavioral biases of investors actually affect prices through their trading activity? Research provides evidence of this by arguing that proprietary traders on the Chicago Board of Trade (which mainly trades derivative securities like options that we will discuss later) take more risk late in the day (as measured by number of trades and trade sizes) to cover their losses in the beginning of the day.[9] This implies loss-averse behavior. Prices are affected by this behavior since the investors are willing to buy contracts at higher prices, and vice versa, than those that prevailed earlier. Stock market participation may be also be influenced by social interactions in that people who are more social, in the sense of interacting more with peers at collective gatherings such as in churches or synagogues, are more likely to invest in the stock market.[10]

Another study shows that reducing investor autonomy by forcing investors by default to participate in a savings plan until they choose to opt out (as opposed to requesting them to enroll in the plan) actually increases their savings rate.[11] Further, more investors who are young and less wealthy hold under-diversified portfolios, suggesting that we (the individual investors) may be exhibiting stronger behavioral biases.[12] And while we prefer stocks with high brand recognition, supporting the familiarity hypothesis,[13] we are also more prone to hold stock in firms that are located close to us—showing a geographic bias in addition to name recognition.[14,15] The individual investor's preference for local stocks extends to professional mutual fund managers, in the sense that such managers tend to show a proclivity for stocks headquartered in the region in which the managers themselves are based.[16] Finally, mutual fund managers are more likely to buy stocks that other managers in the same city are buying, suggesting that one factor impacting portfolio decisions is a word-of-mouth effect by way of social interaction between money managers.[17]

Overall, the evidence on individual investors presented above suggests that we are not particularly sophisticated in designing trading strategies. And, worse, we do not appear to achieve particularly impressive returns. Indeed, one study suggests that there is actually a wealth transfer from individuals to institutions via the stock market—the wrong direction![18] Why then do we trade? Perhaps because for us, individual investors, trading is akin to a consumption good—i.e., we trade for the sheer pleasure that trading provides us in a manner similar to watching a sport or a film, or gambling in Las Vegas, Atlantic City, or in the NCAA betting pool. Further investigation on why we may be willing to trade, while continuing to lose money on average, would be extremely useful.

Stock Indexes: It's All about the Pulse

Have you been paying attention when the evening news comes on and the anchor concludes by saying something like "The Dow ended the day down 20 points and the NASDAQ ended flat." We all hear it and nod our heads sagely, but do we really know what these guys are talking about? They are talking about stock market indexes—and one in particular.

This is nothing but taking the pulse of the patient—the patient being the NYSE and the NASDAQ. The pulse is supposed to capture how the markets performed overall that day in a single number. So, for example, if the NYSE ended the day down, does it mean that every stock trading in the NYSE was down? Not at all!

In fact, it could well be the case that your personal holdings could have had a gang-buster day. The ending value of the pulse and its direction—up or down— from the previous day's closing value is simply a reflection of the overall mood of the market.

To have a better understanding of indexes, first consider the silly, but intuitive, proverb of the blind men and the elephant. Have you heard it? If you haven't, don't feel bad about it. Just read the following box and you will be up to speed.

Here are some common indexes and what they stand for.

The Dow Jones Industrial Average (DJIA)

The oldest and the mother of all indexes, the DJIA, affectionately referred to as the Dow, traces its history back to 1896, when an enterprising reporter named Charles Dow decided to add the closing prices of twelve important stocks of the day, divide the total by 12, and started publishing these numbers on a daily basis. The companies included spanned agricultural products and utilities reflecting the agricultural

Anecdote: Five Blind Men and an Elephant

This (slightly unrealistic) anecdote unfolds as follows. Five blind men (all blind at birth—a fact that is crucial to the story) approach an elephant, touch only one part of it, and then discuss what an elephant is. Since each touches a different part of the beast, they of course disagree. The man who touches the leg says an elephant is like a tree, while the man who touches the trunk says an elephant is like a snake. An elephant is like a rope, says the man who touches its tail; like a wall, says the one who touches its side. You're all wrong, says the man who touches the ear; an elephant is like a big leaf. What is the moral of this proverb?

There is some truth in each of these impressions, but none seems to describe the whole elephant. And it's the same with stock market indexes, each of which tries to describe what's going on in a part of the market. Each has its limitations, but each has its own truth, too.

base of the U.S. economy. Over time, as the economy grew in size and scope, the number of stocks included in the index increased from 12 to 30. Only one company has survived the years since its inception and continues to be included in the index today: General Electric (GE was dropped from the index in 1898 but included again nine years later).

The Dow is the fodder of evening newscasts throughout the U.S. Many news anchors end the newscast with pronouncements like, "The Dow ended the day up 12 points" or "The Dow was choppy today and ended flat." Choppy means uncertainty captured by the standard deviation, or the variance, discussed earlier. It's the ocean analogy. Finance experts in the media are fond of using this term. They feel that it better conveys the uncertainty in the markets. One criticism with the Dow is that it is a simple "price-weighted average." What that means in simple language is that the DJIA simply averages the prices of the 30 stocks so that all stocks within the index have the potential to impact the index equally, independent of their relative size. In reality, intuition suggests that the larger stocks in the index should influence the index more than the relatively smaller stocks .

The Standard & Poor's Index of 500 Stocks (S&P 500)

The S&P 500 index is a comprehensive index of 500 large-company stocks. These stocks make up over 75 percent of the value of the U.S. stock market and hence, is much broader and deeper than the Dow. There is another reason why it is preferred over the Dow by practitioners and researchers. The index is "market value-weighted." That means the biggest companies make up the biggest part of the index, so their price changes move the index the most.

In addition, each stock exchange also has its own index made up of some of its stocks. Here are some examples:

The New York Stock Exchange Market Index is a market value-weighted index of all stocks traded on the NYSE.

The Amex Market Value Index is a market value-weighted index of the American Stock Exchange.

Perhaps the most popular exchange average in recent years is the NASDAQ Composite Index. It is a market value-weighted measure of some stocks traded in the NASDAQ over-the-counter market. Given that the NASDAQ is the home of the technology stocks, the index is loaded with computer and technology companies.

The Russell 3000 is a market value-weighted index of the largest 3,000 companies in the United States. Russell has divided this index into the top 1,000 stocks (the Russell 1000) and the bottom 2,000 stocks (the Russell 2000). The latter index is a popular measure of small company stock activity. Finally, there is the Wilshire 5000. This consists of a market value-weighted measure of all stocks, approximately 8,200, traded on the New York, Amex and NASDAQ stock exchanges. The stock market is some elephant, all right. Each index gives you a different sense of the beast.

Okay, so enough about stock market indexes. What about other kinds of indexes like the Consumer Confidence Index? What does it measure?

Consumer Confidence Index: Information or Noise?

Every month, the two primary measures of U.S. consumer confidence, the University of Michigan's Index of Consumer Sentiment, and the Conference Board's Consumer Confidence Index, are released with much media fanfare. The attention these indexes receive centers on the potential information they contain regarding current and future economic conditions. Changes in the indexes are often described as foreshadowing changes in economic conditions.

What do these indexes measure? And why do they receive so much attention?

Simply stated, consumer confidence is a jazzy phrase for the opinions and attitudes of consumers about the current and future strength of the economy. Since it is basically psychological in nature, it is pretty difficult to measure. The University of Michigan and the Conference Board both measure consumer confidence by asking a random sample of consumers the same questions about current economic conditions and expected future conditions. Consumers are also asked to assess their personal financial situation. Specifically, the questions asked are:

1. We are interested in how people are getting along financially these days. Would you say that you (and your family living there) are better off or worse off financially than you were a year ago?

2. Now looking ahead—do you think that a year from now you (and your family living there) will be better off financially, worse off, or just about the same as now?

3. Now turning to business conditions in the country as a whole, do you think that during the next 12 months we'll have good times financially, or bad times?

4. Looking ahead, which would you say is more likely? That in the country as a whole we'll have continuous good times during the next five years? Or, that we will have periods of widespread unemployment or depression?

5. This question relates to the big things people buy for their homes—such as furniture, a refrigerator, stove, television. Generally speaking, do you think now is a good or bad time for people to buy major household items?

After the surveys are conducted, the responses are aggregated into a single number, called an "index" of consumer confidence. Variation in this index is supposed to measure the variation in overall consumer confidence.

Why does this index receive such attention? It is believed that such an index will provide an early glimpse of the strength of the economy or any impending doom. Another way of saying this is that consumer confidence is believed to predict the state of the economy. Is the infatuation with the index justified?

After much investigation, economists have concluded that while the index has some power to predict the economy, its effect is really quite small. Furthermore, the same studies also conclude that the Consumer Confidence Index does not appear to have much additional information beyond that contained in other common forecasting data. In sum, we may be getting excited about something that is relatively insignificant.

Does Your Ability to Tolerate Risk Remain Constant throughout Your Life?

Academics appear to be divided regarding whether risk tolerance is a genetic and constant personality trait not likely to change over the life of an individual, or is something akin to attitudes and emotions that are likely to change over time and with life experiences. A recent study attempts to tackle this question by investigating the change in financial risk tolerance of scores of individuals over a five-year period and the factors that influence such change. Their results indicate a relatively small change in individuals' financial risk tolerance over time. In particular, the authors find a slight decrease in financial risk tolerance associated with a decrease in household size and after terminating the services of a financial planner. The authors conclude that financial risk tolerance is a stable personality trait and is unlikely to change substantially over the life of an individual.

Reference: G. V. de Venter, D. Michayluck, 2008, A Longitudinal Study of Financial Risk Tolerance, working paper, CFA Institute.

Thought Questions

1. Can ANY company issue stock?

2. What are some of the trade-offs you can think of between a company raising oney through selling shares of itself versus simply borrowing the money from lenders?

3. What would be some potential reasons for companies to underprice their shares in the IPO market?

4. Why would an underwriter try to support a level of price for the newly issued shares in the secondary market?

5. What are some advantages and disadvantages of going public versus staying private?

6. Can you think of some companies you have heard of that are not publicly traded?

7. Why would a company want to control voting rights through issuing multiple classes of shares?

8. What are the main differences between a growth and a value stock?

9. Where did the name "blue chip" stock originate?

10. When is a penny stock right for an investor?

11. Can you think of events in recent history when an entire sector of stocks was affected due to one company's illegal activities?

12. Why are the stocks of emerging markets considered risky?

13. Why is tracking stocks out of favor with investors now? What is an alternative to tracking stocks?

14. With veteran football players, the trade-off is, on one hand, you are getting proven talent while, on the other hand, you never know how many more games they can play. Similarly, what are the trade-offs of investing in penny stocks?

15. What conclusions can you draw about a company that has a very large P/E ratio?

16. How do you rationally explain the stock prices of companies like Google (GOOG) that trade at 100 plus times their earnings?

17. Can you think of other ways (not discussed in this chapter) to identify a potentially hot trend, hot stock, or a hot sector?

18. Do you think the Beardstown ladies did anything unethical? Why or why not?

19. Think carefully about the similarities and differences between Prospect Theory and the Efficient Market Hypothesis. How does it apply to you as an investor?

20. Do the presence of anomalies support, or refute, EMH? Why?

21. Why is a value-weighted index more reasonable than a price-weighted index?

22. What kind of a correlation would you expect between the Consumer Confidence Index and a major stock market index?

Notes

1. Prabhala, N. R., and M. Puri. "Price Support for IPOs Justified" working paper, Stanford University.

2. Shefrin, H., and M. Statman, 1984. "The Disposition to Sell Winners Too Early and Ride Losers Too Long." *Journal of Finance* 40, 777–790.

3. Grinblatt, M. and M. Keloharju, 2001. "How Distance, Language and Culture Influence Stockholdings and Trades." *Journal of Finance* 56, 589–616.

4. Odean, T., 1999. "Do Investors Trade Too Much?" *American Economic Review* 89, 1279–1298.

5. Barber, B., and T. Odean, 2001. "Boys Will Be Boys: Gender, Overconfidence and Common Stock Investment." *Quarterly Journal of Economics* 116, 261–292.

6. Barber, B., and T. Odean, 2002. "Online Investors: Do the Slow Die First?" *Review of Financial Studies* 15, 455–488.

7. Kumar, A., 2006. "Who Gambles in the Stock Market?" working paper, University of Texas, Austin.

8. Hvidkjaer, S., 2006. "A Trade Based Analysis of Momentum." *Review of Financial Studies* 19, 457–491.

9. Coval, J., and T. Shumway, 2005. "Do Behavioral Biases Affect Prices?" *Journal of Finance* 60, 1–34.

10. Hong, H., J. Kubik, and J. Stein, 2004. "Social Interactions and Stock Market Participation." *Journal of Finance* 59, 137–163.

11. Benartzi, S., and R. Thaler, 2004. "Save More Tomorrow: Using Behavioral Economics to Increase Employee Saving." *Journal of Political Economy* 112, 164–187.

12. Goetzman, W. N., and A. Kumar, 2003. "Why Do Individual Investors Hold Underdiversified Portfolios?" working paper, Yale University.

13. Frieder, L., and A. Subrahmanyam, 2005. "Brand Perceptions and the Market for Common Stock." *Journal of Financial and Quantitative Analysis* 40, 57–85.

14. Huberman, G., 2001. "Familiarity Breeds Investment." *Review of Financial Studies* 14, 659–680.

15. Grinblatt, M., and M. Keloharju, 2001. "What Makes Investors Trade?" *Journal of Finance* 56, 589–616.

16. Coval, J., and T. Moskowitz, 1999. "Home Bias at Home: Local Equity Preference in Domestic Portfolios." *Journal of Finance* 54, 145–166.

17. Hong, H., J. Kubik, and J. Stein, 2005. "Thy Neighbor's Portfolio: Word of Mouth Effects in the Holding and Trades of Money Managers." *Journal of Finance* 60, 2801–2824.

18. Barber, B., Y. J. Liu, Y. T. Lee, and T. Odean, 2004. "Who Gains from Trade? Evidence from Taiwan" working paper, University of California at Berkeley.

4

Basket of Stocks—Mutual Funds

Investors should follow the following prescription:
- *A careful selection of a few investments (or a few types of investment) having regard to their cheapness in relation to their probable actual and potential intrinsic value over a period of years ahead and in relation to alternative investments at the time;*
  - *A steadfast holding of these in fairly large units through thick and thin, perhaps for several years, until either they have fulfilled their promise or it is evident that they were purchased on a mistake;*
    - *A balanced investment position, i.e., a variety of risks in spite of individual holdings being large, and if possible, opposed risks.*

—John Maynard Keynes

So far, we have talked about individual stocks. We have discussed how to identify good stocks, their traits, how to trade them, and so on. However, as investors, we do not necessarily have to buy and sell individual stocks. We could buy and sell packages of many stocks, conveniently bundled and ready-made for us. Think of it as pre-packaged food that is ready to eat—the TV-dinners you can buy in your neighborhood grocery stores. The important feature of these packaged dinners is that you do not have to worry about the individual food components of your package. You see that the main ingredient of your dinner is beef (say). You check the back for the total caloric intake and you put it in your basket. It is the same with packaged investments.

Anecdote: Grease Monkey

I am always reminded of a story dating back to when I had just purchased my first car as a graduate student in the U.S. It was a sky-blue Ford Mustang, and I had purchased it with my own saved money. Needless to say, I was very proud of it. This was my baby and I was going to take care of it, change its oil, and so on. Someone had told me that the axles of the car needed greasing at regular intervals. I didn't know what it entailed but, like a new parent, I was determined to be hands-on and involved in my car's future and well-being. Those were the days when you could still work on cars yourself and didn't have to have them hooked to diagnostic machines to determine what was wrong with them. Oh how I miss those butterfly valves in the carburetor.

One day I borrowed a grease gun from a friend. I was going to grease those axles. The following Saturday was D-day (or, should I say, G-day). It was a beautiful summer morning and the birds were singing. Whistling a happy tune myself, I crawled under the car, grease gun in hand. Half an hour later, I emerged from down under. The chassis, unfortunately, was dry while I was greased from head to foot! The moral of the story? There are some jobs that are best left to experts!

What does this mean for investing in mutual funds? Simply that some (stock picking) jobs are perhaps best left to the mutual fund managers.

You see the overall flavor of your investment (chicken, beef, turkey, etc.) and the broad category of risk it carries (calories) and you buy it. In investments, these pre-cooked and pre-packaged dinners are called mutual funds. As it happens, mutual funds are quite the rage these days. We now have well over 8,000 funds in existence and there are even mutual funds of mutual funds. Now, if that is not diversification, I don't know what is.

A mutual fund is simply a pooling of investors' monies in creating a large pot with which to buy lots of different stocks. While this idea of pooling money for investment purposes was first born in Europe in the mid-1800s, the first pooled fund in the U.S. was created in 1893 for the faculty and staff of Harvard College. The problem was if you were not affiliated with Harvard, you were out of luck. The first official mutual fund for the masses was created in 1924 and called the Massachusetts Investors' Trust. By all accounts it was a successful venture because it grew from about $50,000 to almost $400,000 in assets within a year, which in those days was a lot of money. Since its humble beginnings, the mutual fund has come a long way with a mind-dizzying number of them to choose from. Companies like Morningstar have sprung up to help investors make intelligent choices.

Explosive Popularity

Since its humble beginnings in 1924, the mutual fund has come a long way. In the decade of the 1990s itself, the number of available funds increased by about two and a half times from about 3,000 funds in 1990 to about 8,000 plus funds in 2003. Almost three quarters of mutual fund assets are held by individual investors like you and me. Institutions, trustees, and guardians hold the rest. An average household (however defined) has about $25,000 invested in mutual fund shares, and more than one in three households made their first mutual fund purchase between 1990 and 1995.

One reason mutual funds have skyrocketed in popularity could simply be the marketing campaigns that Madison Avenue has waged to lure in investors. Owning mutual funds is now equated with a certain glamorous lifestyle, with professionals working for you, while you are sipping mai tais on some exotic beach with dolphins playing in the background. Let's just say we have bought into the hype. A less cynical explanation could be that as Americans have gotten busier with their lives, mutual funds seem like a convenient way to be investing in the markets without spending a lot of personal time doing the research and making the buy/sell decisions.

Why Mutual Funds?

The common answers I hear when I ask, "Why mutual funds?"

- They are convenient. I have no time to do research.
- I want a diversified portfolio.
- I want to make money.

And my personal favorite:

- I want to have fun!

I have to confess that "fun" threw me for a loop! In all my years of researching and teaching investments, I had not thought of mutual funds as fun. Maybe that is what was missing in my life: Having fun with mutual funds! On a slightly serious note, however, why would anyone ever want to invest in mutual funds?

Diversification

There is no greater advantage to using mutual funds than diversification. Do you honestly believe wealthy investors purchase just a couple of stocks? Of course not! If they are not using mutual funds (many do), they are purchasing a large number of stocks. Smart investors diversify because it greatly reduces risk without sacrificing returns. If the idea of diversification is new to you, think about it this way: You may be dating that cute guy from class, but you are not quite sure if he is the one for you. So, just in case he is not, you are also dating three other guys that you have met in various social events around campus. And none of the guys know about the others. That's pure diversification across assets.

Here is another way to think of diversification: Good football teams also diversify across types of players. Consider the well-known maxim: Offense wins games; defense wins championships. Right there is the notion of diversification. To win games, which in turn gives you a shot at winning championships, you need to have both offense and defense. The Indianapolis Colts exemplified this with their incredible run through the playoffs in 2007. Can you explain why?

Let's consider the diversification issue with regard to investments. Investors like mutual funds because they can invest in a variety of stocks with relatively little money. Buying 100 shares of Microsoft at current prices will cost you about $2,600. With $2,600, you could buy into a mutual fund and invest in literally hundreds of stocks. Diversification is important for investing. More diversification means less risk. Why? If you're invested in one stock and that stock hits a rough spot and takes a dive, it's tough for you to cash out without being hurt. If you are invested in a variety of stocks, you are less likely to be affected by the bad performance of one stock or even a few.

As I briefly alluded to in the beginning of the chapter, these days we are also seeing funds-of-funds: mutual funds comprising other mutual funds in their portfolio. Why do they do this? Primarily to diversify across a manager's investment styles. Think about this for a second. When you buy a single fund, you get a lot of stocks that are a part of the fund's portfolio. So you are diversified across stocks. But you still have a single fund manger (or, a single investment philosophy) that is at work guiding the buying and selling of what goes into the fund's portfolio. But what if you wanted to have exposure to many different investment philosophies simultaneously without taking the trouble of buying many different mutual funds? The answer lies in buying fund-of-funds. The downside, of course, is the second layer of fees that are absent in a regular mutual fund. The underlying funds have a fee just as the overall fund-of-fund manager does. And you have to trust the overall fund-of-fund manager to do a good job of researching the component fund managers' backgrounds and styles, etc. At the end of the day, the investors choose these investment vehicles to obtain stable returns while further reducing risk.

Professional Management

By purchasing mutual funds, you are essentially hiring a professional manager at an inexpensive price. It would be presumptuous of you to think that you know more than the mutual fund manager. These managers have been around the industry for a long time and have the academic credentials to back it up. Saying you could outperform a mutual fund manager is similar to a football fan sitting on his couch saying, "I could have made that catch." Possible? Of course! Likely? Nope!

Even if some of us are better at picking stocks than professionals and their support staff, most of us would not want to spend the amount of time it takes to watch, research and trade in the market on a daily basis.

Because it is convenient, we pay a lot of money to a professional fund manager with an MBA degree who thinks he/she knows all there is to know about investments and can make the stock buying and selling decisions for us. It's not that they are always right. Probably more like 50 percent of the time—which would make their being right or wrong a random process.

Efficiency

By pooling investors' monies together, mutual fund companies can take advantage of economies of scale. With large sums of money to invest, they often trade commission-free and have personal contacts at brokerage firms. In other words, the volume of trading they do entitles them to certain perks which they can then pass on to the fund investors. Another way to look at this is to consider Sam's Club or Costco. Have you ever wondered how you can get things cheap at these places? It's simple really. Sam's buys products in such volume that they can get deep discounts from manufacturers and then pass on those cost savings to you, the end user. But there is a catch: You too have to buy in large quantities. Have you wondered why everything at these places is in such large quantities? Well, now you know. It's the good old volume discount.

Ease of Use

Can you imagine keeping track of a portfolio consisting of hundreds of stocks? The bookkeeping duties involved with stocks are much more complicated than owning a mutual fund. If you are doing your own taxes, or are short on time, this can be a big deal.

If we don't have time to do our own research to pick stocks, then mutual funds are probably the best way to go. It's like paying someone to clean our house for us. Sometimes they work well and our money is well spent and at other times, things break, things go missing, etc. You take the good with the bad. It's the same with investing in mutual funds.

Another reason investors like funds is that they can invest small amounts of money. With some funds, the minimum investment can be as low as $250 for an Individual Retirement Account, or IRA. In fact, some investment advisors recommend that if you have less than $10,000 to invest, a fund may be the only way to go. You'll be properly diversified despite the small amount you're investing.

Liquidity

If you find yourself in need of money in a short period of time, mutual funds are highly liquid. Mutual funds happen to b ehighly liquid (meaning, easily convertible to cash) if you happen to have an urgent liquidity need. Simply put in your sell order during the day and, when the market closes, a check will be sent to you or you can have it wired to a bank account. Stocks can be much more difficult depending on what kinds of stocks you are invested in. Some mutual funds also carry check writing privileges, which means you can actually write checks from the account, similar to your checking account at the bank.

Cost

Mutual funds are excellent for new investors because you can invest small amounts of money and can invest at regular intervals with no trading costs. Stock investing, however, carries high transaction fees, making it difficult for the small investor to make money. If

> ## Focus
>
> There is a sense among novice investors that investing in mutual funds is a safe bet, that we will somehow make money if we only invest in mutual funds. If you buy mutual funds with the hope that you are more or less guaranteed to make money, then you are in for a big unpleasant surprise.

Jane wants to put $100 a month into stocks and the broker charges her $15 per transaction, her investment is automatically down 15 percent every time she invests. That is not a good way for Jane to start off.

Wealthy stock investors get special treatment from brokers and wealthy account holders get special treatment from the banks, but mutual funds are non-discriminatory. It doesn't matter whether you have $50 or $500,000, you are getting the exact same manager, the same account access, and the same investment. In that sense, mutual funds are the great equalizers. We all get the same treatment. Well, almost!

Risk

In general, mutual funds carry a much lower risk than stocks. This is primarily due to diversification. Certain mutual funds can be riskier than individual stocks, but you have to go out of your way to find them. Also, companies like Morningstar have made picking mutual funds easy with their star rating system. As long as you stay with four- and five-star funds, you are generally getting funds that are earning at least as much return as their risk would suggest—and possibly more.

With stocks, one worry is that the company you are investing in will go bankrupt. With mutual funds, that chance is next to nil. Since mutual funds typically hold anywhere from 25 to 5,000 companies, all of the companies would have to go bankrupt. But what happens if your mutual fund company itself were to go bankrupt? It turns out that if that were to happen (very small chance), your money is still safe. Under the Investment Company Act passed in 1940, each mutual fund is set up as an individual corporation complete with its governing board of directors. Hence, if this corporation were to file for bankruptcy, it would be treated as a regular corporation filing for bankruptcy and the fund's assets would be protected.

I won't tell you to never invest in individual stocks, but I do hope you see the advantages of using mutual funds. For international stocks or bonds, mutual funds allow you to invest without worrying about foreign restrictions on buying or selling securities. Also, you don't have to deal with the innumerable regulations that come with investment purchases in foreign countries. Nor do you have to worry about converting to U.S. dollars when you buy and sell. This makes international investing through mutual funds very convenient.

Measuring Fund Performance

But how do we measure fund performance? Unfortunately, we don't have one single measure for funds, because they can invest in any type of asset. For example, there are stock funds, bond funds, real estate funds, funds that invest in specific sectors, and many more. Some funds combine different kinds of assets. On average, fund performance mirrors the performance of the fund's asset class.

For specific asset classes, consistently underperforming funds for the past ten years have been the emerging-market equity funds (emerging-market bond funds have been fine) and precious metal funds. Over the last few years, since the burst of the tech bubble, large-cap equity funds, international funds, high yield bond funds, and technology/communication sector funds have not done so well either.

But what if you wanted to have exposure to the U.S. market as a whole? For example, what if you wanted to have exposure to the NASDAQ market or what if, for some crazy reason, you wanted to invest in the 500 largest companies in the U.S.? You could do so by buying "index" funds. We will discuss these later in the chapter.

It's the Prospectus, Stupid!

Mutual funds have two goals: To make money—both for themselves and for you, the investor. They are notorious for letting you know how good they are without exactly falling over themselves to reveal their weaknesses. After all, the prospectus also serves as an advertisement for the fund. But it does contain useful information if you know what to look for and where to look. The problem lies in the fact that in the good old days, before the advent of the Internet, we would read more and order copies of the glossy promotional material associated with anything in which we invested. Nowadays, everything is kept online and hardly anyone bothers to order printed copies of the prospectus. We may visit the company's Web site and cursorily scroll through the online prospectus but it is nowhere near as thorough a perusal as with a printed copy in our hands. Note that the information provided below has been compiled from a variety of resources including private conversations, Morningstar, Motley Fool, and other mutual fund-related websites on the Internet.

The basics are usually outlined on the cover page, but to really get a feel for the fund, you have to go beyond the covers. One of the major reasons that 90 percent of mutual funds underperform the S&P 500 Index is not that the fund managers are inefficient, but that they charge disproportionately more for the quality of their advice, costs that index funds do not have.

Fund Objectives

The prospectus will not detail actual fund hold-ings, but will describe the fund's objective and how it will attain it. For example, this section might tell you that when the fund says "small-cap," it means any company with a market capi-talization below $1 billion. Also, the fund may plan to have at least 80 percent of its assets invested in small-caps at any given time. There is, however, no guarantee that the fund will sell those stocks that, over time, may go from being a

> ## Questions
>
> All prospectuses should answer these essential questions:
>
> 1. How much is the fund going to make from managing your money?
>
> 2. What returns have the fund deliv-ered for investors in the past, and what does it generally invest in to achieve these results?

small-cap to a medium- or large-cap stock. This could become problematic if you bought the fund attracted by the intrinsic profit potential of small-cap stocks.

Fund Investment Strategy Section

You may want to know what investment strategy the fund uses. If you are a consci-entious investor (unlike me) then you have no doubt determined the type of fund you want (for example, growth and income, growth, or aggressive growth) and then used some kind of a screening tool to find the funds in that category that have deliv-ered the best results in the past. The alternative would be to pick up a fund on a whim without any research (the "life is a box of chocolates" analogy) like throwing a dart at a board with mutual fund names. You could train a chimpanzee to do it.

The sections of the prospectus dealing with the fund's investment strategy and accompanying risks are where you will find the details on who's running the fund and how they're running it. For example, you could find out that the fund manager does not just invest in small-cap growth companies but also engages in a fair amount of gambling by trading futures and options, taking short positions, and using margin trading. We will discuss margin trading formally in Chapter 6 later in the book.

Fund Expenses

Annual management fees are just one of the charges an investor finds in the sec-tion on "Transaction and Fund Expenses." The transaction side tells you about the sales charge or "load" (what it will cost you to buy into the fund), the sales charge to reinvest distributions (what it will cost to reinvest the annual profits the fund distributes to you), the redemption fees (what it will cost you to sell your shares of the fund), and the exchange fee (what it will cost you to move money from one fund to another in the same family of funds).

The first item is the sales charge, or the front-end load, for buying into the fund. Another charge is a back-end load, also known as a redemption fee, or a deferred sales charge. This is a charge for selling your shares in the fund. Often, the charge can run as high as 4 percent to 5 percent, but it is usually reduced the longer you own the fund. Many true no-load funds have no redemption fees, and some funds have no redemption fees except a 1 percent fee for investors who hold shares in the fund for less than 6 to 12 months. These time-sensitive redemption fees are designed to discourage investors from trying to time the market by jumping from one fund to another, since fund managers hate investor redemptions in their funds because it means they may have to sell stock when they least want to in order to come up with the redemption funds.

A fund's operating expenses can be decomposed into the management fee, marketing—or 12b-1—fee, and "other" expenses. Each is measured as a percentage of the fund's average net assets and payable every year. The management fee is what you're paying to fund managers for making the big investment decisions.

A healthy chunk of the expenses goes to 12b-1, which is the SEC rule that permits funds to charge you up to 1 percent of assets per year for the cost of marketing the fund to you and other shareholders. That means funds will actually charge you for the cost of reeling you in. Revenues generated under 12b-1 may go to pay the broker who sold you on the fund, or for that slick advertising on cable that originally caught your eye, or for that glossy brochure the investment company mailed you—all on your dime.

Finally, other expenses include various administrative costs such as keeping shareholder records, sending out financial reports, filing documents with the SEC, and so forth. All of these annual expenses get added up as a percent of assets under management, with a handy table showing what this will cost you in real money per $1,000 over the next few years, so you can compare the operating expenses of different funds. Before you start feeling warm and fuzzy about the funds giving you so much information, keep in mind that it is not purely out of the goodness of their hearts. SEC rules require funds to disclose both shareholder fees and operating expenses in a fee table near the front of a fund's prospectus. Funds are simply following orders.

Other Expense-Related Information

According to the experts, expenses run around 1.5 percent for the average equity fund. You should look for funds with expenses less than 1 percent. The expense ratio should also be declining over the years because, as a fund's assets increase, the investment company should be able to squeeze out additional economies of scale. This is a fancy way of saying that a fund should be able to save money just by virtue of its size. (Remember thoe Costco's and Sam's analogy.)

The ratio of net investment income to average net assets is equivalent to the fund's annual dividend yield. For an income-oriented fund, this varies between 1.5 to 3.5 percent while, for an aggressive growth fund, this number is expected to be closer to 0.5 percent.

Turnover Rate

Another important metric often overlooked by investors is the portfolio turnover rate defined as the percentage of total assets that were shifted from one investment to another over the past year. 100 percent indicates that the entire portfolio was turned over (read active trading strategy and higher costs), whereas a series of years showing low turnover, say around 40 percent, would indicate the fund manager doesn't trade in and out of stocks, but is more comfortable making long-term investments that he/she doesn't have to mess with for a while (read passive investment strategy and lower costs). This is an important measure because the fund manager's trading pattern is one that you can reliably take from the past and extrapolate to the future. And that is something that you cannot necessarily say for past performance predicting future performance.

The pattern of turnover rates also gives you an idea of the kind of a tax bill you will be facing. This is because a fund investor typically pays taxes on the fund's income and capital gains distributions. So a fund that doesn't do a lot of trading should have higher unrealized gains and a smaller tax bill for you (good news). If you have to choose between two funds, one with high turnover and one with low turnover, generating similar total returns, guess which one is better for you. The one with the low turnover, of course, since your tax hit is likely to be smaller. It will be lower also because longer-term holdings will benefit from the lower capital gains tax rate.

In sum, don't under estimate the prospectus. It's not just blatant advertising. There is important information there if you know where to look.

Index Mutual Funds

An index fund is a collection of stocks (or bonds) which track the overall market or a specific segment of the overall market. Arguably the best known index, and certainly the one that gets mentioned in the evening news a lot, is the Dow Jones Industrial Average (DJIA), composed of thirty major stocks across various industries selected by the editors at Dow Jones as best reflecting the U.S. stock market. So a mutual fund tracking the DJIA, for example, will comprise the same thirty stocks in its portfolio. Since the stocks in the DJIA do not get changed much, neither does the index fund tracking it. This last part is very important as we will soon see.

However, a broad-based index of large companies in the U.S. is the S&P 500, whose 500 stocks are selected by the Standard & Poor's based on its internal research related to a company's importance and its ability to represent a given sector of the economy. Collectively these 500 stocks make up 75 percent of the value of the U.S. stock market, so this average is much broader than the Dow's. It is also "market value-weighted," meaning that the biggest companies make up the biggest part of the index and their price changes move the index the most.

So what's so great about these index funds?

Index Funds Have Lower Fees

Index funds can be managed by a much smaller staff than an actively managed fund. Computers do most of the work, so there is no need to hire an expensive fund manager or research analysts. Index funds can have expense ratios as low as 0.18 percent (of the fund's assets), while actively managed funds can have expense ratios over 3.0 percent.

Here are some examples of index funds (with ticker symbols for your convenience):

Fund Name	Ticker	
FUNDS TRACKING THE S&P 500		
CA Inv. S&P 500 Index	SPFIX	http://www.caltrust.com
Dreyfus Basic S&P 500 Index	DSPIX	http://www.dreyfus.com
Dreyfus S&P 500 Index	PEOPX	http://www.dreyfus.com
Fidelity Spartan 500 Index	FSMKX	http://www.fidelity.com
Schwab S&P 500 Select	SWPPX	http://www.schwab.com
Scudder S&P 500	SCPIX	http://www.scudder.com
Fidelity Spartan Total Market Index	FSTMX	http://www.fidelity.com
T. Rowe Price Total Market	POMIX	http://www.troweprice.com
Vanguard Total Stock Market	VTSMX	http://www.vanguard.com
		EXPENSE
OTHER INDEX FUNDS		**RATIO**
Fidelity Spartan Total Market	FSTMX	0.25%
T. Rowe Price Total Market	POMIX	0.40%
Schwab Total Stock Market	SWTIX	0.40%
Vantagepoint Broad Market Index II	VPBMX	0.27%

Index Funds Don't Have Fund Manager Continuity Issues

Have you ever noticed that when the head coach of a professional sports team leaves and a new one is hired to take his place, the organization goes through a period of flux where no one quite knows what is going on? Almost predictably, the team performs poorly for a couple of years until things settle down and performance starts to improve. It's like that with mutual fund management too.

When a fund's manager leaves and a new one takes her place, you are never quite sure of what you will get until some time has elapsed and you have had a chance to see her performance. That is because, even within the broad fund philosophy, each manager has her own philosophy of investing, one that does not change often and can be reliably extrapolated from the past to the future. However, with index funds, this is not an issue.

Why? Simply because if one index fund manger leaves, the one succeeding him/her will simply continue to do what the other one did: maintain the same stocks in the same proportion as the particular index it is mimicking. So, manager continuity is one less thing to worry about with index funds.

Life-Cycle Funds

Life-Cycle refers to the process of the cycle of life for individuals wherein one starts young and then goes through the life process to old age. But, more importantly, as one moves through life, his needs, his available wealth, and his degree of risk aversion all change in predictable ways. Life-Cycle funds simply adjust to the changing needs of the individual. They were first introduced in the early 1990s, and offered investors pre-mixed doses of stocks, bonds, and cash according to their age and risk tolerance.

The Real Deal: Fund-Related Scandals

As with everything else in life, when something becomes very big very quickly with trillions of dollars invested industry-wide, ethical boundaries often get blurred by greed. Recently, scandals involving the mutual fund industry have spread like the wildfires of California and have implicated the biggest players in the mutual fund industry; companies like Putnam Investments, and household names like Merrill Lynch and Bank of America.

The scandals involve trade-related lapses that make money for the mutual fund management at the expense of fund shareholders like you and me. One such practice, known as "late trading" is quite simple to understand when put in the right perspective. Mutual funds, unlike the component stocks, are valued at 4 PM EST when they are legally expected to stop taking buy and sell orders, so a correct fund value can be assigned, and all trades made before that time cleared at that established price. Any orders coming in after 4 PM are expected to be held over for clearance at the next day's closing price. But it turns out that many mutual funds have allowed exceptions to this rule—particularly those funds known as hedge funds which are private little country-club type mutual funds run with small groups of wealthy individuals' monies. The hedge fund managers were allowed to make purchases after 4 PM at the already established price for that day.

Now you may be scratching your head at this point and going, "so?"

The problem is that sometimes news that seriously impacts the price of the component stocks, and hence the fund itself, breaks after 4 PM, or in the "after hours," as it is known. And such news is sure to impact the fund price next day.

So, by buying at the previous days' price illegally, these funds and individuals make money for sure. It's like plucking money off the money tree.

Another practice is known as "market timing." Market timing is nothing but some hedge funds and connected individuals being allowed to trade at stale prices in response to global events after close of market in one region in order to take advantage of markets that are still open in another region. So, for example, major European markets close several hours ahead of the NYSE. If something happened to the NYSE after European markets closed, the European market is sure to be affected similarly when it opens the next day. By trading the European stocks at the stale prices today, one would be perfectly poised to make a nice killing (by selling out at a higher price or by buying at a lower price) when Europe opened for trading the next day.

It's like a crucial fourth-and-one situation in football. The defense has to stop the offense in order to get the ball back and mount its own drive to victory. If they fail, the offense gets a new set of downs and runs off precious minutes of the clock. If the defense gets to know what play the offense will run before they run the play, then it's a no-brainer that the defense will stop the offense from getting the required yardage. But that would be cheating. It's like that with mutual funds too.

Notice that the funds are already premixed and cooked. It's just a matter of allocating the right mix to the individual as a function of his age. Thus, for example, almost all available fund families offer Life-Cycle funds in three broad categories: Aggressive, moderate, and conservative. And you can cycle through these funds (hence the name) as you journey through life—going from the young, aggressive investor to the older and more conservative one. While some Life-Cycle funds are funds of mutual funds, the rest are just regular mutual funds.

All the Life-Cycle funds share the same goal of first increasing and then protecting your wealth. While some track indexes and maintain a more or less static mix of assets, most Life-Cycle funds are more actively managed (read more management fees) by nature. So, for example, Vanguard funds, which advertise a passive indexing strategy in its Life Strategy brochure, invest about a quarter of each life-cycle portfolio in its actively managed Vanguard Asset Allocation fund (ticker: VAAPX).

As an investor, if active fund management makes you nervous, you have the choice of staying with the more passively run index funds.

Exchange Traded Funds (ETF)

Exchange Traded Funds (ETF) are similar to index mutual funds, but are traded more like stocks. ETFs first launched in 1993 and have grown into a $150 billion industry. As their name implies, ETFs represent a basket of securities that are traded on an exchange. As with all investment products, exchange traded funds have their share of advantages and disadvantages.

ETFs are not like your father's mutual funds. For one thing, they trade just like stocks, based on supply and demand. And S&P ETFs tend to be priced efficiently because traders can buy S&P futures or the stocks themselves if they think an ETF has dipped too low in price. Do you know what this practice is called? "Arbitrage." Look it up if it interests you.

Plus, ETFs have certain tax advantages over traditional funds, making it less likely that investors will be hit with huge capital gains distributions if there are mass redemptions, which is a fancy way of saying that many fund shareholders want their money back at the same time.

Recently, SPDRs (ticker symbol, SPY) trading on the American Stock Exchange lowered annual expenses to 0.12 percent. And, Barclays Global Investors, the world's largest manager of index funds, announced that its new Amex-traded iShares (IVV) which will also track the S&P 500, would have expenses of just 0.0945 percent. Is competition good or what? Striking back, Vanguard announced that its S&P Vipers will also be traded on the AMEX. Vanguard has not yet disclosed annual expenses for its S&P Vipers or for other Vipers that will mimic its traditional index mutual funds.

Advantages of Exchange Traded Funds

- Similar to stocks, ETFs offer more flexibility than your typical mutual fund.
- ETFs can be bought and sold throughout the trading day, allowing for intraday trading—rare with mutual funds.

- Traders have the ability to short or buy ETFs on margin.
- Low annual expenses rival the cheapest mutual funds.
- Tax efficiency—Due to SEC regulations, ETFs tend to beat out mutual funds when it comes to tax efficiency (if it is a nontaxable account, they are equal).

Disadvantages of ETFs

Unfortunately, exchange traded funds do have some negatives. For example:

- Commissions—Like stocks, trading ETFs will cost you.
- Only institutions and the extremely wealthy can deal directly with the ETF companies (you must buy them through a broker).
- Unlike mutual funds, ETFs don't necessarily trade at the net asset values of their underlying holdings, meaning an ETF could potentially trade above or below the value of the underlying portfolio.
- Slippage—As with stocks, there is a bid-ask spread, meaning you might buy the ETF for 15.125 but can only sell it for 15 (the difference or the spread is basically a hidden charge).
- Investing directly with a mutual fund company generally beats out ETFs, especially in these situations:

  —Non-taxable accounts.

  —Small investments. If you invest a certain amount each month or are on some sort of automatic investment plan (ETF commissions would kill your investment).

  —Active traders. Although ETFs are primarily geared toward active traders, an active trader might be better off with mutual funds which don't charge commissions (most mutual funds discourage active trading, but some, like Rydex, Profunds and Potomac Funds, encourage it).

However, over the long term, the S&P 500 beats the returns of 80 percent of the actively managed funds (and that isn't even taking into account tax efficiency).

Bond ETFs

Bond ETFs provide the investor with coupon income from the underlying component bonds that mirror a particular government or corporate bond index. As with regular bonds, bond ETFs increase in value when the underlying interest rates decline and vice versa. Here are some examples of high-performing bond ETFs.

The iShares Lehman Aggregate Bond Fund (ticker: AGG) offers investors a comprehensive exposure to corporate, government, mortgage, and asset-backed bonds. For slightly more risk-taking investors, the iShares $ InvesTop Corporate Bond Fund (ticker: LQD) might be an option. For investors wishing to play it safe, the iShares Barclays 7–10 Year Treasury Fund (ticker: IEF) might be another possibility. Another offering is the iShares Barclays TIPS Bond Fund (ticker: TIP) that tracks inflation-protected government notes.

Over time, more ETFs are sure to hit the market so stay tuned! In **Figure 1,** I have plotted the one-year returns on these bond ETFs and compared them to the S&P 500 Index. Notice the inverse nature of the performance of the bond ETFs relative to the S&P Index. When the stock market does well, the bond market is in the tank and vice versa. Therefore, from a diversification standpoint, if you have a stock index and any one of the bond ETFs in your portfolio, you are set.

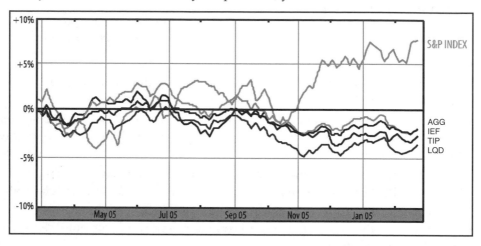

Figure 1: A comparison of 1-year returns of several bond ETFs with the return on the S&P 500 Index.

When Is an ETF Right for You?

If you have an itchy trading finger, ETFs are the way to go. You can sell them whenever the market is open—not just at the close, as with regular mutual funds.

If you happen to pick the Barclay's iShares over SPDRs, you might earn slightly higher returns because they can reinvest dividends. In fact, the Vanguard Index 500 fund has regularly beaten the SPDRs, which must pay out cash dividends quarterly to its shareholders.

But ETFs plainly aren't for everybody. If you're investing a little bit at a time, you're better off investing in index mutual funds.

Rating the ETFs

A recent *Wall Street Journal* article ("How to Rate the ETF Ratings," April 29, 2006, p. B4) states that more than 320 billion dollars of investor money are in ETFs. And with such increasing popularity comes increased attention. Several companies are trying to be the first to provide investment-related guidelines for ETFs much like Morningstar has done for the world of mutual fund investing. In fact, Morningstar has jumped into the fray by assigning its star ratings to ETFs. Other ETF rating firms include Altavista Independent Research, Buyside Research, Standard and Poor's, and Lipper.

It appears that ETFs like SPDR (SPY), the Nasdaq-100 Index tracking (QQQQ), the IShares S&P 500 Index (IVV), the Midcap SPDR (MDY), and the iShares Russell 2000 Index (IWM) top the charts among all five rating agencies. However, investors should not be blinded by the ratings alone. Since ETFs are indexes, check on how an ETF is doing related to the index it most closely resembles. Do your own due diligence before diving into the ETF pool.

Also, ETFs sometimes trade at premiums or discounts to their underlying net asset values. To see how ETFs could be affected, consider the 1987 crash, when the S&P futures closed at a 10 percent discount to their net asset value. Presumably, the ETFs would have been hit just as hard.

In the meantime, you might be better off holding onto your index funds and not diving headlong into the ETF pool. It's like Botox or liposuction. Don't do it until the kinks are ironed out.

Comparing Active Funds versus Passive (like Index) Funds

Actively managed funds have a portfolio manager or a team selecting the investments for the portfolio. Have you ever seen commercials with analysts looking very busy sitting around a large conference table, making cool and pithy comments over cups of coffee about what to buy, what to hold, and what to sell? That is active management. Obviously, for all this work, they charge you a lot of money.

By contrast, index funds mirror well-known stock or bond indexes and are passive funds. Since the composition of the indexes change infrequently, there is no sitting around the conference table and deciding what to buy/sell/hold.

Downside of ETFs

After comparing the advantages and disadvantages of using ETFs, you might conclude that they are a better deal than mutual funds—not true. Commissions make ETFs unattractive. If your portfolio is a tax-deferred investment, like a 401(k) or an IRA, you can avoid paying commissions by investing directly with a mutual fund company. Even in a taxable account, commissions make exchange traded funds look bad.

As an example, consider the following. A lump-sum investment of $10,000 in the iShares S&P 500 Index, with a very low trading cost of $8, would need to be held for two years to beat out the Vanguard 500 Index's costs. If you are investing less than $10,000 and are paying more than $8 commissions, or you are investing more than once, this example would make ETFs look much worse. Note that iShares.com is a valuable resource providing tools, strategy and data on more than 77 iShares ETFs.

Examples of ETFs

ETF TYPE	FULL NAME	TRACKS
DIAMONDs	Diamonds Trust Series I	Dow Jones Industrial Average
FITRs	Fixed income exchange traded securities	Various treasuries (including 1, 2, 5 and 10-year)
HOLDRs	Holding company depository receipts (marketed by Merrill Lynch)	Narrow industry groups (Each initially owns 20 stocks)
QUBEs	Nasdaq-100 tracking stock (QQQQ)	Nasdaq-100 Index
Spiders	Standard & Poor's Depository Receipts (SPDRs)	Track a variety of Standard & Poor's indexes
StreetTracks	State Street Global Advisor ETFs	Various indexes, including Dow Jones-style indexes and Wilshire indexes
VIPERs	Vanguard Index Participation Receipts	Several Vanguard Index funds

Consequently, they are cheap. Also, while index funds perform pretty much like the indexes they track, the performance of actively managed funds can vary.

Critics argue that any measure of fund performance is going to be colored by "survivorship bias." That is, only the funds that survive get measured. In fact, if you include all those funds that don't make it, fund performance, overall, looks a lot worse.

Statistics show convincingly that almost all mutual funds have suffered mightily in the stock market's decline following the tech-bubble burst after March 2000. Fund managers are not miracle workers, even though they would like us to believe they are. If the whole market is down, the chances of any fund doing well are almost zero given that the funds are comprised of the individual stocks that are not doing well to begin with.

Over the long haul, however, studies have shown that the S&P 500 beats out the returns of 80 percent of actively managed funds (and that isn't even taking into account tax efficiency). In sum, invest in mutual funds if you want to expose your money to the stock market without spending too much time doing the research. And, if you do, then make sure you understand that mutual funds do lose money.

There are no guarantees in this business. If there are, you know something you are not supposed to, and you could go to jail for trading on that information. We call that insider trading. Remember Martha Stewart and her doing time in a federal prison in Alderson, West Virginia?

Having said all that, how do you pick the mutual funds that best suit your needs? I wish I could say that it's a super simple task. But it isn't. Sometimes picking a mutual fund is, as Forrest Gump said, "like a box of chocolates—you never know what you are going to get!" First, you need to determine what your investment philosophy is and find a fund that best matches that philosophy. And how do you do that?

Fortunately, many Web sites such as Morningstar, for example, categorize their funds by market capitalization (small, medium and large) and by value, growth and diversified, which reflects the kind of stocks the underlying fund is primarily invested in. From here, try to find a fund whose investment philosophy closely matches yours. It's not easy and requires patience if you want to do it right.

Additionally, these days there are quite a few mutual fund screeners that are absolutely free to all of us. You may have to register for a few of them but it's free registration.

Hedge Fund Protection in Bear Markets for the Retail Investor

Contributed by Greg N. Gregoriou
Professor of Finance
State University of New York (Plattsburgh)

Hedging is frequently defined as using downside risk to achieve portfolio protection in bear markets. To protect their investments (crop), farmers began using futures contracts as a hedge against the instability in price of various commodities such as corn, cattle, etc., since the beginning of the 20th century in the United States. One can further apply this to the area of investments, whereby hedging insulates investors from down markets or more commonly known as bear markets.

Many investors have a hard time understanding the term "hedge fund" because it encompasses numerous manager skill-based dynamic trading strategies. In fact, there is no exact definition of a hedge fund (a misnomer). In essence, hedge funds provide absolute returns rather than returns relative to standard passive benchmarks (i.e. S&P 500 Index, etc.). The goal of hedge funds, or a fund of hedge funds (a basket of hedge funds), is to make money for its investors by taking leveraged positions and trying to capture price inefficiencies of global stock, bond and currency markets. Contrary to the buy-and-hold or static strategies of mutual funds, hedge funds are known to use "dynamic" or "active" strategies, making hedge funds notorious as speculative vehicles. Dynamic strategies implies using options, futures, swaps, and other more complex derivatives instruments to amplify hedge fund returns. Hedge funds are not passive investors like mutual funds and can quickly liquidate their entire portfolio in times of market stress. Mutual funds, on the other hand, sit tight and hope the market turns around.

Modern portfolio theory, as pioneered by Nobel Prize winner Harry Markowitz (1952)[19], provides investors with a essential tool for diversifying traditional stock and bond investment portfolios by combining different assets to maximize return while minimizing risk. However, to attain proper diversification in traditional investment portfolios, hedge funds can further enhance the diversification process due to their low correlation features among hedge fund strategies. Furthermore, the correlations between hedge fund strategies and stock and bond markets tend to provide low positive correlations, while some hedge fund strategies (short sellers) provide a negative correlation.

Who created the first hedge fund? It was Alfred Winslow Jones, an associate editor of *Fortune* magazine, who was responsible for creating the first hedge fund in 1949 through a private investment partnership. Jones hedged the risk of his fund by purchasing stocks he believed were undervalued and short selling stocks he thought were overvalued. His idea of a market-neutral fund was fundamentally to eliminate gains and losses from market fluctuations and provide protection to the investors against drops in the stock market. Using this newly created dynamic trading strategy during bull and bear markets, Jones outperformed the average U.S. equity mutual fund. Jones' use of leverage was also a salient feature in his strategy that distinguished him from the pack by allowing him to magnify the returns of his fund. The number of hedge funds and assets under management increased at a feverish pace during the 1990s with nearly $1.5 trillion in capital at the end of 2006, according to *Business Week* magazine.

It is common knowledge that investing in alternative assets such as hedge funds offers investors low correlation to traditional stock and bond markets. The main advantage of hedge funds is to be less susceptible to the movements of the markets by seeking "absolute returns" and offering unique investment opportunities not available through mutual funds. Hedge funds offer superior risk-return trade-off and provide protection in negative S&P 500 quarters as well as in other developed and emerging markets.

A key feature of hedge funds is that they can reduce the volatility of a global portfolio, increase risk-adjusted returns and enhance performance of traditional investment portfolios. Hedge funds have received in-depth reporting and notoriety in many professional magazines as destabilizing world financial markets and are frequently seen as villains. A well-known example is George Soros' speculative attack on the British sterling in the Fall of 1992 which netted $2 billion dollars for his group of funds in one week. However, there have been some spectacular losses in 1998 and 2006, with Long-Term Capital Management and Amaranth Advisors losing billions.

Hedge funds are regarded as illiquid private investment pools which allow up to a maximum of 99 investors or, alternatively, 499 institutional and high net worth investors (e.g., only for U.S. onshore funds). Hedge funds are not allowed to solicit or advertise to the public and are not regulated like mutual funds or pension funds. Thus, hedge funds do not fall under the control of the Investment Company Act of 1940 and fall outside the regulation of the Securities Act of 1933. They are also exempt from the Securities Exchange Commission (SEC) Act of 1934 and do not have to reveal any of their holdings/positions.

Who typically invests in hedge funds? Investors include high net worth individuals and institutional investors, foundations, pension funds, life insurance companies, endowment funds, and investment banks. Today, U.S. (onshore) hedge funds are limited to accredited investors with a net worth exceeding $1 million, but a fund of hedge funds allows investors with less money, or lower risk tolerance, to enter this world of privately managed money.

Over the last 5 years there has been a tremendous influx of capital migrating towards hedge funds for several reasons, such as recurring currency devaluations and high volatility in world financial markets. In these types of scenarios, hedge funds are regarded as risk management instruments that can provide portfolio protection against downside risk.

Hedge funds are typically seen as innovative financial instruments, and the strategies they employ can provide added liquidity and stability to stock, bond, and currency markets. Numerous studies have concluded that hedge funds and funds of hedge funds offer higher risk-adjusted returns than mutual funds and stock market indexes. With the recent turmoil in global financial markets, hedge funds and funds of hedge funds are becoming an important investment alternative for investors interested in further diversifying their traditional stock and bond portfolios.

The number and popularity of hedge funds have grown at an explosive pace during the past decade, and will certainly rival the mutual fund industry in a few years. Numerous well-known mutual fund managers with solid reputations are leaving the mutual fund industry and setting up hedge funds. Apparently, the brightest brains on Wall Street are migrating, including Fidelity's Jeff Vinik, who left the Magellan Fund to head Vinik Asset Management, a Boston hedge fund.

The financial market meltdown in February 2007 had its origins in China and caused tremors across global markets giving investors a taste of panic and euphoria. The simple mention of a market correction is enough to set vibrations across the entire financial world. How then can an individual investor protect himself from these wild market gyrations and simultaneously provide stability to his portfolio? What strategies can an investor adopt? Bonds, you say! Try again. The answer is hedge funds or a basket of hedge funds more commonly known as a fund of funds (FOFs). This popular strategy (classification) provides a collection of the best hedge fund managers with different strategies all included in one portfolio. The value added by FOFs allows for instant diversification and provides low volatility when compared to traditional mutual funds and stock market indices. In essence, FOFs provide equity-like returns with bond-like (low) volatility. However, this feature comes at a price where typical management and performance fees range from about 2 percent and 20 percent respectively. Furthermore, FOFs have the drawback of another layer of fees whereby the specialist is compensated for hedge fund manager selection and constant monitoring as well as monthly visits to the hedge funds that make up the FOF portfolio. It is very cumbersome and time consuming for the FOF manager to try to siphon through almost 8,000 hedge funds in various hedge fund databases and attempt to select what he believes are the top performing funds, making sure that their individual strategies do not overlap.

Although a great majority of unsophisticated and neophyte investors think that simply holding U.S. stocks, international stocks, and bonds will produce an efficient and well-diversified portfolio, their view is incorrect. A landmark study by Professor Bruno Solink concludes that investors have no place to hide anymore due to the high correlations existing among developed financial markets today.[20] Even thirty years ago, many developed financial markets had low correlations among themselves, but the landscape today seems to be causing all markets to move in tandem whenever there is a market correction. With this in mind, now is an excellent time to add alternative investments (such as hedge funds and FOFs) to traditional portfolios. Typically mutual funds use a relative benchmark to compare their returns. Hedge funds, however, produce absolute returns irrespective of market conditions. When investing in hedge funds or FOFs, the investor typically will sacrifice upside gains for downside protection—a steep price to pay for protection, but well worth it!

How do these absolute return vehicles, which are geared only for sophisticated and high net worth individuals, play a role in unsophisticated and typical investor portfolios in the United States? There are a few FOFs in the U.S. where investors can get in with a minimum investment of $1,000 and Geronimo Funds is one of the firms offering numerous absolute return vehicles for downside equity risk management.

Risks of ETF Investment

As ETFs become popular investment vehicles, it is important to keep in mind the inherent risks of these investment vehicles—especially during moments of market meltdown such as the one we witnessed on February 27 and then again on March

13, 2007. Specifically, on February 27, when stock prices nosedived in China, it had rippling effects around the world, including the U.S. markets.

According to an article in the *Wall Street Journal*,[21] a particular ETF managed by Barclays Global Investors tracking the Chinese stock market closed in the U.S. on February 27 down 9.9 percent even though the index it was tracking fell just 2.1 percent during Chinese trading hours. In another example, the iShares emerging market fund (an ETF) lost about 8.1 percent even though the index it tracked had fallen only about 3.1 percent over the same period.

Although ETFs are advertised as an easy and convenient way for investors to get in and out of the markets, the above examples exemplify an inherent problem with such a strategy. During moments of severe market stress, prices of ETFs might get seriously out of line relative to the index they track, resulting in significant losses for individual investors looking to unload their shares. This aspect of ETF investing has not been talked about a whole lot amid all the talk about their benefits, including their liquidity, flexibility, and their ability to track the market, or sections of it, like index mutual funds. Of course, the fact that the ETF pricing varies so significantly from the inherent index it is tracking at times of high market volatility represents opportunities for arbitrage profits by sophisticated investors. Such profits are out of the purview of ordinary investors who just face the brunt of the high costs associated with volatility without the accompanying benefits of profit.[22]

Due to the increasing popularity of ETFs, the new clientele of ETF investors are the professional investors. While traditional index mutual funds that price once a day are good for individual investors, institutional investors with fast trading strategies find the ability of ETFs to price continuously, and the fact that they can be shorted, to be big advantages allowing them to move in and out of markets, or particular sectors, with ease. Such strategies have the downside of exacerbating volatility—

Critical Information: What Are Fund Screeners?

Fund screeners are nothing more than database mining tools that sort through tons of financial data, a miniscule amount of which would put all of us to sleep instantly, and come up with a list of funds that meet the criteria you have provided. Do you want a fund manager with a lengthy tenure? Do you want an aggressive new fund with an incredible record? Do you want a fund of a certain size?

Interestingly, answering questions like these helps you define your strategy and can be a useful exercise. Start with a fund screener like the ones at Morningstar.com, quicken.com, or stockpoint.com, and start screening right away.

Let's say you are a timid person by nature and all these aggressive screening definitions are leaving you with a sweaty brow and a racing pulse causing you immense stress. Fear not! There is hope even for you. And the answer is Predefined Screens.

Go to MSN MoneyCentral's predefined screen and check it out. Remember that here you are basically trusting someone else's judgment to do what's best for you. It's like a blind date that your friends have set up. Sometimes they work but mostly they don't.

MoneyCentral's predefined screens like "Large Domestic Stock" and "Safe and Steady" will hopefully steer you in the right direction. For the mathematically minded among you, there is also hope. Sites like RiskGrades, Total Sum and Portfolio Science use mathematics to render judgments on funds.

especially in times of market stress such as the kind we observed in February and March of 2007.

Individual investors need to be very careful about the changing demographic of ETF investors and the increase in risk this presents—especially when a stock market somewhere in the world goes temporarily berserk.

Research on Mutual Funds

Economists have long tried to understand how mutual funds could have come into existence. People have argued that under the assumption that investors cannot remain in the market to trade at all times just to trade, there would be a natural incentive to establish trading firms or financial market intermediaries to take over the investors' portfolio while they engage in other activities. These firms therefore exist to simply take orders from their investors and we could interpret such firms or financial intermediaries as mutual funds. Once we think of mutual funds this way, an intuitive rationale for funds differing along the lines of trading styles and size also emerges as a natural way to cater to investors with different styles and risk characteristics.

Why are there so many mutual funds around? What leads the industry to segment itself into an ever-increasing number of mutual fund categories? To address these questions, economists argue that such phenomena can be justified from the point of view of the marketing strategies used by the managing companies to exploit investors' inherent differences (i.e., investor heterogeneity). Consistent with this notion, surveys find that over one-third of respondents say that they have responded to a mutual fund advertisement and over three-fourths of those claim that they have in fact responded to ads in national newspapers like the *Wall Street Journal*.

A group of economists examine the important question of whether mutual fund managers can successfully select stocks that outperform the average stock exhibiting similar characteristics as the chosen stock.[23] Using a large data set, the authors find that while the managers of aggressive growth funds show some "selective" ability, no mutual fund manager displays any significant market timing ability.

Finally, survey research into the typical mutual fund holder demographic also yields fascinating insights. For example, it appears that investors purchasing mutual funds directly from a fund company are more likely to be male while those buying through banks, etc., are equally likely to be male or female. The median age of a typical mutual fund shareholder is about 43 years, which is greater than the median age (38 years) of the U.S. voting age population. Younger investors are more likely to invest in mutual funds through their pension plans (i.e., 401(k) plans that we will discuss later). Mutual fund investors have a median income of about $60,000 relative to a median U.S. household income of a little over $30,000 over approximately the same period reported by the U.S. Census Bureau. Mutual fund investors are also well educated with a majority having at least a college degree. Over 80 percent of the mutual fund investors own their primary residence compared to about 66 percent of the U.S. population. Over 70 percent of the mutual fund investors own stock mutual funds while about 40 percent own money market mutual funds and about a third own bond funds.

Over half the respondents claim to use mutual fund prospectuses to make their mutual fund purchases. Not surprisingly, an overwhelming majority of those making direct purchases of mutual fund shares from fund companies cite the prospectus as their main source of information. Similarly, those purchasing indirectly through brokers or bankers also cite it as their primary source of information for purchase.

Most mutual fund investors appear to know that it is possible to lose money buying stock, bond, and money market mutual funds. College graduates are significantly more likely to believe it is possible to lose money in a stock fund while older investors are more likely to know it is possible to lose money in bond funds. Wealthier investors are more likely to know about possible losses through their mutual funds, while mutual fund investors less than 35 years of age are less likely to believe that one can lose money in a money market mutual fund.

The level of mutual fund expenses seems to have little role to play in a fund purchasing decision for an overwhelming majority of the respondents. Very few respondents appear to know what kind of expenses their invested mutual funds carry although higher income investors were more likely to be aware of their mutual funds' expenses. Almost all investors investing in mutual funds through their pension plans have little to no idea of the kind of expenses generated by the funds in their retirement portfolio. The really scary finding is that less than 15 percent of the respondents were even aware that higher expenses could lead to lower than average returns. Further details on the pattern of mutual fund ownership in the U.S. over the nineties can be found in the footnote reference here.[24]

Summary

While mutual funds still remain the domain of the educated and relatively prosperous investors, in spite of their skyrocketing popularity, the real challenge will lie in educating the less-educated and lower-than-average income earning American families to feel comfortable enough to invest some of their funds in these vehicles so that they too can be a part of the American dream.

Thought Questions

1. Can mutual funds lose money on a regular basis? Why or why not?

2. What is one aspect of mutual funds you can reliably take from the past and extrapolate to the future?

3. What is the relationship between fund activity and fund philosophy?

4. Why is examining current fund manager tenure, when deciding whether to invest in that fund, a useful activity?

5. What is the difference between very large funds (like Fidelity Magellan) and index funds? Which would you prefer and why?

6. When would you prefer a mutual fund over an ETF?

7. Why are mutual fund prospectuses important?

8. What does it say about a fund that has a high expense ratio?

9. Should index funds have a high expense ratio? Why or why not?

10. Why is a 12b-1 fee important for a mutual fund?

11. Why is "market timing" considered a bad thing? Who gets hurt in market timing?

12. What is special about Life-Cycle funds? What are the differences between these funds and index funds? What are some other examples of Life-Cycle funds?

13. What does the evidence, that the S&P 500 index funds beat out over 80 percent of the actively managed funds, suggest to you as an investor?

14. What is the economic rationale for the creation of mutual funds?

Notes

19. Markowitz, H., 1952, Portfolio Selection, *Journal of Finance* 7, 77–91.

20. Solnik, B., 1999, *International Investments*, Fourth Edition, Addison Wesley.

21. "Fast Money Crowd Embraces ETFs, Adding Risk for Individual Investors," *Wall Street Journal*, March 17, 2007, p. 1.

22. In fact, brokerages such as Goldman Sachs have internal teams of traders to take advantage of precisely such arbitrage opportunities.

23. Daniel, K., M. Grinblatt, S. Titman, and R. Wermers, 1997. "Measuring Mutual Fund Performance with Characteristic-based Benchmarks." *Journal of Finance* 52, 1035–1058.

24. Poterba, J. "The Rise of the Equity Culture: U.S. Stockownership Patterns," 1989–1998, unpublished manuscript, MIT.

5

Bonds

The right time for a company to finance its growth is not when it needs capital,
but rather when the market is most receptive to providing capital.
—Mike Milken, The Junk Bond King

Ever borrow money from someone? Sure you have! It happens all the time. Forget your lunch money? Need cab fare? Need to buy a house? A car? Need new land and machinery to grow your small business? These days, people borrow money every day for many reasons.

However, things were not always like this. When I was little, I used to hear people say, "If you can't afford it with cash, don't buy it!" Debt was a four-letter word. My parents bought everything with their savings and paid cash. In England, just a hundred years ago, there were debtors prisons. All in all, society was structured to keep wealth out of the common people's hands. If you weren't born into it, or didn't inherit it, you had no right to it. Borrowing could give everyone a boost in their purchasing power but that would mean the common person might improve his position in life and then demand other things too. That was simply too much for the privileged to bear. So debt became a bad word. But not any more, thankfully! Now, we pride ourselves on our borrowing prowess. We carry all the credit cards we possibly can and proudly show off our cards personalized with pictures of "spaghetti Jimmy" or our favorite pets (I am guilty of that one) to our friends. Going into debt is now hip. We sing cool songs in praise of debt and pay homage to the Debt Gods on a daily basis.

Much like individuals, large organizations such as corporations, the federal government, and state and local governments all need to borrow money occasionally. But they do so through a specific instrument that we, as individuals, do not have access to. Bonds are a form of indebtedness that are sold to the public in set increments, normally in the neighborhood of $1,000. In return for loaning the debtor the money, the lender gets a piece of paper that stipulates how much was lent, the agreed-upon interest rate, how often interest (also known as coupon payments) will be paid, and the term of the loan.

Figure 2 illustrates the three basic bond types. In the first case, coupon payments occur at regular intervals (usually semi-annually) and then, at maturity, the face value of the bond is paid to the investor, usually $1,000 for most bonds issued by corporations. Think of the face value of the bond as the principal in a loan that the borrower returns to the lender when the bond matures.

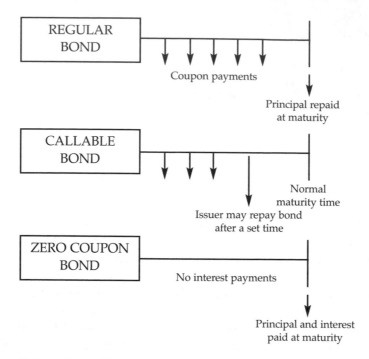

Figure 2. Types of Bonds

In the second case, we have a callable bond where the corporation issuing the bond decides to "call" the bond in and pay the investors the face value of the bond at that point. Why do companies do this? For the same reason we refinance our mortgage loans when interest rates go down: To borrow at newer, cheaper rates. The third example is a zero coupon bond. With these bonds, the issuer pays no coupon interest and simply pays the face value at maturity. The buyers of these bonds buy them at a discount from the face value and then get the face value back at maturity. A lot of the short-term bonds issued by the government are of this type.

The bond was born the first time an ancient monarch borrowed a large sum of money from a rich neighbor, agreed to repay the money with interest, and wrote it up on a piece of parchment. Deficit-laden governments across the world use bonds as a way to finance their operations. Cash-strapped companies sell debt to raise the money they need to expand. Even individuals routinely take out interest-bearing loans, whether they are credit card balances, car loans, or mortgages.

Who Issues Bonds?

Bonds are known as "fixed-income" securities because the amount of income the bond generates each year is "fixed," or set, when the bond is sold. No matter what happens or who holds the bond, it will generate exactly the same amount of money.

The first type of bond is sold by the U.S. Government. These bonds are called Treasuries because they are sold by the Treasury Department. Treasuries come in a variety of different "maturities," or length of time until maturity, ranging from one month to thirty years. Types of Treasuries include Treasury notes, Treasury bills, Treasury bonds, and inflation-indexed notes. These all vary based on maturity and the amount of interest paid. The Treasury Department also sells savings bonds as well as other types of debt through the Bureau of the Public Debt. Treasuries are guaranteed by the U.S. Government and are free of state and local taxes on the interest they pay. Short-term U.S. Treasury bonds are also called risk-free bonds. Do you know why? What are the chances that the U.S. Government will go bankrupt ?

Some government agencies and quasi-government agencies such as the Federal National Mortgage Association (Fannie Mae), the Federal Home Loan Mortgage Corp. (Freddie Mac), and the Government National Mortgage Association (Ginnie Mae) sell bonds backed by the full faith and credit of the U.S. Government for specific purposes such as funding home ownership.

The second type of bond is sold by corporations. Companies sell debt through the public securities markets just as they sell stock. A company has a lot of flexibility about how much debt it can issue and what interest rate it will pay, although it must make the bond attractive enough to interest investors or no one will buy them.

Corporate bonds normally carry higher interest rates than government bonds because there is a risk that the company could go bankrupt and default on the bond, unlike the government, which can just print more money if it really needs it. Can you, however, think of the consequencnes of printing too much money? High-yield bonds, also known as junk bonds, are corporate bonds issued by companies whose credit quality is below investment grade. Some corporate bonds are called convertible bonds because they can be converted into stock if certain provisions are met.

The third type of bond is issued by state and local governments (municipal bonds or munis). Because state and local governments can go bankrupt (ask the holders of Orange County, California, muni bonds if you don't believe that one), they have to offer competitive interest rates just like corporate bonds. Unlike corporations, though, the only way that a state can get more income is to raise taxes on its citizens, always an unpopular move. As a way around this problem, the federal government permits state and local governments to sell bonds that are free of federal income tax on the interest paid. State and local governments can also waive state and local income taxes on the bonds. Even though they pay lower rates of interest, borrowers in high tax brackets can actually have a higher after-tax yield by holding these bonds than they would with other forms of fixed-income investments. Unlike Treasury bills, however, which are risk free, municipal bonds can be quite risky. Do your homework before investing in them.

Par Value, Coupon Rate, Maturity Date, Call, Default . . . Ugh!

There are three important things to know about any bond before you buy it: The par value, the coupon rate, and the maturity date. Knowing these three facts (and a few other odds and ends, depending on what kind of bond you are buying) allows you to analyze the bond and compare it to other potential investments.

Par value is the amount of money the investor will receive once the bond matures, meaning the entity that sold the bond will return to the investor the original amount that was loaned, also called the principal. As mentioned earlier, par value for corporate bonds is normally $1,000, although for certain government bonds it can be much higher.

The coupon rate is the amount of interest that the bondholder will receive expressed as a percentage of the par value. Thus, if a bond has a par value of $1,000 and a coupon rate of 10 percent, the person holding the bond will receive $100 a year. The bond will also specify when the interest is to be paid, whether monthly, quarterly, semiannually, or annually.

The maturity date is the date when the bond issuer has to return the principal to the lender. After the debtor pays back the principal, they are no longer obligated to make interest payments.

Sometimes a company will decide to "call" its bond, meaning that it will be giving the lenders their money back before the maturity date of the bond. All corporate bonds specify whether they can be called and how soon they can be called. Federal government bonds are never called, but state and local government bonds can be called before maturity. The call feature allows the issuing agency to pay the investor the face amount for the bond and buy back the bond before maturity. This allows the issuer to then reissue the bond at lower interest rates.

Bonds: What Are They Good For?

Bonds should fit your investment objective, which is income and safety of principal. If you are looking for long-term growth, bonds may not match your objective. However, if your objective is safety of principal and you want to earn current income from your investments, bonds would very much do the job. For example, a major objective of someone over seventy is to live off her investments and not lose money in case she may need money for health care. Although she may live thirty more years, a portion of her retirement money might be invested for growth in stocks, but a majority should probably be invested for income in bonds that mature at different times, so the principal would be available without loss.

Yet Another Benefit of U.S. Treasury Bonds

Between 1996 and 2000, the U.S. Treasury reduced Bill issuance by about 30 percent and decreased issuance of coupon securities by about 50 percent. This apparently innocent action created shock waves around the world. Why? Among other things, U.S. Treasuries are used as benchmarks for pricing and quotations in the United States, and in international bond markets, are considered safe havens for investors' monies. They are also used as hedges to fixed income positions and are an important component of global bond indexes. And this is because of the liquidity of the U.S. Treasury markets.

The U.S. Treasury made thiedecision to scale back because the Government was running at a surplus budget mode and it seemed to make fiscal sense to reduce new

Bill issuance, i.e., reduce the amount of governmental borrowing. But who could have known that such an action would trigger a domino effect in the rest of the world? That thought in itself is very scary and gives new insight to the cliché: A butterfly flapping its wings in China affecting the weather in North America. Of course, now that we are seriously in deficit, such questions have become more academic than practical. I discuss it here only as an illustration of how seemingly innocent actions can trigger a whole chain of events which may not even have been considered before such decisions were made by policy wonks.

Critical Info

Bonds can diversify an investor's holdings. In fact, a typical graph showing stock and bond market returns over the past 75 years, shows one overwhelming trend: The stock and bond markets tend to move in opposite directions. So, when the stock prices go up, bonds go down; when bonds go up, stocks go down. Over the long haul, this negative correlation between stocks and bonds permits a portfolio of stocks and bonds to even out the highs and lows and can result in an overall higher return at a relatively lower risk.

Interestingly, even while the debate about the decision by the U.S. Treasury to eliminate certain bills was going on, there were at least three reasons cited for why this shrinking supply of Treasuries might be a temporary phenomenon at best.

1. Tax revenues would be significantly below the levels projected by the Congressional Budget Office—especially if the ongoing recession over the period 2000–2004 continued or worsened. Additionally, expenditures could turn out to be significantly greater than expected, due to the current (and future) "war on terrorism," as one example.

2. Longer-term budget projections suggested that U.S. fiscal balance would, under current tax and expenditure policies, eventually reverse course, as will the path of publicly held Treasury debt.

3. The investment policy of the Social Security Trust Fund might be changed to include private assets.

Connection between Treasuries and the Social Security (SS) Trust Fund

The surplus money in the SS Trust Fund is invested in government bonds or T-bills, as opposed to being invested in stocks or corporate bonds or even simply placed in a bank account. So, the extra money is actually already used to finance past government deficit spending. Ergo, the SS Trust Fund owns NO REAL ASSETS.

The SS Trust Fund owns some type of bonds or T-bills, but these "assets" are really just promises to pay, made by a different arm of the government, presumably the Treasury Department. They are assets from the point of view of SS as a program, but they don't actually represent assets from the point of view of the government as a whole.

Current thinking is that the SS Trust Fund should invest in some private assets and use T-bills to finance such purchases.

It is refreshing to see (on some levels) that two out of the three reasons have to come to fruition and the talk about shrinking U.S. Treasuries has receded in the background. But for that brief period in history, the decision to reduce issuance did provide economists with a natural laboratory of what can happen when supplies of U.S. Treasury bonds are artificially reduced. We are unlikely to see a similar event in our lifetimes.

How to Calculate Bond Yields

In case you are scratching your head and wondering what a "yield" is, let me explain. With every investment, you have to have a way of knowing what kind of returns your investments are bringing home for you. In bonds, this can be accomplished through calculating their yield. Knowing your bond's yield also helps you compare it with other potential investments—sort of like an apples-to-apples, if you will. You can calculate the yield on a bond by dividing the amount of interest it will pay over the course of a year by the current price of the bond. Thus, for example, if a bond that cost $1,000 pays $75 a year in interest, then its current yield is $75 divided by $1,000, or 7.5 percent.

However, since we can buy a bond above or below its par value, bond investors often use another kind of yield called "yield to maturity." The yield to maturity includes not only the interest payments you will receive all the way to maturity, but also assumes that you will reinvest the interest payment at the same rate as the current yield on the bond, and takes into account any difference between the current par value of the bond and the actual trading price of the bond in the future.

If you buy a bond at par value, the yield to maturity will be very close to the current yield, which is exactly the same as its coupon rate. Yield to maturity is especially important when looking at zero-coupon bonds. Recall that this is a special type of bond that pays no interest until the maturity date, when you receive all of your principal back plus interest for the the face value of the bond. Because zeros have no current yield, any yield you see associated with them is always a yield to maturity.

Why Bond Yields Can Differ from Coupon Rates

You may ask: "Why not just look at the coupon rate to determine the bond's yield?" And I would say, "Aha! That does not always work!" You see, bond prices fluctuate as interest rates change, so a bond can trade above or below the par value based on what the prevailing interest rates are. If you hold the bond to maturity, you are guaranteed to get your principal back. However, if you sell the bond before it matures, you will have to sell it at the going price, which may be above or below par value.

If in the late 1970s you bought a $1,000 bond with a coupon rate of 10 percent and a maturity date of December 31, 1999, from a company called Yoyo Enterprises, this bond would pay you $100 per year until December 31, 1999, at which time you would get back the $1,000 principal.

Now, say you still own that bond in 1998 (current time), when long-term interest rates touch 5 percent. If issued in 1998, that same bond would only pay $50 a year, not $100. As a reflection of the fact that interest rates have dropped since the coupon rate was set on the bond, you would actually be able to sell your Yoyo Enterprises bond for more than the $1,000 par value. This is because an investor in 1998 would only be expecting a 5 percent yield, so he would pay a premium for a bond that paid 10 percent.

If you hold a bond to maturity, you won't lose your principal if the borrower doesn't default or restructure. If you buy and sell bonds before they mature, you can make or lose money on the bonds themselves completely separate from the interest rates. How much more you are going to get depends on the exact maturity date of the bond, where interest rates have moved, and the transaction costs involved.

How to Make Money from Bonds

Most people assume that there is only one way to make money with bonds: You collect interest. Actually, there are two ways you can make money with bonds. The first is to collect the yield (interest). The second is the gain (or loss) when interest rates fall (or rise). Let's try the easy one first.

You empty out your piggy bank and pay $1,000 for a government bond with a 4 percent coupon and a 10-year maturity. You then get $40 every year for ten years, and your $1,000 back at the end. You buy the bond when it's issued and hold it until maturity, you get interest or yield on your bond, and that's the extent of your return. Many investors buy bonds exclusively for their yield. For high-quality bonds or Treasuries where there is little chance of the issuer going under, you can depend on the interest coming in as agreed.

However, if you buy or sell the bond on the secondary market, things could get a bit hairy. Remember, interest rates go up and down. A bond is priced on the going market interest rate (which changes often). Interest rates may have been 5 percent last year, but investors can only get 3 percent now. There's no reason why you should pay out more interest than the market. So if you sell a $1,000 par value bond with a 5 percent coupon in a 3 percent market, you want to sell it so that it yields 3 percent instead of 5 percent.

The annual interest paid by the issuer is still going to be 5 percent of par, or $50. The issuer has to pay this according to the bond agreement. In order to provide a 3 percent yield, you get to sell the bond for more than you paid—that is, at a premium. You make a capital gain on it. This is true for any bond you sell after interest rates fall. This is counterintuitive so it bears repeating:

> If interest rates go down, the price of your bond goes up.

But the opposite can also happen. What if interest rates go up to 6 percent and you have the same $1,000 par value bond with a 5 percent coupon? The investor who buys it will want his 6 percent yield; otherwise, he will pass on your bond and go elsewhere. To give the buyer a 6 percent yield in a 5 percent market, you have to sell the bond at a discount, or for less than what you paid. Now you have a capital loss.

> Therefore, if interest rates go up, the price of your bond goes down.

Of course, the above example assumes that the underlying company selling the bond will not go bankrupt before the bond matures, and the probability of that happening is determined by the rating of the bond.

The yield to maturity (YTM) tells you what you will earn on the bond if you hold it until it matures. That is, it adds the redemption value to the mix. So if you bought a bond at a discount for $935, when your bond is redeemed by the issuer, you're going to make a capital gain. That is, you only paid $935 for a bond that gets you $1,000. That's a gain of $65. In calculating your total return on this bond, it's important to include this gain. Yield to maturity takes into consideration any gain or loss you make on the bond along with the interest. The yield to maturity calculation is simply the internal rate of return (IRR) calculation, which is the interest rate at which the stream of cash flows associated with the bond equates to zero. Very simply, the YTM calculation takes into account information about price, maturity, annual interest, and what you get at redemption. Then it solves for the rate of return that best fits the cash flows.

In sum, when looking at a bond, it's important to carefully evaluate the yield to maturity. It's the most complete measure (in that it includes gain or loss and yield) of bond return.

Bond Ratings and Trading Strategies

Almost all investors who buy bonds do so because they are generally safe investments. However, except for bonds from the federal government, bonds carry the potential risk of default, no matter how remote that risk might be. Whether it is a high-yield corporate bond or a bond sold by the sovereign state of Virginia, there is always a chance that the entity that borrowed the money will not be able to make the interest payments.

Bond ratings were developed as a way to indicate how financially stable the issuer of the bonds really is. Developed by third parties like Standard and Poor's and Moody's, bond-rating services assign bonds a letter, or a mixed letter and number rating based on the financial soundness of the bond issuer. To complicate things, the rating agencies use entirely different rating systems, making it important to check what the ratings mean before you draw any conclusions. The higher the rating, the higher the quality of the bond, with Treasury bonds rated the highest and "junk" bonds rated the lowest. More details later.

Depending on the bond, it can either trade frequently at a low commission or it may be difficult to find a buyer or seller and therefore involve large transaction costs. "Liquidity" is the term used to describe how easy it is to sell something. Highly liquid bonds include U.S. Treasuries, which trade billions of dollars worth every day. Illiquid bonds would include the bonds of companies viewed as being close to bankruptcy. Because it is no longer a safe investment, only those speculating that there will be a corporate turnaround are willing to buy those bonds, meaning they trade less frequently. Liquidity has a direct effect on the commission you pay to trade a bond, which unlike stocks, rarely trades on a fixed commission schedule. Now let's discuss credit rating and credit rating agencies.

To understand what they are, remember the last time you went to the bank to get a loan? You filled out a long credit application that asked for information about your job and how much money you had. Then the bank did a formal credit check on you through credit rating bureaus, that we will discuss later, in order to get the lowdown on whether you paid all your bills on time, etc. Bond issuers go through the same process (except it's a lot more complex and detailed), and they are given a credit rating based on this financial examination.

Credit rating analysis is done by a few companies, but the best known are Moody's, and Standard and Poor's (yes, of the S&P 500 fame). These credit ratings run pretty much like grades in school. The more A's you get, the better off you are. And, like my high school grades, a C is not acceptable. In fact, anything under BBB for Standard and Poor's and Baa for Moody's is not considered investment grade. Bonds with ratings lower than BBB, or Baa, are classified as high yield, speculative, or junk bonds.

Better credit ratings mean that the company is in better financial shape and there is less default risk in holding its bonds. Remember, you might be holding them for many years. Lower credit ratings mean that buying the company's bonds is more risky. The company might not be able to pay interest. In some cases, you might even lose some or all of your principal.

In order to compensate you for the increased risk, issuers give you a higher interest rate for bonds with lower credit ratings. Spreads—that is, the difference in interest rates between the highest and the lowest quality investment grade bonds—can be 50 basis points, or 0.5 percent. Junk bonds provide yields of 5 percent to 9 percent above investment grade bonds, but have a much higher default rate. It's the old risk and return paradigm again. You need to evaluate whether the return is worth the risk.

Critical Info: Picking a Bond Broker

Bond commissions vary widely from brokerage to brokerage, so it does not hurt to shop around before making your decision. Through a brokerage, you can buy anything from a 30-year Treasury to a 3-month junk bond issued by a corporation on the edge of bankruptcy. You can either participate in the direct offering of the bonds or pick them up in the secondary market, depending on your brokerage.

In an effort to make it easier for citizens to buy U.S. Government bonds, the Bureau of the Public Debt started the TreasuryDirect program. This program enables individuals to purchase bonds directly from the Treasury, completely avoiding brokerage fees. Investors can establish a single TreasuryDirect account that will hold all of their Treasury notes, bills, and bonds. Investors are issued account statements periodically. Interest and the repayment of principal are taken care of electronically via direct deposit to a bank or through a brokerage designated by the account holder. As long as you have enough money, you can buy any type of Treasury security you want. Additionally, you can transfer bonds to and from your account wherever you desire. The Bureau also allows you to direct deposit payments, reinvest money after a bond matures, and sell bonds for a flat fee of $34. To learn more, visit TreasuryDirect on the Internet.

However, the telephone market remains the most popular way to purchase corporate bonds.

Bond Trading Strategies

As we have seen so far, bond prices are sensitive to the prevailing interest rates in the economy. So when the Fed raises or lowers interest rates, bond prices change. If you expect interest rates to go up in the future, one way to take advantage of trading in bonds is to invest in relatively short-term bonds. So, if interest rates do happen to rise, your short-term bonds will have smaller fluctuations (i.e., lower volatility) than longer-term bonds and this is a good thing for you, the investor.

If you are a long-term investor, however, investing in short-term bonds will not be a good thing. for you. Historically, short-term bonds yield less than long-term bonds. So this strategy, even though safer from one angle, turns out to be costly for you in terms of your returns. Also, since rising rates usually signal a stronger economy, as a long-term investor you may also decide to ride out the bond market and, instead, put your money in the equity market and/or mutual, and exchange traded funds.

Another strategy used in bond investing is known as laddering. Laddering is nothing but holding bonds of varying maturities—from short-term to long-term—in order to guard against possible interest rate changes. Laddered bonds in your portfolio should be held to their maturity and should be concentrated on A-rated bonds only.

Bond Ratings

	Moody's	Standard & Poor's	Quality
Investment Grade			
Investment grade best quality. Interest payments are protected by earnings and principal is secure. Actual default rate less than 2 percent.	Aaa	AAA	High Grade
Protection of interest is not as high as Aaa but still high quality. Actual default rate less than 2 percent.	Aa	AA	High grade
Over the long term, some risk to investment. Actual default rate less than 5 percent.	A	A	Medium
Adequate for now but may be unreliable over time. Actual default rate 5 percent.	Baa	BBB	Medium
Below Investment Grade (Junk)			
Future is not certain. Moderate protection of interest and principal. Some speculation. Actual default rate about 17 percent.	Ba	BB	Speculative
Little protection of interest and principal. Actual default rate about 26 percent.	B	B	Speculative
Poor standing. May be in default. Actual default rate over 40 percent.	Caa	CCC	Default
Often in default. Highly speculative.	Ca	CC	Default
Extremely poor prospects.	C	No interest	Poor Investment
	D		In default

For example, you may decide to buy five different Treasury notes or bonds (no default risk), each maturing in the same month every year for five successive years. Then, once a year, each expiring bond is replaced with a new bond maturing in five years.

The benefit of this strategy is that the ladder that you have created should protect you from wild fluctuations in prices and yields that can occur in any one of the bonds. The multiple rungs of a ladder will insure you against such volatility. As an example, the 10-year T-bond yield in 2000 was about 6.8 percent and dropped with each successive new 10-year T-bond issued for three straight years after that to less than 4 percent for those issued in 2003. So, if you bought the 10-year T-bond in 2000, you would enjoy a nice return relative to the same issue a couple of years later. Laddering protects you against such fluctuations because you would have the 2000 issued 10-year T-bond in your portfolio to prop up your return even when the subsequent 10-year bonds in your portfolio were not doing so well. Think of laddering as a bond yield smoothing strategy.

If the above strategies still seem complicated, fear not. Just find yourself a low-fee bond mutual fund. An example is the Vanguard Total Bond Market Index (ticker: VBMFX) yielding around 4.5 percent. While no bond fund manager will ever explicitly claim they have a laddered investment approach, they set up their portfolios so certain bonds become due at certain times. In the case of VBMFX, for example, about 78 percent of the money is in AAA bonds (including Treasuries all of which are AAA). The fund has an average effective maturity of 7.20 years (<10 years makes it an intermediate term bond).Another possibility is the Managers Bond Fund (ticker: MGFIX) with a yield of about 3.6 percent and average maturity of about 5 years.

How Much of Your Portfolio Should Be in Bonds?

The answer will depend on your age, income, and investment objectives. Thus, for example, a February 2003 *Wall Street Journal* survey of portfolio strategists at 16 top brokerage firms showed that, on average, they recommended a portfolio blend of assets that includes 23.16 percent bonds, 68.66 percent stocks, and 6.83 percent cash. Individual firm allocations ranged from as much as 40 percent bonds and 89 percent stocks. Investors should review their portfolios occasionally to make sure their portfolio mix continues to meet their investment objectives. Additionally, feel free to experiment with the percentages in each category depending on how risk averse (or

More on Bond Ladders

Just like stock investing, when investing in bonds, it is good to spread your risk over similar quality bonds maturing at different time intervals. At the same time you work towards maintaining the average maturity of your preference in the portfolio. So, if your comfort zone is between 7–10 years, you set up your portfolio with bonds so that the average maturity of the bonds stays within 7–10 years. When a bond matures, simply replace it with a new one of suitable maturity so your average maturity stays within the same interval.

risk taking) you believe yourself to be. If you are risk averse, you should have more in bonds and cash than in stocks and the opposite if you are a risk taker by nature.

Reverse Repos and the Orange County Fiasco

Have you wondered why we so often hear of shady investment deals involving stocks, whether it is through insider trading or phony analyst ratings, but almost no cases involving bonds? Is it because bonds are so boring that even criminals find it beneath their dignity to be unscrupulous with them? So, I went looking and found something that is sure to stir your interest. It did mine. It is a story of intrigue and corruption and greed and arrogance and, most importantly, involves bond trading. It is a story that took place in Orange County in California—the nation's fifth-largest county and one of its richest—and how it lost more than $2 billion in taxpayer money through risky bond trading.

In December 1994, the world was shocked when Orange County filed for bankruptcy protection. Once the dust settled, there emerged an unlikely villain: Robert L. Citron, the county treasurer also known as "El Wizzo" by his adoring fans (okay, I made that up, but it sounds cool).

About fifteen years before, in the early eighties, Orange County was attracting thousands of residents energized by legislation that limited property taxes. As the county grew so did its need for services including roads, schools, libraries, and other public works. But since property taxes could not be raised, this presented a dilemma to the elected county officials. How to increase the county finances without increasing taxes?

As with other momentous events in history, it seemed like the stage was being set for someone with an audacious vision to come along and provide the solution. It was at this propitious juncture that Robert Citron entered the county stage. As county treasurer, he had access to the county's tax receipts and the proceeds of public bond offerings. And as an investor of these funds, Citron seemed convinced there was only one way to go. If he could somehow borrow money at low, short-term interest rates and invest at higher, longer term interest rates, it might be the answer he was looking for to grow the county funds. Another important belief he held which played such a crucial role, first in his overall investment strategy and then to finally unravel everything he had tried to accomplish, was that interest rates would not increase over the next few years. This is important to note because in bond trading strategies, predicting the future direction of interest rates is crucial and almost all strategies are geared towards that.

Next, Citron made another very risky move. He set out to artificially boost the size of his investment portfolio. We are all familiar with buying stocks on margin. That provides us with leverage and brings with it risks. The way you leverage yourself in bond trading is through a practice known as reverse repurchase agreements (or "reverse repos"). In fact, Citron managed to take the $7.4 billion county fund and create a $20 billion portfolio through reverse repos. In case you are wondering what exactly are reverse repos, let me tell you. However, in order to understand reverse repos, you will have to first understand what a "repo" is. Let us say you need cash for a month. You have a car and you sell the title of the car to the bank (the buyer) for money with the agreement that you will buy back the title in a month for an agreed upon sum of money. If you default on the loan, the bank simply takes possession of your car. This is the essence of a repo. Repos are an alternative to investing in short-term T-bills. A reverse repo is the same as a repo except it is considered from the side of the buyer (or the bank in the above example). Here the buyer trades money for securities agreeing to sell them later. Specifically, Citron pledged his securities as collateral and reinvested the cash thus obtained in new securities—mostly five-year notes issued by government sponsored agencies like the Federal National Mortgage Association (or Fannie Mae). In fact, Citron had a leverage ratio of his portfolio of 5:1 which meant that he had artificially increased the interest rate sensitivity of his portfolio five times (the interest rate sensitivity of a portfolio is also known as its "duration"). So every point of interest move in the wrong direction would magnify portfolio losses by five points. Through his actions, Citron was gambling his investment portfolio on the belief that interest rates were not going to be going up anytime soon.

> ## Duration
>
> Formally, duration measures the sensitivity of a bond's price to changes in the prevailing interest rates. For example, a 5-year duration means the bond will decrease in value by 5 percent if interest rates rise 1 percent and increase in value by 5 percent if interest rates fall 1 percent.

For a while, his investment strategy worked just as drawn up and he was a God. Each year, for more than a decade, he saved Orange County from a budget crunch by producing unexpected interest income. The cash helped save a bunch of popular county initiatives without having to raise taxes. In fact, city officials started taking Citron's magician-like ability to produce extra money for the county for granted. The cry around city hall was, "Bob's a jolly good fellow . . ." Everyone was sharing in the good life and loving it all the way to the bank!

The decade of the '90s began and Citron's performance continued. Articles written over this period reveal that in 1993, for example, the Orange County investment pool returned about 8.5 percent (relative to the state of California making about 4.7 percent on their investment pool). Interestingly, Bob Citron was never really trying to hide his trading strategy. He was a big proponent of the reverse purchase agreements to increase portfolio yields and would talk it up every opportunity he got. And while people around him knew that Citron was using reverse repos to increase yields and some even knew of the inherent risks involved, you know the old adage, "A winner can do no wrong!" As long as the returns were coming in, no one was going to swim against the tide and question, let alone criticize, Citron's investment strategy. The same mentality is at play when we look away or make excuses for the incorrigible (and sometimes illegal) behavior of our entertainers, sports figures, star coaches and even media personalities. As long as the person is a success, and/or a celebrity, he/she can do no wrong.

One contemporary newspaper article, in September, 1993, has Citron on record saying that he did not believe interest rates would increase in the next three years.

And with interest rates at historic lows, his whole strategy of leveraging his portfolio and investing long had worked out like a dream. But, unbeknownst to everyone, dark clouds were gathering on the horizon.

Early in 1994, the first raindrops started falling. The Federal Reserve raised short-term interest rates for the first time since 1989. While publicly stating he was not surprised by the Fed's interest tightening, and that any such effect would be short lived, privately these were unsettling times for Bob Citron. Apparently not used to being questioned about his investing decisions, Citron was starting to feel the heat emanating from his political opponent in the upcoming elections and the somewhat rattled investors.

And then the worst happened. Beginning in February 1994, the Federal Reserve Bank started a series of six consecutive interest rate increases. By Labor Day of that year, investors in Citron's pool were getting downright jittery. Interest rates were rising and no one seemed to know what was happening with the portfolio. What no one knew was that Citron was actually borrowing more money in a last ditch effort to recoup his portfolio losses. But surprisingly, Citron, rather than trying to get out of some of his positions to stem his losses hung on to his belief that the increase in interest rates was at or near its peak and things would get better again soon. Finally, on December 1, 1994, Citron announced that the county investment fund faced a $1.5 billion paper loss. After this announcement things went from bad to worse in a hurry.

On December 4, 1994, Bob Citron resigned and on December 6, Orange County announced it was filing for protection from its creditors under Chapter 11 of the bankruptcy code. In the immediate aftermath of the filing, the county's loss was pegged at a minimum of $2 billion.

But here is the ultimate irony and a valuable lesson in investing. By (some say prematurely) liquidating the investment pool in December 1994, the county locked in an actual loss (as opposed to paper losses) of about $1.6 billion. Unfortunately, soon after the liquidation, interest rates did go back down by about 2.5 percent. The obvious implication of this is that the liquidation of the Orange County portfolio, vis-à-vis its timing, represented a gigantic opportunity cost (and an opportunity lost)—to the order of about $1.4 billion. But remember that this opportunity cost is with the benefit of hindsight which is always 20/20. No one could have foreseen, sitting in the smoldering ruins of a $1.6 billion paper loss in December 1994, that rates would go back down again so soon. And you thought bonds were boring?

Research on Bonds

Research reveals that the extent of liquidity (i.e., trading volume) of a bond determines about 7 percent of the cross sectional variation in bond yields for investment grade bonds and about 22 percent of a bond yield for speculative (or junk) bonds.[25] What are we as investors to make of these findings? Pay attention to the volume of the bond contract that you are interested in transacting—especially if you are interested in transacting speculative, or junk, bonds. Look at Web sites such as http://investinginbonds.com in order to learn more.[26]

Another study examines the reputation of Wall Street dealers who buy and sell Treasury bonds and the effect of this reputation on the trading pattern of these Treasuries.[27] They show that similar trades on similar bonds executed in the same market can have very different volume and volatility patterns depending on which dealer originated the trade. The moral of the story here is that bond dealers are very important. So the next time you are contemplating buying bonds, go to a big and reputed bond dealer like Merrill Lynch, Salomon Smith Barney, Morgan Stanley, etc. It's like going to college—where you go matters. That is why people spend many thousands of dollars to graduate from prestgious universities.

Finally, another paper looks at the corporate, Treasury, and municipal bond markets together.[28] Arguing that the total value of bonds outstanding in these three markets is well over $14 trillion, the paper estimates that the main determinants of bid-ask spreads in the bond market are the time to maturity of the bond, its trading activity (volume) and the bond's credit rating. As an investor, those are the three aspects of your bond you need to pay close attention to in order to minimize your transactions cost. The bottom line is that bonds provide an important safety net in your portfolio. Make sure you have some A-rated corporate bonds and maybe even a few higher yield (and, by extension, lower rated) bonds if you are feeling a tad adventurous. You will not be sorry! It's that offense/defense thing—except this one is within your investment portfolio itself.

Thought Questions

1. Why do companies sometimes choose to issue bonds to raise money rather than issue stocks?

2. Can you think of an example in your own life where you, or someone you know, may have recalled a loan they have? Think of the similarities between that and a company's recalling its bonds.

3. Why are bonds a popular device to raise money by cash-strapped governments, including the United States government?

4. Are bonds issued by corporations any safer than those issued by the government? Why or why not?

5. Can you think of a way junk bonds may have been used to finance corporate-takeovers?

6. Are municipal bonds as safe as U.S. Treasury bonds? Why or why not?

7. Can you identify some years or periods where both bond and stock investments suffered? What drives this phenomenon?

8. Why are the U.S. Treasury securities so important in world economy?

9. Would you buy a bond that is freshly issued or a bond of similar risk that has been around for a while?

10 Can a bond's yield change after its issuance? Why or why not?

11. What happens to your bond's yield if the company declares bankruptcy before the bond matures?

12. How do you make money from your bond investments?

13. What is another term for bond price sensitivity to prevailing interest rate changes?

14. Why do you think bonds are not as popular as stocks?

15. What do bond ratings say about the underlying company?

16. Do you think investing in junk bonds is bad? When can such an investment strategy be lucrative?

17. Why is laddering such an important strategy for bond investors?

Notes

25. Chen L., D. A. Lesmond, J. Wei, 2007. Corporate Yield Spreads and Bond Liquidity. *Journal of Finance* 62, 119–149.

26. http://investinginbonds.com/

27. Massa, M., and A. Simonov, 2003. Reputation and Interdealer Trading: A Microstructure Analysis of the Treasury Bond Market. *Journal of Financial Markets* 6, 99–141.

28. Chakravarty, S., and A. Sarkar, 2003. Trading Costs in Three U.S. Bond Markets. *Journal of Fixed Income*, June, 39–48.

6

Pizza Coupons and Stock Options

If stock options aren't a form of compensation, what are they?
If compensation isn't an expense, what is it? And, if expenses shouldn't go
into the calculation of earnings, whre in the world do they go?
—Warren Buffett, CEO, Berkshire Hathaway

Before reading this section, let's conduct a simple experiment. Pick up your phone and call your insurance agent—the guy who writes your homeowner's and auto policies. The conversation might go something like this:

"Say, Arni (Insurance Agent), I have a question for you. I have been contemplating buying some stocks but, as you know, I am very cautious by nature and hate losing money. Can you sell me insurance of some kind so I can protect my investment?"

Stunned silence at the other end. Eventually, Arni coughs and says,

"Uh, Maggie (that's you), you're kidding me, right? We don't sell policies like that. Listen, I have a client waiting here. Let's talk later about some new policies we have that you shouldn't be without." Click!

You get the picture. Standard insurance companies do not sell investment insurance policies. But does this mean that you cannot have investment insurance?

Sure you can! And here's how.

What Are Options?

Options are simply legal contracts between two entities to buy and sell stock for a fixed price over a given time period.

These contracts are standardized—they control a fixed amount of shares and they expire at the same time. Because of this standardization, they are traded on an exchange, just like shares of stock. The contracts are usually highly liquid, which means there are many buyers and sellers who are willing to buy or sell. You can buy an option contract the same way you buy stock—by calling your broker or going to your online brokerage account.

Options and Pizza Coupons

Options don't just exist in the world of investments. Who among us has not received pizza coupons in the mail? Those glossy advertisements from local pizza establishments stating that one of their coupons entitles you to a large, one-topping pizza for $9.99 and is valid over the next month. The basic idea is the same. You have the right, but are not obliged, to exercise this coupon any time before it expires in order to get your pizza for the price on the coupon regardless of how much it will actually cost in the establishment. Why do you have the right but not the obligation? You may not feel like pizza over the next month, or you may not like the coupon issuer's pizzas. In that case, you will simply ignore the coupon and it will expire unused at the end of the month. This is an example of an option.

Another example of options occurs when you buy a house. Specifically, when you make a bid on the house, you make a down payment of "earnest money" as a sign that you are serious and the house should not be shown to any other prospective buyer. Let's say you agree to buy the house for $200,000 with a down payment of $1,000. You have the right but are not obliged to buy the house. If, in a month, the housing market tumbles, for example, you may feel that the house is now worth $150,000 and you can forfeit your right to purchase it. You will lose your earnest money in the process but, under the circumstances, it might be the best decision. Thus, for $1,000, you had 'in essence' purchased an option to buy the house for $200,000.

How about your annual visit to the doctor? That is an option too because you can postpone the checkup for a while. By delaying, however, you run the risk of harboring something serious. On the other hand, if you exercise your option and go for the checkup, it will cost you money.

One final example deals with computers and when to upgrade. If you exercise your option and buy the computer, you lose out on the opportunity to get an even better one down the road. And as soon as you buy, it is a losing proposition since computer prices are mostly downward sloping. In fact, the optimal time to upgrade is never.

Long Call Options

A call option gives its owner the right, but not the obligation, to buy stock (or "call" it away from the owner) at a specified price over a specified time period.

Options in History

One of the earliest examples of option use comes to us from Greece. The Greek philosopher, Thales(~640–550 BC) (and friend of another more famous philosopher, Aristotle), predicted that the up coming olive harvest would be bountiful. Having faith in his prediction, Thales offered to pay the local olive refineries a fixed sum of money for the right, but not the obligation, to rent their facilities over the duration of the next harvesting season.

Apparently, his hunch paid off and, as the bountiful olive crops arrived in town, the demand for olive presses soared. Not surprisingly, the value to use the olive presses went through the roof—the result of demand far outstripping supply. Thales had, of course, locked up the use of these presses through his "option" contract many months before, much to the press owners' collective dismay. Hopefully, Thales was able to exercise his option on the presses to make some real money in the olive business—either by pressing the olives and selling them for a profit, or by simply selling his right to the presses to some other entrepreneur at a hefty price over what he paid for them earlier. One hopes for Thales's sake that the press owners followed through with the agreement.

In trading lingo, any asset that you buy is called a long position. If you buy a call option, you are the owner, and have a long position in the contract. The owner with the long position has the right, but not the obligation, to buy stock. You are allowed to purchase the stock for a fixed price, but not required to do so. In other words, you have the option to buy—which is where these financial assets get their name.

The price at which you can buy the stock is called the strike price, which was a slang term that came into use because that's the price where the deal—the contract— was struck. Generally, each contract controls 100 shares of stock, called the underlying stock, which we will discuss later. For now, just understand that, unless otherwise stated, each contract controls 100 shares.

Each contract is good only for a certain amount of time. Usually you can find contracts with as little as a couple of weeks to expire and as long as three years of time remaining to expiration. These are standardized time frames, so you can't pick the exact date you want it to expire.

Just as stock is traded in shares, options are traded in units called contracts. If you buy one IBM March $100 call option (one contract), you have the right, but not the obligation, to buy one hundred shares of IBM (the underlying stock) for $100 per share (the strike price) through the expiration date in March—usually the third Friday of the month.

Now when would this call option contract become valuable? Obviously, if IBM's stock price were to rise over $100 before the option expired.

Think of a call option as a coupon giving you the right to buy stock at a fixed price until an expiration date. The big difference between an option represented by a pizza coupon discussed earlier and a call option is that you must pay for the call option while pizza coupons arrive in your mailbox unsolicited and are free.

Put Options—For Investment Insurance

A put option allows the owner to sell the stock ("put" it back somewhere else) for the strike price within a given time. As with call options, the put buyer (long position) has the right, but not the obligation. If you buy an IBM March $100 put, you have the right, but not the obligation, to sell 100 shares of IBM for $100 per share through the third Friday in March.

This put option becomes valuable when IBM stock price goes down below $100. Why? You can still sell IBM shares for $100 when it's trading in the open market for a price below $100. Aren't options wonderful? Yes, but only when things go your way, for you could just as easily be the helpless sap for whom the price went in the opposite direction.

Are you beginning to see how you can have options as an insurance policy for your stock investments? Put options can be used as investment insurance for your stock purchases—assuming, of course, that the stock you are interested in purchasing has options contracts trading on it—not always the case. But, if it does, here is an example of how you might buy a put option contract to give yourself some protection and peace of mind with your stock investments.

Let's say you have just bought 200 shares of MSFT for $25 apiece or $5,000 in total, plus commissions. Having spent so much money, you are justifiably concerned that the MSFT share price may go below $25 in the short term, leading to losses in your investment portfolio. What should you do? Buy two put option contracts on MSFT with a strike price of $25 for $3 apiece, or $600 plus commissions.

Anytime MSFT share price goes below $25, your share portfolio shows a loss but your option portfolio shows a gain to offset the loss in your stocks. So, for $600, you have bought some peace of mind with your 200 shares of MSFT. But, there is a catch. Do you see it?

The option contract that you purchased has a finite life . . . maybe nine months at the most (unless you have those special option contracts known as LEAPS). After nine months, if your stock still hasn't dipped below $25, your option will expire and you will once again be without protection. Depending on your situation then, you may decide to get another option contract at a different strike price in order to be protected again.

However, keep in mind that not all traded stocks have underlying options written on them. You may not have available options in some of the stocks you are interested in. However, it is a safe bet that if it is a liquid stock, it probably does have options trading on it.

So far we have talked about buying options (both calls and puts). It turns out we can also sell (or short) options.

Short Calls and Puts

With either calls or puts, the buyers (the long positions) have the right, but not the obligation, to buy or sell. The investor on the other side (the seller of the option, also called the short position) has the obligation to fulfill the contract. He or she has no choice. If a long call owner decides to buy the stock, the short call trader must oblige and sell. Likewise, if long put owners decide to sell their stock, the short put traders must purchase the stock. Regardless of whether the short option seller is forced to buy or sell stock, the premium received from the initial short trade is theirs to keep. That's their compensation for accepting the risk.

In sum, buying options is far less risky than selling options. Remember this during your forays into the world of options. If you just want to get your feet wet gradually and don't want to play with the big boys, restrict your option trades to BUYING option contracts (as opposed to SELLING calls or puts).

Following is a simple table that summarizes our discussion in terms of rights versus obligations. Think about the differences between the two. What does it mean to say you have a right to do something versus you have an obligation to do the very same thing?

For example, if a fellow student asks you out on a date, do you have the right (or the obligation) to turn him down? Think about it within an option context.

Pricing Options

	Call Option	**Put Option**
Long Position (the buyer)	Right, but not the obligation, to BUY stock at the strike price	Right, but not the obligation, to SELL stock at the strike price
Short Position (the seller)	Possible obligation to SELL stock at the strike price	Possible obligation to BUY stock at the strike price

Pricing options is not an easy task. The reason for this is that options are "derivative" securities—they get their values from the underlying stock. As the stock price changes every second, so do the options that are written on that stock. That said, option prices display certain properties that are fairly easy to see. For example, options prices can never be negative; zero, perhaps, but never negative. Another property is that a call option price can never be worth more than the underlying stock price. A third property is that a put option price can never be more than the strike price associated with the option. These properties all follow from an argument often used in finance to set values of assets known as the "no-arbitrage" principle.

One intuitive, and the simplest, way to price options is to use what is known as the "replicating portfolio" idea. With replicating portfolios, we simply construct a hypothetical portfolio using only stocks, bonds, and/or borrowed cash (all of which are easier to price) such that the portfolio payoff mimics that of the option we are attempting to price. Then, we value the stock-bond portfolio and, by extension, we have the value of the option. Unfortunately, the idea of creating a replicating portfolio to value an option is a static concept and can only get us so far. Since the underlying stock and bond prices are changing constantly, the replicating portfolio becomes too cumbersome a process when used to value options within a dynamic context. This is where multi-period models like the binomial model or the Black-Scholes models of option pricing come in.

There are whole books devoted to such dynamic option pricing approaches so we will not deal with them here, except in an elementary and intuitive way to give you an idea of the kind of animal you are dealing with. If you want further education in the art of option pricing, you should consult these books.

On a very basic level, consider that the stock price path has multiple time steps and at each of these times the stock can take only one of two possible values. For example, if we considered two time steps, 1 and 2, and two possible stock values at each of the two time steps (let's just call them UP and DOWN), we would have a total of four possible terminal values for the stock. These four possible paths could be drawn as a tree

No Arbitrage Principle

Arbitrage means a cost-free way to make money—the good old perpetual money-making machine argument. It will not work except over very small stretches of time because as soon as an arbitrage opportunity arises, everyone will jump in and take advantage of it until it goes away. And the no-arbitrage condition is restored. It turns out that this arbitrage argument, and finding the point of no-arbitrage, is a useful tool to price financial assets or to set bounds on the prices of certain financial assets.

Creators of Option Pricing

The Black-Scholes option pricing formula is named after the two economists, Fischer Black and Myron Scholes, who developed the now-famous formula in a paper published in the *Journal of Political Economy* in 1973.

diagram and the price of the option today can be calculated based on the probabilities we assigned to the likelihood of each of the four states occurring in the future and then discounting them to the present. This is similar to the process we used to value stocks as a discounted stream of future cash flows associated with the stock. The advantage of this process is that it is amenable to being expanded to include many time periods and quick calculations to come up with new option prices as market conditions, and the underlying stock conditions, change. As we increase the number of time steps in the binomial tree mentioned above, the statistical distribution of the stock return becomes a "normal" distribution which has nice properties that are easy to work with. Take my word for it. And with a little more statistical manipulation we arrive at the Black-Scholes option pricing formula.

The Black-Scholes option pricing formula was initially derived for a stylized situation involving a specific type of option and where the underlying stock paid no dividends. The formula has the following as its input:

- The underlying stock price.
- The volatility of the underlying stock price.
- The strike price.
- The time to expiration.
- The interest rate (calculated on the basis of continuous compounding—a time value of money concept).

Properties of the Black-Scholes Option Pricing Formula

The Black-Scholes option pricing formula has some interesting properties outlined below.

- Call prices decrease as the strike price increases.
- Call prices increase as the stock price increases.
- Call prices increase with time to expiration.
- Put prices increase as the strike price increases.
- Put prices decrease as the stock price increases.
- Put prices may increase or decrease with time to expiration.
- Call and put prices both increase as the volatility of the underlying stock increases.
- Calls and puts of a given stock are bound by a relationship known as the "put call parity." This means that if you know the call option price for a given stock, it is easy to figure out the price of the corresponding put option.

Exercising Options

If you wish to buy stock with your call option, or sell stock with your put option, you simply call your broker and tell him you want to exercise the option. Then, three business days later, the transaction will take place. For example, if you own a $50 strike call option and decide to exercise it, your account will be debited for $5,000 ($50 per share times 100 shares per contract) plus commissions and credited 100 shares of stock on the third business day. Similarly, if you own a $50 strike put and exercise it, you will receive $5,000 minus commissions and will be debited for 100 shares of stock on the third business day. Note that you cannot exercise portions of an option—you either buy, or sell, in lots of 100 shares. For instance, if you own one contract, you cannot call your broker and use it to only buy 75 shares. You either buy 100 or none at all. Of course, if you own more than one contract, you can certainly exercise only a portion. If you have five contracts, you could, for example, only exercise two of them and buy 200 underlying shares.

What If You Want Out of Your Contract?

You can always get out of any option contract—long or short—by executing an offsetting position. So, for example, if you are long a March $50 strike call, you can simply sell a March $50 call (called "selling to close") and you no longer have the right to purchase the stock for $50. If you have sold a $75 put (called "selling to open") and no longer want the obligation to buy the stock for $75, you can simply buy a $75 put (buy to close), which relieves you of your obligation.

However, the catch is that the price you receive (or pay) is determined by the market and can be very different from when you entered into the contract.

For example, if you sell a $75 strike put with the stock at $80, you may receive say $6 (per share). Later, if the stock is trading for $70, you may wish to get out of the contract. However, that $75 put may now be trading for $11, meaning you sold for $6 and had to pay $11 to exit: a loss of $5 per contract.

In fact, most options are closed out in the open market this way. Less than 5 percent of the time are contracts actually exercised for stock. The moral of this story is that you can always get out of a contract at any time—it may just cost you a lot of money to do it.

How Are Options Similar to Stocks?

- Options are securities.
- Options trade on national SEC regulated exchanges.
- Option orders are transacted through market-makers and retail participants with bids to buy and offers or asks to sell, and can be traded like any other security.

How Do Options Differ from Stocks?

- Options have an expiration date, while common stocks can be held forever (unless the company goes kaput).[29] If an option is not exercised on or before expiration, it expires worthless.
- Options only exist as a book entry, which means they are held electronically. There are no certificates for options as there are for stocks; so you cannot hang an option certificate on your wall the same way you can, say, a Disney stock certificate.
- There is no limit to the number of options that can be traded on an underlying stock; however, common stocks have a fixed number of shares outstanding.
- Options do not confer voting rights or dividends. They are strictly contracts to buy or sell the underlying stock or index. If you want a dividend or wish to vote the proxy, you need to exercise the call option.

Price Discovery

Price discovery is one of the most important functions of an exchange—whether it is a stock exchange or an option exchange or any other exchange. If a particular venue is associated with price discovery, you can safely take the asset prices from that exchange as indicative of all publicly available information on the underlying company.

If you understood most of what was discussed in this chapter, you are already ahead-of 90 percent of your brethren. Doesn't that make you feel good?

Research on Options

The research on options has focused primarily on the impact of options trading on the corresponding stock prices. Economists refer to it as price discovery. If new information about a company is reflected in the company's option trades, then economists would say that options markets display significant price discovery. Why is this important? If you knew, for example, that new information about a given company always shows up in its option trades and then shows up in its stock prices; then if you saw the company's call options doing well, it might indicate the stock prices are about to go up as well and you could use the information to buy the company's stocks and profit handsomely.

In a recent research paper, three economists show how certain option trades can convey useful information about future stock price movements.[30] Therefore, you would do well to look at a company's option trades in order to form opinions about its future stock prices. By the same token, research has also shown that new information about a given company is reflected in the stock price first and then in the corresponding option trades.[31]

Another research study has applied sophisticated analysis using a large data set over a long time horizon and found evidence that significant price discovery occurs in the option markets.[32] This study has actually quantified the amount of price discovery in the option markets as around 20 percent. The authors also state that the amount of price discovery occurring in the options tends to be greater when option trading volume is higher, when the corresponding stock trading volume is lower, and for stocks with high volatility.

So pay attention to how a company's options are trading before making stock purchasing, or selling, decisions. There is important information about a stock's impending performance in the stock's option trades.

Credit Default Swaps (CDS)

Credit Default Swaps (CDS) have been blamed for the collapse of the global financial markets in the Fall of 2008, lasting well into the first and second quarters of 2009. While the end is not in sight at the writing of this revision of the book, it behooves us to understand the basic nature of these contracts and why we got to where we are today. The definition of a CDS contract is inocuous, giving no hint of its immense potency. It is a contract between two counterparties. The buyer of a CDS contract makes periodic payments to the seller of the CDS contract. In return, the buyer receives an appropriate payoff if the underlying financial instrument defaults in the future. At this point, you are thinking, "isn't this an insurance contract?" And you would be absolutely right. It is!

> ### Definition of a CDS
>
> The definition of a CDS contract is innocent with no hint of the immense potency it has. It is a contract between two counterparties. The buyer of a CDS contract makes periodic payments to the seller of the CDS contract. In return, the buyer receives an appropriate payoff if the underlying financial instrument defaults in the future.

They say that innovations move in light years while regulations move merely in years. Therefore, it is logical that innovations stay a few steps ahead of the law and by the time the cops arrive, the criminals are long gone. Such an analogy is appropriate for the CDS contracts which on their face are regular insurance contracts much like the home insurance policy that you have with your local insurance company. That policy states that if something bad should happen to your property, the company that has sold (or written) the policy will step up and reimburse you for your losses consistent with the conditions of your policy. Critical in this arrangement is the ability of your insurance company to be available with cash when the need arises. Now take this thought a step further. Consider the fact that your insurance company resells your policy to another company across the world. Now when you have a need, it is the new purchaser of the policy that has the responsibility to pony up the money in return for the insurance premium income it is now earning. But what if this company across the world had no way to honor your claims? It bought the policy to simply earn your regular premium payments with no intention of ever paying your claims. And because there was no regulation in place to investigate whether the new buyer had the financial capability to meet its insurance obligation, no one said a word. Now consider the same thing happening to thousands of insurance policies each worth many billions of dollars in assets and you start to understand the magnitude of the problem.

Now you may ask, can your local insurance companies like State Farm or Farm Bureau, or any number of other companies you may be familiar with, that have the word "insurance" in their names, do such a thing? The answer is NO! An insurance company, that declares itself to be an insurance company, cannot indulge in such a practice. The U.S. Congress has enacted legislation that severely curtails what insurance companies can, and cannot, do with your money. The problem is not them. It is companies that pretend to be insurance companies that are behind the mess we are in today. Financial services companies like AIG and others of their ilk were playing at being insurance companies. Since they did not fall under the rubric of a traditional insurance company, the rules that would normally apply to conventional insurance companies did not apply to them. So they could operate right under the noses of the regulators with impunity—and did. Until the sheer size of this market and the unregulated nature of this game, which spanned the globe, simply got out of hand. It may have gone on unnoticed if it were not for the match that lit the proverbial bomb.

That match came in the form of the failure of the subprime mortgage market. As millions of homeowners decided they could not afford the terms of their mortgages anymore and defaulted roughly around the same time the financial services companies that had bought CDS contracts for protection for just such an eventuality turned to companies like AIG and demanded their money. And suddenly everyone realized that these so-called insurance contracts had been sold and resold many times over and no one really knew who the final buyer was or whether this buyer could pay up. In most cases the buyer resided across the world in a country with no jurisdiction to enforce payment.

Madoff: A Path Littered with Clues

Greg N. Gregoriou and Francois-Serge Lhabitant*

On December 10, 2008, Madoff confessed to his two sons, his brother, and his wife that his investment advisory business was "a giant Ponzi scheme." In the evening, his sons turned him in to U.S. authorities. Madoff was arrested the next day and charged with securities fraud. The SEC filed a complaint in federal court in Manhattan seeking an asset freeze and the appointment of a receiver for BMIS.

Flashback to the preceding decade. Bernie had an impeccable reputation on Wall Street. He was on the short list of guests for every family birthday, anniversary, bar mitzvah, wedding and graduation. His firm was ranked as one of the top market makers in NASDAQ stocks. His solid and consistent track record generated a mixture of amazement, fascination, and curiosity. Investing with him was exclusive—a clear sign that one had made it socially. Bernie was truly a legend in the financial industry. Admired by most, venerated by some, his success was such that

> Born on April 29, 1938, Bernard L. Madoff graduated from Far Rockaway High School in 1956. He attended Hofstra University Law School but never graduated. In the early 1960s, he created BMIS with an initial capital of US$ 5,000 earned from working as a lifeguard during the summer and installing refrigeration systems.

* Greg N. Gregoriou is a professor of finance at the State University of New York (Plattsburgh), Plattsburgh; Francois-Serge Lhabitant is a professor of finance at the HEC University of Lausanne and at the EDHEC Business School.

very few dared criticizing him without risking their careers. His house of cards nevertheless crumbled on December 11, 2008, when news broke that the F.B.I. had arrested Madoff and charged him and his brokerage firm Bernard L. Madoff Investment Securities LLC (hereafter: BMIS) with securities fraud. According to the SEC complaint, Madoff himself informed two of his senior employees that his investment advisory business was "just one big lie" and "basically, a giant Ponzi scheme."

All Madoff investors should, in retrospect, kick themselves for not asking more questions prior to investing. As many of them have learned to their regret, there is no substitute for due diligence. Indeed, as discussed in this article, there were a number of red flags in Madoff's investment advisory business that should have been identified as serious concerns and warded off potential clients.

Madoff's Investment Strategy

The strategy officially followed by Madoff was in theory remarkably simple—a combination of a protective put and a covered call. It can be summarized as follows:

1. Buy a basket of stocks highly correlated to the S&P 100 Index.

2. Sell out-of-the-money call options on the S&P 100 with a notional value similar to that of the long equity portfolio. This creates a ceiling value beyond which further gains in the basket of stocks are offset by increasing liability of the short call options.

3. Buy out of the money put options on the S&P 100 with a notional value similar to that of the long equity portfolio. This creates a floor value below which further declines in the value of the basket of stocks is offset by gains in the long put options.

The terminal payoff of the resulting position is illustrated in **Exhibit 1.** Option traders normally refer to it as a "collar" or a "bull spread." Some traders also call it

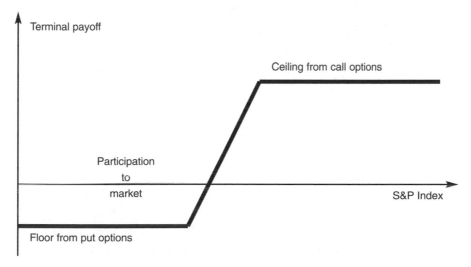

Exhibit 1: Unbundling the split strike conversion portfolio

a "vacation trade" because you can establish the position and not worry about it until the expiration date of the options approaches. Madoff referred to it as a "split strike conversion."

Collars typically aim at providing some downside protection at a cheaper cost than buying puts alone—the cost of purchasing the puts is mitigated by the proceeds from selling the calls. In addition, collars are commonly used to exploit the option skew, i.e., a situation where at-the-money call premiums are higher than the at-the-money put premiums. Overall, the cost of a collar varies as a function of the relative levels of the exercise prices, the implied volatility smiles of the underlying options, and the maturity of the strategy. Officially, Madoff claimed to implement this strategy over short term horizons—typically less than a month. The rest of the time, the portfolio was allegedly in cash.

Madoff's promise was to return 8–12 percent a year reliably, no matter what the markets did. Although results could vary from one feeder to another due to fees, leverage and other factors, all of them did in general show persistently smooth positive returns. Over his seventeen year track record, Madoff would have delivered an impressive total return of 557 percent, with no down year and almost no negative months (less than 5 percent of the time).

The stability of this track record combined with its positive skewness were some of the most compelling arguments to invest with Madoff. Returns were good but not oversized and their consistency made it seem that the outcome of the strategy was almost predictable. A perfect investment for a conservative portfolio and an even more perfect investment to leverage for an aggressive one. . . . As an illustration, **Exhibit 2** compares the cumulative performance of the strategy versus the S&P 100 Index. Returns are comparable (11.2 percent p.a. for the Fairfield Sentry Ltd

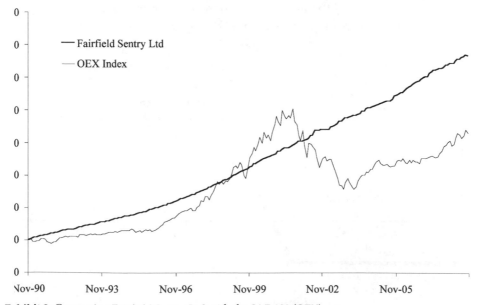

Exhibit 2: Comparing Fairfield Sentry Ltd with the S&P 100 (OEX).

fund versus 8.5 percent p.a. for the S&P 100) but the difference in volatility is striking (2.5 percent p.a. for the fund versus 14.8 percent for the S&P 100). The maximum drawdown difference is also abysmal (-0.6 percent p.a. for the fund versus -49.1 percent for the S&P 100).

Red Flags

Operational Flags

Lack of segregation among service providers

Madoff worked alone with no third party independent oversight. He traded his managed accounts through his affiliated broker-dealer BMIS, which also executed and cleared these trades. More importantly, all assets were administered within his organization, which also produced all documents showing the underlying investments. In a traditional hedge fund, this should have been a clear no-go for all investors, as it allows for performance manipulation and substantially increases the risk for the misappropriation of assets, since there is no third party independently confirming the legal ownership of the Fund's securities.

Obscure auditors

BMIS was audited by a small accountancy firm called Friehling and Horowitz. Although this firm was accredited by the SEC, it was virtually unknown within the investment management industry. Sandwiched between two medical offices it operated from a small 550-square foot office in the Georgetown Office Plaza in New City, New York. Its staff consisted of one partner in his late 70s who lived in Miami (Jerome Horowitz), a secretary, and one active accountant (David Friehling). The firm was not peer reviewed and therefore had no independent check on its quality controls. One should clearly have questioned the choice of such a small audit firm given the large asset base of BMIS. Additional investigations would also have revealed that Friehling and Horowitz had claimed every year since 1993 in writing to the American Institute of Certified Public Accountants that it was not conducting an audit.

Unusual fee structure

Since BMIS was not operating a fund, one should question the way the firm was rewarded for its investment services. Officially, there was no management or performance fee at BMIS—the sole form of compensation according to its Form ADV

> A typical hedge fund uses a network of service providers which normally includes an investment manager to manage the assets, one or several brokers to execute trades, a fund administrator to calculate the NAV, and some custodian(s)/prime broker(s) to custody the positions.

was a "market rate" commission charged on each trade. This allowed the distributor of the feeder funds to charge final investors a management and/or a performance fee—typically 2 percent and 20 percent.

Heavy family influence

Key positions of control at BMIS were held by Madoff family. His brother Peter joined the firm in 1965. He was a Senior Managing Director, the Head of Trading and the Chief Compliance Officer for the investment advisor and the broker dealer businesses. Madoff's nephew, Charles Wiener, joined in 1978 and served as the

Director of Administration. Bernard Madoff's oldest son, Mark, joined the family team in 1986 and was Director of Listed Trading. His youngest son, Andrew, started in 1988 and was Director of NASDAQ. Peter's daughter and Bernard's niece, Shana, joined the firm in 1995 and served as the in-house Legal Council and Rules Compliance Attorney for the market-making arm on the broker-dealer side.

Lack of staff and extreme secrecy

In its regulatory filing, BMIS indicated that he had between one and five employees who performed investment advisory functions, including research. Simultaneously, it disclosed US$ 17 billion of assets under management. How could one believe that such a large sum of money can be managed by such a small group of people?

According to investors, access to Madoff's offices for onsite due diligence was very limited or even denied. Madoff refused to answer questions about his business in general and his investment strategies in particular. He never provided any explanations or monthly performance attribution, even informally, and even threatened to expel some investors who asked too many questions. Such an attitude is very unusual in the hedge fund world. Even the most secretive hedge funds are usually willing to demonstrate to investors that they have quality operations and provide operational transparency. None of this was available with Madoff.

Investments Flags

A black box strategy

Madoff's purported track record was so good and so consistent that it should have become suspect. When applied systematically with a monthly rollover, a split strike conversion strategy can be profitable over long periods but it will also generate some down months and exhibit significant levels of volatility. This was not the case at Madoff, who only had 10 down months out of 215 and a very low volatility. No other split strike conversion manager was able to deliver such a consistent track record.

Several possible explanations have been considered by investors to explain this puzzle. Let us mention some of them:

Market intelligence: Madoff could have added value by stock picking and market timing. Madoff's edge would then have been his ability to gather and process market-order-flow information from the massive amount of order flow BMIS handled each day, and then use this information to implement optimally his split strike option strategy. However, it is unlikely there would not be a single failure of this edge over seventeen years.

Front running: Madoff could have used the information from his market-making division to trade in securities ahead of placing orders he received from clients. However, this would have been illegal in the U.S.

Subsidized returns: Madoff could have used the capital provided by his feeders as pseudo equity, for instance, to leverage some position without having to explicitly borrow, or to conduct more market making by purchasing additional order flow. In exchange, some of the profits made on the market making could have been used to subsidize and smooth the returns of the strategy. However, Madoff himself dismissed this explanation, as his firm used no leverage and had very little inventory.

Market Size

Executing a split strike conversion strategy with over US$ 17 billion of capital would have been prohibitively expensive using S&P 100 options, which are much less used than S&P 500 options. Given the daily trading volume, option prices would have experienced sharp moves in the wrong direction for Madoff. None of that did happen. When questioned about the discrepancy between the daily trading volumes and his alleged needs, Madoff supposedly explained that he used primarily OTC markets. But that explanation is unconvincing. Firstly, there are not so many counterparties that could be consistently ready to sell cheap insurance every month—and lose money for seventeen years by doing so. Secondly, the counterparty credit exposures for firms that could have done such trades were likely to be too large for these firms to approve. And thirdly, some of these counterparties would have hedged their books, and there was no indication of such movements. Not surprisingly, the names of these alleged counterparties could never be confirmed, and no option arbitrageur ever saw one of Madoff's trades. This should have suggested that Madoff could not be doing what he said he was doing.

Incoherent 13F Filings

In the U.S., investment managers who exercise investment discretion over US$ 100 million or more of assets must disclose quarterly their holdings on a 13F Form with the SEC. These 13F Forms, which are publicly available, contain the names and ". . . class of the securities, the CUSIP number, the number of shares owned and the total market value of each security." Interestingly, while Madoff had over US$ 17 billion of positions, his 13F Form usually only contained scatterings of small positions in small (non-S&P 100) equities. Madoff's explanation was that his strategy was mostly in cash at the end of each quarter to avoid publicizing information concerning the securities he was trading on a discretionary basis. Again, this is hard to believe and it would have created massive movements on money markets.

Impending Doom

The most tenacious Madoff opponent turned out to be Harry Markopolis, a former money manager and investment investigator. In May 1999, Markopolis started a campaign to persuade the SEC's Boston office that Madoff's returns could not be legitimate. But his reports were laden with frothy opinions and provided no definitive evidence of a crime, so the SEC paid little attention. Markopolis nevertheless continued his repeated requests, which culminated in November 2005 with a 17-page letter titled "The World's Largest Hedge Fund Is a Fraud." In this letter, Markopolis listed 29 red flags that suggested again that either Madoff was front-running his customer orders, or he was conducting "the world's largest Ponzi scheme." This time, the SEC's New York Office followed up on Markopolis' tips and investigated BMIS and one of its feeders. It found no evidence of front running or of a Ponzi scheme, but a few technical violations surfaced that were rapidly corrected. Since these violations "were not so serious as to warrant an enforcement action," the case was closed. In early 2008, Markopolis tried again to capture the attention of the SEC's Washington office, but obtained no response. These repeated failures by regulators to pursue investigations will certainly be examined and discussed extensively in the near future, but Markopolis' letters should have been a warning sign for investors.

Last but not least, several banks refused to do business with Madoff. One of them in particular black-listed Madoff in its asset management division and banned its brokering side from trading with BMIS. Several professional advisers and due diligence firms attempted to analyze the strategy and/or some of its feeder funds and rejected them from their list of approved investments.

* The above article is an abridged version and is used with the permission of the authors. The complete article appears in *The Journal of Wealth Management*.

References

Arvedlund E. "Don't Ask, Don't Tell," *Barrons*, May 7, 2001, p.1.

Brown S., W. N. Goetzmann, B. Liang, and C. Schwarz. (2008a), "Mandatory Disclosure and Operational Risk: Evidence from Hedge Fund Registration," *The Journal of Finance*, vol. Vol. 63, No. 6 (2008a), pp. 2785–2815.

Brown S., W. N. Goetzmann, B. Liang, and C. Schwarz. "Estimating Operational Risk for Hedge Funds: The _-Score," Yale ICF Working Paper No. 08-08, 2008, New Haven, CT.

Lhabitant F. *The Handbook of Hedge Funds*. London: John Wiley and Sons, 2006.

Markopolis H. "The World's Largest Hedge Fund Is a Fraud," Letter to the S.E.C., 2005.

Markov M. "Madoff: a Tale of Two Funds," MPI Quantitative Research Series, December 2008, New Brunswick, NJ.

SEC, 2004. Available at http://www.sec.gov/answers/form13f.thm.

U.S. District Court for the Southern District of New York (2008), "U.S. v. Madoff (2008)," 08-MAG-02735.

Thought Questions

1. Why is the phrase, "you have the right but not the obligation," so important with call and put options?

2. When do you have the obligation to go through with an option transaction?

3. When purchasing options as an insurance policy, what is the premium for the policy, and how long is the policy valid for?

4. Why is buying options safer as a trading strategy, relative to selling options?

5. Do you always have to exercise your options or let them expire unexercised? What else can you do with your options?

6. Are there options traded on all publicly traded stocks? Why or why not?

7. What can the regulators do to minimize the destructive influence of CDS?

8. Were Bernard Madoff's actions wrong? Should his investors share some of the blame? Why or why not?

Notes

29. Options expire on the Saturday following the third Friday of the expiration month. However, this is for accounting purposes only as there is nothing the option trader can do with an option on Saturday. Thus, the third Friday of the expiration month is the last trading day and for practical purposes, the day you want to consider as the expiration day.

30. Easley, D., M. O'Hara, P. S. Srinivas, 1998. "Option Volume and Stock Prices: Evidence on Where Informed Traders Trade." *Journal of Finance* 48, 1957–1967.

31. Finucane, T. J., 1999. "A New Measure of the Direction and Timing of Information Flow Between Markets." *Journal of Financial Markets* 2, 135–151.

32. Chakravarty, S., H. Gulen, S. Mayhew, 2004. "Informed Trading in Stock and Options Markets." *Journal of Finance* 59, 1235–1258.

7

Trading Assets

Don't try to buy at the bottom and sell at the top. This cannot be done—except by liars.
—Bernard Baruch

If your favorite stock is selling for $50/share one second, what can it change to the next moment? Can it increase to 50\frac{1}{16}$ or decline to 49\frac{15}{16}$? Can it, for example, increase instead to $50.02 or decrease to $49.99? Should we even care? It turns out that we should care for the following reason. How stock prices increase or decrease affects the best prices to buy or sell them at any given time. The difference between the best price to buy and the best price to sell the stock is also known as the stock's bid-ask spread which is an implicit cost incurred by investors for transacting that stock (note that the spread is a cost you incur IN ADDITION TO the commission you are paying your broker to execute your order). Another point to keep in mind is that the ask price is generally higher than the bid price. What it boils down to is we, the investors, are buying at the higher price and selling at the lower price. The difference between the ask and the bid price, i.e., the bid-ask spread, is a cost that we incur for the pleasure of transacting in stocks. The wider the spread, the greater is our cost and the narrower the spread, the smaller is our cost. Naturally, we would want the spread to be at its narrowest at all times. Since we, the investors, are incurring the cost, someone else is earning this cost. Professional market intermediaries who are buying and selling stocks to us are the ones who are earning the spread and the wider the spread, the more profitable it is for them to buy/sell stocks with us. Naturally, they want to keep spreads wide if possible.

The Saga of Wide Spreads

Let us begin with a true story of how important bid-ask spreads are in the markets. Did you know that wider spreads once almost brought the mighty NASDAQ market very

---

Bagehot's Intuition

Economist Jack Treynor, writing under the pseudonym of Bagehot, once intuitively observed that the market-maker (the intermediary in the stock exchange), who trades in any given stock, makes his money mostly by trading against uninformed traders (people like you and me), and loses money trading against informed traders since these traders trade on superior information. On balance, therefore, the market-maker sets his bid-ask prices to minimize losses on his trades with the informed traders and to maximize his gains on trades with the uninformed traders. Hence, spreads should increase when the market-maker believes more informed traders are present in the market and should decrease when more uninformed traders are in the market.

nearly to its knees? It was the result of a couple of academics writing a simple research paper.[33] Did you think academics had no power?

Using a matched sample of 50 NYSE stocks and 50 NASDAQ stocks, the economists found that spreads on NASDAQ stocks were generally wider than their comparable NYSE stocks. This meant that investors had been, on average, paying more to buy NASDAQ stocks and receiving relatively less to sell them. Based on the study's results, the authors concluded that any rational model of price quoting behavior cannot explain the wider spreads and that their finding "raises the question of whether NASDAQ dealers implicitly collude to maintain wide spreads." It is this last statement by the authors that took the trading world by storm and, soon after the study's publication, both the Department of Justice and the Securities and Exchange Commission began broad investigations of the NASDAQ market. In light of such scrutiny, the NASDAQ market underwent a tremendous structural overhaul over the next few years.

The findings of this study and a couple of related ones, subsequently published by Christie and Schultz, were hotly debated for years by academics, practitioners, and regulators alike. Economists published competing research papers aggressively refuting the suggestion of dealer collusion alluded to by the original authors. The underlying point made by the refuting economists centered on the fact that competitive economic factors would explain the difference in spreads uncovered by the original authors and would not necessarily imply collusion by NASDAQ dealers. In addition, two practices prevalent in NASDAQ, known as preferencing and internalization of order flow, would reduce the incentive for a dealer to improve bid and ask prices. That is, if a large fraction of the order flow is preferenced or internalized, a dealer's incentive to improve quotes wanes because posting better prices may not attract additional order flow. Preferencing and internalization of order flow also exist in other markets, such as the NYSE, but not to the same degree. At the end of the day, the original study spawned a whole cottage industry of follow-up studies each refuting parts of the original study's findings and/or the conclusions. We will never really know what went on in NASDAQ. However, one thing is certain. All that attention made NASDAQ a better and a more transparent market. And, that is a good thing!

Preferencing and Internalization

Order flow is preferenced when a broker agrees to route its retail customer order flow to a particular dealer (often in return for a payment), and the dealer agrees to execute that order flow at prices no worse than the best bid or ask, as required by NASDAQ rules. Order flow is internalized when a dealer trades with its own retail customers at prices no worse than the best bid or ask of any dealer.

Decimal Pricing

Decimal pricing is a way of listing the price of something in dollars and cents, with a decimal point rather than in fractions. You will find decimal pricing almost everywhere there are monetary transactions—except in the U.S. securities market where, until recently, fractions (sixteenths-of-a-dollar) were used instead. Thus, for example, if you bought a stock at a price of $50 1/16, under decimal pricing that same stock purchased now will be at $50.06. Recall the questions at the beginning of this chapter?

You might be thinking, why would we want to trade in anything other than decimals? After all, that is how things are priced at supermarkets, department stores, and other places we go to buy things. Why should stocks be any different? It turns out that for over two hundred years stocks have been quoted in fractions. The problem with fractions for most of us is that it is a pesky thing we learned in high school, or even in that introductory math class in college, and then proceeded to forget about right after finals. So, when we encounter a stock price of $36 7/16 we have to find a calculator to figure out what it means in decimals. So why did this practice continue for so long? The easy answer is simply because people were too lazy to change. Actually, it is a little more complicated than that.

When something goes on forever, as was the case with fractional trading, the entire infrastructure grows around it. People, companies, and stock exchanges (our good old stock supermarkets) spend millions of dollars to support all the activities that go on in a large supermarket, all of which are designed to support fractional trading. So given all the money that has been put in, nobody really wants to change it because it will cost a lot of extra money to rebuild the infrastructure around decimal trading. Hence, status quo for years and years.

Eventually Congress got in on the act, decided to play the role of high school principal, and sternly told the exchanges that they had to get with the program or else. Ergo, we got decimal pricing.

The securities industry and regulators have been simplifying the information that investors need. Using more "plain English" in prospectuses and client communications is one example. Decimal pricing is another. It's easier to understand. Decimalization should also help the U.S. markets compete with foreign exchanges, which already use decimals. Our decimalization will reduce the slight disparities that can occur when foreign securities trade in decimals in their home markets and in fractions on a U.S. exchange.

Summary

Preliminary reviews by the SEC and the NASDAQ Stock Market show that decimal trading has substantially narrowed quoted spreads. NASDAQ reports that the average effective spread for its securities has shrunk 50 percent since decimalization went into effect. Similarly, the SEC estimates that the average effective spread for New York Stock Exchange securities shrunk 28 percent. The overall narrowing of spreads makes it likely that retail investors, entering small orders, have experienced reduced trading costs.

Has Decimalization Cut into Wall Street's Profit Margins?

Following is an excerpt from a *Wall Street Journal* story on decimalization:[34]

A just-completed academic study[35] has found that, as expected, the transition to "decimalization" from quoting stocks in fractions is cutting into Wall Street's profit margins. That is, the change is narrowing bid ask spreads, or the difference between the price offered to buy a stock and the price offered to sell it.

The study referred to above goes on to say that on average, quoted bid-ask spreads shrank by about 48 percent for the six American Stock Exchange stocks taking part in a decimalization pilot program that began August 28, 2001, and by 28 percent for the seven NYSE stocks in a concurrent pilot program. The study looked at transaction data before and after the decimalization pilot began and found that bid-ask spreads fell, on average, by about 55 percent at the Amex and 4 percent at the NYSE.

All this is certainly good news for us, the investors. But, here is the problem! While a narrow spread means that investors like you and I are buying stocks more cheaply and selling stocks at higher prices, it is tempting to conclude that the specialists and brokers on Wall Street (collectively known as the institutional traders) must be making less profit. And the thought of making less profit is making these big boys mad! They have money, influence, and good friends in Washington, who in turn have senators as good friends. Therefore, there is intense lobbying going on to roll back decimalization so the institutional investors can make more money than they are making right now. But, wait a minute! Do the institutional investors have a basis to complain about reduced profits?

To answer this very question, three economists investigated institutional trading costs both before and after decimalization using a proprietary database of institutional trades.[36] Their study found that there has been no increase in institutional trading costs following decimalization. Thus, institutions appear to have no basis to complain. The data suggests that they want to roll back decimalization and move to wider minimum tick sizes (like a nickel) just to make a buck!

How Does Decimalization Change the Way We Invest?

The short answer is, it doesn't! Your overall investment strategy should not be affected in the least. However, some procedural aspects of investing have changed.

Specialist Firms on Wall Street

Specialist firms exist on Wall Street to facilitate buyers meeting sellers. Specialist firms have names like Spear, Leeds & Kellogg, Van der Moolen, and LaBranche, and are required to make continuous price quotes on both sides of the market (i.e., act both as buyers and sellers) in all the stocks they are responsible for in order to maintain a fair and orderly market. In so doing, specialists end up acting as both agents and as principals. That is, they sometimes help arrange to bring buyers and sellers together and collect a commission for doing so. Or, they may end up selling stocks from their own inventory, or buying stocks into their personal inventory if there are no other sellers or buyers respectively at that particular point in time. So specialists provide "immediacy" and keep Wall Street humming like a well-oiled machine.

Specialists post demand and supply of the stocks they make markets in and the price at which such demand or supply will be executed. In the same way, parties interested in partaking of matchmaking services post their particulars including the kind of people they would like to meet (sensitive, caring, good teeth and, of course, making good money—this from the women). Then it is up to the individual to take the first step (usually the men) and the horse race is on!

In sum, dating services are to Main Street what market-making firms are to Wall Street!

You will have to get used to placing orders and receiving executions in decimals instead of fractions; and the quotes you get from your brokerage firm, whether electronically or through a broker, will be in decimals.

Trading Places

There are two very important stock markets in the United States—well, three actually, but the third one resembles the first one and is a significantly smaller version of it. The first stock market in the United States is the New York Stock Exchange (NYSE) and is located at the corner of Wall and Broad streets in New York City. It is a physical (read bricks-and-mortar) exchange that meets every day from 9:30 AM EST to 4:00 PM EST. There is "after-hours" trading but the bulk of the day's trading takes place during the day. The NYSE was established in 1792 when 24 New York City stockbrokers and merchants signed an agreement under a buttonwood tree and formed an organization for self-preservation purposes and in order to keep the riff-raff out. This was the precursor to today's stock exchanges. The American Stock Exchange (AMEX) began its existence in 1921 with no desire to compete with its older and bigger rival—the NYSE. The traders in AMEX were enterprising and unconventional and handled stocks of young and marginal companies. The National Association of Securities Dealers Automated Quotation (NASDAQ) Stock Market, founded in 1971, was the world's first electronic stock market and comprised of a bunch of computer terminals networked together. The purpose of the NASDAQ was to popularize (and even legitimize) the OTC (over-the-counter) securities market which, up to that point, had been relatively unknown and unused by investors. Think of OTC stocks as the orphans in the stock world, sort of like the movie "The Cider House Rules." No one really cares about them and banishes them into some street corner to be traded in a hush-hush manner. In essence, a stock is known as an OTC stock mainly because the company is small and does not yet meet the listing criteria of the established exchanges like the NYSE and AMEX. With its first day of trading on February 8, 1971, the NASDAQ system displayed quotes for over 2,500 OTC stocks.

In sum, the U.S. has three major stock exchanges: The bricks-and-mortar NYSE and AMEX, and one electronic or virtual stock exchange, the NASDAQ. Below, we will explore why it is important to know where a stock is listed and whether there is a benefit for the companies and its shareholders to move their primary sources of listing from one exchange to another.

Stock Tickers

Stock tickers are more than a combination of letters denoting a specific company. So, understanding the meaning of the ticker behind a company will help you gain a deeper understanding of the company itself. First, one-letter symbols are rare. They are reserved for the very best companies and convey a certain social status. Some examples are: Citigroup (C), Ford Motor (F), Gillette (G), Kellogg (K), Sears Roebuck (S), AT&T (T), and so on. Some single letters are still up for grabs. It is no secret that the NYSE desperately wants Microsoft to switch from the NASDAQ (which has always been its primary listing exchange) to the NYSE and, until recently, kept aside the symbol M for that possibility. Microsoft will probably never switch!

The general rule governing letter choices for stock tickers is as follows: Stocks having the NYSE as their primary listing venue have one to three characters; stocks trading in the National Market System of the NASDAQ, where the most liquid (and best) stocks trade, have four characters; NASDAQ small- cap stocks (less liquid and smaller in size) have five characters. Finally, mutual funds have five characters with the last always being X.

- NYSE stocks have one to three characters.
- NASDAQ NMS stocks have four characters.
- NASDAQ small-cap stocks have five characters.
- U.S. mutual funds have five characters, the last being X.

These days, when everybody uses search engines to look up just about anything and "Google" is a verb used in everyday communication as in "Let's just Google this," choosing a combination of letters to represent your company has become a science—like jury consultants and the obsession with identifying the perfect jury for the desired verdict. Thus, for example, the Peoria, Illinois-based company Caterpillar has as its ticker symbol CAT. Incidentally, the word CAT is typed into search engines well over a million times a month (it is amazing that someone actually keeps track of such things)—not necessarily by people looking for companies to invest in, but those looking for information about, yes, you guessed it: The feline. By the same token, the toy manufacturer and retailer Toys "R" Us trades in the NYSE with ticker TOY. Guess what comes up every time a parent "Googles" the word TOY in order to find information on toys? In the Internet age, this is an example of ticker symbol optimization! Choosing the right combination of symbols for your company can get you a lot of free publicity, which is a wonderful thing!

Where Your Stock Lists Is Important Too!

So far we have discussed the importance of the specific letters (the number of and so forth) in determining the type of company. But tickers convey more information. For example, where a stock might be listed (its primary exchange) is also conveyed by a stock's ticker. Knowing the listing exchange (i.e., NYSE, AMEX, or NASDAQ) of the company you may be interested in may also suggest subtle, but important, information about the company itself. That is because our two main listing exchanges—the NYSE and NASDAQ (AMEX is very small and mimics the NYSE for the most part)—have very different characteristics and listing requirements. NYSE is the old and established name and has been in existence for over 200 years. By comparison, the NASDAQ is truly the new kid on the block and has been in existence for about 30 years. To belong to the NYSE is like belonging to an old country club, full of tradition and filled with old, but rich, people. In comparison, the NASDAQ has much less stringent listing requirements and almost anybody can get in. It is full of younger, hipper companies representing the casual, dress in jeans and T-shirt mentality. Not surprisingly, most new tech/dot-com companies of the late 1990s were listed in the NASDAQ since none were eligible to be listed in the NYSE. So when the dot-com bubble burst, guess which market got hit the hardest? NASDAQ, of course!

The exchange-listing decision of companies happens to be an important research topic in finance. And this research is done in one of two ways. In the first approach, comparable stocks trading in the NYSE and NASDAQ are examined to see which stocks display favorable qualities, such as lower trading costs, lower volatility (or, choppiness in prices), and lower bid-ask spreads. In the second approach, stocks that switched from one exchange to another are followed in what is known as an "event study" to track how its trade-related characteristics changed from before switching to after switching.

Studies matching NYSE and NASDAQ stocks based on size, shares outstanding, trading volume, and price variability (or, choppiness in prices) find that NYSE stocks show smaller bid-ask spreads and lower trading costs overall than comparable stocks in the NASDAQ. This implies that, all else being equal, NYSE does better for the investor than NASDAQ. That's one for NYSE and zero for NASDAQ. Furthermore, studies that examine stocks that moved from the NASDAQ to the NYSE report that after the switch the same stocks display lower price choppiness, smaller bid-ask spreads, and overall lower trading costs. By my count, that's two for NYSE and zero for NASDAQ. Hence, based on the research evidence, it seems clear that anybody with common sense would want to list in the NYSE, right? Even if you were not eligible to be listed in the NYSE initially, as soon as you became eligible to move to the NYSE, you would do so. I would have thought so too!

But, consider the facts. Between 1986 and 1998, about 2,700 non-financial companies listed in the NASDAQ satisfied the eligibility criteria for listing on the NYSE. Yet, only 460 firms chose to actually move to the NYSE. That is just about 1 in 6 companies. Why? While several plausible theories exist, none are able to provide a definitive answer that fits all stocks/companies. For example, one theory is that a lot of the stocks that can move to the NYSE but choose not to do so, like Microsoft or Intel, are already world leaders in their respective areas and have all the name recognition they want. So they do not see a gain in switching exchanges and simply choose to stay in the NASDAQ, where, incidentally, they are treated like royalty. While this explanation might fit the NASDAQ superstars like Microsoft, Intel and a few others, for the vast majority of companies listing at the NASDAQ that are eligible to move, and choose not to do so, this reasoning does not hold true. They are not the household names that those aforementioned companies are. And they could certainly benefit from the identified benefits of moving their primary listing to the NYSE. And, yet, they don't move. It cannot be inertia or laziness. While you and I can laze around in our pajamas and not go to work, companies for the most part always look at the bottom line and profits. And it is simply not believable that a company would leave money on the table by not switching exchanges if it has the option of doing so.

Yet another plausible explanation, related to tech stocks in particular, is that NASDAQ is considered to be the home of the tech stocks. So, naturally, companies

The Effective Bid–Ask Spread

An effective bid-ask spread or simply an effective spread differs a bit from the quoted bid-ask spreads discussed above. Specifically, when actual trades take place in response to the quoted bid-ask spreads posted by the market-makers in the NYSE, or by the stock dealers in the NASDAQ, the difference between the actual trade price and the quoted bid-ask spread midpoint represents the effective spread and captures "actual," or ex post, cost of trading the stock compared to the theoretical, or ex ante, cost of trading represented by the quoted spreads. Academics prefer to use effective spreads rather than quoted spreads as an accurate estimator of trading costs.

like Microsoft and Intel would like to belong with their peer group. Again, this rationale is flawed for the following reason. Large and well-known companies don't have to be with their peer group to be legitimate. They are already legitimate companies and so, while this argument might hold for a fledgling tech company (that would not be eligible to be listed in the NYSE anyway), it certainly does not hold for the tech giants that most of these NYSE-eligible companies are.

And here is another twist. Recently, Sears, the retail giant, declared that they were moving from the NYSE to the NAS-DAQ! And, what makes the move interesting is the fact that Sears is a single-lettered stock (ticker: S) in the NYSE. So they are throwing away their glamorous position in the NYSE to move to the NASDAQ (trading in a single-letter ticker for four letters). In a convoluted way, this move reinforces the argument I was making above about large and well-known companies not being burdened by issues of peer-group location and name recognition factors in deciding which exchange to call home.

Put differently, Sears does not believe that it loses anything by moving to the NASDAQ from the NYSE. Some say that Sears is trying to distance itself from the aura of being established to embrace the freshness and vitality of youth. By joining the home of Amazon and eBay, the company is saying, "Look, we're hip too!"

And you thought only men have midlife crises?

Why Bid-Ask Spreads May Have Been Higher in the 1990s

In the section entitled "The Saga of Wide Spreads" earlier in this chapter, we learned about how a couple of academics reported on the quoted bid-ask spreads in NAS-DAQ stocks being greater than similar stocks trading in the NYSE. The academics concluded that a rational explanation was there was collusion among the dealers in the NASDAQ resulting in the spreads remaining wide.

That study was published in 1994 and generated a lot of heat for the NASDAQ for the remainder of the decade. The Department of Justice (DOJ) opened an investigation in 1996 as did the Securities and Exchange Commission that included taped conversations among traders employed by the NASDAQ market-makers or dealers. These recordings revealed that there might have been some arm-twisting going on in order to keep those bid-ask spreads wide.

The bigger question: Was collusion the only reason NASDAQ spreads were higher relative to NYSE stocks? The reason this is important for us investors is, if this happens to be generally true, then every time we buy and sell a stock listed in the NASDAQ (which covers almost everything in the tech sector, for example) we might be paying more to buy and getting less to sell. This is not good! A recent study published by two academics provides a second explanation.[37] They argue that the high spreads observed in the NASDAQ might have been the work of day traders trading in the NASDAQ's small order execution system (SOES). These traders were called SOES bandits. Basically, these SOES bandits took advantage of a loophole in the NASDAQ trading system whereby they could quickly buy and sell those lower trading volume stocks whose prices may not have been updated by the dealers in a timely manner, in order to quickly exploit changing market conditions.

Therefore, faced with the prospect of not knowing which stocks would be the target of these bandits at any point in the trading day, the NASDAQ dealers may have kept the quoted spreads wider in order to compensate themselves for the added risk they perceived they were facing from the SOES bandits. Professors Benston and Wood analyzed market data over thirteen years between 1987 and 1999 and concluded that trading by the SOES bandits is an important reason for the relative increase in both the quoted and effective bid-ask spreads in the NASDAQ, but not in the NYSE where such bandits were not active.

How to Reduce Excess Volatility in Our Stock Markets

Our finance theories and models are fairly well calibrated to explain stock price behavior in the long run. Daily, weekly, monthly—these are all fairly well understood. What we have almost no handle on are how stock prices, and the markets overall, behave in the short run—in the split seconds, within a minute, etc. Now technology has driven the markets to where things happen in nanoseconds. Everything has accelerated to the point where, much like laws governing classical and quantum physics, there is a whole set of "quantum laws" that are governing stock price behavior within very short time intervals that are totally different from the long time frame equilibrium stock price behavior that we teach our undergraduates and graduates. For example, according to Robert Schwartz, an economist at Baruch College, the three most volatile minutes within a trading day are the first two minutes every morning when markets open (at 9:30 AM EST) and the final minute before markets close (4 PM EST). He asserts also that markets are not efficient—certainly not in the short run. It is those huge swings in price that occur within a few seconds or minutes that fall right outside the rubric of finance theory as we understand it. Schwartz argues that inaccurate price discovery contributes to volatility. If there are piles upon piles of information cascades each buffeting stock prices each nanosecond then uncertainty builds up and eventually blows up the market, taking everything in its path—much like the tsunami. Technology has contributed to the current state of our markets: technology and the democratization of markets, whereby individuals and institutions all have access to the same set of tools to affect trades. The ability of thousands of individuals to jump in and out of trades instantaneously counters the effect of a single institutional trade and affords individuals power as a group. The downside of this power is the increase in volatility that we have seen in recent years. This problem will only get worse as technology improves further and allows us to do things at even smaller snapshots of time.

One possible remedy to bring volatility under control is to slow things down by bringing back the call auction trading in a big way. It exists currently but only under very special circumstances. For example, when there is a trading halt on a particular stock, when trading resumes it does so with a call auction. When trading begins every morning in the NYSE at 9:30 AM, it does so with a call auction. At almost every other time, trading occurs on a continuous basis. The argument can be made that if we have call auctions on every stock once every hour (say) then a price discovery process occurs at that point in time. Such a mechanism would immediately lead to a reduction in volatility without sacrificing price discovery. Skeptics will point to the remaining minutes within each hour with no explicit price discovery, even though it is unclear what a supposed price discovery process every second of the hour accomplishes.

Another way to reduce volatility, as proposed by Robert Schwartz, is to establish well-defined stabilization funds that would buy and sell equity shares according to clearly stated procedures. These would be run by third party fiduciaries and would be responsible for buying shares in a falling market and selling shares in a rising market. This would be accomplished at regular intervals in pre-specified amounts through call auctions.

To summarize, regulation is not the answer to our problems and neither is unrestricted free markets. These are polar cases and both can lead to problems. A well balanced combination of the two can help the markets deal with the excessive volatility issue without sacrificing price discovery.

How to Narrow Down Your List of Stocks

Now that you have an appreciation for the importance of bid-ask spreads in determining trading costs, let us turn to ways in which you can narrow down your potential stock purchases.

Before you actually shoot your first deer, however, you have to understand your equipment—the gun. First, you spend countless hours understanding how to take care of it, how to clean it and how to lock it and put it away safely. Then one day, after you have given up all hope of ever actually using the gun, your father announces that today is the day you two will be going hunting in the woods for deer. Similarly, if you are taking driving lessons, you have to do quite a bit of preparatory work before you are actually allowed to get in the vehicle with the big flashy sign proudly proclaiming you to be a "Student Driver."

It is the same with investing. You have to understand the terrain you will be playing in before delving into any specific investment. You also need to understand the language of investing—the jargon and the important question: What to invest in?

Surprisingly, this seemingly innocent question freezes many beginners into instant paralysis. My response is to say, "In the beginning, don't sweat the small stuff." Start with the familiar. For a novice, the differences between a researched pick and a pick through familiarity will be miniscule. You might as well flip a coin to pick a familiar stock. Or, if you have a pet monkey, have it pick a few.

So what is a good stock to put all of your $640 in? Is Coca-Cola a good stock? You like the Pepsi commercials—especially the ones around Super Bowl time. Is Pepsi a good investment? How about Hewlett-Packard? You like Abercrombie clothes. Should you invest in the company's stock? You eat a bagel every morning with your coffee. Should you invest in a bagel chain? Your iPod Nano is like a tumor on your arm these days. Is Apple (the company that makes them) a good bet? The bottom line is that, barring a few bad stocks in the absolute sense, whether a stock is good or bad really depends on whether it meets YOUR needs at that moment.

The basic rule of thumb is the following: If you have a long-term perspective in your investment approach, you could take a chance with a long shot that is not so hot today but could win the big one in a few years. These are not stocks that are going to pay any dividends (dividends are denominated in dollars and represent your share of the profits the company made the previous quarter); your only hope of making money with these is through stock price appreciation over time. Think of those early investors who believed in Microsoft back in 1982. Another example is Amazon. How about Google? Do you think Google, at $400 a share, has the potential to further increase in value?

On the other hand, if you are older and want something that will be a winner right away, you may want to confine your attention to a solid Old Economy stock with a consistent record of dividend payments. Think IBM here. Maybe even Intel. How about General Electric or Exxon Mobil?

The first place to start is with the familiar. Trying to find the perfect stock in the beginning will only scare you into inaction. So, I say, jump in and swim!

Do you remember your first swimming lessons where your father had to nearly drag you into the deep end of the pool? Remember the helpless feeling that would come over you as you realized it was either sink or swim? Actually, I think it is my childhood I am thinking of. Even if you did your homework meticulously and studied the market for a long time, at some point you will have to make that leap of faith. It is inevitable. It is the same with your personal relationships. You can go out a person all you want but, at some point, you will have to make the leap of faith. It is no different with stocks!

Go ahead; ask around for some initial recommendations. Ask your parents, significant others, priests, or even family pets if you wish, for their recommendations (and do not be shocked if Nabisco is pawed). Any brand of clothing you like. Any brand of food you like. Look up the parent company. Any particular medication you take frequently and think the world of? Put them all on your list. We will begin our research from this list.

Fast forward a few weeks. You now have your preliminary stock picks. Let's assume your list is as follows: Harley Davidson (ticker: HDI, boyfriend's pick), GlaxoSmithKline

> ## Caution
>
> While there are no rules on how long you need to hold for your strategy to be termed buy-and-hold, I like to suggest at least one year so you are eligible for the long-term capital gains tax rate which is lower than your usual (or, short-term) capital gains tax rate.

(ticker: GSK), makers of Geritol (gramps came in with that one), and Sirius Satellite Radio (ticker: SIRI, your baby brother's choice). What now?

The next logical step is to decide if any of these companies are worth your hard-earned money. To do so, we go to the Internet Web site: http://finance.yahoo.com/. There are many other similar (or even better) sites available, so you could just as easily go to any of them. I will use the Yahoo! site as an illustration. Best of all, IT IS FREE! A couple of clicks at the Yahoo! site brings up the following Summary screen for GlaxoSmithKline.

What if you know the company you want to check out, but don't know its ticker? Fortunately, that is an easy problem to solve. In the Yahoo! site, for example, all you need to do is go to Symbol Lookup where you type in the company name (or as much of the company name as you can remember) and Yahoo! will find all the companies that match your query and their respective tickers. Simply pick the one that corresponds to the company you are interested in.

Before deciding which of our stocks is worth investing in, let us first understand what some of the key numbers are telling us. Not all the numbers in the table are relevant for the beginning investor and we will not discuss them. For the moment, we will simply focus on the ones we must understand now in order to make a reasonably intelligent initial stock purchasing decision.

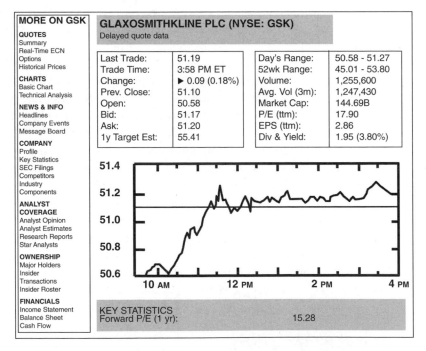

Figure 3: Summary Screen for GSK

Last Trade, in Figure 3, simply means the time and price of the last trade in this stock. Change means the percentage change in the Last Trade price from the previous day's closing price. Prev Close provides the previous day's closing price. Notice that in this case, the Prev Close is 51.10 and the Last Trade is 51.19 so that Change is 0.09. Make sense? Open provides the current day's opening price, which is $50.58. Volume shows the current cumulative trading volume in the stock in number of shares. Day's Range implies the price fluctuation in the stock from the opening to the Last Trade. Bid and Ask are important to get a good handle on. Recall that the Ask is nearly always as great (or greater) than the Bid and denotes the price we have to pay to buy a share of stock at that moment in time. Similarly, the Bid is the price we would receive per share if we sold this company's shares at that point in time. The difference between the Ask and Bid is known as the Bid-Ask spread (3 cents in this example) and is a measure of uncertainty or prevailing risk in that stock at that point in time. The wider the spread, the greater the uncertainty, and the more expensive it is for us to trade in that company's shares. The wider the average spread for a stock, the more we are paying to buy the stock and the less we are getting from selling it (relative to a stock with a narrower spread).

P/E is the price-earnings ratio which for this stock is 17.90, implying that the consensus belief of the market is that the current stock price is almost 18 times its earnings. The higher this number the more optimistic investors are about the potential of the company. Note that this P/E ratio is based on the company's prior 52-week earnings. It is therefore a backward-looking P/E ratio. (By contrast, stock analysts and other market professionals like to use a P/E ratio where the earnings are the forecasted next year's earnings—a forward-looking P/E ratio.) And the P/E ratio using the forward 1-year projected earnings is also provided on the same screen and is 15.28. Market Cap denotes the market value of the company. In the case of GlaxoSmithKline it is at $144.69B. This is a large-size company by any definition. (Recall the definitions of small, medium and large-size companies?)

Finally, Div & Yield denotes the dollar dividend per share paid by the company over the previous 52 weeks and the yield denotes the dollar dividend divided by the current stock price which, in this case, is 3.8 percent. Avg Vol (3m) denotes the average daily trading volume of this stock in number of shares over the prior 3 months while Volume denotes the trading volume of this stock that particular day. 52wk Range implies the low and high prices of the stock over the previous 52 weeks. Finally, 1y Target Est denotes the estimated stock price 1 year from now. This is what the stock price is estimated to be a year from now by the stock analysts. Notice that there are other numbers in the tables that we will ignore for the moment.

The next screen we will examine pertains to company profitability. Ideally, want to see companies making profits and, more importantly, that there is an upward trend in their earnings pattern. One click on the Income Statement button pulls up the following screen for GSK.

MORE ON GSK	GLAXOSMITHKLINE PLC - Income Statement			
QUOTES				
Summary				
Real-Time ECN				
Options	**Period Eding**	**31 Dec 04**	**31 Dec 03**	**31 Dec 02**
Historical Prices	Total Revenue	39,223,649	38,266,206	34,032,533
CHARTS	Cost of Revenue	8,301,719	8,081,504	7,373,822
Basic Chart	Gross Profit	30,921,930	30,184,702	26,658,710
Technical Analysis	Operating Expenses			
NEWS & INFO	Research Development	5,469,617	4,963,794	4,789,134
Headlines	Selling General & Administrative Non	14,605,555	13,404,555	13,521,883
Company Events	Recurring	446,971	(174,293)	(29,879)
Message Board	Others	2,714,579	5,572,041	6,730,458
COMPANY	Total Operating Expenses	23,236,723	23,766,096	25,012,596
Profile	Operating Income or Loss	7,685,207	6,418,607	1,646,114
Key Statistics	Income from Continuing Operations			
SEC Filings	Total Other Income/Expenses Net	379,540	131,609	146,000
Competitors	Earnings before Interest and Taxes	8,064,748	6,560,216	1,792,115
Industry	Interest Expense	587,513	357,479	308,045
Components	Income before Tax	7,477,135	6,192,737	1,484,070
ANALYST	Income Tax Expense	2,022,930	1,700,246	468,485
COVERAGE	Minority Interest	(190,733)	(167,179)	(176,484)
Analyst Opinion	Net Income from Continuing Ops	5,263,471	4,325,471	839,101
Analyst Estimates	Non-recurring Events			
Research Reports	Discontinued Operations	—	—	—
Star Analysts	Extraordinary Items	—	—	—
OWNERSHIP	Effect of Accounting Changes	—	—	(144,396)
Major Holders	Other Items	—	—	—
Insider Transactions	Net Income	5,263,471	4,325,312	694,705
Insider Roster				
FINANCIALS				
Income Statement				
Balance Sheet				
Cash Flow				

Figure 4: Income Statement for GSK

From the above, we see that GSK has made a net profit in each of the 3 previous years and displays a pattern of increasing net income over the 3 years. Both are good signs for the company. Keep in mind that when evaluating technology companies you may not see any profits. In such cases, you will have to put more weight on the other screens.

At this point, it is instructive to see how the analysts come down on the stock. If your stock is a relatively established company, chances are that it is followed by analysts. By contrast, if your stock is relatively new, or a very small company, chances are no analysts are following it. It might be wise to steer clear of such stocks if you are new to the markets. Clicking on "Analyst Opinion" on the side brings up the following screen. Typically, we want the current mean recommendation as close to 1 (Strong Buy) as possible. Also, the change from the previous week should be 0 or negative.

MORE ON GSK	GLAXOSMITHKLINE PLC - Analyst Opinion			
QUOTES Summary Real-Time ECN Options Historical Prices				
	RECOMMENDATION	**SUMMARY***	**PRICE TARGET**	**SUMMARY**
CHARTS Basic Chart Technical Analysis	Mean Recommendation (this week)	2.5	Mean Target	55.41
	Mean Recommendation (last week)	2.5	Median Target	55.32
NEWS & INFO Headlines Company Events Message Board	Change	0.0	High Target	58.00
	Industry Mean		Low Target	53.00
	Sector Mean		No. of Brokers	4
COMPANY Profile Key Statistics SEC Filings Competitors Industry Components	S & P 500 Mean	2.47	Data provided by Thomson/First Call	
	* (Strong Buy) 2.0 - 5.0 (Strong Sell)			

UPGRADES & DOWNGRADES HISTORY

Date	Research Firm	Action	From	To
3 Feb 06	Leerink Swann	Downgrade	Mkt Perform	Underperform
21 Nov 05	CSFB	Downgrade	Outperform	Neutral
3 Nov 05	Bear Stearns	Upgrade	Underperform	Peer Perform
18 Aug 05	JP Morgan	Upgrade	Underweight	Neutral
10 Jun 05	Bear Stearns	Downgrade	Peer Perform	Underperform
4 Mar 05	Prudential	Downgrade	Neutral	Underweight
10 Jan 05	Morgan Stanley	Downgrade	Equal-weight	Underweight
14 Sep 04	Lehman Brothers Smith Barney	Upgrade	Equal-weight	Overweight
24 Jun 04	Citigroup	Downgrade	Buy	Hold
18 Feb 04	CIBC Wrld Mkts	Upgrade	Sector Underperform	Sector Underperform

(Side navigation column also lists: ANALYST COVERAGE — Analyst Opinion, Analyst Estimates, Research Reports, Star Analysts; OWNERSHIP — Major Holders, Insider Transactions, Insider Roster; FINANCIALS — Income Statement, Balance Sheet, Cash Flow)

Figure 5: Analyst Opinion for GSK

We will now move to another screen. Click on "Major Holders" on the side and a screen like the following pops up.

MORE ON GSK	GLAXOSMITHKLINE PLC — Major Holders			
QUOTES Summary Real-Time ECN Options Historical Prices				
	BREAKDOWN			
CHARTS Basic Chart Technical Analysis	% of Shares Held by All Insider and 5% Owners			0%
	% of Shares Held by Institutional & Mutual Fund Owners			10%
NEWS & INFO Headlines Company Events Message Board	% of Float Held by Institutional & Mutual Fund Owners			10%
	Number of Institutions Holding Shares			483

MAJOR DIRECT HOLDERS (FORMS 3 & 4)

Holder	Shares		Reported	

TOP INSTITUTIONAL HOLDERS

Holder	Shares	% Out	Value*	Reported
MORGAN STANLEY	33,228,858	1.12	$1,703,975,838	30 Sep 05
DODGE & COX INC	30,946,025	1.04	$1,586,912,162	30 Sep 05
STATE ST CORP	19,173,998	.65	$983,242,617	30 Sep 05
LORD ABBETT & CO	14,537,592	.49	$745,487,717	30 Sep 05
BRANDES INVEST- MENT PARTNERS L.P.	12,223,498	.41	$626,820,977	30 Sep 05
AMVESCAP PLC	12,080,878	.41	$619,507,423	30 Sep 05
CITIGROUP INC.	11,960,036	.40	$613,310,646	30 Sep 05
WACHOVIA CORP NEW	11,318,738	.38	$580,424,884	30 Sep 05
MELLON FINANCIAL CORP	9,624,736	.32	$493,556,462	30 Sep 05
WELLINGTON MGMT CO, LLP	7,998,981	.27	$410,187,745	30 Sep 05

(Side navigation column also lists: COMPANY — Profile, Key Statistics, SEC Filings, Competitors, Industry, Components; ANALYST COVERAGE — Analyst Opinion, Analyst Estimates, Research Reports, Star Analysts; OWNERSHIP — Major Holders, Insider Transactions, Insider Roster; FINANCIALS — Income Statement, Balance Sheet, Cash Flow)

Figure 6: Major Holders for GSK

Notice above that this page provides a snapshot of the percentage of shares held by large shareholders and the percentage of shares held by institutions and mutual funds. In this case, 10 percent of the shares are held by mutual funds and institutions. The term "float" simply means shares that are available to be traded in secondary markets and is a reflection of the liquidity of the stock.

Next, we click over to the page entitled "Insider Transactions." Here is a reproduction of the page.

MORE ON GSK	GLAXOSMITHKLINE PLC — Insider Transactions					
QUOTES Summary Real-Time ECN Options Historical Prices						
CHARTS Basic Chart Technical Analysis	**NET SHARE PURCHASE ACTIVITY** Insider Purchases—Last 6 Months			**NET INSTITUTIONAL PURCHASES** Prior Qtr to Latest Qtr		
NEWS & INFO Headlines Company Events Message Board		Shares	Trans			Shares
	Purchases	N/A	0	Net Shares Purchased (Sold)		4,528,020
	Sales	N/A	0	% Change in Institutional		1.6%
	Net Shares Purchased (Sold)	N/A	0	Shares Held		
COMPANY Profile Key Statistics SEC Filings Competitors Industry Components	Total Insider Shares Held	226.12K	N/A			
	% Net Shares Purchased (Sold)	0.0%	N/A			
ANALYST	**INSIDER & RULE 144 TRANSACTIONS REPORTED—LAST TWO YEARS**					
COVERAGE Analyst Opinion Analyst Estimates Research Reports Star Analysts	Date	Insider	Shares	Type	Transaction	Value
	19 Dec 05	Ziegler, John	29,417	Direct	Planned Sale	$1,537,038
	6 Dec 05	Yamada, Tadatak	74,866	Direct	Planned Sale	$3,760,733
OWNERSHIP Major Holders Insider Transactions Insider Roster	28 Oct 05	Ziegler, John	21,596	Direct	Planned Sale	$1,133,790
	14 Dec 04	Garnier, Jean Chief Executive Officer	79,054	Direct	Planned Sale	$3,744,037
	24 Nov 04	Phelan, Daniel	22,923	Direct	Planned Sale	$ 977,895
FINANCIALS Income Statement Balance Sheet Cash Flow	17 Sep 04	Stout, David Officer	34,904	Direct	Planned Sale	$1,500,872

Figure 7: Insider Transactions for GSK

This page summarizes company insiders' activities as well as institutional activity in GSK. Insiders and institutions have been shown in many finance research articles to be associated with information about the prospects of the firm. In other words, senior company officials, as well as large institutional investors, know things about the firm before they are public information and their trading patterns can provide valuable insight to us little folks about how the company may do in the near future. For GSK, we see that no company insiders either bought or sold shares in the last six months. And institutions collectively increased their holdings by 1.6 percent. Both are good news.

One final screen I want to point out relates to "Competitors." When evaluating companies for possible investment, it is always instructive to see how the candidate company's numbers measure up to its main competitors and to the industry the candidate belongs to. So, for example, GSK by itself may look just fine but it is possible that it is not doing as well as its competitors in which case one may want to rethink about investing in GSK in favor of, maybe even, the competition. A click on the "Competitors" button for GSK brings up the following screen.

MORE ON GSK	GLAXOSMITHKLINE PLC — Competitors				
QUOTES Summary Real-Time ECN Options Historical Prices **CHARTS** Basic Chart Technical Analysis **NEWS & INFO** Headlines Company Events Message Board **COMPANY** Profile Key Statistics SEC Filings Competitors Industry Components **ANALYST** **COVERAGE** Analyst Opinion Analyst Estimates Research Reports Star Analysts **OWNERSHIP** Major Holders Insider Transactions Insider Roster **FINANCIALS** Income Statement Balance Sheet Cash Flow					

DIRECT COMPETITOR COMPARISON

	GSK	NVS	PFE	SGP	Industry
Market Cap	144.55B	128.27B	196.08B	28.01B	12.55B
Employees	N/A	90.924	N/A	N/A	27
Qtrly Rev Growth (yoy)	10.80%	14.10%	-8.90%	6.40%	13.50%
Revenue (ttm)	37.79B	32.53B	51.30B	9.51B	9.51B
Gross Margin (ttm)	78.01%	72.74%	83.77%	64.81%	72.38%
EBITDA (ttm)	13.50B	8.50B	20.86B	1.26B	148.08M
Oper Margins (ttm)	30.40%	21.54%	29.90%	-0.81%	18.04%
Net Income (ttm)	8.18B	5.19B	8.09B	183.00M	86.41M
EPS (ttm)	2.86	2.22	1.091	0.123	0.33
P/E (ttm)	17.90	24.73	24.38	154.07	20.39
PEG (5 yr expected)	2.65	1.67	2.43	1.66	1.76
P/S (ttm)	3.81	3.90	3.79	2.92	4.04

NVS = Novartis AG
PFE = Pfizer Inc.
SGP = Schering-Plough Corp.
Industry = Drug Manufacturers - Major

BIOTECHNOLOGY COMPANIES RANKED BY SALES

Company	Symbol	Price	Change	Market Cap	P/E
Amgen Inc	AMGN	75.48	0.98%	93.17B	25.81
Genentech Inc.	DNA	86.09	1.34%	90.73B	72.77
Biogen Idec Inc.	BIIB	50.10	1.05%	17.00B	107.97
Genzyme Corp.	GENZ	70.00	0.01%	18.08B	42.45
Serono SA	SRA	17.74	-2.26%	18.80B	N/A
Applera Corporation	Private—View Profile				
Chiron Corp.	CHIR	45.70	0.62%	8.62B	47.06
Gilead Sciences Inc.	GILD	63.67	3.26%	29.16B	37.10
Medimmune Inc.	MEDI	37.38	1.55%	9.20B	N/A
Invitrogen Corp.	IVGN	70.31	0.82%	3.72B	34.60

Figure 7: Insider Transactions for GSK

This screen provides a fascinating picture of GSK vis-à-vis its competitors and the industry group (drug manufacturers) as a whole. First, notice that GSK (a large-cap firm by any measure) has a quarterly revenue growth that is lagging the industry group, and at least one of its competitors, NVS. Second, its earnings before interest and taxes (EBITA) over the past 12 months, while exceeding that of NVS, lags behind another competitor, PFE. The operating margin of GSK is also greater than that of its competitors.

A firm's PEG Ratio is its P/E ratio divided by its annual earnings growth rate. PEG was popularized by the famed mutual fund manager, Peter Lynch, who took the Fidelity Magellan Fund from obscurity to superstardom and, in the process, became somewhat of a legend himself in professional investing circles. These days, he is featured in Fidelity's commercials where he appears looking sage in his snow-white hair. The intuition behind PEG is that a company that is valued fairly (and that is the million dollar issue) will have its earnings growth rate equal its P/E ratio. Hence, when the P/E ratio is significantly greater than its earnings growth (i.e., PEG significantly greater than 1), the company could be overvalued. Similarly, when

PEG Ratio

A firm's P/E ratio divided by its earnings growth rate. Rule of thumb: PEG greater than 1 implies an overvalued company, while PEG less than 1 implies an undervalued company.

the P/E ratio is significantly less than its growth rate of earnings (i.e., PEG significantly less than 1), the company is undervalued and a buying opportunity. By that yardstick, GSK, with its PEG at 2.65, is overvalued relative to the industry as a whole (1.76); overvalued relative to PFE and certainly overvalued relative to NVS.

Returning to the two remaining stocks in our list, without going into the details, I will simply provide the "Competitors" screen for HDI and SIRI as a way to summarize most of the pertinent information about these two stocks.

MORE ON GSK

QUOTES
Summary
Real-Time ECN
Options
Historical Prices

CHARTS
Basic Chart
Technical Analysis

NEWS & INFO
Headlines
Company Events
Message Board

COMPANY
Profile
Key Statistics
SEC Filings
Competitors

Harley Davidson Inc. (HDI)—Competitors

DIRECT COMPETITOR COMPARISON

	HDI	Pvt1	PII	Pvt2	Industry
Market Cap	14.51B	N/A	2.09B	N/A	12.55B
Employees	N/A	105,9721	3,600	5101	27
Qtrly Rev Growth (yoy)	10.20%	N/A	6.80%	N/A	13.50%
Revenue (ttm)	5.67B	60.47B1	1.92B	9.51B	9.51B
Gross Margin (ttm)	39.34%	N/A	24.75%	N/A	72.38%
EBITDA (ttm)	1.68B	N/A	290.78B	N/A	148.08M
Oper Margins (ttm)	25.91%	N/A	11.81%	N/A	18.05%
Net Income (ttm)	959.60B	3.03B1	148.05M	-600.00K1	2.65B
EPS (ttm)	3.415	N/A	3.301	N/A	0.33
P/E (ttm)	15.48	N/A	15.20	N/A	20.39
PEG (5 yr expected)	1.23	N/A	1.09	N/A	1.76
P/S (ttm)	2.58	N/A	1.10	N/A	4.04

Pvt1 = Baverische Motoren Werke AG   PII = Polaris Industries
Pvt2 = Triumph Motorcycles Limited (privately held)   Industry = Recreational Vehicles
1 = As of 2004

Figure 9: Competitors for HDI

MORE ON GSK

QUOTES
Summary
Real-Time ECN
Options
Historical Prices

CHARTS
Basic Chart
Technical Analysis

NEWS & INFO
Headlines
Company Events
Message Board

COMPANY
Profile
Key Statistics
SEC Filings
Competitors

SIRIUS SATELLITE RADIO INC. (SIRI)—Competitors

DIRECT COMPETITOR COMPARISON

	SIRI	CCU	CMLS	XMSR	Industry
Market Cap	6.86B	15.21B	742.37B	4.92B	610.62M
Employees	N/A	N/A	2,900	N/A	27
Qtrly Rev Growth (yoy)	217.30%	-24.10%	1.60%	113.10%	5.60%
Revenue (ttm)	242.24B	6.61B	329.28B	558.27B	329.28B
Gross Margin (ttm)	23.65%	62.68%	32.08%	27.40%	37.60%
EBITDA (ttm)	-574.45B	2.15B	88.51B	-375.83M 8	8.51M
Oper Margins (ttm)	-342.27%	21.52%	19.38%	-92.84%	25.37%
Net Income (ttm)	-863.00M	635.15M	14.83M	-675.31M	11.63M
EPS (ttm)	-0.651	1.710	0.212	-3.075	0.44
P/E (ttm)	N/A	16.46	54.67	N/A	21.73
PEG (5 yr expected)	N/A	1.79	3.31	N/A	3.31
P/S (ttm)	28.75	2.31	2.29	8.63	2.40

CCU = Clear Channel Communications Inc.   CMLS = Cumulus Media Inc.
XMSR = XM Sattelite Radio Holdings Inc.   Industry = Broadcasting - Radio

Figure 10: Competitors for SIRI

I also have a return (i.e., price change) graph of the three stocks: SIRI, GSK and HDI, along with the S&P 500 Market Index graph (GSPC) which shows how they have performed over the past 2 years. From the graph it appears as though HDI has an inverse relationship with the economy. When the economy does poorly, HDI does well and vice versa. Could it be that Harleys sell well when the economy is in the tank as people ride bikes more in order to conserve on gasoline expenses and to generally feel better about themselves? Something to think about!

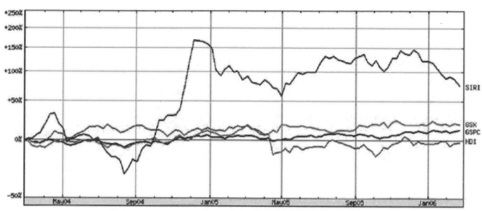

Figure 11: Return information for GSK, HDI, SIRI and S&P 500 Index

Google Finance Web Site—An Example of Technology Convergence

A recent alternative to the Yahoo finance website is the Google finance site (http://www.google.com/finance). It is organized differently and some readers may find it to be more to their liking. It also provides video clips on important financial events of the day and you can chart pre-opening and after-close happenings in what is known as after-hours trading. This is interesting because a lot of market-moving events happen after markets close at 4 PM EST or before its open at 9:30 AM EST. Many companies delay announcing major corporate events until after markets close. These announcements impact after-hours trading and can be seen clearly when plotting pre-market, and after-hours, trading on the Google Web site. This will give an investor time to think about her strategy when markets formally open.

The "top movers" stock list is a nice addition. There is a market summary module as well as a sector summary module. The latter is particularly useful if you want a bird's-eye view of a given section to decide whether or not to get into that sector's ETF.

For individual stocks, the site allows you to easily graph up to 40 years of historical daily data in order to form an opinion about the long-term trends of a stock.

This is particularly useful for stocks like IBM or GE that have been the mainstays of the U.S. economy for decades. For the relatively newer companies like Microsoft, Intel, or Amazon, this feature is less relevant. Another interesting feature on the site is the ease with which you can now see stock splits or dividends when you are looking at a stock chart.

Overall, the charting and viewing capabilities of the Google Finance page might be better than those of the Yahoo! Finance page. What I like in particular about individual stock graphing is the ability to see the impact of company-specific news on the stock price right on the graph itself. So, for example, I chart GSK on the Google page for a side-by-side horse race with the Yahoo! Finance Web site. **Figure 12** provides the opening shots of the stock much like Figure 3 under the Yahoo! Finance site.

Figure 12: GSK in Google Finance

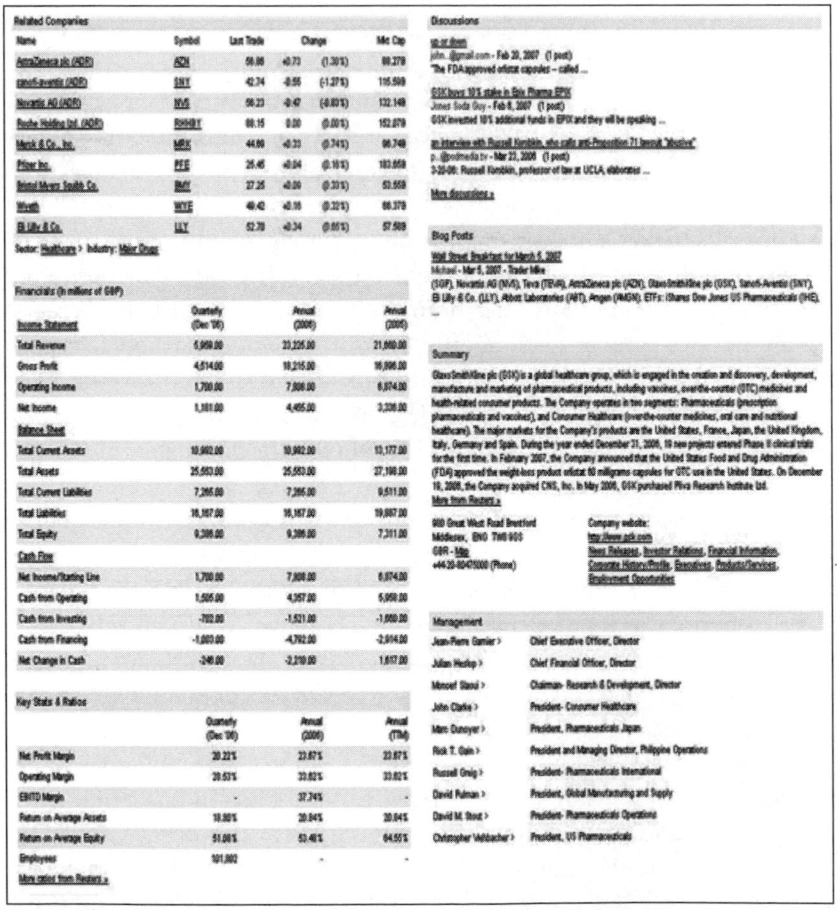

Figure 13: Remainder of GSK page on the Google Finance page

Notice, however, the subtle difference in Figure 12. The impact of GSK-specific news is mapped directly on the graph so you can clearly see its impact on the stock price. Specifically, within the time period window over which I have chosen for the stock price to be displayed notice the impact of news A and B on GSK price. Other windows will reveal the impact of news C, D, etc. on GSK price over that time period. This is a very useful feature. In **Figure 13,** I reproduce the rest of the GSK page.

The Google Finance page doesn't have any more or less information than the Yahoo! pages for the same stock. Although some of the innovations in Google such as blog posts and discussions are not in Yahoo! yet, I suspect they are just around the corner since these websites tend to copy one another. It's like the Windows operating system. With each successive update, Microsoft has included features that were staples of the Mac operating system and now there is little difference in the front end of the latest version of Windows and Mac OS X. It's what I call the convergence of technology.

Basic Rules of Trading and Investing

Earlier we covered some important metrics of stocks using information that is freely available on the Internet. Let us apply these measures to the three stocks, GSK, HDI,

Anecdote: Foreigner in Water-Cooler Land

When I came to the United States as a graduate student many years ago I was confused by many things. But, mainly, I was confused with — yes, drinking fountains! I had never encountered them in my country and was clueless about how to drink out of them. And I was too proud to ask someone to show me how to operate them. I was afraid people would think I was stupid or something and laugh at me.

One day I decided to crack the mystery even if it killed me. Okay, maybe nothing so dramatic. Accordingly, that afternoon, I parked myself in the vicinity of the fountain near my department and, while humming a carefree tune, kept one eye peeled on the contraption.

A few minutes passed and I was running out of humming material. A girl came by and stood in front of the fountain. The moment was here! I was quivering in anticipation.

Then something happened. What? Darn! I had missed the moment! Water came spurting out. She drank and walked away.

I was devastated. What could she have done to make the water emerge?

After she left, I strolled casually by the fountain and, without breaking stride, tried to see if there was a lever of some sort around the faucet that would make the water flow out. None was visible. Hell!

So I went back to my perch and continued the vigil. A second student came by after a few minutes and I edged closer. As God was my witness, I was going to crack it this time. But once again, the guy just stood there and water appeared to magically squirt out. What on earth were these people doing?

Well, to make a long story short, I wasted the better part of an afternoon trying to figure out how to work the water fountain, simply because of my stupid pride. Can you guess what made the water discharge?

It was a semi-disguised foot pedal, which is why I could not see anything obvious sticking out during my hurriedly casual inspections.

In sum, do not be afraid to ask others for help getting started on something. Don't let pride get in your way. You will save a lot of time by doing things that are useful rather than standing around waiting for water to stream out of the fountain.

and SIRI. One belongs to the Drug Manufacturers Sector (GSK), another to the Recreational Vehicles Sector (HDI), while the third belongs to the Broadcasting Sector (SIRI). Together, they represent very different segments of the market. Understand, however, that you could do everything I suggest here and still come out losing money. I can promise you this, however. If you follow the few basic rules that I outline below, you should be able to eliminate a big chunk of the blunders made by novice investors. That is not to say that you will never lose any money by investing.

My suggestions encompass "investing" metrics and "trading" metrics. Recall that pure investors are those who intend to be in the markets once in a while and buy primarily to hold. Pure traders, on the other hand, plan to be in the market buying and selling on a regular basis—sometimes many times within a single trading day. Some of these traders are known as "day traders." Most of us will probably fall in between these two extremes and possess characteristics of both investor and trader. As pure investors, we will look for only those measures that capture the long-term viability of a stock while as pure traders we will set aside all long-term measures and instead focus on only the short-term aspects of a stock. Let's first examine some of the important trading measures of a stock.

The first trading rule for a trading newbie is not to touch anything that is trading around or above its 52 week high. Chances are these stocks are overpriced and will fall in value in the coming days. Instead, try to locate stocks that are trading around their 52 week lows.

My second trading rule is to choose stocks that have at least one million shares in daily trading volume. Stocks with relatively high trading volume are easier and cheaper to buy and sell and are less prone to uncertainty (read price swings) than stocks that have very thin trading volume. Avoid stocks with daily trading volume of less than 100,000 shares unless you are a seasoned investor.

My third trading rule for the novice investor is to initially avoid small- and mid-cap stocks, i.e., stocks with market values less than $5 billion. These are relatively risky (read higher volatility) and you should only focus on these when you have more confidence in the market and have been trading for a while. To start with, focus on large-cap stocks only (read lower volatility). These are the most established companies in their respective market sectors and have the most written about them. Relatively they are the safest stocks to put your money in.

My fourth trading rule relates to the opinion of the analysts. Remember, the closer the consensus value is to 1 the better it is for the stock's future prospects. Closer to 5

Day Traders

Day traders buy and sell stocks quickly throughout the day—sometimes holding a position for a few seconds and making a couple of cents in profits per stock. But in doing it often over the course of a single day, they hope it will all add up to a meaningful profit in the aggregate. Most of the time they have no information about the companies they are buying and selling. They are just tickers on the screen.

Officially, under the rules of the NYSE and NASDAQ, trades deemed "pattern day traders" must have at least $25,000 in their trading accounts and can only trade in margin accounts.

spells trouble and closer to 3 is about neutral. More importantly, you want to see a negative change in the consensus value from last week to the current week, indicating a move towards 1. Pick stocks with overall analyst recommendations between 1 and less than 3, preferably closest to 1, and one where the change from the previous week is nonpositive (i.e., either negative or 0). So much for traders who intend to trade relatively frequently.

> ## Recall
>
> Analysts do not like saying "Sell" unless they absolutely have to. A "Hold" is as good as a "Sell" pronouncement. They are just being polite about it by say-ing "Hold". If you see a "Hold," It may not exactly be time to jump ship although it's certainly not the right time to buy it.

For investors—those intending to be in the market once in a long while—the above measures are less important than measures that reflect on the long-term prosperity of the underlying company.

Accordingly, my first investing rule is to check the stock's P/E ratio based on the trailing 12 months (ttm) as well as its forward P/E ratio (based on next year's expected earnings). First check to see where the ttm P/E ratio ranks relative to its competitors and the industry as a whole. Ideally, you want it to be lower than both its competitors and the industry as a whole. Also, you want the forward P/E ratio to be significantly less than the trailing P/E. If the projected P/E is greater than (or about the same as) the trailing P/E, the projected earnings are less than (or about the same as) the trailing earnings and that is not a good sign. Some analysts also swear by the "Rule of 20" which means that for stocks in the Tech or Tech-Related Sectors, a forward P/E greater than 20 implies overvalued while less than 20 implies undervalued stock.

My second investing rule is to examine the firm's trailing net income pattern to see if a) there are profits, and b) the profits exhibit an increasing pattern over this period. Yahoo! allows you to see the three previous years' income (or loss) or just the three prior quarters. There should be signs that the company's income has an increasing pattern or that the losses exhibit a declining pattern. The latter is especially valid for new companies without established earnings patterns. Google's (ticker: GOOG) net income over 2002–2005 was almost non-existent; $381,000 over the third quarter of 2005—a mere pittance for a $115B market value company.

My third investing rule concerns what company insiders are up to. Research suggests that when company insiders are lining up to sell their own company shares, even if it's under the guise of needing money for unrelated expenses (they have to declare a reason for wanting to sell shares) such as an upcoming wedding, it's not good news for the company. After all, selling is selling no matter how it is dressed up. My mother (who has no idea of finance and could not recognize a stock if her life depended on it) is fond of saying: "Let's call a spade a spade!" On the other hand, if company insiders are generally buying, it is good news. So, click on Insider Transactions. Ideally, we want insiders to buy or at least, to not line up in droves to sell company shares. Unchanged insider activity, i.e., no buys or sells, is also good news. Also, check out what the institutions are doing. There is a lot of research suggesting that institutions are smart investors and usually know what is going on with the companies they invest in. If they are net buyers that might imply good things on the horizon, while the opposite might be the case if they are net sellers. Preferably, you want the institutions to be net buyers in a stock you are thinking of purchasing.

Remember, the weight you give to each of these rules depends on whether you aim to be an investor or a trader. If you want to have elements of each in your trading/investing then give them equal weights. Let's now use these simple rules to see if we can distinguish between the three stocks we started off the chapter with: GSK, HDI, and SIRI. GSK's current price at $51.65 is fairly close to its 52 week high of $53.80 which should give us pause if we are not intending to invest in GSK over the long haul. In comparison, HDI (current price: $51.54 versus 52 week high: $62.47) seems to have some wiggle room at the top. SIRI (current price: $5.08 versus 52 week high: $7.98) also has some room to grow at the high end in the short run. In sum, Trading Rule 1 favors both HDI and SIRI and probably sidelines GSK for the moment.

With Trading Rule 2, SIRI passes easily, while GSK (avg. daily vol: 1.245 million shares) just makes the cut and HDI (avg. daily vol: 2 million shares) clears it with a bit more room. Under Trading Rule 3, both GSK and HDI are clearly large-cap stocks and therefore easily clear the firm size bar. SIRI is a little questionable, being closest in market cap to the $5 billion cut-off, of the three companies on our list and is a judgment call. We will accept this one in the mix, given the newness of the technology it markets, although such decisions will have to be made on a case-by-case basis.

With Trading Rule 4, HDI's mean recommendation is about a neutral 2.9 and unchanged from the previous week. Its current price is also close to its mean price target. GSK's mean recommendation is a little better at 2.5 and also unchanged from the previous week. SIRI's mean recommendation is a 2.1 and is clearly the best of the three. Its current price is also significantly lower than its mean price target of $7.55.

In sum, based on the four trading rules (keeping in mind that stock selection is not an exact science), SIRI is first, HDI second and GSK is a clear third. Let us now turn to examining the long-term prospects of these three stocks based on the three investment rules.

According to Investing Rule 1, GSK has the clear low trailing P/E ratio (17.90) relative to its competitors and the industry as a whole, while its forward P/E ratio (15.28) is significantly lower. HDI's trailing P/E ratio (14.95) is also significantly higher than its forward P/E (12.52), while being a little lower than its competitor (Polaris) and quite a bit lower than its industry group. Finally, SIRI's trailing and forward P/E numbers are not available because the company has had no earnings and is not expected to have any over the coming year. The same is true for its nearest Satellite competitor, XM Satellite Radio (ticker: XMSR).

According to Investing Rule 2, GSK demonstrates a pattern of increasing net income over the three previous years, while HDI shows a similar pattern of increasing net income although its growth rate of net income over the three most recent years is significantly smaller than that of GSK. By contrast, SIRI has had losses over the last three years—not surprising given the nature of the emergent technology. A closer look at the three most recent quarters of SIRI, however, shows a pattern of decreasing (or unchanged) losses which might be encouraging. In sum, Rule 2 clearly favors GSK, followed by HDI with SIRI a distant third.

Finally, according to Investing Rule 3, GSK insiders neither bought nor sold company shares over the previous six months (a good sign) while institutions were net purchasers over the same period (another good sign). By comparison, HDI insiders were net sellers to the tune of 19 percent (bad sign) while institutions were net purchasers of HDI (a good sign). Finally, SIRI insiders were net sellers while institutions were net buyers by a large amount (a very good sign). In sum, Rule 3 favors GSK while HDI and SIRI emit mixed signals.

Overall, the conservative long-term pick would be GSK. HDI is a weak possibility. However, if you have a bit of a gambling streak, and you believe that Satellite Radio technology is an emergent area that will take over the market in the next few years, then SIRI could be a long-shot pick. What makes SIRI slightly more attractive, in my opinion, relative to its rival, XMSR, is the simple fact that SIRI is seriously cheaper than XMSR: As I write this, SIRI is currently trading around $3 a share compared to about $11 a share for XMSR.

Shopping for Stocks

When you want to buy groceries, you walk into your friendly neighborhood grocery store, take stuff from the shelves and throw it in your shopping cart with careless abandon. You do not bother to check the price and just pick whatever comes first or whatever catches your eye. You run to the checkout lane that says "20 items or less," even though you have at least 30 items. You just hope the checkout person cannot count very well. You zap your credit card and get out of the store as soon as possible. No, that is just me!

How do we buy stocks? Is it the same as buying milk and cereal? In a previous chapter, we discussed how stocks sell in their own special supermarkets known as the NYSE, AMEX or the NASDAQ. Are the rules the same? Can we just go in one of these places and fill our stock needs? Turns out, we cannot! Unlike our neighborhood supermarket or department store, where we walk in and pay for purchases ourselves at the counter (unless you are trying to sneak it out under your jacket), we are not really allowed inside a stock supermarket.

Only special people, let's call them our personal shoppers, who have lots of money and have paid lots of money for the privilege of entering the supermarket, are allowed inside. So we give our personal shoppers the list of stuff we want to buy and then press our noses against the glass windows while they march right in with our lists and buy the stocks for us. Then they come out and hand us our stocks and we pay the shoppers a commission. These personal shoppers, to whom we pay a commission to do our stock shopping for us, are known as brokers.

Just who are these brokers? They have all kinds of fancy names like Merrill Lynch, Prudential, Charles Schwab, E-trade, Dean Witter, Fidelity, and so on. They all have commercials that depict them as conscientious with your money and sitting around trying to find the best possible way to help you "one investor at a time." A complete list of brokers (or, your personal stock shoppers) can be found at http://www. dmoz.org/Business/Investing/ Brokerages/. Now that we have our personal shoppers ready to buy stocks for us on commission, the question is: what kind of instructions do we give our shopper? Unlike the grocery store, where the prices of individual items are clearly marked on the shelves, the stock supermarket does not have fixed prices. In fact, the stock prices keep changing every second that the stock supermarket is open. Houston, we have a problem!

How do we convey to our personal shopper what we are willing to pay for our purchases? We need to give him clear instructions on what to do once he is inside the stock supermarket. Otherwise, a lot of time and money will be spent in futility. For example, are we in such a hurry that we don't want him (or her) to waste a whole lot of time shopping inside for a better price; or, do we have some time to kill and don't want the shopper to rush his purchases? Should we allow him to take his time to see if he can find a good deal for us (and, if so, what price do we consider a good deal)? Or, should we just allow him to buy for us immediately at our chosen price? And if he is unable to execute the order immediately, should he simply tear up our list and walk out of the supermarket? These are some of the points we need to instruct our shoppers on in order for them to do their job efficiently.

As luck would have it, this information has been standardized into order types that take away any possible ambiguities in our instructions to our shoppers. Two of the simplest instructions are "market" and "limit" orders.

A market order is where you tell your shopper that it is okay to buy the stock at the best possible price that he can get for you. This is the most general instruction for buying (or selling) stocks that you can give your shopper. For example, if you want him to buy 100 shares of MSFT, you simply put in a market buy for 100 shares of MSFT as your instruction to your broker. The implicit understanding is that your broker will get your shares at the best price available at the time he runs your order through. While you know your order will execute, and you can guess the price your order will be executed at by studying market activity around the time of your order, you can never be certain of the "fill price" until you receive a confirmation from your broker notifying you of the exact price at which your order executed. An economist's way of expressing a market order is "execution certain, price uncertain."

Then there is the slightly more sophisticated limit order. A limit order is an instruction to your shopper to buy a specified quantity of a security at (or below) a price that you specify to him (or, at or above your specified price if you were selling). Unlike the market order, a limit order tells your shopper how much of a stock you would like to buy at what price. For example, you place a limit buy order to sell 100 shares of MSFT at a limit price of $27.00 per share. What you are telling your broker is that he has the freedom to sell on your behalf 100 shares of MSFT at $27 or higher. Under no circumstances will you take less than $27 for your shares.

What happens if your shopper cannot find the price you want? Very simple! Your order does not get bought (or sold if you execute). And therein lies the crucial difference between market and limit orders. Limit orders are "price certain, execution uncertain." If they execute, you get the price you want (or better). But there is no guarantee of execution.

If your limit order cannot be executed at the price you want, the question is how long will your shopper try to get it executed? That will depend on your limit order instructions. You could, for example, make it a "Day" limit order in which case your broker will only try to execute your order as long as markets are open that day (until 4:00 PM EST). And, if your order is unexecuted at the end of the trading day, it is automatically deleted from the records. The next day you have to start all over if you still want to buy or sell that stock. Or, you could make it a "Good Till Canceled" (GTC) limit order in which case your broker will keep trying to execute your order the same day and the next day and the next day . . . until you actually cancel the instruction. That is a lot of hard work for your shopper. Not surprisingly, placing a limit order with your shopper will cost you more than if you were to place a market order. Can you really blame your shopper? The poor guy has to work much harder to do your stock shopping with a limit order and demands to be compensated more for it.

Our instructions to the brokers do not end here. There is more! Another relatively common instruction involves what is called a "Stop Loss" order. Let us say that you bought Chuck E. Cheese (your favorite pizza place) stock for $25 a share. After a few months, Chuck E. Cheese is trading at $35 a share and you are afraid one bad day in the market might wipe out all your paper gains. What do you do? You can place a stop loss order at $32 (say). Where you pick the stop loss price is entirely up to you but it does matter as we will soon see. Your broker understands your order as follows: If Chuck E. Cheese were to slide down and hit $32, your stop loss order would activate immediately and become a market order. Your broker would then treat this as such and sell you out ASAP in the vicinity of $32 thereby allowing you to protect most of your gains.

The big question is where do you put the stop loss price? Here is the tradeoff you face. If you set it too close to the current price, there is a possibility that the stock might dip momentarily to that price, thereby activating your order, and then go back up again. In that case, you will look (and feel) stupid since you cannot participate in the stock's upward move anymore because you sold your stock and are out of the market. On the other hand, if you place the stop price too low, you do not protect your potential gains very well. Overall, where you put your stop price is a function of how risk tolerant you are and what you expect to happen to the stock in the short run. As Charlie Weis, coach of the Notre Dame football team said, "play-calling in football is more an art than a science." And in a previous chapter, I made the statement that ascribing the "right" price to a stock is more of an art than science. The same claim can be made for choosing the stop price.

While we are on the topic of choosing stop loss prices, a related question is, when should you put in a stop loss order versus a limit sell order? Consider the fact that when you place a limit sell order, you are unable to participate in further gains of the stock above the limit price because you are sold out. In a stop loss order, on the other hand, you do not lose any money below the stop loss price because you are sold out. Based on this, you can characterize a limit sell order as an offensive strategy and a stop loss order as a defensive strategy. In addition, to push the football analogy a bit further, whether or not a football coach will elect to go for a one-point or a two-point play after a touchdown is, among other things, a function of whether or not he is defensive- or offensive-minded. For instance, Mike Martz, one-time coach of the St. Louis Rams might go for a two-point conversion (read offensive-minded, risk-taking) after a touchdown while someone like the Indianapolis Colts' Tony Dungy might go for one (read defensive-minded, plays it safe). So too is your choice a function of how you approach your investing. If you are offensive-minded by nature, you may be more inclined to favor limit sell orders. If, on the other hand, you are defensive-minded, you will be more likely to protect your gains through placing of stop loss orders below the current price of the stock. Other less common trading instructions are, fill-or-kill,[38] Market-on-Close,[39] At-the-Open,[40] and a Contingent order.[41] These are orders used by experienced professional investors that you do not need to mess with as you get started on your journey. But, someday soon, these advanced orders might well become a part of your repertoire.

Buying on Margin and Short Selling

So far, we have looked at how to provide standardized instructions to our broker on how to buy or sell our stocks for us. Here we will study other ways to buy or sell stocks. These are aggressive strategies and should be left alone when you are a novice. But after you have quelled your fear of the markets and are starting to feel confident, here are some advanced stock transaction tips.

When you want to buy a new car, but do not have the money to pay for the whole purchase price yourself, what do you do? You walk into your friendly neighborhood bank and ask for a loan, of course. The loan officer makes some inquiries and, if you have been good (no black marks against you by other merchants), she approves the loan and you get the rest of the money you need for your car. You can purchase stocks the same way—well, almost!

The idea behind buying on margin is the same as above. You want to buy shares but don't have the entire purchase price in your trading account. So you ask your broker for a loan. The broker says, "Okay, I will give you 50 percent of the purchase price while you need to put forward the other 50 percent." If you agree, then the broker advances you the 50 percent and you are able to make your purchase. How is this beneficial for you? Here's a concrete example.

Let's say you want to buy 100 shares of MSFT XYZ at $25 a share (total purchase price is $2,500). When you buy on margin, you pay $1,250 and your broker lends you the other $1,250. You are lucky and MSFT rises 50 percent to $37.50 a share, making your total investment $3,750, and you decide to sell. With the proceeds, you first pay your broker the $1,250 (plus interest and commissions) you owe, and you keep the remaining $2,500 (minus interest and commissions) for yourself. Given that your initial investment was $1,250, you make about 100 percent on your investment (before interest and commissions). This is the good scenario.

What if you were wrong and MSFT falls 50 percent to $12.50 soon after your purchase? This is where the big risk of buying on margin rears its ugly head in the form of a "margin call" from your broker. Typically, if the value of your investment falls below 50 percent of its original value, your broker will issue a margin call, which means you have to put more money into your margin account. What if you don't have the money to put in your account? Very simple! Your broker will immediately liquidate your stocks and pay himself back his principle, interest and fines, and commissions, and whatever else he can charge you with. He will also come after you for anything he cannot recover from the stock sale.

Buying on margin is also called leveraged buying. The term leveraging implies that you can buy more than you could afford with the money you are actually investing (in the above example, $1,250). Leveraging can magnify your profits as well as your losses. To see this, consider the above example. When MSFT goes up 50 percent in value, the return on your investment is 100 percent. However, consider the downside too. When MSFT falls 50 percent in value, your losses are 100 percent. That, my friends, is leveraging!

In the area of leveraged investing, let us consider a risky investment tactic: short selling. Very simply, short selling involves selling shares of stock that you do not own personally but borrowed from someone who does own them (like your broker). Ideally, what you want to do is to be able to buy back these shares in the near future at a cheaper price ("cover your shorts") and give the shares back to your lender (along with fees and commissions, of course). While with margin buying your broker lent you money, with short selling, your broker lends you shares of stock instead.

> # History of Margin Trading
>
> When the stock market dropped about 12 percent on October 29, 1929, one of the factors blamed for the market plunge was the fact that, according to the prevalent rules of the day, investors could borrow up to 90 percent of the purchase price. Therefore, the market was highly overleveraged. In the wake of the crash, many of the market rules were changed. The margin requirements were dropped from 90 percent to 50 percent which is where it stands today.

This is another example of leveraged investing—something that magnifies your profits and your losses. People short sell in order to make money in falling markets. There is something macabre about it that offends many people. It is like making money out of someone's misery.

Keep in mind that the money from a short sale is not available to you for spending. The broker would be stupid to allow you to do that. Instead, the proceeds are held in escrow as collateral for the lender of the shares (i.e., the broker). You are not earning any interest on this money and you have to pay any dividends that may be paid on those shares while they are in your control. There are also tax considerations to factor in.

Short selling has a polemic history in America. In the 1860s Jay Gould, arguably the most unethical of the robber barons of the nineteenth century, became known for his questionable acquisition of Erie Railroad from the clutches of Cornelius Vanderbilt through shady investment practices that also involved copious amounts of short selling. In modern times, institutional short selling was among the culprits blamed for the stock market crash of 1987. In its wake, new rules were passed limiting the scope of short selling. For example, short selling is not permitted in falling markets. You can only short sell a stock while it is rising in value (on the "up tick") or is stable (at "zero tick").

Here is the research evidence. A recent paper[42] investigating the information content of short sell orders reports several interesting (at least, they were interesting to me) findings. It appears that almost 13 percent of all NYSE trading volume involves a short seller. They also found something else interesting. Large short sell orders are informative (especially the institutional short sells) and that stocks with heavy shorting underperform stocks that are lightly shorted by over 1 percent. The conclusion is that institutions who are short selling seem to know what they are doing. We, the small investors, would do well to keep track of institutional short selling. That is, however, not an easy task.

When to Buy

With so many people with itchy trading fingers, the stock market horizon has changed drastically. Market watchers often report serious upward and downward swings in stock prices as millions of traders sit in front of their terminals, in dark bedrooms and basements, jumping in and out of stocks as a result of gossip and rumors originating in chat rooms (i.e., the bling-bling traders). These are mostly young people for whom computers are extensions of their arms. The older population, by contrast, largely fears the computer and has as little as possible to do with them.

Even casual followers of the stock market have noticed how volatile (or jumpy) the market has become since the late 1990s as more and more bling-bling traders jump in and out of the stock markets at a moment's notice. In fact, these days, it is not uncommon to see the major market indexes (for the current discussion, indexes

---

Five-Minute Break Risk Arbitrage and Gekko-isms

There is a great scene in the movie *Wall Street* where Gordon Gekko, played by Michael Douglas, gets up in a shareholder's meeting of Teldar Papers to give a speech. For the uninitiated, Gordon Gekko is a Wall Street mogul who has traded his way to wealth by indulging in risk arbitrage and his character is based on Ivan Boesky, the notorious risk arbitrage (also known as "risk-arb") trader of the 1980s.

Risk arbitrage attempts to profit from selling short the stock of an acquiring company and buying the stock of the acquired. This is coined "arbitrage" due to the fact that companies will often finance takeovers through the issuance of more stock, thus diluting the value of the existing float (i.e., shares that are freely available for buying and selling), and offer a premium over the current share price of the firm they are acquiring, based upon expected future revenues and profits. In addition, shareholders of the takeover target face little risk, as they typically receive a premium for the shares they hold, while the acquiring company faces the operational and business risk from having to integrate the acquired's business into its own fold.

Back to Gekko. He is an unapologetic champion of wealth, greed and capitalism. "Greed is good, greed works, greed clarifies and cuts to the essence. . . .," he states in his speech. If you haven't seen this scene, rent the video and watch it. It captures corporate greed in a real way. Another famous Gekko-ism: "If you need a friend, get a dog."

measure the overall market pulse) jump by as much as 3 percent in a single day, something unheard of ten years ago. A study by the New York Stock Exchange shows that the last few years stand out as being the most volatile since the 1970s. Then, the instability was from shocks related to world events, oil price shortages, etc. These days it appears to be a direct result of bling-bling trading. Obviously such volatility is not good, because excess jumpiness in markets means that the average investor usually loses money. The loss usually comes from buying too high and selling too low.

Volatility is a way to measure the rate and magnitude of changes in the price of anything—in our case, stocks. High volatility means greater uncertainty because you don't know what the stock is going to do minute-by-minute. Investors don't like uncertainty. Risk-averse investors hate uncertainty. They like to make money but hate having to take risks in order to do so. Sure sounds like my father! He too hated taking risks (especially after that Ponzi scheme we discussed earlier).

The hallmark of a stable stock exchange is one where volatility is held at a minimum. This gives investors the confidence to invest their money in stocks listed on that exchange. One of the reasons the United States stock markets are so attractive to investors the world over is precisely because our markets are relatively less volatile than stock markets elsewhere. The catchword is "relatively." U.S. markets have gotten significantly more volatile than they were even ten years ago. And it will only get worse!

Now more than ever (isn't that a song?) we need to understand when to get out of markets.

When to Sell

Deciding when to sell is one of the most difficult questions in investments. And believe me, nobody has the definitive answer. Even Wall Street is strangely quiet on this topic. One of the major reasons knowing when to sell is difficult is that, as human beings, hope springs eternal! Can you believe Scott Peterson is still getting letters from female fans while he sits in jail awaiting execution for the murder of his pregnant wife?

Behavioral finance experts will tell you that we hold on to losers too long and sell winners too early. Remember that incurring losses is an integral part of investing. It's as certain as death and taxes. What is important, however, is to keep those losses at a minimum. Make sense?

More about Volatility

Research by economists has shown that stock market volatility tends to be persistent. That is, periods of high volatility, as well as low volatility, tend to last for months. And periods of high volatility tend to occur when stock prices are falling—including recessions. Stock market volatility is also positively related to volatility in economic variables like inflation, industrial production, and the amount of debt carried by the big companies. Since 1962, there appears to have been a steady decline in the common part of the volatility that is shared across returns on different stocks. By contrast, the volatility attributed to firm-specific sources has increased.

The implication for investors, then, is to hold more stocks in their portfolios in order to achieve proper diversification.

Anecdote: My Mother—An Unlikely Bling-Bling Trader!

A few years ago, my mother decided she needed to learn to use the computer and guess who got drafted to teach her? All the basics went down quite smoothly, and I was just beginning to congratulate myself on an assignment well done, when suddenly I saw her arching her entire body as she moved her mouse. I had to actually hold her down while she moved her mouse in order to convince her that she did not need to physically move with her mouse.

Next, we had to tackle the equally thorny issue of running out of mouse real estate before the cursor reached where she wanted it placed on the computer screen! I found her a couple of hours later, still sitting patiently with the mouse at the very edge of the mouse pad, puzzling over what to do next. Obviously the idea of simply picking up the mouse and starting over to reach her desired location on the computer screen had not yet occurred to her. So it's fairly safe to say that itchy trading fingers will not afflict my mother (and maybe even yours?) any time soon.

And how do you do that? Sell stocks to cut losses. For this, you will have to have a predefined rule set up BEFORE you begin investing and YOU HAVE TO STICK TO IT, EVEN IF IT KILLS YOU!

You could, for example, decide that if the stock price falls $2 below your purchase price, you will sell. When that day comes, you will have to sell it. No wavering. Or, you could have a rule that says that once a company misses its earnings estimates, you will dump it. This one is actually followed by a few professional money managers, so you are in good company. Some investors use complex rules related to whether the stock price is too high relative to earnings growth. For example, you might sell a stock if its price is substantially more than twice its expected earnings growth over the next twelve months. So, if the stock is expected to grow its earnings by 10 percent next year, you will sell when the stock price passes twenty times its estimated earnings.

The moral of the story is that you need to have predefined rules for bailing out and be brutal when it comes time to dump either that errant stock or boyfriend, whichever comes first. Do not try to make excuses to hang onto it or him when that day comes. Remember that, as human beings, we can rationalize anything under the sun. That still does not change a loser.

Trading on Trends

Consider the assumption that stock prices show trends—either upward or downward. Of course, the immediate question is, What comprises a trend? You might naïvely say that an upward trend is formed when the most recent price is greater than the past price, or that a downward trend is formed when the most recent price is less than the past price. And, eyeballing a chart to spot a trend might be fraught (yes, I wanted to throw in that word) with inaccuracies. But fear not! There is a more accurate way of spotting trends (upward or downward) that statisticians have used for a long time—moving averages (MA). Using moving averages takes the guesswork out of spotting trends.

Moving averages are simple averages of the prices over a trailing period. For example a 50-day moving average is simply the average of the past 50 days' stock prices. So every day, the 50th day is thrown out and replaced by the most recent day, and the 49th-day price the day before becomes the 50th-day price today.

A very basic decision rule is to buy when the stock's current price penetrates its moving average curve on the upside; if the stock's current price penetrates its moving average curve on the downside, sell the stock. The rationale behind such a rule is really quite intuitive. The average is nothing but a simple centering of past prices. So, if a stock's current price moves above the level it reached in the immediate past, then we can assume that an uptrend in the stock has begun. The investor then seeks to take advantage of the situation by buying early. Similarly, when the current price of the stock moves below its moving average, then it is an indication that a downtrend has started and it is appropriate to sell the stock.

Of course, things have gotten just a tad sophisticated since these simple pronouncements and most market pros I know of use the trailing 50-day moving average as a benchmark for establishing short-term trends and use a 200-day moving average as a benchmark for establishing long-term trends. An easy way to spot these two kinds of moving averages is from the fact that the 50-day average is usually more choppy (less smooth) than the 200-day moving average.

Here then is a revised course of action. Study the trailing 50- and 200-day averages for any stock you are interested in buying or selling. These are easily graphed on any webpage that has charting services freely available (for example, http://www. stockcharts. com). It's probably a good time to buy when the stock price is above both the 200-day MA and the 50-day MA. For a conservative sell signal, any time the stock has dipped below its 200-day MA line might be a good time to let it go.

As an example, I have plotted the daily prices of Microsoft for a whole year and overlaid it with its 50-day MA and 200-day MA plots. Notice that the 50-day MA graph is choppier than the 200-day MA graph. Furthermore, Microsoft's current stock price lies below both these averages and has for a while. A reasonable conclusion is that it might be a good time to consider accumulating Microsoft stock.

Are Moving Averages an Effective Investment Tool? The Research Evidence

What does the research have to say about the efficacy of using moving averages as a buy/sell tool? In an old research study done in the late 1960s using month-end

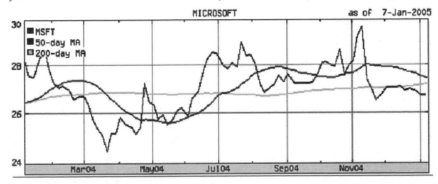

Figure 14: MSFT price path and moving averages

stock prices, a simple experiment was designed.[43] Each stock in the study was followed as though it were observed by an investor who could either take a position in the stock or hold cash. The starting investment sum in each stock was $100 (a pretty large sum forty years ago). At the beginning, a moving average number for each stock, based on its previous six-month month-end values, was computed. In each following month, the initial number was updated by including the most recent month-end value and throwing out the oldest month value in the series. If the current price had moved up above the moving average value then as many shares of the stock as could be purchased with $100 was purchased. The position was then held until the price movement reversed itself, at which time the position was closed out. This strategy was compared against a simple buy-and-hold strategy of the same stocks. The results show that an investor using the moving average decision rule on the stocks would, on average, be significantly worse off than if he simply bought the security and held it.

Interestingly, these results have been used by opponents of the moving average method of investing for years to argue against the technique. I find that amazing due to a number of reasons, not the least of which is that none of these critics seem to have actually read the original paper. If they had, they would have realized that the comparisons were made with monthly stock prices (i.e., using the last price of the stock on the last business day of the month). This is unthinkable in today's world where we have second-by-second stock prices available and intra-day trends are established on a regular basis, which would lead to a very different scenario than the one prevailing forty years ago when the experiment described above was performed. In short, it is entirely possible that an intra-daily moving average price series would lead to very different findings. The author of the original article says so himself in his conclusions. Yet, this latter fact is conveniently ignored by the critics claiming that moving averages are not a good investment strategy.

Thought Questions

1. Why is the ask price generally greater than the bid price?

2. Can the bid price ever be greater than the ask price? Can this condition be sustainable?

3. Why did it take over 200 years of trading for the minimum price ticks to change from $1/8 to 1 cent?

4. Why are institutions so against decimal pricing?

5. Identify a few other companies trading in the NASDAQ that could be moving to the NYSE but are choosing to stay in the NASDAQ. What could be their reasoning?

6. Why do you think the 24 merchants initially signed the agreement to create a cartel that eventually became known as the NYSE?

7. Knowing how stock tickers are allocated across exchanges, can you articulate why the NYSE was impacted much less by the collapse of the dot-com bubble than the NASDAQ?

8. What are the inherent differences between established companies and the newer firms? Think about IBM and Google and see if your reasons fit these two companies.

9. Do you think it is important for a stock to have a large float? Why or why not?

10. Sirius Satellite Radio seems to have done reasonably well over the last two years. What are some of the reasons you can think of that would give you pause in buying SIRI stock?

11. Can you think of another emergent technology that might get popular in the next five years? What companies are behind this technology? Are they publicly traded yet?

12. Why is high trading volume in a stock important for a small investor?

13. What does it mean for a stock to have a large bid-ask spread? All else being equal, should you invest in a stock with a large spread or one with a small spread?

14. Why are institutions (rather than individuals) considered to be smart, or informed, investors?

15. What are the main trade-offs between market and limit orders?

16. If you are trading in a high volume stock, are you more likely to use a market or a limit order? How about a stock with relatively little trading volume?

17. What are the main differences between a stop-loss order and a limit-sell order?

18. Why is leveraging oneself a risky strategy?

19. What do you think market volatility was like during the dot-com boom of the late nineties?

20. Why are American stock markets less volatile than markets elsewhere?

Notes

33. Christie, W. J., and P. Schultz, 1994. "Why Do NASDAQ Market Makers Avoid Odd-Eighth Quotes?" *Journal of Finance* 42, 1813–1840.

34. Ceron, Gaslon F. "Decimalization Cuts Wall Street Profit, Narrowing Bid-Ask Spreads, Says Study." *Wall Street Journal*, September 8, 2000.

35. Chakravarty, S., R. A. Wood and R. Van Ness, 2004. "Decimals and Liquidity: A Study of the NYSE." *Journal of Financial Research* 27, 75–94.

36. Chakravarty, S., V. Panchapagesan, and R. A. Wood, 2005. "Has Decimalization Hurt Institutional Investors? An Investigation into Trading Costs and Order Routing Practices of Buy-Side Institutions." *Journal of Financial Markets* 8, 400–420.

37. Benston, G. J., and R. A. Wood, 2008. "Why Effective Spreads on NASDAQ Were Higher Than on the New York Stock Exchange in the 1990s." *Journal of Empirical Finance* 15, 17–40.

38. Usually meant for a large limit order which must be filled in entirety or canceled (killed).

39. A market order to be executed at the end of the trading day.

40. An order specifying execution at the opening of the market.

41. An order whose execution depends on the execution or the price of another traded security.

42. Boehmer, E., C. M. Jones, and X. Zhang, 2005. " Which Shorts are Informed?" unpublished manuscript, Texas A&M University.

43. James, F. E., 1968. "Monthly Moving Averages—An Effective Investment Tool?," *Journal of Financial and Quantitative Analysis* 3, 315–326.

8

Advanced Topics

To paraphrase Oscar Wilde, a speculator is a man who knows
the price of everything and the value of nothing.

—Justyn Walsh,

Stock Analysts

Stock analysts are professional stock researchers who are supposed to go through the minutiae of company profit and loss statements and other accounting data, talk to top company officials, perform all kinds of research, and come up with pronouncements of "BUY," "SELL," or "HOLD." In fact, a groundbreaking study published in the *Journal of Finance* in the mid-1990s, using a large sample of analyst recommendations, concluded that analyst recommendation changes were accompanied by a tremendous trading volume increase and positive abnormal returns.[44] In simple English, the findings implied that analyst recommendations are not cosmetic but, rather, "informed" events. Further translation: These analysts know what they are talking about and are not simply blowing smoke up our chimneys. Naturally, investors paid a lot of attention to what these analysts said.

There was a problem, however. Stock analysts, for the most part, are employed by big brokerage houses like Merrill Lynch, A.G. Edwards, Morgan Stanley, Goldman Sachs, etc. These same brokerage houses also make a lot of money from investment banking services which involve bringing a company public (read the section on IPOs if you have no clue what this means) and having its shares trade in the stock exchanges (by some estimates, almost 70 percent of a brokerage firm's profits come from such activities). Now if you're like me, you are shaking your head and going, "Hmmmm! Doesn't there seem to be a conflict of interest here? Isn't it more like the fox guarding the henhouse?" Well, the brokerages will all tell you emphatically, and often, that they have a "Chinese wall" between their analyst department and their investment banking group so that one group does not talk to the other group. Ergo, no conflict. Yeah, right!

This situation is not unlike that prevailing in the National Football League where the coaches all look out for each other. The bias/conflict lies in the fact that a hiring decision made by a current NFL head coach will, in turn, affect his own employment in the future. So, for instance, the head coach for the Browns gets fired and promptly gets hired as a defensive coordinator of the Buffalo Bills (usually by the same guy who once worked for the fired coach as an assistant in another NFL franchise). Then the Bills do well for a couple of years and the assistant coach's stock increases and he is hired back as a head coach with the Colts (say). Of course, he promptly hires on to his staff the rejected head coaches from losing franchises (who, may well have hired him earlier in other NFL openings) and who were recently fired from their respective positions. Thus, the circle of life at the NFL continues unabated. The bottom line is that conflict of interest and/or bias is everywhere. Why blame Wall Street for it?

In the go-go years of the dot-com boom, analysts like Merrill Lynch's Henry Blodgett and Morgan Stanley's Mary Meeker became household names and held almost rock-star status. They made TV appearances and their proclamations about various stocks were eagerly consumed by millions of adoring fans eager to ride the gravy train to fortune.

Predictions have a self-fulfilling aspect. If I pronounce a stock to be a great buy and then a few thousand of you run out and buy a hundred shares each, soon it DOES become a great buy. Not because it was a great buy to begin with, but because all of you helped to make it so. Life was great for Blodgett and Meeker and they could do no wrong. They were making millions of dollars in salaries and bonuses from their respective brokerage companies. However, within the din of adoration, there were a few spoilsports who were accusing these star analysts of being more like cheerleaders for the firms they were supposed to be analyzing than unbiased analysts. But nobody listened! And here is the interesting bit. Many of the stocks these analysts were bullish on kept going down in price. Worse, many of them were ones the analyst's parent company happened to be in an investment banking relationship with. Shocked?

For example, Morgan Stanley's star analyst, Mary Meeker, made an impassioned pitch for Priceline, the company that her own firm had helped bring to the market as a publicly traded company (through an IPO). Meeker was bullish on Priceline, then trading for $134 a share. Even when the stock fell almost 50 percent to about $77, she continued to recommend a BUY for Priceline. When the stock plunged to less than $3 a share, she continued to repeat her BUY mantra! Brokerage firms continued to deny any connection between their analysts and their investment banking activity. Remember that Chinese wall?

Analysts as a group fell out of favor when the dot-com boom collapsed in early 2000. Mary Meeker now loudly professes her innocence and talks (for a hefty fee, of course) about the evils perpetrated by brokers everywhere. Most of the star brokers (including Meeker, Blodgett and Jack Grubmann) have been fired by their original companies and have found employment elsewhere—but not at the ungodly salaries they once commanded.

To Blodgett a Stock

Henry Blodgett was so insistent with his bullish predictions that Wall Street professionals coined the phrase: "To blodgett a stock." Blodgett, of course, claims he based his predictions on sound analysis.

Recently, the attorney general of New York, Eliot Spitzer, while he served as New york's attorney general, made it his mission to go after corporate crime including analysts and the brokerage firms that employed them, making them rich. Among other things, he accused these firms, and their star analysts, of publicizing stocks that they had an investment banking relationship with, to the point where objectivity was sacrificed. Some have compared Spitzer's zeal to Superman using his superpowers for good rather than evil. Spitzer comes from a privileged family. His father is an Austrian immigrant and self-made real estate mogul. Eliot attended Princeton and Harvard and appears to have the pedigree to go after this powerful lobby. Unfortunately, he has now dropped out of favor for being involved with a prostitute.

In the course of their investigation sometime in 2002, Spitzer's staff came across internal e-mail among Merrill analysts that they downgraded a stock, not because there was anything fundamentally wrong with it, but because the company would not do business with Merrill.

Even before analyst bashing became America's favorite pastime, after Oprah and Jerry Springer, academic research had examined the effect of equity buy/sell recommendations by financial analysts in equity markets. As mentioned earlier, an interesting article published in the *Journal of Finance* by Kent Womack of Dartmouth College in 1996 essentially concluded that recommendation changes embodied valuable information for which a brokerage firm should be compensated. More recently, however, another research study concluded that analyst recommendation changes are inherently uninformed liquidity enhancing events.[45] Don't you wish life were simpler?

> **Fun Fax**
>
> Economics is the only discipline where two people can share a Nobel Prize for saying completely opposite things. For example, Friedrich von Hayek and Gunnar Myrdal shared the 1974 Noble Prize in Economics for saying completely opposite things. So the million dollar question: Why does economics exist? The answer: To help make our sports prognosticators on ESPN feel better about themselves.

Leveling the Playing Field through Regulation FD

Adopted in October 2000, the U.S. Security and Exchange Commission's (SEC) Regulation Fair Disclosure, also known as Reg FD, was meant to level the playing field of information dissemination and make it easier for the little guys (that would be you and me) to play in the same field as the big boys. At a meeting with small investors following the adoption of this regulation, then-SEC Chairman Arthur Levitt said: "You are now privy to the same information, and at the same time, as analysts, investment bankers, and every other professional on Wall Street." Most observers concede that Reg FD largely accomplished its goal of removing the selective disclosure of inside information whereby some analysts allowed themselves to be spoon-fed information by companies in return for special access to the highest echelons of the company. But what about the quality of the information itself that is now coming out of the companies?

Interestingly, academic research,[46] using a large sample of earnings forecasts made by analysts around the passage of Reg FD, finds that analyst forecasts have become less accurate (read less reliable) both individually as well as in the aggregate, after the passage of Reg FD and relatively less reliable for forecasts made on small companies compared to those made on large firms. In balance, as the regulatory body has mandated a more democratic way of disseminating information, the quality of the information publicly disseminated appears to have decreased. This is not good news for small investors.

Stock Splits

As stocks increase in price, some companies will split their stock. In simple terms, the company will say that for every share a shareholder owns, after a certain day, also known as the ex-date, it will be replaced by two or three new shares (or, more). In the former case, it is a 2-for-1 split and in the latter case, a 3-for-1 split. Nothing changes except that on the ex-date the stock trades at half the price (in case of a 2-for-1 split) and you own twice the number of shares you owned before the split. From a theoretical standpoint, a stock split is a non-event. While the split reduces the share of the company each share of stock represents, each shareholder in turn gets enough extra shares so his fraction of the company owned remains the same as before the split. In addition, on the day of the split (i.e., the ex-date), the stock price is proportionately adjusted so the market value of the company remains exactly the same.

Why Do Companies Split Their Shares?

There have been suggestions that companies split their shares to signal future profitability. One study in particular examines 1,275 2-for-1 stock splits initiated by New York Stock Exchange stocks over 1975–1990 and reports a post-split excess return of about 8 percent in the first year and over 12 percent in the first three years following the split. The authors conclude that while splits realign prices to a lower trading range, the managers of the companies undertaking these splits self-select by conditioning the decision to split on expected future performance.[47]

There have also been suggestions that minimum price variation rules (or minimum tick sizes that we saw earlier) may have a role to play in companies' decisions to split their shares. In particular, if the exchange mandated minimum tick size (currently one penny) stays fixed while the stock price changes constantly, the relative tick size of the stock—1 penny divided by the stock price—changes constantly too. It is this relative tick size of a stock that declines as the stock's price increases. And as the relative tick size declines, so does the incentive for investors to provide liquidity in the stock. Thus, liquidity suffers. Ergo, these stocks declare stock splits to increase the relative tick size and thereby increase their liquidity.[48] Additional research by other economists suggests that firms with very low levels of institutional ownership prior to the split appear to gain in liquidity following splits and that a higher fraction of post-split trades are made by less sophisticated investors—that is, it is investors like you and me—who dive into these stocks following splits. Something to think about.

The most interesting reason for companies splitting shares, however, may be related to the psychological effect it has on investors. Studies show that individual investors like you and me prefer to trade shares in the $20–60 range. So if a company wants new individual investors to own shares of the company, they will regularly split their shares as they increase beyond the normal trading range in order to force the stock price back into the investors' comfort zone. Contrarily, if a company does not want individual investors in its ownership demographic, it may never split. The classic example of the latter is the Warren Buffet-owned Berkshire Hathaway shares. Currently, each share trades for about $90,000. It is clear that Buffet, in spite of his folksy attitude, would rather have institutions and wealthy individuals as his sole shareholders. By contrast, Microsoft is an example of a company that wants individual investors in its shareholder base. It has, over the course of its existence, routinely split its stock. The magnitude of Microsoft's splits over the years of its existence as a publicly traded company can be understood with the following example. If you spent a couple of thousand dollars buying Microsoft shares in 1982 and held on to it, you would be worth in the neighborhood of $2 million today.

Reverse Stock Splits

Reverse stock splits are used when a company tries to artificially increase its stock price. For example, if a company declares a 1-for-20 reverse split, for every 20 shares you owned before the split, you would own 1 new share after the split. The stock price would also be adjusted upward 20 times relative to the pre-split price. Usually when a company announces a reverse split, it is not good news. It means that the company is teetering on the brink and is giving a last ditch effort to stay afloat and, more importantly, to stay listed in organized stock exchanges like the NASDAQ. Most companies announcing reverse splits see their stock prices go down eventually to less than a dollar per share. These are usually very thinly traded and are consigned to be in the basement of organized trading exchanges (known as pink sheet stocks, for example). In the short run, however, things might look rosy. A study investigating the liquidity effects of reverse stock splits reports that bid-ask spreads decrease and trading volume increases immediately following reverse stock splits. Thus, in the short run, reverse stock splits might enhance the liquidity of a stock.[49] All things considered, it might be wise to stay away from them.

In sum, while stock splits may be good news, the long-term prognosis of reverse stock splits is not good. The initial good news following reverse stock splits might just be the calm before the storm!

Insider Trading

Insider trading occurs when someone with privileged information about a company (and, by extension, its stock) trades on the information for personal profit. Before 1968, insider trading was common and generally accepted by society. In recent years, however, two schools of thought have developed. One group of scholars and practitioners claims that insider trading does not hurt any single individual in the market and argue that insider trading helps prices find their "correct" value. In other words, insider trading helps to make prices efficient. They also argue that allowing insiders to trade and profit is a form of incentive compensation for top management of a company—an argument that has recently taken a beating due to the plethora of scandals involving stock options and company insiders. Experts say that the strongest argument against insider trading as compensation is the difficulty of measuring and benchmarking entitlement and rewards.

The second school of thought argues that allowing insider trading is psychologically harmful to the investor community at large. If it is common knowledge that insiders are trading, then everyone else may be reluctant to trade in what they see as an unfair market. Then market liquidity is compromised and society as a whole suffers. This is the "market confidence" argument that the Securities and Exchange Commission (SEC)—a regulatory arm of the federal government—has used for years.

A more credible reason for prohibiting insider trading is the so-called "adverse selection" theory. In simple terms, this theory implies that when investors are faced with the prospect of trading against traders with superior information about a company, they (the investors) have an incentive to become defensive and provide inferior prices to the market at large in order to protect themselves from incurring certain losses. Thus, everyone is hurt, since we pay relatively more to buy stock and get relatively less when selling stock (i.e., bid-ask spreads widen). Unfortunately, this argument, while certainly plausible, is not backed by hard data. All this begs the question: Does insider trading really hurt the average investor?

If insider information leads to gain, it is logical to impose a monetary penalty to remove the gain and punish the individual(s) who benefited from the insider information (it may or may not be appropriate to institute criminal penalties for this). However, the thrust of the insider trading laws rests on the assumption that insider trading hurts the markets and other people trading in the markets who do not have access to the same information. The SEC spends millions of our tax dollars annually in the name of oversight aimed at investigating, curbing, and prosecuting insider trading based on the assumption that insider trading is bad. Unfortunately, the assumption itself has little empirical validation.

In a collection of research studies, economists Sugato Chakravarty and John McConnell have shown that insider trading does not appear to increase trading costs.[50,51] The authors analyze insider trading data from a well-known inside trader, Ivan Boesky, pertaining to Boesky's purchase of Carnation Company shares in the summer of 1984, just prior to Carnation being bought out by Swiss food company Nestle SA. The two economists show that Boesky's trades in Carnation shares based on illegal inside information did not move stock prices any more than other simultaneous buyers of the same stock at the same time who did not have private information. This is an important discovery, since it establishes that insider trading does not have any more impact on stock prices than non-insider trades.

Chakravarty and McConnell also find that Boesky's insider trading in Carnation stock had little effect on its bid-ask spread, and no effect on market depth. Moreover, the effect of Boesky's trading was actually positive on both the bid-ask spread and market depth. That is, market liquidity either increased or stayed the same during Boesky's trading. There were no ill effects of Boesky's trading on the other consumers active in this stock, as presumed by insider trading laws. A detailed examination of the spreads in Carnation stock on Boesky-trading and on non-Boesky-trading days revealed that not only did Boesky's trades have no effect on bid-ask spreads, but the minimal effect that Boesky's trades did have on market depth were in a direction that would help the uninformed trader. Boesky's trades increased market depth by making more shares available.

Such evidence notwithstanding, experts say there is yet another justification for insider trading, and this one may explain why corporations did not regulate the practice themselves before the SEC got into the act. Management and shareholders of large, publicly held corporations have a strong common interest in the accurate pricing of the company's shares. If pricing is not reliable, investors will demand a higher return in order to be compensated for assuming this added risk. Thus, all other things being equal, the shares of a company with reliable pricing will sell for more than otherwise identical shares.

> ## Recall
>
> The bid (ask) is the price at which the market maker is willing to buy (sell) a stock. The deeper the market, the narrower the spread and the cheaper it is for investors to transact. Market depth is the number of shares available at each bid and ask price. The greater the number of shares available at each such price, the deeper the market.

Lack of confidence in the reliability of a share's price, reflected in a higher risk premium, will have several negative effects. The company will have to pay more for new capital, boards of directors and the managers themselves will have less reliable feedback on managerial performance, managers' professional reputations will suffer, and the managers will be at greater risk of displacement.

The fact that insiders, who may not even be in managerial positions, profit from the system does not mean that they necessarily understand, or care, about the economic importance of reliable pricing. Nor does it mean that their gain detracts from

Up Close: Ivan Boesky and Carnation

During a three-month period in 1984, Ivan Boesky accumulated 1.7 million shares of Carnation stock, just below 5 percent of all outstanding shares. As a result of a subsequent offer from Nestle to purchase all Carnation shares for a significant premium, Boesky made a significant gain. Unfortunately (for Boesky), his gain was not seen as an outcome of luck or superior market analysis and insight. The SEC charged him with "insider trading" for gaining from illegal information. Boesky later acknowledged that he had received such insider information about the takeover of Carnation from an investment banker at Kidder, Peabody & Company.

Insider trading is a violation of SEC Rule 10b-5 known as the "disclose or abstain" rule. These rules have their roots in the Securities Act of 1934, which prohibits companies and individuals from engaging in fraudulent and unfair behavior and insider trading is but one example. In addition to the criminal sanctions against insider trading authorized by 10b-5, the Insider Trading Sanctions Act (ITSA) of 1984 provided for civil penalties (payable to the government) of up to three times the profit gained, or loss avoided, in insider trading.

Because of his trading, based on inside information, Boesky profited about $50 million. In 1986, as a result of government action against him, Ivan Boesky pled guilty and agreed to pay back the $50 million in profits and another $50 million as civil penalty. He also pled guilty on one count of an unspecified criminal charge that resulted in the SEC barring him from the securities industry for life. Boesky received a 3-year jail sentence in a minimum security prison.

the benefits others receive from the system. The system would not work unless they profited, but there is no need for them to understand the larger picture.

If, on the other hand, insider trading is allowed, there are no delays or uncertainties about what has to be disclosed. There are no issues about when information must be published, or in what form. There is no need to regulate investment bankers, auditors, or stock analysts. The evaluation of new information will be done efficiently through a pure market process. Investors will receive full disclosures in the form of immediate, and correct, price adjustments, at least in theory.

Martha Stewart and Insider Trading

Remember Martha Stewart and the pharmaceutical company ImClone? For those who were hibernating and missed it, here are the highlights, or the lowlights, depending on your point of view.

On Christmas day in 2001, ImClone chief operating officer Harlan Waksal received a phone call informing him that the Food and Drug Administration (FDA) would be rejecting the company's hot new cancer drug, Erbitux. This news must have devastated Waksal because he happened to be leveraged to the hilt with $80 million in debt, $65 million of which was on margin, secured by his stock. The stock itself, as any student of finance knows, was sure to tank when the FDA made its announcement publicly. His monthly interest payment on the margin was about $800,000. If ImClone collapsed, Waksal would be ruined. Waksal and his brother were friends of Martha Stewart who owned about 4,000 shares of ImClone herself. At a price of $75 a share reached just weeks before, Martha's investment in ImClone was about $300,000.

Martha is accused of having received news about ImClone's impending demise well before the public announcement by the FDA, and selling her entire holding in ImClone through her brokers, Merrill Lynch. The very next day, the FDA faxed a letter of rejection to ImClone offices. ImClone announced the news after the market's close. In the wake of the news, ImClone's stock price plunged 16 percent. These days, ImClone trades at around $35 after dropping to about $9 right after the scandal broke. Martha Stewart spent time in prison for her efforts.

The Fascinating Saga of a High School Trader

There was a young lad named Jonathan Lebed who, at sixteen years of age, made a lot of money buying stocks and then taking advantage of Internet chat rooms in order to drive up demand in these same stocks. He would plaster Internet message boards with extremely bullish predictions on the stocks and then sell out quickly once other investors bit on it and started buying the stocks, thereby pushing their prices up.

Lebed's modus operandi included, for example, identifying companies like Yes Entertainment, Inc., and Havana Republic, Inc., low in price and trading activity, according to the SEC. This is because it is easier to move the price of a small company than a big one, such as IBM. He would buy shares of the small company he had targeted, then plaster Internet message boards with postings—sometimes hundreds of them—hyping the stock on Silicon Investor and Yahoo!

He touted one company as the "next stock to gain 1,000 percent" and as "the most undervalued stock ever." Often he would use numerous aliases, creating the impression that many other investors were interested in a single stock and when other investors took the bait, and the stock rose in price, Lebed would unload his position in the stock.

Among the message-board names that Lebed used were "charmdw," "wmmkjj" and "dmaj431." On the Yahoo! message board for Firetector Inc., "charmdw" wrote, for example, "This stock will explode this week." Lebed bought 20,000 Firetector shares the day of the posting and sold soon thereafter—at a profit. Eventually, the SEC forced Lebed to cough up some of his ill-gotten gains to the tune of $285,000—but he actually made over $800,000 in profits. So he got to keep over $500,000 in gains.

Interestingly, Lebed had been on the SEC's radar for several years before formal charges were brought against him. Beginning in early 1998, when he was only thirteen, he was regularly writing on Silicon Investor, a financial Web site, and had formed a stock-picking Web site called StockDogs.com. The SEC had called the youth's parents frequently to warn them that their son's activities might not be appropriate. When the Web site continued to tout stocks, the young man was called in to meet with enforcement attorneys at the SEC's New York office. At his mother's urging, Lebed shut down his Web site, but continued his trading activity. Lebed's lawyer does not deny that his client made exaggerated statements in postings about the potential of stock prices for individual companies, but contends that it isn't illegal. "It's in the nature of puffing— it's an opinion," his lawyer says. "Some of his more enthusiastic statements or predictions about where the price might go could be seen as misleading. It's difficult to characterize those statements as false."

Lebed's defense was that he hyped the stocks but did nothing wrong. His lawyer echoed those sentiments, adding that Lebed's online messages almost always offered a disclaimer that investors should do their own research, and claims that his

Example of Insider Trading

Recently, a manager in Sepracor's accounting department, told his father that Eli Lilly & Co. might terminate a licensing agreement with Sepracor involving a new version of Lilly's widely sold antidepressant, Prozac.

The story goes that the father quickly purchased put options on Sepracor stock. (Note that put options give the holder the right to sell stock at a given price.) After Lilly announced the agreement's termination on October 19, 2000, dad sold the put options for a profit of $55,000 after the value of Sepracor stock plunged. Several months later, the older man transferred $55,000 to his son. Naturally, the SEC was not happy with the father-son team and wanted the return of related profits and civil monetary penalties of up to three times that amount. Then a federal grand jury indicted the son on related criminal charges of insider trading and conspiracy to commit securities fraud.

The defense argument is that the son is innocent because he was not aware of the insider information before it was made public. What do you think?

client did a lot of research, spoke to company chief executives, and even visited some of the companies he promoted.

The SEC maintains there is a big difference between the normal stock-touting messages on the Internet, and what Lebed was doing. Regulators say they aren't interested in, and don't have the resources for, probing every message that hypes a stock. The SEC claims that they see outrageous pitches all the time, many of which have absolutely no impact. Message board participants shoot them down and discredit them immediately.

Hype crosses the line and becomes illegal, the SEC says, when someone knowingly provides false or misleading statements with the clear intent to affect a stock's price, and then defrauds others by trading the shares.

The huge volume of Lebed's Internet postings indicated his intent to move the market, the SEC alleges. He would sometimes put out as many as 500 messages under different names. It is clear that Lebed wanted to create an illusion that this was a good stock and it was not just one person's opinion.

When Lebed predicted—without any basis, according to the SEC—that a stock would climb to $20 from $2, or that it would increase 1,000 percent, he may have violated the law. The SEC alleges that if someone puts in a recommendation with a price prediction that a stock will double, triple, or quadruple, without a reasonable basis, it is illegal. In SEC settlements, defendants usually agree not to talk about the case. So, why has Lebed's lawyer been calling attention to the fact that the SEC settlement didn't force his client to give back all of his profits, only $285,000 of it? What do you think?

Stealth Trading

If you were an investor with valuable information about a stock, what would you do? Would you, for example, trade openly on the information so that others could take advantage of your information, piggyback off you and make profits? Or, would you trade secretively so that no one else finds out what you know, at least till your trading is done? I don't know about you, but I would certainly choose the latter option—to trade stealthily on my information to the extent possible.

Now consider an alternative scenario. What if you did not have valuable information about any stock but just wanted to trade a large quantity of some stock. In trading jargon, you are a large uninformed trader. What would your incentive be? Would you try to trade stealthily as if you were an informed trader? Maybe you would try to pre-announce your trade as a "sunshine trader" would.

Your intrinsic character as an informed trader might decide for you what course of action you want to follow—stealth trading or sunshine trading. Keep in mind that the fact that you are a large trader wanting to trade is valuable information in itself. If someone just has this piece of information in advance, they can profit by it.

Let's assume that you were recognized as an informed trader. When other investors saw you were about to buy a particular stock, what do you think would happen? The moment you stepped up to the plate to execute your trade, a mad rush would ensue and everyone would want a piece of the same action. Prices would rise before you could carry out your trade and you would have to pay through your nose (through increased stock price). Get the picture? You would need to hide—and hide well.

And one way investors with private information might choose to trade is by breaking up their intended trades into smaller sized chunks so that they can hide behind other small traders (of whom there are plenty). Important research by two economists established that informed traders would indeed have the incentive to break down their orders into intermediate-sized chunks, not so big as to give them away and not so small as to take an excruciatingly long time to execute (translation, very costly).[52] In fact, their analysis reveals that it is the medium-sized trades, defined as trades of 500 shares, to 9,999 shares, where most of the informed trading action would be cen-

---

Sunshine Trading

Sunshine trading has its origins with portfolio insurance in the mid-1980s and consists of pre-announcing a particular basket, or index, trading plan before any orders are executed. Thus, the order would be entered between the bid and ask at the announced day and time, and any untraded portion of the order would be withdrawn and re-entered according to the pre-announced schedule until the order was completely executed. The underlying intuition for this technique is that the other market participants are less likely to mistake the order for an informed trader thereby attenuating the market impact associated with the execution of a large informed trade. The technique is not without its flaws since the fact that someone wants to trade is a valuable piece of information by itself regardless of the informed or uninformed nature of the trade.

---

tered. Of course, the markets are not stupid. They know that this is what the informed intend to do. This is analogous to movie stars disguising themselves in sweatpants, baseball caps, and sunglasses in order to try to fool the paparazzi camped outside their houses.

Does it work? Perhaps, but only until the paparazzi figure it out. The stock market works essentially the same way. We know that some of the medium-sized trades are disguised trades from informed investors—we just do not know exactly which ones they are. Therefore, we treat all medium-sized trades with an increased degree

of scrutiny and suspicion, which would result in their displaying an increased price response relative to small- and large-sized trades. Put differently, stock prices will jump up disproportionately after a medium buy and fall disproportionately after a medium sell. This is exactly what the research has shown.

Side Note

The term *paparazzi* originates from Paparazzo, the name of a freelance photographer character in Felini's 1960 film *La Dolce Vita*. The term "Paparazzo" literally means "a buzzing insect."

In later follow-up research, another economist showed stealth trading is associated with the medium-size trades of institutional traders (rather than trades from individual investors).[53] Even more recently, two economists have shown that stealth trading is not just limited to the stock markets but is common in options markets too.[54] In fact, research has uncovered the presence of stealth trading in Australian and Japanese markets. The evidence continues to come in from other Asian and European markets as well. Stealth trading, therefore, appears to be a robust phenomenon

executed by strategic traders to hide their intentions in all markets—here in the
United States and in markets around the world.

Intermarket Sweep Orders (ISO)

Attempting to understand the robustness of our financial markets has never been
more timely in the wake of the recent Wall Street meltdown and the continual gyra-
tion of the markets overall. The recent implementation of Regulation NMS, completed in October of 2007, represents one of the most significant changes in the structure of equity markets in recent memory. While the regulation consists for four main
parts, perhaps the most controversial new rule is Rule 611, the Order Protection
Rule. The essence of the Order Protection Rule is that market orders be routed to the
market center posting the best price. There are several exemptions to the Order
Protection Rule identified in section 611(b) of the regulation. One such exception is
the Intermarket Sweep Order (ISO).

ISO orders are marketable limit orders that allow traders to process demand in
parallel rather than the sequential processing of regular non-ISO orders. To high-
light the differences in the ISO and non-ISO orders, consider a trader that wishes to
purchase 10,000 shares and chooses to "work" the order. The trader divides the total
demand into many small marketable limit buy orders. If the orders are all designated as non-ISO orders and submitted to the market, then the orders will execute
sequentially, being routed to the market center that posts the best execution price,
which can change during the execution of the order set.

Alternatively, the trader can choose to designate the orders as ISO orders and
route these orders to several market centers simultaneously. As each order arrives
at a market center it is immediately executed at the best price, up to the limit price
of the ISO, offered by the selected market center. ISO orders are not redirected to
other exchanges that may have a better posted price and can trade through the
National Best Bid and Offer (NBBO) price. While, for a given market center, orders
are processed sequentially, the fact that ISO orders from a single trader can be
queued in many markets allows for a parallel processing, and a quicker execution,
of the total demand.

Recent research finds that ISO orders are small in size (averaging around 179
shares).[55] Note that such trades differ from the medium-sized stealth trades.
Interestingly these small-sized trades appear to be informed trades indicating that
informed traders may be using such orders—sometimes maybe even over stealth
trading, which are informed traders using medium-size trades.

In sum, as the trading marketplace changes, informed or strategic traders are
finding increasingly creative ways to trade and hide behind uninformed traders. As
small investors ourselves, we have to be careful how we trade and make sure we
don't lose money by being caught in the crossfire of games played by more sophisticated investors.

Games that Large Investors Play

In the fall of 1998, two Stanford University graduate students left the university and formed a company they called Google. Almost 10 years later, shares of Google were trading around $700 per share and the company was worth over $200 billion. All that is public information. It appears however that Google stock may have been the victim of stock price manipulation by powerful Wall Street firms. Research has uncovered that these large investors may have been using small investors in the company's stock as pawns in their quest for high investment returns. Such behavior also explains why such firms are able to pay millions of dollars in salaries and bonuses to their employees and how that money may be earned at the expense of naïve small investors.

Using data from both the stock and options trades in Google over an extended period, the trades of large investors show that they are able to accurately predict the post earnings release price of the company and use this information to make profitable trades in the options markets. So, for example, institutional investors appear to accurately buy call options in Google before a price rise and put options before a price decline. The research appears to find evidence that in the few quarters where the institutional option trades did not appear to be profitable initially, suddenly and almost inexplicably the stock price appeared to veer and head in the needed direction for profit.

In sum, there is compelling evidence to suggest that large institutional traders appear to "know" the post earnings stock prices. In anticipation of this, they sell options with strike prices that later become out of money (i.e., useless). The high success rate of such activities rules out pure chance. Overall, there appear to be good reasons to believe that there are significant price manipulations going on in stock and options markets in ways that benefit large traders at the expense of smaller individual investors like you and me.

Shifting Gears

We have arrived at the end of our investment-related adventures and it's time to move on to the other pillars of personal finance: credit, insurance, and retirement, which are addressed in upcoming chapters.

Jim Cramer's Play

In March 2007, Jim Cramer, the host of CNBC's Mad Money program boasted on-air about manipulating stock prices in a video Interview with TheSteet.com. Cramer bragged how easy it is to move stock prices up, down, or any other way, with the cooperation of the financial press. He talked about specific stocks and how he could spend a few million dollars to knock a company out by driving their stock prices down and harm the "moron longs." Cramer went on to say that he would do this in conjunction with placing large put orders on the company's stock.

Source: Liu, J.W., 2008, Option market and smart traders, working paper, California State University – East Bay.

We have reviewed some of the common investment vehicles you could use to increase your net worth. It is important to look at all investments within a common risk-return continuum as a whole, not as distinct vehicles—like a holistic approach to investing. In spite of superficial differences in pricing and how they are traded, there is little difference between stocks, bonds, mutual funds, options, ETFs, and unit trusts, etc., except in the potential risk and the corresponding returns. This is an important Zen lesson that I want you to understand. It is so important that it bears repeating.

Different Rules, Same Game. All financial instruments covered in this book are only superficially different—in the ways they are traded, in unit sizes, and so on. Think of these simply as rules of the game; the game itself stays the same. It's a continuum between risk and return: How much risk are you comfortable taking, and how much are you willing to gamble for it? Your returns, in turn, are commensurate with the risk you take. That's all there is to it. Once you see the universality of investments, all you will need to understand are the new trading rules for the various games in town and the inherent risks involved: Stocks, bonds, options, mutual funds, and so on.

A second lesson is the following: Practice Makes Perfect. As you read, invest, and try out new ideas, you will get better at it. Of course, there is a difference between working hard and working smart. I was raised by parents who were academics by profession. We were not wealthy by any stretch of the imagination, but we were financially comfortable. My parents believed that wealth itself was somehow obscene but, by the same token, seemed to enjoy the finer things of life. Accordingly, I was raised with this inherent confusion. Is too much wealth good or bad? Is it obscene if it comes to you easily? Is working hard better than working smart? These were questions for which I had no clear answer. I now believe that one can do both. The trick is to work smart and to do so harder. Both have important roles to play in building wealth which, in turn, can provide you with the freedom to smell the roses, so to speak.

Philosophers have long argued that wealth in itself is meaningless; it's what we do with wealth that gives it value. If we use it solely for our personal gratification, it is probably obscene and a waste. But if we use some of it to make a difference for others, it can be a wonderful thing. And when we have the luxury of doing that, it is like arriving at the Promised Land. Think of Warren Buffet's recent decision to give away the bulk of his 40 plus billion dollar fortune to charity.

The hallmark of successful people, whether they are great investors, painters, inventors, salesmen, or engineers, is that they all have a tremendous work ethic and do not take no for an answer. Discipline and tenacity! When I was young I thought I knew it all, and my father used to say, "There is no shortcut to success." I laughed at him then, but it is the truth. Sadly, he is no longer around for me to say thank you for all I learned from him. The Zen story that most closely exemplifies the concept of working hard and succeeding goes as follows: A long time ago in China (of course, it is China!), a martial arts student went up to his teacher and asked, "I am very eager to study your martial arts, but how long will it take for me to master it?"

Anecdote: The Chinese Singer

A classical singer in ancient China was studying under a strict teacher who insisted that the student rehearse the same passage over and over again, day after day, without being permitted to go any further. Finally, overwhelmed and frustrated, the young student went AWOL and found himself another profession. Then one night, while passing an inn, he stumbled upon a singing contest. Having some time to kill, he entered the competition and sang the one passage that he knew so well. When he had finished, the sponsor of the contest praised his performance. Despite the student's embarrassed objections, the sponsor refused to believe that he had just heard a novice performance. "Tell me," the sponsor asked, "Who is your teacher? He must be a great master." This student later became known as the great performer Koshiji. And what is the moral of this story?

Hard work always pays off in the future. You may not realize it at the time you put in the effort. Your friends may laugh at you for being so stupid as to work on something that seems pointless. But, if you persevere, good things will happen.

The teacher looked at the prospect with little interest (those were the days before teaching evaluations) and replied, "Well, maybe ten years, maybe fifteen, maybe twenty." The student was beside himself. But he persisted. "What if I study really hard, practice twice as hard as your best student every day of the week, and take no time off for myself? How long will it take then?" The teacher looked at the student absent-mindedly and replied, "Maybe thirty years." Maybe the Master was a tenured professor already and above teaching evaluations? But, seriously, what do you think the Zen master was trying to tell this impatient student?

An important lesson to take away from the Investment section of this book (and a Zen lesson as well) is to try and master the art of self-control; i.e., control the desire to indulge in bling-bling investing. Strive to get away from the glamorous aspects of investments and have a more utilitarian approach; i.e., don't get greedy! Jesse Livermore, the most famous speculator this country has ever produced, who started with nothing and made and lost his fortune several times over his lifetime before finally taking his own life, used to say that in order to be a successful investor, we have to learn to take our emotions out of investing. We have to learn to become the ultimate disciplinarian. Conquering our emotions is the key to success—at least in investments where emotions can get in the way of rational decision making.

At the end of the day, however, riches and all things material are only superficial; they cannot buy true happiness. Our investment strategies should be geared toward making us comfortable, not necessarily toward making us rich. If we approach investments with the idea of becoming rich, "the home run" mindset, we are setting ourselves up for failure. If we happen to make a lot of money by some stroke of luck and hard work, so be it. But let's not set out with that goal in mind. All too often we forget that prosperity is not just about our bank balances and our houses and cars. True prosperity comes from within. You can have all the toys in the world and still be the unhappiest person on earth.

So now that we have seen ways to increase your wealth, we will turn to the other important aspects of personal finance—those that are designed to protect that which we have built, those that will provide us with a temporary boost to our purchasing power, and those that will help us in our golden years. Recall the football analogy once again: "Offense wins games; defense wins championships."

Anecdote: The Circle of Life

A rich man once asked a Zen master to write something down that would encourage the prosperity of his family for years to come. It would be something that the family could cherish for generations. On a large piece of paper, the master wrote, "First, father dies, then son dies, then grandson dies." The rich man became angry when he saw the master's words. "I asked you to write something down that could bring happiness and prosperity to my family. Why do you give me such a depressing message?" The Zen master said, "Should your son die before you, it would bring you and your family unbearable grief. Should your grandson die before your son, it too would bring your family great sorrow. However, should your family, generation after generation, disappear in the order I have described, it will complete the true circle of life. And that is true happiness and prosperity."

Thought Questions

1. Do you believe analysts' recommendations have value? Why or why not?

2. What do you think are the long-term implications (if any) of Eliot Spitzer's actions on the brokerage industry?

3. In balance, do you think Reg FD has helped or hurt the common investor?

4. If you somehow knew (or suspected) that a stock you are interested in was about to split, how would it alter your investing decision?

5. What are the main arguments for and against banning insider trading? Do you agree with them?

6. Did Martha Stewart do anything wrong? What would you have done in her shoes?

7. Was Jonathan Lebed innocent or was he manipulating the market?

8. Can you think of other areas where people behave stealthily in order to disguise their true motives?

9. Under what conditions are you likely to invest in a stock that has just had a reverse stock split?

10. What is the relationship between the available liquidity of a stock and its relative tick size?

Notes

44. Womack, Kent, 1996. "Do Brokerage Analysts' Recommendations Have Investment Value?" *Journal of Finance* 54, pp. 137–157.

45. Anand, A., S. G. Badrinath, S. Chakravarty, and R. A. Wood, 2006. "Is It Prudent to Trade around Analyst Recommendation Changes? An Analysis of Transaction Costs." *Journal of Trading* 1, 22–37.

46. Agrawal, A., S. Chadha, and M. Chen, 2005. "Who Is Afraid of Reg FD? The Behavior and Performance of Sell Side Analysts Following the SEC's Fair Disclosure Rules." working paper, University of Alabama. http://papers.ssrn.com/sol3/papers.cfm?abstract_id=738685

47. Ikenberry, D. L., G. Rankine, and E. K. Stice, 1996. "What Do Stock Splits Really Signal?" *Journal of Financial and Quantitative Analysis* 31, 357–375.

48. Angel, J. J., 1997. "Tick Size, Share Prices and Stock Splits." *Journal of Finance* 52, 655–681.

49. Han, K. C., 1995. "The Effects of Reverse Stock Splits on the Liquidity of the Stock." *Journal of Financial and Quantitative Analysis* 30, 159–169.

50. Chakravarty, S., and McConnell, J. J., 1997. "An Analysis of Prices, Bid-Ask Spreads, and Bid and Ask Depths Surrounding Ivan Boesky's Illegal Trading in Carnation's Stock." *Financial Management* 26: 18–34.

51. Chakravarty, S., and McConnell, J. J., 1999. "Does Insider Trading Really Move Stock Prices?" *Journal of Financial and Quantitative Analysis* 34: 191–210.

52. Barclay, M. J., and J. Warner, 1993. "Stealth Trading and Volatility: Which Trades Move Prices?" *Journal of Financial Economics* 34, 281–305.

53. Chakravarty, S., 2001. "Stealth Trading: Which Traders' Trades Move Stock Prices?" *Journal of Financial Economics* 61, 289–307.

54. Anand, A., and S. Chakravarty, 2007. "Stealth Trading in Options Markets." *Journal of Financial and Quantitative Analysis* 42, 167–188.

55. Chakravarty, S., P. K. Jain, J. Upson, and R. A. Wood, 2009. Clean Sweep: Informed Trading through Intermarket Sweep Orders, working paper, University of Memphis.

Section A: Action Plan

Here is an action plan to put you on the road to financial health and freedom. The plan is not only for you. You should try to implement a similar plan for anyone in your family, or other loved ones, who would benefit.

1. Think about starting an investment account. People often make the mistake of thinking they need lots of money in order to start one but $500 is enough to get started. Go online to any one of the well-known brokerages like Schwab, TD Ameritrade, or Scottrade and open an account. It is very easy, quick, and you can accomplish everything online.

2. Once you are set up with an online account, begin investing with an index mutual fund or a sector ETF. Then, as you accumulate more wealth, think about a bond mutual fund and even a gold and precious metal ETF. Remember to have no more than 10 percent of your assets in precious metals.

3. Make it a habit to put away a few dollars every month in your investment account. It can be $50 or it can be more. The discipline of regularly putting money in your investment account is the important thing.

4. Get in the habit of reading newspapers like the *Wall Street Journal* or *Barron's* and try to interpret what the various world and national events may mean to your investment portfolio. You should think about and analyze question like: What does this particular event mean for my investment portfolio? What could I buy at this point to make my portfolio grow? Should I get in or out of bond funds? Should I have more gold-related investments in my portfolio?

SECTION B: CREDIT

9

Consumer Credit

What is a bank? It is nothing more than a bunch of loans. How safe are these loans?
--Mike Milken

It is fascinating to look back and realize how far we have come in our civilization. Thousands of years ago when we lived in caves, we simply threw rocks at whatever we wanted. There was no haggling over price and the notion of "one rock fits all" prevailed. We made a quantum leap in our development when we moved up to using bovines and poultry as currency to obtain our daily needs—like aftershave and milk. The problem with such a bulky medium of exchange was that people had to wear long baggy clothes to carry their chickens and cows in order to buy groceries at the local market. Sometimes the "money" would escape from one's pocket and bedlam would ensue. Those were chaotic times!

As we evolved over time, we started buying and selling with pieces of gold, silver, and copper. One needed smaller pockets to carry the money and so people started wearing light clothing with belts and boots. However, since hauling all this metal was still tough, people got into the habit of walking with a slight stoop. You see it in all the period paintings. The rich, however, made their flunkeys carry all the metal, and develop the stoop while the rich enjoyed a fun and "upright" lifestyle. Gradually, people moved to paper money which is easier to carry and transport in little bags we stick over our hind-quarters. Anthropologists opine that the particular location chosen to carry our wallets springs from our primitive instincts to save our posteriors from stray arrows. The interesting thing about paper currency is that paper by itself has no intrinsic value unlike a metal like gold. But as long as we can all agree that it is valuable, guess what, it is! The latest innovation in the evolution of currency is plastic. All the money now lives within plastic and we can "charge" stuff way beyond what we can afford or could afford to buy with cows and chickens. And credit cards are glittery with holograms and, as we all know, our basic instinct is to gravitate towards glittery stuff to pick up and bring home where we can all admire it just like birds. And nowhere is the desire for shiny and glittery stuff more acute than among our young. Just look at a teenager's glittery makeup and you will know what I mean. Credit card companies that issue these shiny pieces of plastic have figured it out too and have started giving away credit cards on America's college campuses.

Every fall semester when the weather is nice and crisp, they come in droves, set up in various parts of the college campuses, and sign up the young for more glittery

The NFL Draft and Credit

Even big NFL sports franchises use a form of credit to trade with one another in order to "draft up" for rookie talent coming out of the universities. Specifically, let us assume that a particular sports franchise has the twentieth pick in the draft. But they want a particular player who they know will help them build their team in the near future. However, there are other teams picking ahead who also want this particular athlete and our team knows that if they simply wait their turn to pick, they might as well kiss this athlete good bye. So what should they do?

Our team may call another team picking significantly ahead and get into a trade agreement with them. In return for surrendering that pick to our team, our team will surrender its second and third round picks to the other team and maybe even give up a couple of first round picks in the next two drafts down the road. A heavy price to pay for one talent who may, or may not, work out. A good example of this is the Indianapolis Colts who a few years ago traded their star running back, Marshall Faulk, to the St. Louis Rams. As it turns out, the Rams made out like bandits. Marshall gave them five years of great performance. The Colts got a couple of players in return who were gone within five years and a lot of experts questioned the benefit to the Colts of such a trade—although hindsight, as they say, is always 20/20.

plastic credit cards—which leads to a pet peeve of mine. All universities that allow credit card companies to sign up students on their campuses should rethink this policy—millions of dollars in scholarships and other monies that these companies are providing for the universities notwithstanding. Students are young and impressionable and credit card companies are shrewd and calculating. It's a volatile mix that can be lethal to students over the long term. More on this later.

Banking in a Different Culture

I grew up in a country where credit was shunned. If you had any debt, you had to walk down the street with your head covered in shame while kids and stray animals pointed at you and made debt jokes. In fact, growing up, we did not have credit cards; all transactions were in cash and a very few with checks. Some transactions even involved livestock and fierce animals.

My father would go to the bank every Monday morning. It was an event. He would bathe and put on a newly ironed shirt and say a prayer to the money gods. Next, he would carefully make a list of how much he would need for the week. Having made sure the timing was auspicious he would step out of the house. If I was lucky and had no school, I would get to accompany him.

Traditionally, banking in India is a leisurely business and does not get going until about noon. Before that, there is much heated discussion and debate about sports and current affairs. During cricket season (cricket is similar to baseball and is played in the commonwealth countries), game scores are analyzed in excruciating detail.

The bank itself was located in a high-ceilinged British colonial style building with large windows and ceiling fans that would creak and rotate ponderously, weighed down with age, dust and grime accumulated through the years. The hum and creaking of these fans nicely complemented the buzz of a teeming mass of humanity scurrying around—where to, I have no idea. It was like going to a social club and my dad would greet and exchange pleasantries with all the people he knew from the bank and neighbors and friends who were also there to withdraw, or deposit, money. A dozen or so chaprasis (waiters) would be bustling around in their dirty uniforms with funny caps carrying tea and snacks on trays to various rooms and cubicles around the large floor.

Through all this hustle and bustle, my father would methodically fill out the paperwork with his fountain pen and then turn it into one of the metal cages behind which most of the banking business would be carried out. Because there was so much cash involved in the day-to-day transactions of the bank, I suppose they did not want people to get ideas and try and rob the bank. To minimize temptation, a uniformed, mustachioed guard with a large ancient gun would stand watch at the front door. I used to wonder if the gun would actually work if someone did try and steal the money. Sadly, no one ever tried while I was present and my childish curiosity was unsatisfied.

After the withdrawal forms had been submitted to one of the cages on the floor, we would commence another round of waiting. The clerks would methodically enter the request for withdrawal in one of the large green bound leather ledgers. It was a time-consuming process and, after what seemed like an eternity, my dad's name would be called and a metal token with a number handed to him for the final round of operations. We would now move over to another section of the floor near a second set of metal cages where the actual financial transaction would occur. After about a half-hour of social chit-chatting, our number would finally be called and my dad and I would head to the metal cage where a lady in a colorful sari with long black shiny hair—perfumed, fragrant and glistening with flavored hair oil— would be seated, surrounded by stacks of currency.

I was not quite tall enough to see past the counters and metal bars of the cages but, standing on tiptoes, I could just see the teller's desk under the metal structure with a small opening for transactions. She would meticulously count out the money, frequently moistening her fingers on a sponge so as to be able to rifle quickly through the stack of bills. I was mesmerized by her deft fingers as she flicked through the pile of notes without missing a single one and knew to the last bill how much she had in her hand. Finally she had counted, and double-checked, the amount she needed to hand back to my father who would then himself carefully count through the notes to make sure he had received the correct amount before stepping back from the cage opening. There was a window of opportunity (no pun intended) of only a few seconds to spot any mistakes in the amount handed over, after which all transactions were final. Customer service was an alien concept. The banking operation itself, from arrival to departure, would take almost two hours.

Fast-Forward to the Present: Why Do We Need Credit?

There are several primary reasons for using credit. For one, you don't have to pay cash for large purchases. Economists call that "shifting consumption from the future to the present." Think of it as a fancy way of saying if we have too much fun now, we will have to pay for it later. The Roman Catholic priests in my high school kept telling me the same thing and I never believed it. Now I know they were only trying to warn me about credit and credit cards.

You can also use credit in financial emergencies. So, if you run out of sugar, for example, rather than knocking on your neighbor's door, you can simply charge the sugar. You can also use credit for investment purposes. For example, you could borrow money from your broker and buy stocks—a practice known as "buying on margin. "

If used properly, credit can be instrumental in helping you achieve your personal financial goals. But there is also pain involved because if you cannot repay your debt with interest your creditors can make your life a "sticky wicket," as the British are fond of saying. If you are not British, just take it from me that sticky wickets are not nice and may involve large men with sunglasses hounding you at work or wherever you live.

While credit can help you buy that house you have always wanted or that car you need so badly, there are certain things credit should not be routinely used for. Things like routine household expenses should not be met with credit. And if your favorite toy poodle, Mr. Peepers, is used to getting regular pedicures and daylong stays at the beauty parlor, try not to charge that. The underlying assumption is that you will not pay off your entire balance in full at the end of the month and such expenses will grow and eventually become unmanageable. For the same reason, impulse purchases using your credit cards should be kept to a minimum. Some will say even fancy restaurant meals should be paid in cash and not charged. Credit is such a convenient device that, like a drug addict or driving a fast car, unless you control your behavior, you can get hooked very easily and rapidly destroy your credit (among other things) through purchases that you can ill afford and for which you will pay a hefty price in the future.

To summarize, credit is a powerful tool but it should be used with caution, keeping in mind that whatever you borrow today will need to be paid back with interest in the near to intermediate future. Try to not get carried away!

Credit Use in the United States

We Americans have been using our credit cards more and more in the last twenty years. Credit cards have become a kind of status symbol as each of us vies with our friends and colleagues on the number, and color, of credit cards we carry in our wallets. If we have an American Express Black card, for example, it signals to our peers that we have arrived. In essence, we are rewarded for spending money (we need to be spending over $15,000 a month for over 3 years before we are eligible for the Black card). Furthermore, credit card companies have a special name for those of us who pay off our balances in full every month—i.e., do the right thing. We are referred to as "deadbeats." That, in a word, sums up the upside-down mentality of the credit card issuers.

According to the most recent publicly available version of the Survey of Consumer Finances, a comprehensive survey of the habits of American families compiled by the Federal Reserve every four years, over 66 percent of American households have a bank-issued credit card, compared to about 43 percent 20 years ago. A majority of the households with credit cards are not paying off their bills in full every month and are "credit revolvers." The credit card companies love these people because they get to make lots of money off revolvers. And the reported credit card debt appears to be sizable: The median outstanding credit card

Credit Card Commandment

If you are a deadbeat in the eyes of credit card companies, you are not interest rate, or fee, sensitive. You are more interested in the goodies a card can offer you like points towards a gift certificate at Barnes and Noble or frequent-flier miles.

If you are going to be a revolver, know what you are getting yourself into by way of interest rates and fees and be prepared to jump ship to a new card with an attractive introductory rate.

balance according to the survey is about $1,800. The median interest paid on credit cards by households is around 15 percent, which is far greater than the returns earned on investment assets by these families. Early on, the credit card companies figured out something really important. If the minimum monthly payments could be lowered to a small dollar amount, it would psychologically induce consumers to hold more debt on their credit card accounts. Boy, were they right!

Researchers have also shown a puzzling connection between a household's credit card debt and its liquid assets in low interest rate accounts, such as savings accounts, coexisting simultaneously. This is known as the "household debt paradox." While the obvious explanation of the paradox is irrational human behavior, ranking right alongside human's barking up trees and sniffing bushes, somehow it leaves us unsatisfied since irrationality can be used as a catchall for anything that does not look "normal." A rational economic explanation for the debt puzzle was needed. A study done by the Federal Reserve found that American credit card holders are actually aware of the rates on their credit cards. It is argued that households contemplating bankruptcy may run their tab up on unsecured debt but convert liquid assets into bankruptcy-exempt assets (like housing and automobiles) before declaring bankruptcy to shield them from repossession.

Yet another explanation of the existence of the debt puzzle lies with the notion that an individual's saving and consumption decisions, normally made simultaneously,

Caution

A lower mandatory monthly dollar payment equals more debt accumulating on your credit cards.

may not actually be simultaneous in the presence of credit cards. If the saving decision and the consumption decision are made by different individuals of the household (say the savings decision is made by the wife while the husband uses the credit limit afforded by the credit cards to decide how much to consume), then credit card (i.e., high interest rate) debt and (low interest rate) asset accounts could easily coexist.

Critical Info: Who Are the Credit Revolvers?

Studies show that bank-issued credit cards are more likely to be held by married and highly educated households with higher incomes. The heads of these households are likely to be either less than 35 or above 65 years old. By contrast, younger and less educated households with lower incomes are less likely to hold credit cards—although a higher percentage of those who do have credit cards are likely to use them for revolving credit.

Is All Credit Created Equal?

One type of credit is Open Account Credit where credit is extended to the borrower in advance of any transaction. Each borrower has a maximum amount she can borrow, also known as the credit limit. Usually interest on the amount borrowed (or charged) can be avoided by paying back the full amount charged at the end of each billing cycle. Credit cards work this way and it's something most of us are familiar with. Usually banks issue these credit cards, and the line of credit extended depends on the applicant's financial status and his ability to pay. Other features that come with credit cards include cash advances (not a good deal because of the high interest rates), and other services or rebates we may get for flying certain airlines or patronizing certain restaurants or shopping in certain stores.

The advantages of credit cards include a short-term interest free loan (this is what we get for paying off our entire balance at the end of each billing cycle and being called deadbeats), and simplified record keeping where you get monthly statements with your charges neatly categorized into categories like gas/automotive, payments and credits, home improvement, restaurants, merchandise/retail, and services. Additionally, suppose we buy an item from a questionable source, want to return it but can't get through to the merchant's toll-free phone line, and can't get a refund for our purchase. All we have to do is call the credit card dispute line. They will take up the dispute on our behalf and give us credit for the merchandise until the dispute is resolved. Chances are that it will be resolved in our favor since most of these questionable merchants back down when faced with the credit card company's legal arm.

Recently, due to intense competition among the various credit card companies for essentially the same pool of potential card holders, credit cards have increasingly been reinvented as a multipurpose tool designed to help out the card holder in a number of different areas of his life—sort of like a one-stop shop. In fact, competition has gotten so bad lately, I would not be surprised if they started offering cash incentives to consumers to switch from one card to another—kind of like the long distance telephone battles that AT&T, Sprint, and MCI fought with each other in the late nineties.

With so many advantages associated with credit cards, there are bound to be some serious disadvantages, right? There are. For one, such a convenience is, in itself, a disadvantage because it can lead to serious overspending. And if you have a compulsive personality, a credit card could lead

Caution

Here's a general rule of thumb for the use of credit: The product purchased should outlive the credit payments! If you think that is not likely to be the case with a particular item, do not charge it and, even if you do, pay it off before the item gets outdated.

to serious spending-related problems. You can, for example, find yourself maxed out on your credit limit when the credit card company suddenly does a "Dr. Jekyll-Mr. Hyde" switch and comes after you with all their legal might. You get reported to the credit bureaus (thereby badly damaging your ability to get further loans from banks and other financial institutions), and you have your credit card charges to pay off which keep growing exponentially due to the high interest rates triggered by what is called the default interest rate which runs about 34 percent—not to mention other penalties.

Let's start by asking a question. What do you think lenders are looking for when they are trying to decide whether to give you money? The simple answer: whether you will be able to pay it back complete with interest.

That's all there is to it. So anything you can do to enhance potential lenders' confidence in your ability to pay their money back (with interest of course), the greater are your chances of getting the loan. What do they look for specifically? They want to know how you have done with past loans, or your credit history. But what if you have no credit history? Get one and get one quickly. How? One relatively easy way is to take out a loan secured by money in your savings account and pay it back over the course of the next 12–18 months, making sure you make every payment on time. This will build your credit profile and ensure you get other loans that you really need, under favorable terms. I can personally verify this method works because I did it myself fresh out of college when no respectable lender would touch me otherwise.

> ## Fun Fax: David Bowie and Credit
>
> Did you know that rock star, David Bowie, opened his own online bank in 2000 known as Bowiebanc.com? It was the Internet's first private label bank. Customers of Bowiebanc.com were issued checks and bankcards bearing the superstar's image. It gave him a platform to market his music directly to his fans and cut out the fat cat music distributors in the middle. Although a novel concept, the bank was soon saddled with growing debt and fell out of favor with the Federal Reserve (America's Central Bank). It closed soon after.

How Lenders Use Your Credit Score

With every sport we play or watch, there is a score. The final score decides who wins and who loses. The goal with sports is to have the winning score at the end. That signals to you and the world that you won.

It's the same way with life and, in particular, with credit. There is a score known as the credit score. The goal in the game of life is to have the highest possible credit score at all times. That signals to potential lenders that you are a winner and opens many doors for you. Have you ever wondered what exactly is going through a potential lender's head when he is deciding whether or not to give you that money?

Very simply, the lender wants to know if he lent money to 100 or 1,000 or 10,000 borrowers with a certain set of characteristics, would 90 percent, 95 percent, or 99 percent repay. It's basically a statistical calculation and the kind of thinking that lies behind the creation of the credit score.

The Credit Report: Make Sure You Know Its Contents

The contents of your credit report, which determines your credit score, affects more than your financial life. It could affect your education, career, and even your love life. That's because your credit report is used by not only lenders but also by insurers, potential employers, and even some educational institutions.

The report affects the rates you'll pay on everything from life insurance to homeowner's insurance. It may tell a college if you're a good risk for some student financial assistance programs. If you're applying for a job, your credit report may be checked as a character reference. And couples planning to apply jointly for mortgages may face a rude relationship shock if one partner has kept his or her past credit problems a secret.

Three major credit reporting bureaus keep track of the credit reports of millions of Americans:

- Equifax: www.equifax.com
- Experian: www.experian.com
- TransUnion: www.tuc.com

Typically, all have the same information, except that some companies are stronger in certain geographic areas and thus may receive reports on your credit status from local merchants. So, in reality, the three companies may end up having different subsets of your credit profile, sometimes with very different conclusions.

Overall, the guts of a credit report is made up of the four sections shown in this graphic.

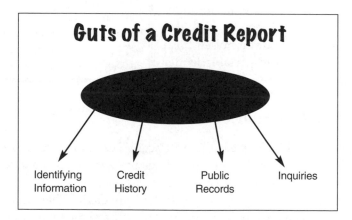

The Identifying Information section provides information to identify you. You need to examine this section to ensure that it is accurate. It will not be unusual to see two or more ways to spell your name or more than one Social Security number if you have had them or used multiple spellings of your name in the past. Other information in this section will include your current and previous addresses, date of birth, telephone numbers, driver's license numbers, your employer and your spouse's name.

Under the Credit History section, each credit account you have had will be listed, including the creditor's name and a scrambled version of the account number for security reasons. If you have multiple accounts with a creditor, those will be listed too. For each account, you will see when you opened the account, the kind of credit it is (such as mortgage or a car loan, or a revolving loan like department store credit), whether the account is in your name or jointly held, the total amount of the loan, the highest balance on the card, how much of the loan you still owe, the fixed monthly payments, the status of the account (whether it is open, inactive, closed, paid, etc.), and most importantly, how well you have serviced the account. In the report from Experian, for example, the latter is expressed in terms simple to understand, such as "never pays late," or "typically pays 30 days late." If the account is sent for internal collection or charged off as a bad loan, it will be indicated too. Reports from other credit bureaus usually use payment codes ranging from 1 to 9, where 1 indicates good payment history and 9 indicates the worst.

The Public Records section is one you want to show up as blank. Anything here is bad news. It typically lists financial data like bankruptcies, judgments and tax liens.

Finally, the fourth section is Inquiries. This section lists everyone who has asked to see your report. If you call the credit bureau and ask to see your own file it will be listed there too. Inquiries are divided into two sections: Hard inquiries and soft inquiries. Hard inquiries are the ones you initiate by filling out a loan application form or by actions such as visiting the doctor's office or a dentist or an optometrist, etc. Soft inquiries are from companies that want to send out promotional materials to a pre-qualified group of people or current creditors monitoring your account to determine if your perceived risk has increased (or decreased). It is the soft inquiries that show up on reports released to consumers. You may have heard that too many inquiries into your account could have a negative impact on your credit score. This is not totally accurate! The fact of the matter is that the vast majority of inquiries are ignored by the FICO credit scoring model. Thus, for example, the FICO scores have around a 30-day buffer where auto and mortgage inquiries are not counted. The model also counts two or more hard inquiries over a given 14-day window as only one inquiry. So, you could have thirty such inquiries over this period, the model will only count one for the purposes of determining your credit score.

Understand that your score is not being generated every day of your life. Rather, your credit report and, by extension, your credit score, is not generated until someone—either an authorized user like a credit-granting merchant or you—requests a look at it. Then the computer pulls together all this information, along with the credit bureau's explanation of its system.

If you see incorrect information on your credit report— such as an account that was closed in bad standing or one you never opened—you should contact the merchant immediately, as well as the credit bureau. By some estimates, as many as 80 percent of all credit reports have errors. A vast majority are, however, innocuous and do not affect anything in any significant way. For the more serious errors, realize that only the initiating merchant can make the correction. But you can initiate a dispute with the merchant by contacting the credit bureau. They'll contact the merchant to expedite a resolution to your problem. The merchant then has thirty days to respond. If you've been the victim of "identity theft"—someone has used your name and Social Security number to open accounts—the credit bureau will "flag" your name and stop new accounts from being opened.

If, after investigation, you still dispute an item on your credit report, you have the right to post a short explanatory statement that will be sent to anyone requesting the report. You can do this online or by mail. It's better to resolve disputes directly with the merchant instead of letting bills go unpaid, which could really ruin your credit.

Most negative information stays on your credit report for seven years; a bankruptcy (and related information) stays for ten years. But lenders often take an interest in your most recent payment patterns. Hence, even after a bankruptcy, if you can get a secured credit card (backed up by, say, a savings deposit at the issuing institution) and make regular and on-time payments, you can rebuild your credit without waiting seven or ten years. Furthermore, in today's competitive environment, in an effort to gain new customers, credit card companies are increasingly willing to give credit cards to people with questionable pasts. So, take heart!

How Do You Score?

The sometimes sad truth is that you are judged by the all important number generated from the information in your credit report: your credit score. For years, this number was a highly guarded secret. Now, however, the veil of secrecy is being lifted—in part due to considerable prodding by consumer groups and by Congress. Fair, Isaac & Co., the California company that originally developed the original credit score, is working with Equifax to make the data available.

Fair, Isaac & Co. created the FICO scores to help lenders gauge the likelihood of a loan being repaid. Over the past 25 years, the scoring process has become so sophisticated that at least 75 percent of all mortgage lending approvals are based in part on a FICO score. But while your credit report is a fairly straightforward compilation of your payment history on all credit accounts, the FICO score is a complicated algorithm—or, computerized model—that evaluates many factors from your credit report in different weighting combinations.

Critical Info

FICO scores consider five main categories for scoring purposes: Payment History has about a 35 percent weight; Length of Payment History gets a 15 percent weight; Amounts Owed gets 30 percent; New Credit gets 10 percent; and Types of Credit gets the remaining 10 percent.

Thus, your credit score could be exactly the same as your neighbor's but for completely different reasons. And that credit score is only one of the factors considered when granting a loan. For example, two people with the same credit score might apply for a mortgage with the same lender. One applicant has a 20 percent down payment, while the other is planning to put only 10 percent down. Or, one is applying for a jumbo mortgage, while the other needs only a $150,000 loan. Those additional factors will also affect the credit decision.

The availability of FICO scores to consumers, along with online credit reports, means you have new ways to check on your financial status—and to protect (or improve) it. But first you must understand these reports, along with your rights and your ability to affect the information in them.

While your credit report is a direct reflection of your financial activities, your credit score is, as we've said, a complicated analysis of the patterns of your financial life. All of the information used to create your FICO score is drawn from your credit report.

One important thing to understand is that your credit score changes relatively infrequently and checking your credit score about once a year is more than sufficient for most people. With regard to payment history carrying the most weight in determining your credit score, here is the most important message:

Pay Your Bills on Time!

Any negative statements associated with your bill payment screw-ups will show up in your credit report for about seven and one-half years. But, given that you have already messed up, your most recent mess-up in the bill payment department carries more weight than an indiscretion a few years ago. If you fumbled the credit-ball but have been on good behavior since then, your scores will likely go up. And, if you cannot make payments, make sure you talk to your creditors. Don't just leave town, change your phone number and hope that it will all go away. It won't! Negotiating with creditors will improve your scores in the long run if you are able to even partially remedy the situation.

Length of credit history is important and, if you have to close credit accounts you may not be using, be sure you close the more recently opened accounts first. But here is the interesting conundrum on having lots of open accounts in good standing that you may not be using. While closing some of them will lead to a reduction in your credit score, closing them may be a precondition to your qualifying for a mortgage or a car loan from a bank because an open account, even if unused, reflects your debt and raises your debt-to-equity ratio. Hence, closing these accounts improves your ratio which improves your chances of getting these loans—but lowers your scores too!

> ## Credit Conundrum
>
> When you close your unused credit card accounts, you are lowering your credit used to credit available ratio which could lower your credit score in the short run. But it also increases your chances of getting the loan you really need in the future.

In terms of amount owed, carrying a large balance on your credit cards does not mean a low score necessarily as long as these accounts are in good standing. But it certainly implies an increased risk of loan default and may give pause to loan officers to extend further credit to you—which may stymie your desire to get that new giant plasma TV. The bottom line is that not all your actions will increase your scores and make you attractive to loan officers at the same time. Sometimes you may have to lower your scores in order to be an attractive loan recipient.

What determines how much credit is too much for you? Closing a lot of credit accounts with zero balances and in good standing will not raise your credit score but your credit scores do take into account how much you owe on installment loans (secured) versus credit card loans (unsecured).

Also, how much of your available credit is being used by you is important too. The consensus seems to be that about 50 percent of available credit should be the target usage. That is why it may not be a good idea to close unused credit accounts in order to increase your scores because it may lead to exactly the opposite effect since your debt-to-credit ratio will increase. However, as I have said above, not closing some of these accounts might stand in the way of your getting some of the attractive loans that you may really want. So, closing unused credit accounts is really a double-edged sword. The damage was already done when you agreed to too many credit accounts in the first place!

You should pay down all revolving credit rather than transferring balances. That is the most effective way to increase your credit score. While closing unused credit accounts will not increase your score, opening a number of new credit cards just to increase your available credit is not a good idea either.

Critical Info

FICO credit scores range from 300 to 850. The median FICO score in the U.S. is about 723. Only about 11 percent of the surveyed population rank above 800; about 20 percent of the population rank between 740 and 780. If your score is below 620, you are in the bottom 20 percent of the population. Get help, ASAP!

New credit accounts for a 10 percent weight in computing your credit score and remember, if you are shopping around for a loan, many inquiries for your credit file will not necessarily decrease your credit score since many inquiries for similar loans made over a two-week period will be counted as a single inquiry. And all such inquiries made within a two-year period remain in your file, although the last twelve months are the most critical. Requesting your own file does not constitute an inquiry.

Types of credit in use also have a 10 percent of the weight and usually includes loans from retailers, finance companies, installment loans, and loans like mortgage and auto loans. While the mix is not that important (as demonstrated by the small weight) under normal circumstances, sometimes in the absence of other relevant information it may take on a whole new dimension.

Finally, these days all three credit rating agencies also compute their own scores which are different from the FICO scores. Why the difference? Turns out that different companies have different information available about you which affect the scores differently. But most lenders look at all three scores and take the middle score (median) as representative.

Another way to think about FICO scores is to look back and think about how your SAT scores affected your college admission and possibly the direction of your future career. Your FICO scores will affect your financial future in much the same way. Score high and the sky is your limit. You can get credit at competitive rates; score low and you may not get that credit and, even if you do, it will be at higher rates or come with many strings attached. So be very careful with how you approach your FICO scores and make sure that you have the winning mentality as if you were playing a sport.

Credit Score Computation Is Top Secret

Even though we know the categories and the overall weights of each category as discussed above, the exact formula employed by FICO is a closely guarded secret. Can you guess why? If we all knew the exact formula, we could take every good (or bad) debt, plug it in the formula and calculate exactly what it would do to our credit score. We would know exactly what to do to make ourselves look good in the eyes of potential lenders and, more importantly, do only as much as it takes to satisfy potential lenders, and no more. This practice is called "gaming the system." If, on the other hand, the exact formula is unknown, or known only in general terms, then we have an incentive to work over and beyond what we may have normally done. In fact, in contract theory, there is research suggesting that relatively vague contracting terms will actually elicit extra effort on the part of one, or both, parties. The same applies to the process of tenure, which all academics have to go through. Exact criteria for tenure are never fully disclosed. Instead, all tenure-track faculty are given general guidelines within which to prove their "tenure-worthiness."

Even though we do not know how to compute our exact score, some things are quite obvious. A high income earns more points than a low income. Fewer credit cards are better than several cards. Paying on time is a must. Also, the more your profile resembles people who pay their bills on time, the more likely it is that the computer will approve your application for credit.

Some of the things that weigh heavily on a good credit rating are stability—both at home and on the job—and a good payment history. The scoring system looks at how close you are to the limits on your cards, what you spend money on, and how much you ask for in cash advances. Pay attention, but don't despair. No matter how bad it looks, there are ways you can rebuild your credit and improve your score.

The Invasion of the Credit Cards

Gone are the days when you had a vanilla credit card with an annual fee that allowed you to buy things on credit. These days, credit cards are a competitive business and companies are fighting over the same segment of the population and hell-bent on stealing customers from each other. We consumers are the net beneficiaries as long as we watch those credit potholes and traps that the credit companies have laid out for us. It's like an obstacle course: You have to delicately dance around the edges to avoid falling into the black hole of hidden charges and stratospheric interest rates.

Credit card companies have gotten smarter and wilier over the years. They will lure you in with promises of 0 percent rates, etc., but buried in fine print somewhere in the back of your agreement form are the details on what will trigger the default interest rate (to the tune of 30–35 percent) if your "perceived" credit risk goes up. And, silly as it may sound, the zero interest rate can go away just like that with something as simple as your inquiring about a car loan for a car you are considering purchasing. Note that you don't even have to buy the car; mere inquiry is sufficient for them to conclude you are a higher risk and trip the default rate. And with everything being online and interconnected these days, credit card companies can easily mine the data from the credit bureaus and keep track of everything you are doing and use it to ratchet up your rates at every opportunity. Keep track of good deals with credit cards at certain Web sites, such as http://cardweb.com or http://CreditCards.com and don't be afraid of changing cards as often as you can in order to take advantage of deals. It's like a fencing match. You and the credit card companies are engaged in delicate parrying and you should not hesitate to dump one company for another for the right terms. They will never show you mercy and neither should you. It's the kill-or-be-killed jungle mentality.

And what if you have bad credit? Don't worry; there is hope for you too. Here is an example of a secured credit card that will help you build your credit profile so that in time you can re-qualify for the regular unsecured credit cards. There are others too, so don't stop looking.

Today there are easily more than one billion cards in circulation—four for every man, woman, and child—with the average cardholder carrying a $6,000 balance from month to month and paying about 17.8 percent in interest to do so.[55] And, what if you wanted to end the flood of prescreened credit card offers? The three main

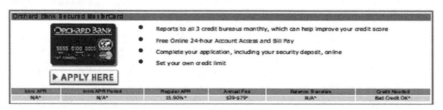

Figure 15: Orchard Bank Secured MasterCard

XXXX Bank Platinum MasterCard: Salient Features

Card benefits include the following: No up-front fees. Platinum benefits include purchase protection. Strengthen your credit reports to all 3 credit bureaus monthly, which can help improve your credit score. Low annual fee of $39–$59. No processing or application fee.

Card Details: Variable purchase APR as low as 10.65%. Online services for account management and payment 24 hours a day. Note! This is not a secured credit card. If you are not approved for the XXXX Bank Platinum MasterCard you may be offered other XXXX Bank Credit Cards with different fee and rate structures.

Application Requirements: In order to apply for a credit card, you must be at least of legal age in the state of your residence, your annual salary must be at least $12,000 (for an unsecured card), you must have a telephone in your residence, reside in the United States, and have a valid Social Security number. Credit approval will be determined upon review of a current credit bureau report and other information bearing on your creditworthiness.

credit bureaus in the United States have established a system so that consumers may remove themselves from all prescreened credit offer lists via notification to any of these three bureaus. Removal from these lists is effective for two years after the request is made. The credit bureaus each have extensive Web sites which explain marketing list opt-outs and how to request them. Unfortunately, you cannot opt out online—at least, not yet.

Thanks to amendments to the Fair Credit Reporting Act which went into effect September 30, 1997, there are steps consumers can take to avoid fraudulent reports and damaged credit ratings. The amended Fair Credit Reporting Act shifts responsibility to retailers and lenders who provide credit information to credit bureaus to ensure that the information they provide is accurate. Also, you have the right to see your credit report to make sure it is complete and correct—your report is no longer the hazy record it has been in the past.

> ## Wait for the Right Card
>
> Watch out for those outrageous annual fees and low-interest rate offers that last less than 6 months. It's only a matter of days before the right offer comes along—one with no annual fee and at least a 25-day grace period. As my mother is fond of saying in her broken English, "plenty fish in sea!"

New Rules to Increase the Minimum Payments on Your Credit Card Balance

Early in the genesis of credit cards, someone had the bright idea of making the minimum required payments on their credit card bills a very low amount (2 percent of their outstanding balance) in order to encourage Americans to use their credit cards more by making it seem like their payments were manageable. Of course, this ploy worked beyond anyone's wildest imaginations as millions of Americans embraced this seemingly affordable source of credit with both arms and racked up ever increasing quantities of debt. Customers' minimum payments were often less than the finance charges for that month which meant they would be paying off their credit card bills deep in the future, even beyond the useful life of the appliance or gadget they were charging in the first place. These were the favored customers for the credit card companies (as opposed to the "deadbeats" who paid off their entire balance at the end of the month); the credit card companies made money hand over fist and

Critical Info

As far as being inundated with unsolicited offers, Amendment Section 604, § 1681e of the FCRA, "Election of Consumer to Be Excluded from Lists," has been a godsend. Under this amendment: "A consumer may elect to have the consumer's name and address excluded from any list provided by a consumer reporting agency . . . in connection with a credit or insurance transaction that is not initiated by the consumer by notifying the agency...that the consumer does not consent to any use of a consumer report relating to the consumer in connection with any credit or insurance transaction that is not initiated by the consumer. . . . Each consumer reporting agency that compiles and maintains files on consumers on a nationwide basis shall establish and maintain a notification system...jointly with other such consumer reporting agencies."

everyone was happy—for a while. Then the government started getting concerned. The credit card companies were increasingly focusing their attention on the high-risk segment of society, often the most vulnerable and least educated, about what they should, or should not, be doing. Why would this worry the regulators? Regulators were concerned that banks, by focusing solely on high-risk borrowers, would be faced with a situation where such people would be unable to make the payments resulting in a surge of defaults as people lined up to file for bankruptcy; and banks would eventually end up having a higher than normal charge-off (this is when a loan is written off as a bad loan) which would hurt the economy overall.

So, the government decided to enforce an advisory passed a few years ago forcing banks to clean up their underperforming loan portfolios of people making only the minimum payment or less. Overall, the Comptroller of Currency has begun enforcing the advisory in order to prevent people from getting too deep in the hole. Specifically, they are increasing the minimum payments from 2 percent to 4 percent of all outstanding balances and also enforcing the requirement for all late fees to be paid off at the month of occurrence. Unfortunately, while this will force banks to tow the line (a good thing), it will also hurt the segment of the population that is already in credit trouble (a bad thing). At the end of the day, it is the people who can least afford to pay who will be squeezed the most.

Credit Factoid

It used to be the case that the credit card companies wanted you, the user, to charge big ticket items on their credit cards, like airplane tickets, appliances, etc. Now the trend is to have you put all your small expense items on your credit cards. So when you go to McDonald's, for example, you can pay for your $2.99 burger with your credit card. A market research firm estimates that such small payments ("micro payments" as they are called) will grow beyond $11 billion within the U.S. in the next 2–3 years.

Pay One Bill Late, Get Punished by All: Universal Default

You have to hand it to the credit card companies. They are always thinking of new ways to outwit consumers and make more money for themselves. It is this same entrepreneurial spirit that made America great. The latest in this series of creative ways to make money is called "universal default. " More than a third of the major credit card issuers now appear to act on this clause. If you miss a payment—any payment, then your interest rate on that card and ALL OTHER CARDS YOU CARRY could go up two to three times their respective regular rates. What is scary is that the late payment could occur over a small amount like a $10 Blockbuster video rental charge and your credit card rates, all of them, could jump to about 30–35 percent. Your universal default rates could go into effect if you applied for a loan for a car. If you happen to be a deadbeat in the credit card world, of course, you may not care so much. But if you happen to be a revolver of credit, such increases can really apply the hammer on your financial freedom.

What can you do? The obvious solution is to make sure your credit card does not carry the universal default provision. If it does, it may be time to switch to a new

card. Go to Web sites like cardweb.com and find another card without such a provision. Above all, try not to be late with your bill payments. Use a bill payment service to ensure timely payments. Caveat Emptor!

Eleven Ways to Repair Credit and Pay Back Credit Card Debt

You can be in denial all you want and you can even pretend to be a baby kanga-
roo sticking your head in the sand (or are those baby ostriches?), but you won't be
able to make your debt go away. The bad credit you have gotten yourself into will
not erase itself.

It will take initiative on your part. The longer you stay curled up in a fetal position in the middle of the living room floor, the quicker it will grow and become your
personal *Little Shop of Horrors* by costing you about 30-plus percent compounded
monthly, month-in and month-out. You can't wish, or pray, it away. But you can pay
it down with determination and the good graces of a few wealthy (and/or gullible)
relatives. Here are some relatively achiev-
able ways to repair your damaged credit
and get out of debt:

1. Lock your cards away. As with a drug
   habit, you first need to take away the
   source of the problem. But do not close
   all your credit accounts. If your credit
   rating has taken a nosedive you may
   need a couple of those credit cards—to
   be used judiciously, of course. However,
   if self-control is a problem for you, it

> **Important Credit Tip**
>
> If you know that you will be a revolver of cred-
> it and, hence, sensitive to the interest rates
> charged on your account, read ALL OF THE
> FINE PRINT, when you sign up for a credit
> card. Never forget that when you sign up for
> one, you are entering a legally binding and
> enforceable contract. So, know what you are
> getting into!

   might be necessary to get rid of the cards altogether. That is a case-by-case decision. Just put them away for the moment while you figure things out.

2. Budget in order to figure out where you stand. I know you hate budgets and
   planning. I do too. But, like medicines that don't taste good, sometimes they are
   exactly what we need. Behavioral researchers tell us that often it is not that we
   don't know what is good for us, but we have a mental block about doing it—particularly if we know what is staring us in the face. But you need to see the cold
   hard facts on paper before planning your battle. It's the same as people going on
   diets. You have to know your starting point in order to chart your destination.

3. Pay more than the minimum. Break the habit of only paying the minimum
   required each month because paying the minimum (4 percent of the outstanding
   balance these days) only prolongs the agony. And it plays right into their hands
   since you pay huge amounts in fees.[57] If your minimum payment is $60, try to
   double that to $120 or more. Borrow from friends or loved ones if you need to.
   Examine your normal expenses. You may be able to squeeze out the extra payments by cutting corners elsewhere. For example, stop going out to lunch everyday; bring it from home instead. Eliminate those trips to Starbucks. Give up

happy hour. Those increased payments will save you hundreds, if not thousands, in interest payments and enable you to get out of the hole you have dug for yourself sooner.

4. Move your balances to a lower-interest card. Examine all your credit cards to find the one with the lowest interest rate. If you have a card or cards with zero introductory rates for six months (say), switch your balance to that card if you have to, and watch for other similar deals to move to when the original welcome mat wears out. Remember the eyeball on the dollar bill? Use your eyeballs to find these deals.

5. Cash in your savings account. You could use the cash in your savings and investments for debt repayment. Think about it in terms of economics 101. Since your credit card is charging you 30 percent interest, you will have to be earning a sensational 45-plus percent return on your savings/investment account before taxes to keep it going in the face of such huge drainage. Close the latter to pay down the former. Don't fall into the trap of the household debt paradox—low interest earning accounts co-existing with high interest rate debt—discussed earlier. It's as simple as that!

6. Borrow against your life insurance. Do you have life insurance that has a cash value? If so, you may want to consider borrowing against the policy. The interest rate is around secured interest rates (well below credit card interest rates), and you can take your time repaying the loan. You may want to repay it, however. If you happen to die before it's repaid, the outstanding balance plus interest will be deducted from the face value of the policy payable to the beneficiary.

7. See if you can get a home-equity loan. Do you own your own home and have equity that's accumulated through the years as you've paid off the mortgage? If so, now is the time to consider a home equity (HEL) line of credit for the maximum amount you can get to pay off your credit card balance. A HEL enables you to kill two birds with one stone. First, you use the loan proceeds to pay down your debt, thus trading something like a 25 percent loan for a 6 percent loan. Second, most homeowners itemize on their income tax returns. HEL interest in most circumstances is a tax deductible item. In a 28 percent marginal tax bracket that means the 6 percent loan really has an effective rate of 4.3 percent, and that is probably the cheapest interest rate you'll ever see on personal indebtedness.[58]

8. Look into borrowing from your 401(k). Do you participate in a 401(k) qualified retirement plan at work? Most 401(k) plans have a loan feature that lets you borrow up to 50 percent of the account's value or $50,000, whichever is smaller. Interest rates usually are a point or two above prime, which usually makes them significantly cheaper than those found on credit cards. Thus, 401(k) plan loans may be a smart solution to debt repayment. Not only is the interest typically much lower than that on credit cards, the best part is you pay it to yourself. Every dime in interest paid on a 401(k) loan goes directly into the borrower's

401(k) account, not into the lender's which further acts to your benefit.[59]

9. Renegotiate the terms of your loan with your creditors. Tell them you've done all you can. Savings are gone, all your friends have abandoned you, relatives are threatening to take you to court, you are living out of a box, and you have no 401(k) to borrow against. Remember Eddie Murphy living out of a box in *Trading Places*? What do you do now? How about threatening bankruptcy? Let your creditors know your situation. Tell them that if you are unable to renegotiate terms, you may have no other recourse but to declare bankruptcy. Ask for a new and lower repayment schedule, request a lower interest rate, and appeal to their desire to receive payment. Faced with the prospect that you may resort to such a drastic step (game theorists call this a "credible threat") creditors will do what they can to protect themselves against a total loss. Indeed, many will negotiate away the

> ## Loan Flipping
>
> Loan flipping is one way of managing excessive debt where the debt-burdened moves the loan balance from a higher interest-bearing account to a lower introductory rate and then repeats the strategy after the introductory rate expires. A lot of young people burdened with excessive debt appear to have become quite proficient at flipping and moving from one introductory card rate to another and managing their debt.
>
> Flipping can also take the form of a mortgage broker repeatedly refinancing a mortgage loan on behalf of a client within a short period of time with little or no tangible net benefit to the client (borrower). Mortgage brokers and lenders who flip loans tend to charge high origination fees with each successive refinancing, and may charge these fees based on the entire amount of the new loan (not on the loan differential through flipping). Each refinancing may also trigger prepayment penalties, which could be financed as part of the total loan amount, adding to the borrower's debt burden.

proverbial farm before they write off your debt. It is certainly worth a shot. And if you don't wish to do this yourself, there are organizations that can do it for you. Nonprofit organizations like the Consumer Credit Counseling Services (CCCS), funded by the credit card issuers, exist in all major cities in the United States. Take advantage of them, if necessary.

10. Add pertinent information to your credit file. True to the "dog that did not bark" syndrome, your credit report could be damaging to you as much by the information that is omitted as by the negative information that is found there. You are entitled to add information presenting your side of the dispute if you feel this will help you with potential lenders who will be reading your file. Regulations permit you to write a letter of up to one hundred words regarding any credit dispute and the agency must provide this information to any creditors who ask for your report.

11. If all else fails, file for bankruptcy. If you decide you can't pay down your debt using any of the methods listed above, the absolute last resort is bankruptcy. However, there are significant drawbacks to using this avenue of relief. Apart from the fact that bankruptcy filing (especially under Chapter 7) has become considerably more difficult (see later in this chapter), and the fact that filing for

bankruptcy costs money that you don't have (anywhere from $1,500 to $3,000), your credit record will contain this information for ten years, thus ensuring that you will have a tough time obtaining affordable credit during that period. But lenders know that you cannot file for another bankruptcy until seven years have passed and they are not so worried about your pulling the same stunt twice. So, in a perverse way, you become a better credit risk.

Bankruptcy (as a Way Out of Debt) May Have Just Gotten Harder!

In March of 2005, the Republican-controlled Senate, sidestepping a flurry of last minute Democratic challenges, passed a bill that would require more people who file for personal bankruptcy protection to be responsible for repaying a part of their debts. President George W. Bush quickly signed the bill into law. Before passage of this bill, it was the job of a Federal bankruptcy court judge to determine if people had to pay all, or part, of their debts. Under the new law, low income people and those with few assets can still file under Chapter 7 and, if approved by the judge, can still wipe their debt slates clean after certain assets are surrendered. However, the crucial difference lies in Chapter 7 filers with incomes higher than their particular state's median income, and who can pay at least $6,000 over five years. They will now be forced to file under Chapter 13 where a judge has more discretion in deciding on a payment plan to partially pay off an individual's debts. Filers would also be required to pay for credit counseling six months before actually filing for bankruptcy. And certain types of debts like child support, alimony, student loans, and taxes will not be wiped out under any circumstances. It is estimated that between 4 and 20 percent of those who would normally (i.e., before passage of the law) be eligible to file under Chapter 7 would be disqualified under the new law.

Not surprisingly, supporters of this law include credit card companies, banks, and other retailers who have long been financially hurt by fiscally irresponsible clients who go on a spending spree and then conveniently seek bankruptcy protection as a way to get out of debt.

Critical Info

Negative information can be maintained on your report for seven years; bankruptcies, for ten years. But many creditors weigh new information more heavily.

It is clear what the arguments by the proponents and the opponents of the law are likely to be. The proponents will argue that this law will ameliorate the loophole used by deadbeat dads, compulsive shoppers and wealthy individuals who use the system to their advantage while opponents will point to the fact that middle to low income workers, single mothers, minorities and the elderly who may have lost their jobs or have huge medical bills, will have the safety net yanked from under them. Unfortunately, no solution is universally acceptable to all constituents and this law is but one example.

The Look-Alikes: Debit Cards

They look like credit cards, taste like credit cards, and they even have the little logo for either Visa or MasterCard on them for good measure. But, repeat after me: All cards that say Visa or MasterCard aren't always "credit" cards. Debit cards and secured credit cards look just like conventional credit cards, but they work very differently. Okay, you can stop repeating after me now.

Debit cards withdraw money directly from your checking account. When you use a debit card, you are paying with cash. Using a debit card can keep you within your means, provided you don't accidentally spend your rent on bar tabs and related goodies.

Bankruptcy Filing Statistics

In 2005, about 1 out of every 60 households filed for bankruptcy protection in the U.S. In terms of states, Indiana tops the list at 2.9 families filing for every 100 households, followed by Ohio at 2.69 families, and Utah at 2.53 families. At the other end of the spectrum, South Carolina has the lowest individual bankruptcy filings at 0.81 families filing per 100 households, followed by Alaska, Vermont, District of Columbia and Hawaii.

Source: "Bankruptcy Filings Soaring Again." MSN Money

But be aware that debit cards don't always offer the same conveniences, services, and protections as conventional credit cards. For instance, there is no grace period—or float—from the time you put something on plastic to the time you actually pay for it. And depending on your bank's policies, you may be charged a fee every time you use your debit card.

Critical Info: Types of (Non-Corporate) Bankruptcies

There are two types of personal bankruptcy relief, Chapter 7 and Chapter 13. Chapter 7 is straight bankruptcy that allows the discharge of almost all debts. Those that aren't discharged are alimony, child support, taxes, loans obtained through filing false financial statements, loans not listed in the bankruptcy petition, legal judgments against the petitioner, and student loans. While Chapter 7 relieves you of the responsibility of repaying most creditors, you may also have to surrender much of the property you own to help satisfy the debt. If you have a hot tub, fancy furniture, flat screen TVs, you can kiss them goodbye. Most people, however, want to know if they can keep their house and their car. The answer to the former is it depends on your state of residency. Some states, like Arizona, have a homestead exemption of a certain dollar value, like $150,000. Other states—like Texas, Florida, Kansas and Iowa—have unlimited homestead exemptions. As to whether you can keep your car, the answer is, once again, a function of exemption laws in your state of residence. You have to calculate your equity in the car from a reliable source like Kelly Blue Book and subtract from it the amount you owe. If you have a car worth $12,000 and you owe $10,000 on it, it is likely you will be able to keep it. Most bankruptcy courts understand you need your car to get to work and to help you get back on your feet. As for the rest of your assets, apply common sense to figure out if you will be able to keep them.

Chapter 13, sometimes called the "wage-earner plan," is different. Under Chapter 13, you keep your property but surrender control of your finances to the bankruptcy court. The court approves a repayment plan based on your financial resources that provides for repayment of all or part of your debt over a three- to five-year period. During that time, your creditors may not harass you for repayment. You also do not incur interest charges on your debt. When all conditions of the court-approved plan have been fulfilled, you emerge debt free from bankruptcy.

In the Wake of the New Bankruptcy

Consumers rushing to beat the October 17, 2005, implementation deadline flooded the court system and around 620,000 bankruptcy filings took place in October, 2005, alone (out of a total of over 2 million filings over the entire 2005). The extra filings represent those who otherwise wouldn't have filed for another 12 to 24 months. Sobering statistics!

Source: "Bankruptcy Filings Soaring Again." MSN Money

Many debit cards limit the amount you may purchase on the card to $1,000 per day, even if you have a checking account flush with cash. So a $1,500 Donna Karan leather skirt will require one debit card transaction and either a check (if the store accepts it) or a trip to the ATM. And if you don't have sufficient funds in your checking account for the skirt, you'll be liable for the transaction and slapped with some pretty serious overdraft fees.

Debit cards may not offer the same rights consumers have with credit cards regarding purchase problems. Say the course on improving your memory that you purchased during a late-night TV shopping spree turns out to be a single cassette and one page of typed instructions. If you paid for it with a debit card, you may have no way to stop payment to Memory Moguls.

Let's say a stranger in dark glasses and a baseball cap takes down your debit card number as you're frantically phoning the Moguls. You may be stuck with unlimited liability for losses should you fail to report the theft within a certain period of time (anywhere from two to sixty days). A lost debit card is like cash to a thief—they simply have to forge your signature to use it. (Customers get a $50 maximum liability with most credit cards, as long as the loss is reported promptly. Otherwise, they can be responsible for up to $500 in fraudulent debit card charges.) Consumers recently raised a stink about this, and debit card issuers like Visa and MasterCard have made moves to improve security and liability. Still, read the fine print and make sure your lender offers you the same protections as those of a standard credit card.

Caution!

Identity theft, when someone opens an account with your name, Social Security number, or other identifying information, is a growing problem. You have seen the advertisements run by Citibank where a girl is sitting around talking funny and boasting about how she is going to buy a sixty-five-inch plasma TV with a fake identity and a credit card that is not hers. One way this happens is when the thief puts his own address on the "special offer" you threw in the trash can and sends it in. The card is delivered and maxed out, and you may never know about it until you get bills for things you never bought or your loan is denied due to unpaid credit card bills. Law enforcement agencies and credit bureaus are just beginning to grasp the extent of this type of fraud, but the National Fraud Information Center says it costs financial institutions over a billion dollars a year. By law, consumers cannot be held responsible for more than $50 if they are the victims of fraud and report the theft promptly. However, banks and creditors simply pass the buck and get us all to ultimately pay with higher fees and interest rates.

As I said earlier, secured credit cards also look like standard Visa and MasterCards. They let consumers with shaky credit histories deposit money into an account and charge for goods and services anywhere from 50 percent to 100 percent of the amount. Some even charge nonrefundable fees to apply for the card. Stay away from such deals even if you are desperate.

Credit Counseling

Debt happens and we have to live with it but there are a lot of organizations that want to help you get out of it. The best known nationwide credit counseling service is the CCCS (Consumer Credit Counseling Service). It promotes itself as a nonprofit debt counseling service and has provided much-needed advice to those in serious debt.

If you are in big trouble with your credit, CCCS will help develop a debt repayment plan for a reasonable monthly fee, based on your overall debts and income. CCCS then contacts your creditors on your behalf and gets them to lower monthly payment requirements and either notch down interest rates or do away with them altogether. CCCS is funded by credit card issuers for one important reason alone. Creditors don't want you declaring bankruptcy and defaulting on the debt altogether. It is far cheaper for them to negotiate with you through CCCS than for them to hire expensive lawyers and take you to court.

Critics of the CCCS system allege that the organization is more concerned with getting the creditor paid off quickly than ensuring that the debtor has enough monthly income on which to live. The debt repayment plans they peddle encourage customers to turn over their paychecks each month for CCCS to dole out among creditors. The organization decides whom to pay and how much.

One compromise is to listen to their advice, adapt it to your needs, but never hand over control of your monthly income. In many instances you can negotiate lower rates on your own. But if your creditors number in the double digits, you may find it exceedingly difficult to get all of them to lower interest rates or to work out an

Summary

There are only two things that will improve a bad credit record: Time and reestablished credit. Debt doctors, credit repair clinics, and such organizations cannot remove negative information from your credit report if it is accurate, no matter how much you pay them. If you find information on your credit report that is outdated or inaccurate, contact the credit bureau directly to have it changed.

acceptable payment schedule. That's where the services of CCCS can come in handy. It has relationships with nearly all unsecured creditors and can usually negotiate lower rates.

If you do sign up for a debt repayment plan from CCCS or any other organization, follow through. It's like joining Alcoholics Anonymous. Also, should you renege on the plan, it can show up as uncollected debt on your credit report for seven years—a flag almost as bad as bankruptcy.

CCCS and other organizations like it, develop debt repayment programs. Other companies are out there that offer to repair your credit rating—usually for a large up-front fee. Never sign up for such offers! At the end of the day, companies that promise you freedom from debt with no personal pain are promising pies in the sky. They will take your money and you will continue to be in the same bad situation.

What You Can Do to Protect Yourself against Identity Theft

Abstain from giving out your Social Security number and any personal information to any organization that you can't check on. Concerned by the potential for fraud, the Social Security Administration's Office of the Inspector General has issued an alert, warning people about the dangers of disclosing their Social Security numbers without verification. The agency's Web site also features a page entitled "When Someone Misuses Your Number," which offers tips on how to protect the data, how to tell if it has been stolen, and what to do if it has.

However, Social Security officials cannot help straighten out damaged credit histories, and the agency won't issue a new Social Security number unless it can be proven that an individual is being disadvantaged or harmed because someone has improperly used their Social Security number. Consumers also can take steps to monitor whether their Social Security number has been obtained and their identity stolen.

The Federal Trade Commission's Web site urges the following steps:

- Never respond to e-mails or other online solicitations that claim to need your Social Security number or other sensitive information to "verify" anything. If you do business with the organization in question, contact them by telephone immediately to report the e-mail.

- Order a copy of your credit report from the three major credit reporting agencies every year. Make sure it's accurate and includes only accounts you've authorized.

- Pay attention to your billing cycles and use online accounts to track your spending. Follow up with creditors if bills don't arrive on time.

- Ask to use digits or alphanumeric characters other than your Social Security number to access account information on financial, health care, and government Web sites. Provide this information online only when absolutely necessary.

- Keep items with personal information in a safe place; tear them up when you don't need them anymore. Make sure charge receipts, copies of credit applications, insurance forms, bank checks and statements, expired charge cards, and credit offers you get in the mail are disposed of properly. You may want to consider purchasing an inexpensive home-office paper shredder.

Credit Cardholders' Bill of Rights Act of 2009

This act passed the U.S. House of Representatives on April 30, 2009, bringing some much needed relief to consumers. The credit card lobby had fought hard to prevent it from passing but did not succeed.

How Social Security Numbers Play a Big Role in Web Identity Theft

Since their inception in 1936, Social Security numbers have successfully linked millions of people to retirement and disability benefits. In recent years, however, those nine-digit numbers have developed a life of their own as a universal identifier for the purposes of taxes, employment, financial accounts, banking, medical benefits, etc. And with its growing importance, online hackers have increasingly focused their energies on obtaining people's SS numbers. Once they do, it is a matter of time before they open fraudulent accounts in the victim's name in order to steal money, goods, or services. What is somewhat surprising is that, in addition to hackers stealing SS numbers online, a great deal of identity theft still occurs by low-tech means such as stealing traditional mail or dumpster diving—thieves digging through your trash looking for discarded insurance and financial account statements that may contain SS numbers. So make sure you buy a cheap shredder from Office Max, or a similar store, and shred all your financial documents before putting them out in the trash.

Under this act, a credit card issuer is not allowed to increase the APR except under the following circumstances:

1. The increase is due to circumstances not controlled by the issuer and is also available to the general public

2. The increase is solely due to the expiration of a promotional rate

3. The increase results from a failure on the part of the consumer to comply with a negotiated workout plan

4. The increase is due solely to the fact that a consumer's minimum payment has not been received within 30 days after the due date for such minimum payment.

The following provisions are also included:

Any increases in the APR can only take place after the issuer has provided a written notice at least 45 days before the change takes effect.

Two-cycle billing is prohibited (some exceptions to this relate to return of payment for insufficient funds or following resolution of a billing error dispute).

A written payment warning will be included in every statement to the effect: Making the minimum payment will increase the interest you pay and the time it takes to repay your balance.

At least once every three months, the billing statement would also include repayment information including (a) the number of months it would take, (b) the total cost to the customer, and (c) the monthly payment amount to eliminate the outstanding balance in 12, 24, and 36 months to pay the entire balance if the customer paid the minimum monthly payment and no further charges were made.

Each monthly statement from the issuer has to contain a toll-free telephone number, the Internet address, and the Web site at which the customer may request the payoff balance on the account. Additionally, each bill will contain a date by which the next periodic payment in the account will need to be paid to avoid being considered a late payment.

At least 21 days of grace period will have to be provided by the issuer before payment is due for the current billing cycle.

Something for College Students

Given that the 16–25 population segment is an appealing demographic target for credit card companies, the act has provisions to safeguard their interests as well. These include the following:

No credit card may be knowingly issued to a customer who is under 18 years of age.

Amount of credit extended to a full time college student may not exceed the greater of (20% of the AGI of the student; $500).

No credit card will be granted to a student whose total debt ceiling including the current card would exceed 30% of the AGI of the student in the most recent year.

A college student will be permitted to have only one credit card account. A student who has no verifiable AGI, or who already has one existing credit card, will not be issued a new credit card.

In summary, this is the first time in almost 30 years that major credit card reform has been enacted in Congress. It should be a welcome relief for millions of Americans of all ages and stripes who have been at the mercy of the credit card companies for decades.

What Does It Mean for You

In the short run, credit card companies will try to make as much profit as they can before the new law goes into effect. That means, fewer questionable credit card approvals, quicker increase of rates and rates themselves that will go higher than normal. If you have a questionable credit record, you may not be approved for a credit card. Also notice that Congress did not put a ceiling on the interest rates that credit card issuers can charge customers. That gives issuers a lot of leeway for interest rates which are sure to go up—both in the near future and after the new law goes into effect.

Street Smarts: A Real-Life Example

Below is a table of relevant terms for three different credit cards each offering a 0 percent interest rate over an introductory period (which itself varies between the three cards). I received all three in the mail and decided to use them here as a case study. The question is, if you had a choice between these three credit cards, which one would you choose?

The answer, unfortunately, is not simple and depends on your particular circumstances. So, let us review the salient features and you can decide which one may be rigt for you.

First, if you are a "deadbeat" like me, then you are basically indifferent to these options since the annual fee of all three cards is zero and you can pick the one that will give you the highest credit line. If you are a revolver, however, there are several options to consider. The default APR is what you should be most concerned with since it will trigger if you are late in your payments or do not make the minimum monthly payment, or you exceed your credit line or make a payment with a check that bounces. You get the idea! The default APR for Amazon and Citi are about the same while Capital One does not have any explicit default APR—although the company reserves the right to change your terms, which may include a default APR in the thirty-plus percent range. It is better to check on that explicitly before signing on, since that may be a deciding factor. So, Capital One gets 1 and the rest get 0. Next,

	Capital One	**Amazon.com**	**Citi Simplicity**
APR for purchases	0% for 9 months. After that, 17.24% variable	0% for 12 months. After that, 14.24% variable	0% for 12 months. After that, 10.24% variable.
Other APRs	Balance transfer APR: Same as purchases. Cash advance APR: 19.9% variable. Default APR: None provided.	Balance transfer APR: Same as purchases. Cash advance APR: 23.24% variable. Default APR: 31.24% variable.	Balance transfer APR: same as purchases. Cash advance APR: 22.49% variable. Default APR: 31.49% variable.
Grace period for repayment of purchase balances	25 days from the date of periodic statement	At least 20 days	At least 20 days
Method of computing balance for purchases	ADB (including new purchases)	2-cycle ADB (including new purchases)	ADB (including new purchases)
Annual Fee	None	None	None
Transaction fee for balance transfers	None	3% of the amount of each transaction, but not less than $5.00 or more than $75	3% of the amount of each transaction, but not less than $5.00 or more than $75
Rates, fees, and terms may change	Variable rates could go up or down when Prime changes. We reserve the right to change the terms of your account, including APRs and fees, for any time for any reason, including changes to competitive or general economic conditions.	We reserve the right to change the account terms (including APRs) at any time for any reason. For example, we may change the terms based on information in your credit report, such as the number of other credit card accounts you have and their balances.	We may change the rates, fees, and terms of your account at any time for any reason. These reasons may be based on the information in your credit report, such as your failure to make payments to another creditor when due, amounts owed to other creditors, the number of credit accounts outstanding, or the number of credit inquiries. The reasons may also include competitive and market related factors.
Other	We do not engage in a practice known as "universal default."		

Figure 16: Comparison across Credit Cards

Yet Another Credit Card Trap

As the Federal Reserve raises its short-term interest rates, credit card companies issue new cards at variable rates of interest which allows them to quickly bump up the offered rates without notifying cardholders.

By contrast, when the Federal Reserve lowers its short-term rates, more credit card issuers switch to fixed-rate cards which means that issuers can delay in passing on the new lower rates to consumers.

As a revolver, you need to be aware of what kind of interest rate climate you are in and of the above-mentioned practices of the credit card issuers.

look for universal default clauses. Capital One states clearly they don't engage in universal default, which is good. By contrast, Citi Simplicity states it will change APRs and fees if someone makes a credit inquiry on you that shows up in your credit report. That smacks of universal default. So, you may want to leave that one aside. Between Capital One and Amazon, a careful reading of the terms under "Rates, fees, and terms may change," shows that Capital One may have slightly less stringent provisions to bump up your rates than Amazon. Capital One also appears to have a 25-day grace period relative to 20 days for Amazon and Citi Simplicity. Finally, Capital One uses an ADB for calculating balance outstanding for purchases while Amazon uses a 2-cycle ADB which is worse from the consumer's standpoint (relative to just an ADB). Specifically, with a 2-cycle ADB, the grace period (of approximately 20 days) is wiped out. If the bill is not paid in full at the first billing, interest charges become retroactive and the interest clock starts ticking from the purchase date itself. And every time you carry a balance, the meter starts running from the day of each new purchase. So you can see that banks

Actual Example of How Interest Starts Piling up with a Two-Cycle Balance Calculation

Imagine starting off the month of December with a zero balance on a credit card. A purchase is then made with the card on December 10 and is not paid off in full with a billing statement that arrives in early January. With average daily balance, because you started at zero, the interest clock won't start ticking until January 1. When the February credit card bill arrives, interest will be charged based on the daily balance held on the account through the month of January, minus any payments. With a two-cycle average daily balance, on the other hand, the February bill will have finance charges based on the average daily balance since the purchase date of December 10.

make more money from the revolvers using this method of billing and it is becoming increasingly popular with issuers as a result. By contrast, an ADB is determined by adding each day's balance and then dividing that total by the number of days in a billing cycle. The average daily balance is then multiplied by a card's monthly periodic rate, which is calculated by dividing the annual percentage rate by twelve.

In conclusion, it appears that Capital One might have the edge between the three choices. Learn to read the salient terms as above so you can make smart choices with your credit cards.

But what if you don't have choices with credit cards? Can you afford to be picky? You have to take pretty much what they give you. Credit card companies are big and powerful and know the right people in Congress to get their way. It is the power of the lobbyists (remember the notorious lobbyist, Jack Abramov?). All we can do is to be smart about their ways and able to walk away from a card with terms that are likely to hurt us in the long term. If you know you are likely to be a credit revolver it is imperative to look through the agreement in order to know the salient features of your agreement: Fees, interest rates and the default rate, and how it will be triggered.

Research on Consumer Lending

Do relationships with your bank help in lowering your loan interest rates? Think about it. What if you had a relationship with your neighborhood bank where you have had an account over a long period of time, or have multiple accounts with them like savings, checking, line of credit and so on? You also stop by the bank from time to time so that the loan officers know you in person and make small talk with you about your family and so on. Do you think that kind of interaction with your bank might actually help you to get a lower interest rate when you next need to borrow money for a car or to buy your next house? Academic research says, YES! But let's start at the very beginning.

In 1981, research by two economists, Joseph Stiglitz and Andrew Weiss, showed theoretically how banks may decide to deny credit to some borrowers who look like big risks to the bank even if these borrowers offered to pay a high interest rate as befitted a high-risk borrower. Stiglitz and Weiss termed this "credit rationing." Under credit rationing, banks, rather than raise interest rates, would keep the rate fixed and, instead, deny some people the opportunity to borrow. Why would a bank do that?

The bank would rather ration credit than raise borrowing interest rates because of two problems: Moral hazard and adverse selection. Moral hazard is also known as hidden action. Under this theory, a borrower could conceivably take the money (at the high interest rate) and then do a switch, unbeknownst to the bank, and put it in a high-risk project (with a correspondingly high return) with a high probability of failure. And adverse selection, also known as hidden information, basically means that the borrower knows more about her personal intentions than does the bank.[60]

Over a span of ten years or so beginning in the early 1990s, many economists wrote papers showing how banks could reduce credit rationing by lowering the adverse selection problem they face, by developing "relationships" with potential borrowers.[61,62] Relationships can encompass a variety of soft information including the length of time that a potential borrower has had an association with a lender, the number of different accounts that a borrower may have with a bank, whether or not the borrower does his or her banking personally or by telephone or through the Internet and so on. Basically, the idea behind relationships is to capture the "soft" information that banks collect either formally or informally about a potential borrower over time and then use it to make credit-related decisions down the road.

It is important to stress that relationships, even if they exist, should work only at the margin. What I mean by that is that if you have a horrible track record with your existing, and past, loans, you are probably not going to get another loan no matter how good your relationship is with your bank. By the same token, if you make lots of money or have lots of property, you will probably get the loan even if you have no relationship with a bank. It is people who are at the margins who might get pushed over into getting a loan because of that relationship: People who, if they didn't have that relationship, may not get approved for the loan. Make sense?

Two economists have recently shown with fairly complex econometric analysis that it is not the loan rates that are lowered by an ongoing relationship with your bank but the possibility (or not) of getting approved for the loan in the first place.[63,64] Basically, think of the overall loan process as comprised of multiple stages, with the first stage consisting of being approved (or not) for the loan and then, conditional on being approved for the loan in the first stage, the loan interest rate is decided by the bank in the second stage. The authors then go on to show that relationships matter only in the first stage loan approval/rejection decision. Conditional on being approved for the loan, loan rates are not driven by relationships.

So, if you are now scratching your head wondering what to believe, let me simplify this for you. Relationships are still important! But not in the same way they were once thought to be. Now what would you do armed with this research evidence? I don't know about you, but I would still work with my local banks to develop presonal relationships.

Stay Clear of the Rule of 78

Some auto loans still use the dangerous Rule of 78 in order to compute your "rebate" for paying off your loan early. The problem is that what is actually presented to you as a rebate is more like a prepayment penalty dressed as a rebate.

The origin of the Rule of 78 goes back to the dark days before computers were invented and provided lenders with a quick way to figure out payout amounts when borrowers wanted to pay off a loan ahead of schedule. You get 78 by adding 1+2+3+4+...+12 = 78, where 1, 2, etc., are the months of the year.

In case you are still wondering where the problem is, calculating your loan payout amount in case of early repayment of your loan, using the Rule of 78 packs more interest in the early months of the loan and much less on the later months. Typically, a lender might get over 75 percent of a loan's interest within the first half of the loan term.

As auto loans go, there are two garden variety types: Simple interest loans and pre-computed loans. The Rule of 78 can be applied to compute the payout of pre-computed loans. Specifically, when you take out a pre-computed auto loan, you have committed to pay the loan principal and the entire accumulated interest over the entire period of the loan—all figured in advance at the start of the loan. By comparison, with a simple interest loan, your interest is calculated daily based on the amount you owe. So, if you pay off such a loan early, and there are no prepayment penalties, you are actually ahead.

As an example, assume you have taken out a 5-year (60-month) pre-computed loan and then decide you want to pay off the loan early after 36 months. Contractually you are obliged to pay off the interest on all 60 months regardless, but your lender might decide to do you a favor by determining your payout minus the 24 months of finance charges you avoid by paying off the loan early. If the lender then uses the Rule of 78 to determine this so-called rebate, you will still pay significantly more for the loan since the Rule applies more of your earlier payments towards interest and less towards principal repayment. Because less is paid off, your principal, or the amount you owe, would be greater than normal. And the earlier you pay it off, the more costly it is for you.

Thought Questions

1. How does credit work in an NFL draft?

2. Can you predict anything about a country's economy overall by looking at its banking system? Why or why not?

3. How do you use credit currently? What are some of the ways you could use credit more eficiently based on the discussions in this chapter?

4. What are some things that should not be purchased with credit? Why?

5. Why are credit card interest rates so high?

6. What is good credit versus bad credit?

7. In the past, when credit was neither widely available nor cheap, how did the we cope?

8. Is it necessarily bad to have the credit payments stretch beyond the life of the item it was used to purchase?

9. Why is it important for you to know the contents of your credit files even if you have not had a credit card in your life or taken out a loan?

10. How do you build a credit profile if you have never borrowed money before?

11. What is the single most important thing affecting your credit score?

12. How would your behavior change if you knew exactly how your score was being computed?

13. Why was the minimum payment on your credit cards originally fixed at 2 percent of the outstanding balance?

14. How has the same low minimum monthly payment become a headache for the government?

15. Why don't a lot of businesses accept Discover card?

16. Why do card issuers love universal default?

17. Has technology helped or hurt the average revolving-credit consumer?

18. Why would you ever use a debit card?

19. Under what circumstances would a debit card be preferable to a credit card?

20. What can you do to minimize identity theft?

21. What are some of the things you would do if your identity were stolen?

22. How does budgeting help you stay out of credit card related troubles?

23. If you have amassed a lot of credit card debt, how would you start paying it down?

24. Should flipping be a part of your debt management strategy?

25. Should you purchase those credit card protection plans most banks want you to buy?

26. Why would a bank not advance a willing high-risk borrower a loan at a very high rate of interest?

27. After reading this chapter how would you summarize the importance (or the lack thereof) of maintaining a good relationship with your local bank?

28. What does relationship mean if you believe only in electronic banking and not in face-to-face traditional banking in a bricks-and-mortar bank branch?

29. According to the research findings presented, do good relationships help everybody in obtaining loans?

Notes

56. Note that we were referring to the mean, or average credit card balance here. Previously, we referred to the median credit card balance of $1,800.

57. So, for example, if you have an outstanding credit card debt of about $8,500 and you made only the minimum payment every month, at 24 percent interest, it will take you 31 years to pay off your debt and, in the process, you would have paid about $16,000 (not adjusted for time value) with about half of that in interest payments. Try to avoid it if you can. Instead, pay as much as you can each month.

58. The danger here is in not learning from your past experience and repeating the same pattern of behavior that got you into the jam to begin with. So, for example, you get yourself a HEL, pay off existing debt, and then ring up charges on the credit cards all over again. Now you have a HEL to repay on top of the credit cards. If, however, you have atoned for your sins, you would use the HEL to pay off the credit cards and then keep them paid off until your HEL is repaid or there will be HELL to pay.

59. But, as with any good thing in life (read chocolates and French-fries), there are some drawbacks. First, the loan and interest will be repaid with after-tax dollars, but the interest will be taxed again when you finally withdraw money from the 401(k) many years later. Additionally, you must repay this loan in five years or less. If you leave your employment prior to full repayment, the outstanding balance becomes due and payable immediately. If it's not repaid, that amount will be treated as a distribution to you. Translation, you will be taxed on the amount at ordinary income tax rates. That is not all, however. If you're under the age of fifty-nine and one-half, you will also be assessed an additional 10 percent excise tax as a penalty for an early withdrawal of retirement funds. Therefore, repay any 401(k) loans before you leave your job.

60. Stiglitz, J. and A. Weiss, 1981. "Credit Rationing in Markets With Imperfect Information." *American Economic Review*, 71: 393–410.

61. Berger, A. N. and G. F. Udell, 1995. "Relationship Lending and Lines of Credit in Small Firm Finance." *Journal of Business* 68: 351–382.

62. Petersen, M. A. and R. G. Rajan, 1994. "The Benefits of Lending Relationships: Evidence from Small Business Data." *Journal of Finance* 49: 3–37.

63. Chakravarty, S. and J. S. Scott, 1999. "Relationship and Rationing in Consumer Loans." *Journal of Business* 72: 523–544.

64. Chakravarty, S. and T. Yilmazer, 2009. "A Multistage Model of Loans and the Rate of Relationships." Forthcoming, *Financial Management*.

Appendix A to Chapter 9

Important Credit Definitions

Acceleration Clause: Allows the lender to require entire repayment of the loan as soon as you are in default (see also Demand Feature).

Add-On Interest: One method of calculating installment-loan finance charges, with interest calculated on the full amount borrowed over the life of the loan. Lenders are required to quote rates in terms of annual interest, so you can compare the true cost of this type of financing with simple interest financing, which computes interest only on the outstanding balance. An 8 percent add-on interest loan for thirty-six months is equivalent to annual simple interest of 14.54 percent.

Adjusted Balance: A method of calculating an open-end finance charge (such as on a charge account) by subtracting payments made during the billing period and applying the interest rate to the balance.

Adverse Action Notice: Reports a lender's decision to refuse, end, or reduce your credit. It must disclose the reason.

Annual Percentage Rate (APR): It is the cost of credit over a full year. The law requires lenders to express financing terms of the APR.

Average Daily Balance: A method of computing the figure on which the finance charge for credit card financing will be based. The account balances for each day in the billing period are totaled and divided by the number of days in the period.

Balloon Note Financing: Allows a final loan payment substantially larger than regular periodic payments.

Collateral (also called security): The property that backs up a loan. It becomes the lender's property if you don't repay the loan.

Co-signer (sometimes called co-maker): The second person who enters into a loan agreement, guaranteeing to make the payments if the borrower defaults. A young person who hasn't established credit or a person with a poor credit rating may need a co-signer.

Credit Bureau: A reporting agency that assembles information on borrowers to help lenders evaluate credit worthiness. You are entitled to see your credit report and dispute or add to the information you feel is erroneous. Your objection(s) must be filed in writing with the report.

Credit Disability and Credit Life Insurance: An optional insurance that makes loan payments if an illness or accident hinders your ability to earn income or pays the remaining balance if you die. Generally, this insurance is included in the monthly payments.

Default: The failure to carry out the terms of a loan contract; for example, missing one or more loan payments. It could apply to any part of the loan agreement.

Delinquency: The failure to make a loan payment on time. You may be required to pay a late fee, expressed as a flat fee or a percentage of the amount due.

Demand Feature: Allows the lender to call for repayment of the full balance owed under specified conditions; for example, if your income decreases or your security (collateral) declines in value.

Disclosure Statement: A document prepared by lenders that must explain certain applicable terms such as the APR, payment schedule, periodic rate, finance charge, principal and other fees associated with the loan.

Equity: The amount of loan principal paid—represents degree of ownership.

Escrow: A payment, usually included in mortgage payments, held by the lender to meet property taxes and insurance premiums for property securing the loan.

Finance Charge: The total dollar cost of credit, including interest and other defined charges. Certain fees not included in the finance charge must appear separately in the disclosure statement.

Grace Period: The time period an open-ended credit loan can be repaid without incurring a finance charge.

High Balance Charge: A fee that may be assessed when you exceed your open-end credit limit.

Lien: A creditor's claim on a debtor's collateral.

Loan Value: The amount financial institutions will lend on a particular item. For example, lenders will usually lend no more than the "blue book" value on a used car.

Net Payoff: The amount owed on a loan, excluding prepaid interest and insurance premiums.

Periodic Rate: The APR divided by the days, weeks or months in a year. An APR of 18 percent has a monthly rate of 1.5 percent and a daily rate of 0.0493 percent, etc.

Prepayment Penalty: A fee charged by some lenders for early payment of a loan balance as compensation for lost interest income.

Security Interest: The lender's right to claim collateral and sell it to recover a defaulted loan balance.

Signature Loan: A loan made without collateral.

Total of Payments: The sum of all installments on a loan.

Truth-in-Lending Act: The federal law requiring lenders to disclose full financing information to the borrower.

Variable Rate Loan: A loan whose APR fluctuates according to certain economic indicators. The lender must disclose what indicators would cause the rate to increase, what limits apply and how the number or amount of payments would be affected.

Appendix B to Chapter 9

Here are some useful links related to online fraud.

- Social Security Administration. When someone misuses your number http://www.ssa.gov/pubs/10064.html

- Identity Theft. http://www.ssa.gov/pubs/idtheft.htm

- I.D. Theft—U.S. http://www.consumer.gov/idtheft/

- Identitytheft.org. http://www.identitytheft.org/

- Privacy Rights Clearinghouse. http://www.privacyrights.org/identity.htm

- Identity Theft Resource Center. http://www.idtheftcenter.org/

Understanding Finance Charges

Now that we understand how and what we can do to make sure that we are able to borrow when we want to and at the lowest rate possible we must remember that being able to borrow is not the end of the story. In some sense, it is the beginning of the story. Don't forget that credit generally comes at a cost; usually finance charges. So we need to understand how finance charges are computed by our lenders.

Computing Finance Charges

The interest rate is applied to the outstanding balance, and the outstanding balance is generally determined using one of four variations of the Average Daily Balance (ADB) method:

- ADB excluding new purchases (the most consumer- friendly)

- ADB including new purchases (most frequently used—no grace period on new purchases if you carry a balance)

- Two-cycle ADB excluding new purchases (calculated using last two billing cycles)

- Two-cycle ADB including new purchases (least consumer-friendly method)

Average Daily Balance Method

- Every day, the bank adds your charges and payments to learn what you owed it that day. It adds these totals and divides that figure by the number of days in the month to determine your average daily balance.

- Then the bank divides its annual interest rate by 12 (the number of months in the year) to get a "monthly interest rate." For example, an 18 percent interest rate divided by 12 equals a monthly rate of 1.5 percent.

- The bank multiplies your average daily balance by the monthly interest rate to obtain the finance charge for that month.

In calculating your daily balance, most banks include charges made during the month ("average daily balance, including new purchases"). Others exclude those charges until the next statement ("average daily balance, excluding new purchases"), which is to your benefit. Remember that finance charges add up quickly, and the longer you take to pay off an account balance, the more you will pay overall.

Two-Cycle Billing Method

Some banks retroactively eliminate the grace period by using a "two-cycle billing method." If you don't pay the entire balance, the finance charge is based on the sum of the average daily balances for both the previous and current months. You are only charged for a two-month time period in the first month if you don't pay all charges. People who sometimes pay in full and sometimes leave a balance will pay about the same amount under the two-cycle method as with a card with no grace period.

THE BOTTOM LINE: YOU SHOULD KNOW HOW YOUR BANK CALCULATES FINANCE CHARGES.

Here is an actual example of how a bank might calculate finance charges.

Calculate the finance charges using the average daily balance method including new purchases. Interest rate is 18% per year. Use ADB including new purchases:

No. of days (1)	Balance (2)	Weighted balance (1 x 2)
5	$ 582	$ 2,910
7	932	6,524
15	986	14,790
4	961	3,844
Total: 31		$28,068

ADB   = $28,068 ÷ 31 = $905.42
Monthly APR   =   0.18 ÷ 12 = .015 or 1.5%
Finance charge = $905.42 x .015 = $13.58

Credit Card Offenses to Watch For

Here is a list of offenses that some credit card companies are sometimes guilty of. Watch out for them and if any of the above happen to you, cancel the card and get a new one from www.cardweb.com.

- Going after the non-credit-worthy. Creditors often prey on those who are least credit-worthy by scanning credit records for telltale signs. If you are a student with no income or have recently emerged from bankruptcy, credit card companies want you badly. They know that the recently bankrupt can't declare bankruptcy for another seven years and that you probably don't know the first thing about budgeting.

- The magically appearing annual fee. You signed up for a card with no annual fee. Yet, it appears on your statement. Some lenders start charging an annual fee to their customers who pay their bill off every month.

- A sliding credit line. One detestable practice is to entice a customer to use a cash advance check or a skip-a-month payment offer and then lower the credit limit on them. The maxed-out customer is then charged an additional fee for being above it. A related tactic is to simply lower the customer's credit limit once they reach it.

- Mysterious fees. You may not have to pay a finance charge to get a cash advance. But most banks charge hefty transaction fees, which can be around 2 percent of the total amount and no less than $10. Also watch out for transaction fees for calling the toll-free number to check your balance, and penalty fees for account inactivity.

- The disappearing grace period. Watch out for lenders who pull the grace period out from under you—especially if you are someone who pays their balance in full every month (i.e., a deadbeat). If your grace period is eliminated, you'll accrue interest from the day you make a purchase. The only way to avoid a finance charge would be to pay your bill before you received it.

Critical Info: Cardholder Protections

Federal law protects your use of credit cards. Here are some of the ways you are protected when you use your credit card for making purchases.

- Errors on your bill. If you find a mistake in your credit card statement, you can dispute the charge. The issuer will take that item out of your bill while the matter is being investigated. In such cases, the issuer will have you fill out (usually online) a form with details of the transaction and ask you to provide in writing any information you may have concerning the purchase in question.

- Unauthorized charges. If your card is used without your permission, you are liable for up to $50. If you report the card missing before any charges are made on it, you are not responsible for anything. But if the perpetrator uses your card before you report it missing, you owe at most $50. Report your card missing as soon as you discover it is gone. These days, a lot of credit card issuers will try and get you to buy a card protection plan for anywhere between $5 and $10 a month. You don't need it. It protects the issuers, not you. Your liability is limited to $50 by law.

• Dispute about merchandise or services. If you are not happy with what you bought, or the item arrived in bad shape, or the seller misrepresented the item and now won't talk to you, you can refuse payment with your credit card company. First, you must have made a good faith attempt to resolve the matter directly with the merchant. The card issuer will initiate discussions with your merchant on your behalf and take the amount off your bill while the investigation is ongoing.

SECTION B: ACTION PLAN

- Examine all the credit cards in your purse or wallet. If you have more than two credit cards you have too many.

- Cancel the remaining cards by calling their toll-free numbers. Understand that the customer service representative will pull out all the stops, in an effort to keep you as a customer. This is standard operating procedure such as throwing all kinds of offers your way. You will have to be strong and make sure you get them to cancel the card.

- If you are carrying credit card debt, think about paying it off if you can, or pay off as much as you can right away.

- For the remainder of your debt, look for a new credit card with low introductory rates and switch your balance to the new card. Remember, the introductory rate is only for a few months and could also go away if you are late with any payments. So make your monthly payments on time!

- Continue to look for ways to lower or eliminate your credit card debt using one or more of the tools described in this chapter.

Section C: Insurance

10

Life Insurance

*Insurance: An ingenious modern game of chance in which the player
is permitted to enjoy the comfortable conviction that he is beating
the man who keeps the table.*

—Ambrose Bierce

We have spent time discussing how to build our wealth. That was the offensive part of our overall strategy if you'll recall. It's now time to play some defense. We have that Super Bowl of life to win, remember? As we traipse through life, we have to find that balance between focusing in on the details and stepping back to take in the big picture. It is not a matter of either-or but understanding that we need to have both in our lives. Sometimes, attention to detail is important and sometimes stepping back to take stock and regrouping is key. The trick is to find our own balance.

Like it or not, we live in a litigious society and one accident, illness, or liability lawsuit that is not protected by insurance could wipe us out for good. While growing up in a foreign country, insurance was not an everyday word. My parents certainly did not have homeowner's insurance but may have carried life insurance from their respective employers. Then, there was some health insurance, once again through work, but that was all. There was no auto insurance. Labor costs were (and continue to be today) very cheap. So, if your car was in an accident, you simply took it to your neighborhood auto mechanic who was an expert in repairing stuff with paperclips and rat tails in a way that would make MacGyver proud. While a lot of rats went with little or no tails as a result, the cars ran wonderfully. Health insurance was not necessary if one was willing to be happy with the care provided by the government. For private nursing homes, which were relatively expensive, one did need health insurance or a lot of family money. Finally, lawsuits were almost unheard of. Disagreements were settled with fists and occasional references to one's lineage and potential connection to primates. That took care of a major chunk of why we need insurance in the United States and why insurance itself is so expensive: To fend off frivolous lawsuits.

But insurance is a crucial element of personal finance in the United States so it is imperative that you understand every dimension of insurance and how you can use it to protect your nest egg. With that in mind, we will explore the various standard insurance contracts available to us and try to understand them intuitively. The bottom line is to be protected against the very small likelihood of very large losses. That may seem like a paradox at first blush. You might make a face upon reading this and think to yourself, "Why would I need protection from something that, by definition, has a very small likelihood of happening?" The reason you would need insurance for those precise moments is because while they are rare occurrences, they are also

> ## The Goal of Insurance
>
> The goal of insurance is to be protected from very large losses which have a very small likelihood of occurrence.

horribly expensive when they do happen. The fact that they are rare is what makes them affordable insurances to have. Let me explain! The cost of insurance is related to what statisticians call "expected loss." Expected loss is computed as the dollar loss incurred times the probability of that loss from occurring. So, if the dollar loss is large and the probability of it happening is small, then the product of the two is also a small number. Ergo, low expected loss and, therefore, low cost!

Unfortunately, most of us forget this important lesson and get insurance protection for relatively smaller (read affordable) dollar losses which have a higher frequency of occurrence, thereby affecting us in two ways. One, they are relatively expensive because the expected loss is relatively large (a relatively small dollar loss multiplied by a relatively large probability of occurrence still makes the product of the two a relatively large number). And more expensive! Second, obtaining such insurance policies leaves us exposed to vital holes in other important areas in our lives. After reading this chapter, you will have a better understanding of which insurance contracts to focus on and which ones to avoid in order to maximize your wealth. In other words, do not buy contact lens insurance. If they tear or get lost, just buy a new pair—with your own money.

Risk: How to Deal with It?

What is risk? Risk is defined as uncertainty with respect to economic loss. Put differently, risk is the possibility of occurrence of an adverse event. An adverse event is an event that results in unexpected cash outflow and the amount of cash flow will, in turn, determine whether you are financially ruined or not. So it is important that you are protected for that small chance of a large loss. At the end of the day, that is what insurance is all about.

Risk can be dealt with in the following ways: You can avoid participating in activities that carry a risk of loss. This is known as Risk Avoidance. For example, if you are a college student, you do not stay in a bar past midnight for research has shown that most bar fights happen between 1:00 and 4:00 AM. By leaving the bar before this dangerous period you are avoiding risky behavior. Or, if you have coyotes living in your backyard, you get the professionals to exterminate them before they can cause harm to you and your family. You get the idea?

Of course, it is not always possible to avoid risk. So, the next best thing is Risk Control. Through risk control, you lessen the likelihood of a loss occurring. For example, you drive within the speed limit thereby reducing the likelihood of an accident. Wearing a seat belt while driving might reduce the severity of an injury if you have an accident. Or, you might decide to bear the risk of loss yourself. This is known as Risk Assumption. Many times you buy an appliance and don't get the extended service warranty beyond the manufacturer's warranty. Beyond a certain point in time, you assume the risk of the appliance breaking down. In ancient cultures there were no insurance policies and very bad water. People always assumed all the risk themselves and died at twenty—of diarrhea. We have come a long way since those days. Now we have useless paper currency and live until the ripe old age of ninety in a nursing home surrounded by strangers!

Finally, we have the mother of all ways to deal with risk: Risk Transfer. This is where you pay someone to assume your risk—the house-cleaner approach. We do this with an insurance company that takes on your risk for a fee, much like a bookie in Las Vegas would accept your bet. In this case, you are saying something like, "I bet I die this coming year!" The insurance company says, "Not so fast! I bet you don't!" If you win (i.e., die) then your beneficiary gets paid the amount of the bet. If you lose (i.e., you live) then the bookie keeps your betting money. Since losing means you did not die, you should be pleased at not winning. How much does it cost you to place this bet? That depends on the odds that the bookie places on you. If you are deemed healthy, then your cost is small to play this game. If you are deemed a high-risk by the bookie, it could be prohibitively expensive to participate in the betting contest! That implies, under certain circumstances, that you may not be able to afford insurance. Unfortunately, millions of Americans at this very moment are feeling this very pain.

What Is Underwriting?

Underwriting is the process by which an insurance company decides whom to insure and the rate to charge that person. In the process (think about the Las Vegas bookie analogy), they (the insurers) have to protect themselves from two issues.

First, they have to guard against adverse selection, which means "hidden information." Within the scope of insurance and insurance companies, adverse selection means insurance companies protecting themselves against too many clients with bad health (read high-risk). People who are interested in buying insurance policies know about their risks better than the insurance company. So, for example, for a health insurance policy, the applicant might have a better idea of her health and may be interested in buying a health insurance policy simply because she expects to fall ill in the near future. Remember, the insurance company needs to have a balanced mix of healthy and sick people. Ideally, the insurance company would, of course, prefer to have only healthy people—people who would not need to file a claim. That way, the insurance company will get to keep all the premium dollars and not give anything back. Total profits! At the other extreme, if the insurance company sells policies to sick people only, they will be out of business. The company will also have to price these policies just right. If it charges too little for higher risk individuals then the company will lose money on those policies. If it charges too much for low-risk individuals then these individuals will not buy policies. It's a delicate balancing act. Economists call that finding the indifference point between pricing too high and pricing too low.

Second, they have to protect themselves against moral hazard (i.e. hidden action). That means we could do things that adversely affect the outcome and then deny we ever did it as long as we are not caught by a hidden camera or an eyewitness. So, for example, you have insurance on your car and drive it to the big city, leave it unlocked somewhere, and go away for a couple of hours. You come back and, predictably, the local bad guys have stripped the car bare of its essentials leaving it sitting on its frame minus the wheels. You file a police report and swear on your dead grandmother that you locked the car, took all precautions, and you are just as shocked as they are about how, or why, the car got vandalized. The insurance company has its own suspicions about what may have happened but knows it cannot prove it in court. They decide it is cheaper to pay out and you get away with negligence.

All this, however, begs the question of why it is feasible for insurance companies to assume your risk—even for money. What happens if they take your money and then you and everybody else files a claim? Won't the insurance company go out of business? Actually, the company is betting on the fact that, in a normal year, the number of people filing claims will be relatively small compared to the number of people with policies who are not filing claims. As long as this is true, everything works like a charm and insurance companies can spend millions of dollars advertising how great they are and constantly asking if you are in good hands. Occasionally, they will go through a lean year when a lot of people file claims all at once and then the insurance company will complain about it and the government will step in and bail them out. For example, when Hurricane Katrina devastated Louisiana and millions of people were hit simultaneously, the insurance companies made some of the payments, but then the government had to step in and bail out the families whose homeowner's policies did not have explicit flood coverage.

The bottom line is that insurance companies do provide a level of protection although you need to be cautious about the quality of the company itself when you buy a policy. There are organizations that rate bonds issued by corporations, states, and municipalities. After all, you want the insurance company to be around when you do have to make a claim and you also want them to have the financial strength to pay you. One of the more established rating agencies is A.M. Best Company founded in 1899 with the goal of detecting insurer insolvency. The following table from Best's Web site summarizes their rankings of insurance companies.

Secure	Vulnerable
A++, A+ (Superior)	B, B- (Fair)
A, A- (Excellent)	C++, C+ (Marginal)
B++, B+ (Very Good)	C, C- (Weak)
	D (Poor)
	E (Under Regulatory Supervision)
	F (In Liquidation)
	S (Rating Suspended)

Figure 17: Insurance Company Rankings

If you are contemplating buying an insurance policy from a company that is not well known, you should go to Best's Web site at http://www.ambest.com and check out the company's financial stability.

Whole Life Policies

Life insurance policies provide security to the families of people who die—as well as address some of the problems of that basic assurance. In ancient Rome, the legionnaires' pledge (see the text box) worked essentially like term insurance. It acknowl-

> **Book Smarts: A Bit of History**
>
> The origin of modern life insurance goes back to the days of the Roman Empire, when legionnaires pledged to one another that they would care for the families of fallen comrades. Needless to say, insurance for the foot soldiers (or anybody else for that matter) was not high on Caesar's list of priorities. Having a spear rip through your arm simply meant splashing some high potency alcohol on it and continuing to fight till death.

edged that someone might suffer an untimely death, leaving surviving family members with sizable financial obligations. And if a large group of people agreed to pay just a little money each, they could help the hapless families pay their bills.

Today's insurance works much the same way, spreading risk among a large pool of similarly situated individuals. The larger the pool of people, the smaller the amount everyone pays in premiums. "Term" refers to the period of time the policy will be in force.

Bottom line: Insurance is about RISK POOLING. The larger the pool, the smaller the amount each individual has to pay into the pool for a given level of benefits. And that is why companies with global operations (read larger pool) survive natural disasters and calamities that may financially wipe out smaller insurance companies (read small pool). As a consumer fish you definitely want to be swimming in the bigger insurance pool.

It bears repeating that the life insurance process is somewhat like a bet you'd lay down in Las Vegas. Both sides place their bets, with the understanding that the "winner" gets big money. Since you can win by dying, you may not be too depressed at losing. But then again if you are competitive like me, who knows! The fact is that, in such betting games, most of the time you will end up losing. The insurance company will say something like, "see ya, sucker!" and keep your premium dollars. How much you bet and get if you win also depends on the odds. In the case of life insurance, the odds assigned to your winning the bet are based on your health and other factors like lifestyle choices. The life insurance odds maker is called an actuary. The actuary goes through a complicated mathematical analysis of mortality rates—that's an abbreviated way of saying how many people your age die each year—and lifestyle characteristics in order to set the premium rate applicable to you.

For example, if you are buying term insurance when you are young and healthy, the odds are slim that you'll die in the year your policy is in force. So your bet is going to be similar to one you might place at the roulette wheel: You put down a small amount. It will be lost if you don't die. If you do die, the insurer will pay you—or, rather, your beneficiaries—a "jackpot" of between ten and one hundred times the amount of your bet. Not bad for one night's work—or death! As you age, and if you adopt unhealthy or dangerous habits such as smoking, overeating, or sky diving, for example, the amount of your bet—your premium rate—will rise, because the chance of your dying begins to increase. For that reason, term insurance becomes increasingly expensive as you get older.

Assume we want to determine the cost of a $250,000 term insurance policy. A healthy 35-year-old woman would pay $170 annually for a fifteen-year level-premium policy, according to Insurance Quote Services, an online insurance shopping service. But a healthy 70-year-old woman would pay more than ten times as much—$1,950 a year— for the same type of policy.

Can you see an inherent problem with term insurance? The older you are, the more expensive it gets. Translation, for older Americans, term insurance can get prohibitively expensive. The insurance companies saw it too.

Trade-Offs with Term Insurance

While term insurance does get more expensive as you age, because the probability of your dying increases, your need for life insurance also declines with age since your children grow up, leave the nest, and become financially independent.

Recognizing that term insurance could become unbearably expensive long before most people would need it to protect their families, insurance companies set to work on an alternative. What they came up with is something called Whole Life.

The calculations behind Whole Life start with the assumption that life starts at zero and ends at age one hundred. So, if you buy a policy somewhere between ages zero and one hundred, you can fund (a part of) your death benefit yourself, based on specific calculations. In essence, you buy a hybrid product that's part insurance, part savings account. Each year, a portion of your premium goes to fund the insurance, which, like a basic term policy, covers the death benefit for those who die prematurely. The other portion of your premium accumulates in a tax-deferred savings account. If you die before the policy matures, your beneficiary will receive a death benefit that comes partly from the insurance company and partly from the savings accumulated in your account. If you die young, the bulk of your death benefit will come from the insurance company; if you die old, the bulk of the death benefit will come from your own savings.

Figure 18 illustrates this. Let's say you started a Whole Life policy, with a certain face value, at 20 years of age. By the time you are 30, the accumulated cash value is very small, as you can see. Should something happen to you then, the insurance company will take the small cash value accumulated and add its own money to make up the face value to pay your beneficiary. Fast forward to when you are 70. By then, a significant amount of cash value has built up in your account. So if something should happen to you then, the insurance company takes this accumulated cash value and adds the rest from its own funds to make up the face value and pay off your dependents. If you should live to be 100, then the cash value buildup equals the face value of the policy and the insurance company incurs no expense to pay off your beneficiary.

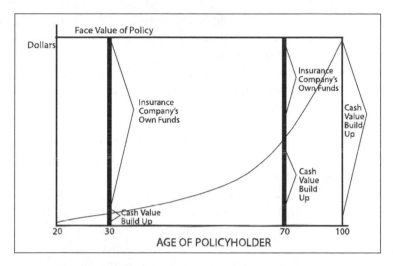

Figure 18: Relationship between age and insurance company payouts

Based on the previous discussion, can you tell me if the insurance companies want you to live longer or die quicker? Live longer, of course, because most of the face value they will be paying out to your chosen beneficiary will come from your own cash value. So, "only the good die young" is not a credo the insurance companies want you to live by. Rather, they want you stay "forever young" if possible! At the extreme end of the spectrum, if you live to be a hundred, they have to pay nothing out of their pockets. You fund the entire death benefit yourself. The insurance company gets to keep all the profits.

Usually, young families have huge insurance needs. They have lots of obligations—children to feed, clothe, and get through school, a mortgage, and, possibly, credit card, or student loan, debts. What makes matters worse is that these same families usually have very few assets, such as savings or stocks, to meet those obligations should the family breadwinner die.

On average, a guaranteed-renewable, term-life policy might cost between 80 cents and $1.50 for each $1,000 in insurance, whereas the premium for a traditional cash-value policy—called Whole Life—would run about $13 to $15 per $1,000 insured. The difference, after paying off insurance agents' commissions and other administrative costs, accumulates in the savings component of your policy. To further illustrate what the choices might be, let's say that you're a healthy 35-year-old man who needs $250,000 in insurance. Depending on the insurer and the options you want on your policy, term insurance would cost between $150 and $350 per year. A cash-value policy would cost about $3,000 to $4,000 per year.

Evolution of Life Insurance Policies

As a general rule, mortality rates are low for those who are younger and rise with time. And as the savings portion of your account grows, you need less term insurance coverage. So, later in life, at a time when more people in your age group are dying, the cost of the insurance portion of your policy shouldn't be rising very fast, if at all, through the magic of subsidization.

For the same money you are spending for a Whole Life insurance policy, you could have bought ten times as much term. The rule of thumb suggests that, up to age fifty, you really should buy the maximum amount of insurance you can afford to protect your family and your income. That means term.

However, as you age, your need for insurance will usually diminish. Your kids will be older and less dependent on you and hopefully you would have paid down some of your outstanding debts. You may have also accumulated some assets. A diminishing need also argues for term over Whole Life, since the Whole Life policy usually can't be canceled without loss during the first several years. However, if you are older and looking for a modest amount of insurance combined with a tax favored investment vehicle, some type of cash-value policy might be just right for you. But with these (Whole Life) policies, too, there is a problem.

A lot of people don't like Whole Life insurance policies. First, they are hard to understand, sort of like math for most people. It's like a big jumble of incomprehensible symbols you encountered in class when you were eight and continued on through college. Although consumers know it's both insurance and investment, they don't know what portion of the premium is going to which part of the policy. Insurance companies tell them, but only after the year is over, the mortality figures are in, and it's largely too late to do anything about it. And, besides, you already have a headache.

Second, the policies are inflexible. Because of the way they are structured, the consumer needs to pay a set premium each year. Your policy lapses if you can't afford the cost one year. If you have accumulated money in the savings portion of the policy at that point, you get this money back. But if the policy lapses in the first few years, the amount you get back is likely to be small relative to what you paid in premiums. The insurance companies knew they had a problem. Their answer was Universal Life.

Universal Life works much the same way as Whole Life, but the policy is more transparent. Companies spell out how much of each year's premiums will be eaten up in mortality fees and expenses and how much will be invested. If you can't afford the whole premium in some years, this policy offers an option. As long as you pay enough to cover the insurance portion of the policy, you can keep the policy in force. In good years, you might decide to over-finance the investment side of your policy, paying a higher premium so more of your money will be invested. In a lean year, you might pay less or nothing at all, letting the premium come from the savings accumulation within the policy itself rather than from you.

The downside of Universal Life policies is that the invested portion of the policy is being handled by an insurance company, which buys fixed-income instruments such as low-risk bonds. This produces only steady, but modest, returns—a problem for younger clients who think bonds are boring and stocks are sexy.

In the early 1980s when the stock market began to take off, investors noticed that they could make a lot more in the stock market than in an insurance contract. The mantra became: Forget permanent insurance. Buy term, and invest the rest. It is always cheaper to do on your own what the insurance companies are doing for you. Have term insurance for the unlikely possibility of an early death, then reduce your need for insurance over time by accumulating savings that could be used to cover your family's financial obligations when you die of old age.

It does not take a rocket scientist to realize that if you invested $1,000 in stocks and earned an average of 8 percent on your money, you'd be doing better than if you invested $1,000 through an insurer who would put the money in bonds earning an average of 4 percent or less. Logically, the term insurance should cost the same whether you bought it alone or through a hybrid type of policy. (That's not, in fact, true.) So the only difference between this and buying a Universal Life policy would be how much you earned on the invested dollars.

> ## In Shopping for Life Insurance, You Should:
>
> - Know the amount and type of coverage you need.
> - Compare costs.
> - Select a large, highly rated, financially secure company.
> - Select a reputable agent.

Insurers responded with a new product, Variable Universal Life, that allowed consumers to invest the dollars accumulating in their cash value accounts in just about anything, including high-risk/high-return stock and bond funds. Still, even Variable Universal Life couldn't answer all of the consumers' needs; i.e., for tax-favored retirement vehicles, products that aided in estate planning, coverage for specific obligations such as home mortgages, or for specific risks such as the loss of a job or one's mental capacity as evidenced by an insane desire to obsessively trap wild mice. So, insurance contract designers continued creating an array of products to address nearly every need out there—including insuring circuses against liability or for owners of dogs deemed dangerous, like pit bulls. These days, even if you drive a rickshaw and are looking for insurance, fear not—there is an insurance company for you. There are variable annuities for those who are so well heeled that they're maxed out on all other tax-favored retirement plans; there are products aimed at estate planning, including "second-to-die" policies that pay benefits to your other heirs rather than to your spouse. There's the garden variety vacation insurance, pet insurance, disability and workers' compensation insurance, and there's insurance to cover nursing home expenses. The list goes on!

You must determine what you need a policy to accomplish. Are you buying insurance for short-term peace of mind or for long-term financial planning? If you are interested in long-term planning, you should consider a form of cash-value insurance. But if you buy a cash-value policy, you have to be certain you'll stick with it long enough to have it pay off for you.

At the end of the day, insurance should be used as a protection of your valuable assets and to protect your loved ones and dependants, should something happen to you. Everything else that comes with insurance products, like tax-deferred growth of the cash value component, should just be treated as icing on the cake. As long as the cake itself is made with solid ingredients, it will be a tasty treat! Consider this discussion on Whole Life, Universal Life and Variable Universal Life policies as hors d'oeuvres to the detailed discussion of these policies next.

The Seamier Side of Whole Life

There is nothing complicated about cash value policies. One part of your premium goes into a savings component and another part goes toward death protection. Yet, there appears to be a lot of confusion about them. For example, having taken this course, and knowing about death protection and cash-value buildup, let's say you buy a Whole Life policy and ask your agent, "How much of my premium is paying for the insurance portion and how much will be invested?" There is a good chance that your agent couldn't tell you either. He could guess, but the answer could not be determined until a year after you bought the policy.

In addition, there is no clear answer for what rate of return you will earn on the invested portion of your account. It is worse than the National Security Agency (NSA) wiretaps. No one knows what is going on. Once a year, the company will tell you what your policy's cash value is, and they'll tell you how much you need to pay in premiums. Economists call this a "black box," but no one knows the contents. A few things about Whole Life policies are clear, however. Premium payments for this type of insurance are a constant. If they start at $5,000 a year, you will be paying that throughout the life of the policy. If you can't pay the premium in a given year, the policy will lapse and you'll get the accumulated cash value back, minus any cancellation fees.

In addition, with Whole Life you are likely to lose the full amount of premiums you've paid if you cancel in the early years of your policy. That's because the cost of writing these policies—the agent's commission, the underwriting fees and expenses—are front-loaded. In simple English, that means that your insurance agent is making out like a bandit with your premium dollars and there is very little of your premium dollars going into the cash value compartment of your policy. Thus, the cash value of your Whole Life policy after the first few years is likely to be zero. And, for the first several years, it is likely to remain a fraction of what you've paid in premiums. Statistics from the American Council of Life Insurance indicate that slightly less than 20 percent of Whole Life consumers cancel within the first two years. If you are one of those, consider all your premium dollars gone for good. It's the black hole of insurance.

Universal Life Policies

Universal Life differs from traditional Whole Life policies in two ways: greater flexibility and greater transparency.

Whole Life policies have always been accused of two major problems: They are hard to understand and inflexible. Insurance agents had a hard time selling these policies after they explained that the premium would always be the same but the investment returns would be impossible to predict. This caused severe heartburn among policyholders and Maalox was flying off the shelves. Agents were also the targets of heinous crimes like toilet-papering and squirrel-dropping. To deal with the general unhappiness, actuaries came up with Universal Life. Universal Life works much the same way as Whole Life. The premium more than covers the requisite death benefit, and the money that isn't used to pay expenses and mortality fees is invested. That investment builds up cash value that eventually chips away at the amount of pure death protection the policyholder will need as she ages.

But the big difference lies in the fact that a Universal Life policy is unbundled to indicate which portion of the premium is paying only for insurance, which portion is paying for fees, and how much is going into the savings element of the policy. In addition, these policies allow individuals to adjust the premium and death benefit. Why is this important? If your circumstances change significantly, leaving you with less or more insurance needs, you can cut or increase the death benefit component of your Universal Life policy. If, however, you're adding to the death benefit, you may be subject to additional physical examinations to prove that you are still healthy and haven't been hit with the caribou flu.

Meanwhile, this type of policy gives you the ability to invest more money and let the cash buildup accrue on a tax-deferred basis if you like the investment returns you're earning. If, on the other hand, you aren't impressed with the investment returns, or if you simply can't afford the entire premium during a given year, you can use the cash buildup in your account to pay the death benefit part of the policy and expenses (i.e., the term insurance part). Translation: Universal Life is flexible.

Because a portion of the policy's cash value is likely to come from investment returns that grow on a tax-deferred basis, you can, in effect, pay for the term insurance portion of the policy with pretax dollars. But this also reduces the amount of cash value in the policy and that could eventually cause the policy to lapse if the investment returns fall behind on the expenses coming out of it.

The cash value of a Universal Life policy is invested in bonds, mortgages, and other fixed-income instruments. Still boring! Thus, the popularity of these policies is still limited to the highly risk averse people who dislike taking any chances with their insurance money. The stock market, by contrast, has grown in leaps and bounds but such policies do not invest there. This means that the younger and hipper crowd has no interest in these policies.

Furthermore, the high rates of inflation in the late 1970s and early 1980s resulted in fixed-income investments (like bonds) posting double-digit returns making the returns on cash-value policies—Whole Life and Universal Life—impressive. But by the mid-1980s, interest rates had dropped dramatically as inflation was gradually brought under control. Someone's blessing became someone else's curse! Returns on fixed-income instruments became lackluster. And as the stock market began taking off, investing money through an insurance policy locked into fixed-income securities seemed stupid.

But the insurance gods were watching from their mountain-top retreats. They jumped in and began promoting an exciting new version of the boring old Universal Life policies: Variable Universal Life, in order to reel in the younger crowd.

Variable Universal Life Policies

The investment portion of the Variable Universal Life policy resembles a 401(k) retirement plan. Policyholders get investment options that range from the safe, but often low-yielding, fixed-income mutual funds to the higher risk, higher reward options, such as small stock funds and high-yield bond funds. You could invest all of the cash buildup in your policy in one option or in some combination of options. And if you wanted to switch investments, you could do that too—without triggering a gain from the sale that could be taxed—as long as you chose another investment offered through the policy itself. But do you see a potential downside? The resulting cash buildup in the policy couldn't be predicted, and it would vary based on the investment choices you made and how well those investments fared. The bottom line with these policies is that you are buying term insurance and investing the rest. But you're doing it through an insurance vehicle, which gives you tax-favored status.

One downside of these products is the fees. When you buy an insurance product that is so closely associated with an investment product, you are hit with fees to pay the insurance company and insurance agents, and fees that pay the investment companies and investment managers. So your returns, net of fees, may not be that great.

With some policies, fees are relatively low. An experienced investor may find that the tax benefit of investing through an insurance policy outweighs the additional costs, so Variable Universal Life works better than other investment alternatives. However, that may not be true with higher cost policies, or if an investor has less need for the insurance guarantees or the tax benefits.

Borrowing from Insurance

Did you know that you could borrow from your life insurance policy (from its cash value)? What may be the most widely offered and least understood of policy options within a cash-value life insurance policy is the ability to borrow against the cash value accumulated in your account. Although the vast majority of insurers offer this benefit, many consumers don't fully understand how these loans work.

When you take out a loan against the cash value buildup in your policy, there's no set repayment schedule. In fact, if you don't feel like it, you needn't pay back the loan at all. If you are wondering, "if something is too good to be true, it probably is," you would be right. Remember the loan is written against your cash value buildup that serves as the collateral to your loan. If you take a loan out and do not repay it, the death benefit from the policy is scaled down accordingly. Also, the interest rate may be slightly higher than comparable market rates (explanation below). Some people think that since they are taking out "their own money," there should be no interest on the loan. The reason the loan carries any interest at all is because technically the money is not coming from your own cash value; the insurance company is actually forwarding you the loan with the cash value buildup held as collateral. This aspect of borrowing from your insurance policy is very important and can have adverse consequences as we will see below. And, like any other collateralized loan there is interest to be paid. Some policy loans are a tremendous bargain and others come at a tremendous cost. Before you take out a loan, you need to find out the facts. What do you need to know? Here are some questions you may want to ask.

How Much Can You Borrow from Your Insurance Policy?

In most cases, you can borrow an amount equivalent to the full cash value accumulated in your account. If, for example, you have a $500,000 policy with a $75,000 accumulated cash value, you could borrow as much as $75,000. And it's real simple to get the loan, as it turns out. Usually all you need to do is call your insurance agent. It can take up to two weeks to process the check, but in an emergency, a loan can sometimes be processed in as little as three days or less.

You may be scratching your head and wondering, "what interest rate do I pay on the loan?" The answer to that question is not so clear. There is always a stated rate of interest, but frequently there will be hidden costs that can boost the effective interest rate. It is usually around the "going" rate of interest. Unlike credit card loans, however, once you take out the loan, the interest rate is locked in. And since there is no set payoff date for your loan, if interest rates rise in the future, the insurer would be forced to pay you more on the accumulated cash value in your account than you were paying on the loan, so the insurer would be taking a loss on the deal, and vice versa. The insurer has to factor in these scenarios when deciding how much to charge you for the loan.

Here is an example of how borrowing against your Universal Life policy actually works. Let's say you have $75,000 in the invested portion of your account. You want to borrow $10,000. The insurer advances you the money and simultaneously takes $10,000 out of your policy's investment account, where it might be earning, say, 4 percent annually, and puts it into a "guaranteed" fund, where the money earns just 2.5 percent per year. Such measures are necessary because insurance money is deemed sacred by the regulators given the sensitive nature of insurance in this country. Let's say the insurer decides to charge you a 3.5 percent rate of interest.

Does that mean you're paying just 3.5 percent to borrow that money? No, since the return on the guaranteed account is 1.5 percentage point lower than the return on the investment account where it had previously been invested—and because moving it into the 2.5 percent guaranteed fund is required, not optional, your true interest rate on the loan is closer to 5 percent—the 3.5 percent you are charged plus the 1.5 percent opportunity cost.

Warning about Borrowing

The outstanding loan balance from your insurance policy may trigger a tax event which means the issuance of an IRS Form 1099, should you choose to cash in your policy at a later date.

But here is the kicker. When you normally cash in your policy or even "annuitize" it by asking the insurer to pay you the accumulated cash value of the policy over time, you are responsible for paying taxes on the profit built up in the account at your ordinary income tax rates (example provided below).

So, if you have borrowed from your account, that taxable profit could amount to nothing more than a paper entry; yet, you may have very real taxes that are due on it.

In most cases, an insurer will let you keep the loan outstanding for as long as your policy is in force. You won't even be required to make any kind of monthly payment on it. You can opt to pay as much or as little as you like. But if you don't pay at least enough to cover the interest payments, the amount of unpaid interest will accrue and be added to the loan balance. As that balance increases, the interest you owe increases with it. If the loan balance goes high enough, it will eat up the cash value in your account, causing the policy to lapse.

You could also pay the loan interest with the accumulated dividends building up in your account, and this may be a smart way to go because it allows you to use pretax dollars—investment income earned in an insurance policy is not taxed until the money is withdrawn from the policy. But again, you need to be sure you are paying at least enough to cover the interest or your loan amount will increase. And if you die while you have a loan outstanding, the death benefit will be reduced by the amount of the loan and any unpaid interest.

An Example of the Adverse Tax Consequences of Borrowing from Insurance

Let's take the case of Sara who borrows $50,000 from her cash value life insurance policy. Assume that the accumulated cash value in her policy at this point is $60,000—enough to ensure that the policy premiums are paid so that Sara does not have to make any payments on her loan for a while. Also, recall from our previous discussion that when she borrows from her life insurance policy she is not actually borrowing her own money; she is borrowing from her insurance company with her money as collateral. Why is this important? On paper, the cash value in her policy continues to grow. A few years later, assume that the cash value in her policy has grown to $100,000 (this is her new cash value) while the balance outstanding on her loan has grown to $103,000. Since insurers will only allow her to borrow up to 100 percent of the cash value in her account, she will get a bill from the insurance company asking her to immediately pay the difference; i.e., $3,000. And what happens if she doesn't comply? The insurance company will report to the IRS a taxable income based on the excess of her cash value at the point of taking out the loan—about $40,000 in this case. So Sara has to pay income taxes on her $40,000 phantom gain. Something to think about!

An Insurance Mistake to Avoid

One mistake people often make is to assume that life insurance proceeds are free of tax. The word on the street is that if you inherit life insurance money from your favorite Aunt Emma, you have won the jackpot. While it is true that you, Aunt Emma's chosen beneficiary, receive the face value without having to pay any income tax, whether or not the money is subject to estate taxes is a function of whether Aunt Emma owned the policy at the time of her death. If she did, you have to pay estate taxes on it. If, on the other hand, she had transferred ownership of the policy to you (her favorite nephew) prior to her death, making you both the beneficiary and the policy owner, then there are no estate taxes to worry about. If you own the policy, however, you also have to make the premium payments. For that, Aunt Emma could gift you money (up to $12,000 per person in 2007) to take care of all, or some, of the payments.

As a case study of how improper transfers of insurance ownership can hurt survivors, an insured person had transferred ownership of a $1 million policy to a life insurance trust but failed to make the trust the beneficiary. He also happened to die within 3 years of the transfer (believe me, you don't want to do that!). His mistake (in improper transfer—not in dying) cost his heirs $450,000 in estate taxes that might have gone to them if things had been handled properly.

Do You Really Need Life Insurance?

This is the big question, and the answer depends on whether you have dependents—children, a spouse, or other people who rely on you for financial support. Now, I have a few dogs and a cat that totally depend on me for their dog and cat treats and chew toys but sadly they don't count. This is for human dependents only! If you have any of the two-legged variety of dependents and want to protect their financial health after you die, the answer is yes. If you don't, life insurance is unnecessary. It's really that simple.

The tricky part is determining exactly how much insurance you might need, because life insurance is designed to fill a gap between the financial resources your family would have after you died and what they would need. To know the size of this gap, you must know how much you own, how much you owe and how much you spend. And all those components are dynamic, meaning they change throughout your life. But it's possible to get a fairly accurate idea of needs. And once you have figured them out, the rest is simple!

Start with a copy of your household budget and a net worth statement—a simple listing of your assets and liabilities. If you have no idea of what you own and what you are spending money on, you may have other more pressing issues to deal with than figuring out your life insurance needs. Get your most recent mortgage statement (showing its retirement), your most recent statement from your brokerage account (if you have one), and your most recent bank statement showing how much you have in your checking and savings accounts.

From your list of assets, consider: What tangible assets could you sell for cash, if necessary? What assets are you willing to liquidate? What current debts could be paid off with the proceeds? Are the debts bigger than the anticipated proceeds, or would the proceeds be sufficient to pay off the debts?

If your calculations include the sale of a home, be sure to estimate the home's value conservatively (use the lowest of all possible values). Remember, though, that even in the best of circumstances, a house is not a liquid asset. Translation: It cannot be converted to cash (i.e., sold) quickly. Allow anywhere from one month to nine months before a house is sold to receive close to what you may ideally want from it.

Now from your budget, consider what expenses would disappear if you or your spouse died. What continuing expenses would the survivor be willing and able to cut? What added expenses might you face if one of you died?

Normally, you can expect that certain expenditures—food, clothing, and transportation—would be likely to decline somewhat when one member of a household died. Other expenditures would not. Chances are your rent or mortgage expenses would stay the same and that your child care bills would go up. This again depends on specific circumstances; one size definitely does not fit all.

When doing this planning, inexperienced couples might easily forget to factor in the cash equivalent of the stay-at-home spouse raising children and doing the housework like cooking and cleaning, which would need to be paid for if that spouse were to die. How accurately you are able to estimate all this will determine how accurately you are able to predict your family's life insurance needs and how much monthly income your survivors would need if something were to happen to you in the near future.

Now, consider how long the survivors would need that income. How old are your children? Are they so young that the surviving spouse would face either a day-care or a financial crisis if he (or she) had to work more hours to help close the economic gap your death would leave? Would your children's college plans be likely to be affected by your death? How would your death affect your spouse's retirement plans?

If your spouse is not currently working, would he or she be employable today or in the near future without job training or further education? How long would it take to make your spouse employable? How long would it take before your spouse's income could more than make up for the income he or she would lose if you were to die soon?

The length of time your survivors will need income will have a big role in determining how much insurance you need. Some families will need income from insurance proceeds for a few years and others will need income for life. Most will fall between these two extremes.

With the information you've gleaned from going through the previous steps, fill out the following work sheet to come up with a rough estimate of how much life insurance you should buy. Remember, this is not an exact science. Feel free to approximate the figures to the nearest nice-looking number. If you come up with a number like $836,285.93, it might make sense to look for insurance with a face value of $1 million if you can afford the premium payments.

A Specific Boilerplate to Calculate Need

I know that some of you will be unhappy with the previous discussion and will want a relatively precise prescription of how to approach a "needs" calculation. For you, here is one such prescription. Again, this is not the only way, but it will yield a rough estimate of your life insurance needs. For single parents, the steps will be more complicated, partly because the financial issues will depend on the children's ages and guardians.

1. Calculate your current monthly expenses. If you are married, record the number twice, so you can calculate the insurance need for each spouse.

2. Estimate expenses that would be eliminated if one spouse died. (For example, if you would jettison one of two cars, eliminate that car payment. If you have assets that could easily be liquidated to pay off some of your debts to reduce your monthly expenditures, factor that in.)

3. Estimate the increased monthly expenses you might have if one spouse died. (Be sure to consider items such as child care.)

4. Record the income each spouse contributes to the family budget to determine how much income would be lost in the event of either spouse's death.

5. Using the previous information, estimate what each spouse's monthly expenses, and income, would be if the other spouse were to die. Subtract expenses from income to determine whether survivors would have a gap between the income they need and what they're likely to have in the event of a death. If you come up with a negative number, you have an insurance need.

6. For simplicity's sake, multiply the gap figure by the number of months you expect this gap to continue, for a rough estimate of how much insurance you need. (For instance, a family may figure that their income would be lower than expenses for a few years, when the children need day care and financial support, but would diminish once they became independent.) If you would expect to need income from the insurance for more than five years, you should perform the calculation explained in step 7.

7. To calculate a long-term insurance need, multiply your current monthly gap by twelve to come up with an annual amount. Finally make sure you account for time value of money by discounting the dollar sum appropriately to get a realistic present value.

Viatical Insurance

In the mid-eighties, as the AIDS epidemic gripped the world and millions of people across the world became victims to it, a new problem faced the insurance community. Thousands of young men and women were afflicted with a deadly disease with no cure and needed a lot of money for their medical treatment. Many of them, ironically, had life-insurance policies which would pay off large sums at their deaths but were of little use to them while alive. The same was true of people suffering from cancer and other forms of terminal illness. It was frustrating but, as with any free society, when a need arises, institutions rise to meet it. In this case, companies sprang up to offer terminally afflicted people a cash buyout of their insurance policies at pennies to a dollar—say fifty cents to a dollar—so that a million dollar face value policy could be bought up for say $500,000. In return for the cash payment, the original policy holder would make the buyer (the company) the beneficiary of the policy upon his death. The company would have the responsibility of making the premium payments to keep the policy active and upon the policyholder's death (a few months to a few years later) would get the face value of the million dollars. It was a win-win for everybody. The afflicted got their much-needed money for medical treatments, while the buyer got a decent return on the investment. As with any new industry, initially there was little regulation of the practices, which led to fraudulent actions by some. Over time, however, everyone wised up to them and such buyouts became fairly standardized. Insurance companies, not wanting to be left out of the action, came up with innovations of their own which included an "Accelerated Benefits" provision in the life insurance policy which would offer anywhere from about 25 to 100 percent of the death benefit as early payment, but policyholders could collect only under very specific circumstances. In most cases, the insurance company would reduce the benefits provided the policyholder before death in order to compensate itself for the interest it would lose through early payout.

In 1997, Congress weighed in by changing the tax code such that the proceeds from either accelerated benefits, or viatical settlements, were tax-exempt as long as the claimant's life expectancy was less than two years and the viatical settlement company was licensed. State taxes are another matter though. While most states have made these settlements tax exempt, some have not. Make sure to check with your local taxing authority.

Investing in Viatical Schemes

Would you like to invest in death and dying and make a return doing so? Some find the idea of investing in such schemes distasteful while others consider it just another investment with its inherent risks and returns. If you belong to the latter group, be careful about evaluating the risks of viatical investments. There have been network TV shows like *20/20* that have showcased individuals who put down a significant amount of cash in the hope of turning a quick profit only to be disappointed and frustrated when the dying refused to die, thanks to improved treatments of terminal illnesses, thereby jeopardizing the possibility of recouping their initial investment.

In sum, do your own homework before investing in a viatical scheme. Invest only in policies from A-rated (or better) insurance companies. Avoid policies less than two years old. Finally, try to buy into a viatical insurance pool (i.e., diversify) rather than dealing one-on-one with one terminally ill patient.

Insurance Advice for Young Couples

When you are starting off with a young family, with pressing needs and little discretionary income, term insurance is the best life insurance policy to buy since, dollar-for-dollar, it's the cheapest and most efficient policy for you.

Lately, however, the government has been forcing insurance companies to get more reinsurance on the insurance products they are selling to the public so that they can readily pay off anybody with a claim. Increase in such reserve costs for insurance companies implies that we, the customers, are paying more for policies.

Insurance companies have also increased the standards of qualification for their best rates for term life insurance. There used to be two rates: one for smokers and one for non-smokers. Those days are gone!

Now, insurance companies look at family health history (including those of your grandparents), your driving record (more than one violation in your record over the last three years and you can kiss those favored rates goodbye), stricter standards for your height/weight ratio, your cholesterol and blood pressure. Only if you have all of these in the best shape possible will you get favored rates for your term life insurance policies.

So, get in the gym and start working out!

Thought Questions

1. What would happen to your insurance premiums if you lived a lifestyle with a high probability of a large dollar loss?

2. Can you think of examples in your everyday life where you routinely use the concepts of adverse selection and moral hazard?

3. Why can't you buy insurance for activities like riverboat gambling or horse-racing?

4. Why do insurance companies accept your risk?

5. What would happen to the world if it were populated only by risk averse people? Hint: Think of a world comprised of only risk averse and risk seeking people. How does insurance fit in this model?

6. What would happen to your insurance policy if the underwriting company declared bankruptcy?

7. When in your life cycle should you switch from no insurance to term insurance to a cash-value insurance?

8. Why do insurance needs decline as you age?

9. What are the risks involved in viatical investments?

10. What are the similarities and differences between investing in a funeral home and in a viatical scheme?

11. Why are inflexibility and opacity, associated with Whole Life policies, a bad thing?

12. What is the dominant characteristic of a Variable Life policy? Does it violate the basic tenets of insurance?

13. Can you think of any circumstances in which you might need life insurance even if you had no dependents?

14. What role, if any, does life insurance play in your retirement planning?

15. Can you think of a few other examples of adverse selection and moral hazard in your life?

Appendix to Chapter 10

Insurance Terms

Beneficiary clause specifies person(s) to receive benefits after the death of the insured.

Change of policy provision permits the policyholder to switch policy forms.

Disability clause may include waiver of premium benefit and/or a disability income portion.

Exclusions stipulate other circumstances in which benefits will not be paid.

Grace period permits the policyholder to retain full coverage for a short period of time after missing a due date for a premium payment.

Guaranteed purchase options enable the insured to purchase additional coverage without providing evidence of insurability.

Living benefits allow the insured to receive a portion of benefits prior to death.

Multiple indemnity increases the face value of the policy by a multiplier (usually 2 or 3) if the insured dies in an accident.

Nonforfeiture options provide a cash value life insurance policyholder with some benefits, even when the policy is terminated prior to its maturity.

Participating policies enable the policyholder to receive dividends that reflect the difference between premiums charged and the actual amount needed to fund the mortality experience of the company.

Payment of premiums specifies when premium payments are due.

Policy loan provisions are loans secured by the cash value of the policy.

Policy reinstatement revives the original contractual relationship between the insurance company and the insured.

Settlement options specify the way that benefits will be paid after the death of the insured.

Suicide clause specifies benefits will not be paid if the insured commits suicide within a specified amount of time after policy inception.

Summary of Life Insurance Contracts

Term Insurance

- Benefit paid if insured dies during the policy period.

- No savings component.

- Economical way for young families to purchase large amounts of life insurance.

Types of Term Insurance

- Straight term coverage remains the same while premiums increase.

- Decreasing term premiums remain the same while coverage decreases.

Features to Look for in Term Insurance

- Renewability allows insured to renew policy without evidence of insurability.

- Convertibility allows insured to convert to Whole Life policy without evidence of insurability.

Whole Life Insurance

- Provides death protection plus a savings feature called cash value.

- If policy canceled prior to death, insured has the right to the cash value of the policy. This is also known as the nonforfeiture right.

Types of Whole Life Insurance

- Continuous premium level premiums are paid until death or cancellation of policy.

- Limited payment level premiums are paid for a specified number of years; insurance remains in force until death.

- Single premium lifetime coverage is purchased with a single premium.

Advantages of Whole Life

- It provides a savings vehicle.

- Cash value can be borrowed against.

- Premiums remain constant.

- Cash value accumulates tax free until redeemed.

Disadvantages of Whole Life

- This insurance provides much less death protection than term insurance.

- Provides lower returns than other savings vehicles.

- Loans must be repaid with interest.

- Tax penalties may be assessed on cash values withdrawn early.

- If you have a loan outstanding when you die, that amount is subtracted from the face value of your policy.

Universal Life Insurance

- This insurance provides death protection plus a savings feature.

- Premiums are "unbundled" into two separate accounts.

- Savings grow at the current interest rate.

- Provides flexibility in premiums paid and death benefit.

- Understand the risks before you buy!

Other Types of Life Insurance

- Variable and Variable Universal Life.

- Insurance on multiple lives.

- Group life insurance.

11

Health and Property Insurance

Are you in good hands? (Allstate commercial)
Before you invite too many cooks in your kitchen to make broth,
make sure you have adequate homeowner's insurance.
—Sugato Chakravarty

Sobering Statistics

A report published by the U.S. Department of Commerce in 2004 shows that about 15.6 percent of the population, or about 45 million people, were without health insurance coverage in 2003, up from 15.2 percent and 43.6 million people, in 2002. Furthermore, the percentage and number of people covered by employment-based health insurance fell between 2002 and 2003 from about 61.3 percent and 175.3 million to 60.4 percent and 174 million. When examined from a different angle, the likelihood of being covered by health insurance rises with household income. Among people in households with annual incomes of less than $25,000 in 2003, about 75.8 percent had health insurance while for those with incomes of $75,000 or more, about 92 percent had health insurance. Looking at the data state-by-state over a three year period from 2001–2003, Texas (24.6 percent) and New Mexico (21.3 percent) had the highest and second highest proportions of uninsured while Minnesota (8.2 percent) had the lowest. Indiana had a 12.9 percent uninsured rate over the same period. Any way we look at it, these are sobering numbers and underscore the need for major health care reform in this country.

There is nothing magical about health insurance relative to other kinds of insurance. It is based on the same risk-pooling concept we have discussed regarding life insurance. The same problems of moral hazard and adverse selection apply here as well. For example, the insurance company would like to keep out the sick people and insure as many healthy people as they can. From the consumer's standpoint, the people who know they are likely to fall ill are the ones who are more enthusiastic about buying health insurance policies than people who consider themselves healthy. However, health insurance has its own terminology which will be covered here so that you will know your stuff when you are sitting across from your insurance agent and he starts using fancy words.

The wide variety in types of policies and quality of coverage can make choosing a health care plan very complicated. In selecting one, it is important to be aware of

239

the types of plans that are available, as well as the features that characterize each type of plan. These are summarized below.

Optimal Design of Health Insurance Contracts

The underpinning of a well-designed health insurance policy is such that there is an appropriate trade-off between risk sharing and moral hazard on the one hand—the perverse incentive of people to seek more care when they are insured. That is, every time they feel a twinge they visit their doctor to have it checked out and demand supplementary tests etc. that can slow the system and make it difficult for real patients to be adequately treated—and the incentive of physicians to encourage such hypochondriac behavior knowing they will be well reimbursed.

Therefore the challenge is to design appropriate coinsurance arrangements where patients pay for care up to the point where the marginal gains from less risk sharing are just offset by the marginal benefits of less wasteful care being provided. The available data shows that both moral hazard and demand-inducement are quantitatively important. Coinsurance-based control on expenditure is a crude incentive mechanism. It also has an added problem in that it does not adequately incentivize the physicians who are the ones making the expenditure-related decisions (i.e., by ordering more tests and prescribing expensive medication). Therefore, the goal is to adequately motivate physicians to buy into the supply side cost containment measures by financially rewarding such behavior.

How does one operate in such an insurance market? Naturally, the economists' approach is to provide the patients with choices through a surge of managed care choices and allow each service-providing entity to compete freely in the market. This allows patients to choose the plan that best fits their budgets at costs that are reasonable.

However, the choice in health insurance is a mixed blessing because of adverse selection problems—the tendency for the sick to choose more generous insurance than the healthy. When the sick and the healthy enroll in different plans, plans that are heavier on the relatively sick (poor risk) would have to charge more to be profitable relative to plans that comprise an average (or better) mix of sick over healthy. The resulting high premiums serve to discourage those who are currently healthier but would prefer generous care from enrolling in those plans (because the premiums are so high), while simultaneously encouraging plans to device strategies that discourage the sick or sickly from enrolling so that the overall costs are reduced.

The welfare losses from adverse selection are large in practice. Added to them are further losses from having premiums that vary with observable health status. Because insurance contracts are annually renewable, patients are denied a "futures contract" insurance: The right to buy health coverage at average rates in the future if they got sick today. As genetic treatments and other forms of medical diagnosis get better and the ability to predict a patient's future health status increases, this lack of futures health care insurance policies could become a significant issue.

At the end of the day, we have to be clear in our minds about what exactly does insurance do and how it relates to expenditures in the health care market. If that crucial link between the two is better health for the covered citizenry then we will need to have a serious debate about whether the health care system today is promoting better health at affordable costs. Consistent with the confusion in public policy, the current research is not clear about which specific approach to health care insurance (universal coverage or some other formula) might promote health in the most cost effective manner. Resolving this question will be the central focus of policy makers and politicians in the years to come.

Reference

Cutler, D.M. and R. J. Zeckhauser, 1999, The Anatomy of Health Insurance, NBER working paper #7176, Boston, MA.

Traditional Indemnity Plans

- These are also called fee-for-service plans.

- You typically choose the doctors and hospitals, pay for the service, and then get paid back by the insurance company.

Managed Care Plans

- Users make monthly payments directly to health care providers.

- A designated group of doctors and hospitals provide services.

- No deductibles are changed, just low co-payments for services.

Types of Managed Care Plans

- Health Maintenance Organizations (HMOs). Comprehensive services are usually at one facility.

- Individual Practice Associations (IPAs). Physicians operate out of their own offices and community hospitals.

- Preferred Provider Organizations (PPOs). Broader network of "approved" physicians allowing use of out-of-network providers.

Major Providers of Health Insurance

The major providers of health care insurance in the United States can be broadly divided in three components: private insurers, government agencies and workman's compensation. Other sources of health care insurance include homeowner's and automobile insurance policies containing limited amounts of medical coverage, and other government health programs at the federal, state, and local levels, including Medicaid and programs for military personnel.

Private Insurers

- Insurance companies
- Managed care organizations
- Blue Cross/Blue Shield (prepaid expense plans)
- Group plans (may incorporate any of the above)

Government Agencies

- Social Security's Medicare program
  —Part A—basic hospital insurance for those sixty-five and over who are qualified
  —Part B—supplementary medical insurance; optional coverage available for a monthly premium to those eligible for Part A

Workers' Compensation Insurance

- Premiums paid by employers for workers injured on the job
- Coverage includes:
  —Medical and rehabilitation expenses
  —Disability income
  —Lump-sum payments for death or dismemberment
  —Second-injury funds

Types of Medical Expense Coverage

Just as health care plans differ, so do the types of medical expense coverage they provide. Here are some examples of types of medical expense coverage:

- Hospital insurance. Pays a portion of per-day room-and-board charges, use of hospital facilities, and selected other services.
- Dental insurance. Covers necessary dental care and some dental injuries. It is usually offered through group insurance plans.
- Surgical expense insurance. Pays cost of surgery either in or out of the hospital. However, not all procedures, such as cosmetic or experimental surgeries, are covered.
- Physicians' expense insurance. Pays physician fees for nonsurgical care in the hospital, including consultation with specialists and lab tests.
- Major medical insurance. Provides broad coverage for illnesses and injuries of a catastrophic nature. Amount of coverage is large.
- Comprehensive major medical. The most desirable coverage, it combines major medical with basic hospital, surgical, and physicians' expense coverage. This type of coverage is usually offered through group plans with a low deductible.

Health Insurance Coverage You Don't Need

Interestingly, health care plans may also offer coverage that you don't need. Here are some examples:

- Accident policies. These only cover certain types of accidents, usually travel-related. Here is how an advertisement for Personal Accident Health Insurance goes:

  "Insures you for accidents *anywhere*: Your home, your yard, at your work, at play, playing sports (there are some exceptions), skiing, bicycling, driving your car, etc.—Anywhere! Anyhow: Break a leg, slice a finger, chip a tooth, crack a rib, pull a hamstring, sprain an ankle, rack your back, whack your head, etc.— Anytime! As long as it is accidental (there are a few other exceptions. Call for details)!"

  Such policies can cost around $25 per month for individuals and about $30 a month for families and provide about $2,500 in benefits with a $100 deductible. Higher benefits cost more, but you get the picture.

- Hospital income policies. These policies provide a specified pre-determined amount for each day of a covered hospital confinement. They also provide limited additional benefits for intensive care, emergencies, extended care, and out-patient surgeries.

  To receive $250 per day in hospital benefits (up to a hospital stay of 365 days), a 45-year-old male living in Indiana will have to pay an annual premium of about $325. A 20-year-old female will have to pay around $290 annually for the same per diem payout. However, statistics provided by the Department of Health and Human Services indicate that the average length of hospital stay in the U.S. is in the neighborhood of 4 days. Do you think you really need this policy?

- Travel Insurance. Provides insurance coverage for foreign trips. Covers medical assistance or transport back home following illness or accident or if you have a serious illness of a close relative back home. Coverage includes emergency medical services on foreign soil and payout for dismemberment, hospital stay, loss of baggage, passport, etc.

  For example, the cost of insurance for a one-week trip to Europe for a single individual is about $20 without winter sports–related coverage and about $40 with winter sports coverage included. Those ski trips to Gstaad can get expensive real fast.

- Cancer Insurance. It is estimated that over 10 million people in the U.S. have cancer insurance policies. They are usually sold through employee benefit plans. Cancer insurance policies promise to provide cash benefits for cancer-related medical expenses such as hospitalization, surgery, anesthesia, chemotherapy, radiation and preventative care. Commonly reported problems associated with this policy include:

Critical Info: Smoking—The Great Elevator of Health Insurance Rates

Smoking is the great Satan, as far as your health insurance rates go. If you don't believe me, go to http://www.quotesmith.com and observe how sensitive your insurance rates are to the various health-related questions you are prompted to answer before representative quotes pop up on the screen. Among the many questions asked are: "Are you a smoker?" If you say "yes" your rates go up by at least twice relative to if you said "no". What is interesting is that if you claim (in one of the other questions) that you are an intravenous drug user (but not a smoker) your rates hardly change. Simply stated, according to the insurance companies, being a smoker is far worse than shooting up on a regular basis.

The bottom line is if you want your insurance rates down, stay off the cigarettes.

Pre-existing Conditions. Most policies will deny coverage for pre-existing conditions. Some cancer insurance policies will deny claims even if the person did not know they were sick when they applied.

Limited Outpatient Coverage. Many cancer insurance policies only cover procedures and treatment that occur during hospitalization. However, many of today's treatments, such as chemotherapy and radiation, are done on an outpatient basis. Translation: You are denied coverage.

Narrow Definitions of Terms. Some insurers have strict, narrow definitions of the conditions and treatment they will cover. For example, a cancer insurance policy may limit coverage for Stage A prostate cancer or exempt certain forms of skin cancer from coverage.

Secondary Illness. Cancer insurance policies often do not cover secondary or cancer-related illnesses and injury such as infection, diabetes or pneumonia.

Critical Info

Insurance Companies try to keep costs down in policies through:
- Preadmission certification.
- Continued-stay review.
- Second surgical opinions.
- Caseworkers.
- Waiver of coinsurance.

Here are the cold hard facts. Cancer insurance will provide coverage only for cancer and it is subject to meeting all of the above hurdles to qualify. Also, according to the National Association of Insurance Commissioners, cancer treatment accounts for approximately 10 percent of U.S. health expenses.

Overall, instead of buying the above policies piecemeal consider having one major medical policy that will pay you more in covered costs for any of the above issues and much more. They also have the benefit of providing significantly higher maximum dollar benefits—sometimes to the tune of $1 million. In addition, major medical policies have the added benefit of covering you (and your family) for any accident and illness, including cancer. They cost more than these policies bought individually but provide significantly more.

Long-Term Care Insurance

An estimated 15 million Americans need assistance from others to carry out everyday activities. Most, but not all, persons in need of long-term care are elderly. Approximately 53 percent are persons aged 65 and older; 44 percent are working-age adults aged 18 to 64; and 3 percent are children under age 18. 40 percent of the older population with long-term care needs are poor or near poor (with incomes below 150 percent of the federal poverty level).

Many major health care insurers still do not cover costs related to long-term medical and personal care. Thus, the market for long-term care insurance is evolving.

Long-term care coverage provides for delivery of medical and personal care, other than hospital care, to persons with chronic medical conditions due to illness or frailty. Policy provisions that should be considered in selecting a long-term care plan include:

- Care. What types and levels of care are covered?

- Benefits. What are the eligibility requirements? How much is the daily benefit and how long will it last?

- Waiting period. Once eligible, how long before the payments begin?

- Renewability. Is the policy guaranteed renewable?

- Pre-existing conditions. How will they be handled?

> ### Do You Need Long-Term Care Insurance?
>
> In determining whether or not you need long-term care insurance, ask yourself the following questions: Do I have a lot of assets to preserve for my dependents? Can I afford the premiums? Is there a family history of disabling disease? Will my family be able to care for me? Based on your answers, it should be obvious to you if you need long-term care insurance.

- Premiums. How much are they? Will they increase? Is there an inflation clause built into the policy?

Other Considerations in Purchasing Long-Term Care Insurance

- Buy the policy while you are healthy.

- Don't buy more coverage than you need. (But how much is that?)

- Increase the waiting period if you can cover costs yourself for a certain time period.

- Understand the policy provisions and when benefits are paid.

Age	Death	Disability
25	24.1%	34.8%
30	23.5%	33.1%
35	22.8%	31.3%
40	21.8%	29.1%
45	20.4%	26.3%
50	18.3%	22.6%
55	14.9%	17.6%
60	9.3%	10.6%

Figure 19: Probability of death vs. a disability between the age shown and age 65.

Disability Income Insurance

There are two threats to your ability to earn an income—death and disability. Death we have already dealt with; here, we deal with disability. Funny thing is we don't know when death will occur, but we know it is inevitable. Disability, on the other hand, isn't a certainty. But what are the chances that you will be disabled before age sixty-five? The table above puts it in perspective. The bottom line, is that you are more likely to become disabled than to outright die!

Disability insurance provides families with weekly or monthly income to replace income lost when the insured is unable to work due to an illness or injury. When estimating disability needs:

1. Estimate monthly living expenses.

2. Estimate existing benefits such as:
   - Social Security
   - Other government benefits
   - Company benefits
   - Group disability policy benefits

3. Subtract (2) from (1).

Property Insurance

Now we turn to another application of the insurance principles we covered earlier: Property insurance and especially, homeowner's insurance. This area of insurance, which most of you will deal with in one form or another, has its own distinct vocabulary and it is essential that you don't run out screaming when your insurance agent starts dropping those terms in conversations with you.

To make decisions regarding the types of property insurance you need, you must first understand the types of losses to which you may be exposed and how these potential losses can best be covered. There are two primary types of exposure that most people face:

Critical Info

The cost of disability insurance, as well as the amount of coverage provided, is dependent on the provisions of the plan. Disability income insurance provisions generally include:

- Definition of disability. "Own occupation" is most desirable (this implies that anytime you are unable to perform the duties of the occupation that you are trained and qualified for, you are considered disabled).
- Benefits. How much will they be and how long will they last?
- Probationary period. How long is it after policy is issued before benefits are available?
- Waiting period. Once disabled, how long is it before benefits begin?
- Renewability. Is it guaranteed renewable or non-cancelable?
- Other features. Look for cost-of-living adjustment, guaranteed insurability option, waiver of premium.

General Considerations in Shopping for Insurance

- Consider your needs.
- How much can you afford?
- What can you do to lower your health care needs?
- Compare policies and costs.
- What does your employer provide?
- Select a quality company (consult A.M. Best ratings) with a good agent.

- Property loss—economic loss because your property is damaged, destroyed, or stolen.
- Liability—damage you cause others, either through your actions or through negligence.

Most property and liability insurance contracts are founded on the principle of indemnity. This principle says that:

- The insured is entitled to payment from the insurance company only if a loss has been suffered.
- The amount of payment should not be greater than the economic value of the loss.

The following concepts are related to the principle of indemnity:

- Insurable interest. You can only insure property in which you have an interest.
- Actual cash value. You can collect, at most, the depreciated value of your property unless you have replacement cost coverage.
- Subrogation. You give your right to collect damages from the person who harmed you to the insurance company once the company has paid you.
- Other insurance. If multiple companies insure the property, the companies together will not pay you more than your economic loss.

Property insurance contracts generally have co-insurance provisions, which require that: (1) You must buy insurance in an amount equal to at least a certain percentage of the replacement value of your property. (2) Otherwise, the insurance company will not fully repay you for your loss. You will have become the "co-insured" and must bear part of the loss.

Homeowner's Insurance

Usually, a person's home is among her most valuable possessions. Therefore, it is important to make sure it is sufficiently protected. Recent statistics released by the Insurance Information Institute show that the nationwide average expenditure for homeowners' insurance is about $600 annually. State Farm Mutual Group appears to be the largest writer of homeowner's insurance bringing in over $11 billion in annual premiums. Allstate is a distant second at around $5.5 billion in annual premiums. American Family Insurance ranks a distant ninth at about $1.2 billion in annual premiums. Finally, the latest data shows that homeowners' claims accounted for about $78 out of every $100 in insurance premiums. Almost all of the remainder goes toward commissions, general overhead expenses, state premium taxes, licenses and fees.

> ### Critical Info
>
> There are several types of homeowner's insurance policies available. These include:
> • HO-4—renter's insurance
> • HO-5 -homeowner's insurance[1]
> • HO- 6—condo owner's insurance
> _____
> 1. Most homeowner's policies are now automatically adjusted so you have coverage for at least 80 percent of the property value. Standard HO policies are sold for replacement at actual cash value. For older homes, policies are sold at replacement cost up to a pre-stated maximum dollar value. Check with your insurance agent before signing on if you happen to have an older home.

Homeowner's insurance policies state the conditions (perils) under which the policy will pay and also stipulate the property that's covered and the extent to which it's covered. Specifically, homeowner's insurance policy provisions include:

Perils and Property Covered

This part is divided into two sections.

- Section I deals with loss to your property, under what conditions it will be covered, and the extent of coverage.
- Section II deals with liability, which may arise in connection with this property, either through your actions or through negligence.
- Perils which are rarely covered are flood, earthquake, and acts of war. Your policy may also exclude other perils. Additional coverage can be obtained through the purchasing of "endorsements. "[64]
- Limits are placed on the property covered. For example, reimbursement for furnishings and personal property in your home will be limited to 75 percent of the policy amount.

Persons Covered

- States who is covered under the policy such as the homeowner and residents of the household. Coverage for guests may be limited.

Locations Covered

- Most policies cover your personal property worldwide even in a second home (although the second home dwelling structure is not covered). Factors that limit homeowner's insurance payments:

  —Insurable interest.
  —Subrogation
  —Other insurance

- Replacement cost is the amount necessary to restore your property at today's prices. All homeowner's policies are now automatically sold at replacement cost unless you happen to live in a designated "older" home.

- Policy limits: For example, the maximum payable on furnishings would be 75 percent of the policy amount. For large dollar items that leave the home (examples are watches, rings, jewelry, golf clubs), consider adding a Personal Property Floater (PPF).

- Internal Limits apply to specific items.[65] For example:
  —Money $200
  —Securities $1,000
  —Watercraft $1,000
  —Jewelry $1,000
  —Firearms $2,000
  —Silverware $2,500
  —Home Computer $5,000

Deductibles help hold down insurance costs because they eliminate frequent small loss claims which are proportionately more expensive to administer. Having higher policy deductibles helps lower premium costs on the one hand and minimizes frivolous claims on the other.

Homeowner's insurance premiums differ from company to company, differ depending on location, and differ on discounts offered, such as for nonsmokers or for security systems. Bottom line is SHOP AROUND before you settle on an insurance company and the specific policy.

Insurance Claim Statistics

How exactly do insurance losses break out by categories? Data over a 4-year period between 1999 and 2003 shows that nationwide about one-third of the claims related to fire, lightning and debris removal, about 25 percent of the claims related to wind and hail related damage, and water and freezing related damages accounted for about 22 percent of the claims. Other property damage accounted for about 10 percent of the claims, while theft resulted in only about 3.5 percent of the claims, and bodily injury resulted in about 4 percent of the claims. Medical payments related to homeowners insurance accounted for less than 1 percent of the claims.

In terms of frequency of perils (leading to homeowners insurance claims), the data indicates that about 25 percent of the occurrences relate to lightning and hail,

17 percent from water due to a failure of indoor appliances or plumbing, 14 percent from theft, 8 percent from damage related to snow and ice, only about 7 percent from fire related damages, 7 percent from water from heavy rain and/or flooding, 3 percent from water from sewers or drains or sump pump overflow, 3 percent from liability resulting in injury to others, and 1 percent from mold. So keep these in mind when you decide whether to purchase additional coverage through your homeowners' policy. Finally, about 27 percent of homeowners had made at least one claim on their home or condo policy in the past ten years, according to a recent survey conducted by an Insurance Research Group.

Insurance agents always caution against filing false claims. If the claim itself is not a large one, false filers may be able to slide by the first time—but even that is not certain since the damage assessors can get involved and awkward questions can be asked. Chances are that it will be discovered and you could be dropped from coverage. People also try to get the insurance company to pay for normal wear-and-ear damage and damage caused by the elements. Word of advice: DON'T! Chances are you will be caught and there are serious consequences to misrepresentation. The analogy is with shoplifting. If you get caught, it is seriously embarrassing and you will have a high price to pay just to save a few dollars. It's not worth it! Finally, don't turn in the small claims. Take large deductibles. Insurance companies reason that those who turn in nickel-and-dime claims are much more likely to have additional claims down the road and your rates could go up as a result.

Mortgage Insurance

Have you ever wondered about mortgage insurance? It's basically like this. The bank loans you the money against a property that serves as the collateral. And mortgage insurance covers the mortgage lender against loss caused by a mortgager's default. It may cover all or part of the loss, and it may not relieve any liability on the borrower's part if the mortgage is defaulted on.

Private mortgage insurance was developed to help borrowers purchase a home without putting 20 percent down as was required by banks and lenders many years ago. Different types of loans have different requirements for the amount of coverage needed, but it essentially serves the same purpose. It helps protect the lender. Note, however, that not all loans require mortgage insurance and the premium varies due to different criteria.

The bank has somehow determined that if you cannot fork out at least 20 percent of the purchase price of the house as down payment they can ask you to get mortgage insurance (as a part of your mortgage loan approval). But why 20 percent? Why not 15 percent or 25 percent? And why is it that if you are unable to come up with 20 percent down, you are somehow at a greater risk of not making the mortgage payments than if you did have the money to reach the magical 20 percent mark?

In any event, mortgage insurance is here to stay and we might as well deal with it. The trick is to avoid paying it if we can. There are a number of ways borrowers can avoid, or reduce, the amount of insurance typically required.

Avoid Paying Mortgage Insurance

Put 20 percent down on a conventional loan. The down payment may be a gift from a relative or it may be borrowed against the your own assets, such as a loan against your 401(k) or automobile. Have your lender or mortgage broker set up two loans: The first mortgage of 80 percent and a "second" for 10 percent or 15 percent. The first mortgage can then be sold by the bank to some national mortgage company while they keep the second loan in house. Apply for an 80 percent mortgage and have the seller carry back a second mortgage (also known as a line-of- credit that is junior to the first mortgage). What does it mean to say that the seller carries back a mortgage? Simply that the seller helps finance the buyer's purchase by loaning the buyer part of his equity, instead of receiving all cash from the buyer at the time of sale. So a carry back does not mean the seller takes out an additional mortgage before selling. Note that the seller may wish to do this only if he or she is desperate to sell the house. Have the lender set up Lender Paid Mortgage insurance and build it in your mortgage. Since the mortgage insurance is built into the interest rate, it may be tax deductible. The downside to this is that since there is no mortgage insurance, you can't really drop it when the property value reaches 80 percent. Anytime mortgage insurance is required on a home loan, discuss with your lender or mortgage broker what other options and loan programs may be available to reduce, or even avoid, mortgage insurance. My experience has been that competition among lenders forces banks to be extremely proactive in working with you to avoid paying PMI (private mortgage insurance).

Conventional Mortgages

When the loan-to-value for an owner-occupied residence is more than 80 percent (or the borrower is putting less than 20 percent down) then private mortgage insurance (PMI) may be required. The premium may be paid on an annual, monthly, or single-premium plan. The premiums are based on the amount and terms of the loan and may vary according to the loan-to-value, type of loan, term of loan, and the amount of coverage required by the lender. The less the borrower puts down, the higher the premium. PMI may be waived when the loan reaches 80 percent of the value of the property.

Woes of the Subprime Borrowers

If you happen to be someone with a spotty credit history and an irregular employment record or someone with a lot of debt and not a whole lot of income to pay it off with, welcome to the real world! You are what lenders refer to as a "subprime borrower." As a subprime borrower, the loans you get from banks or other financial institutions come with a lot of strings attached that other borrowers don't have to deal with. For example, it is not cheap for subprime borrowers to refinance their mortgages at new lower rates. Why, you ask? Prepaying those loans comes with thousands of dollars in fees (also known as prepayment penalties).

These prepayment penalties, all but gone from the mortgages taken by the average (read non-subprime) homebuyers, are alive and well among those who don't qualify for conventional financing. About 80 percent of mortgages in the subprime market carried prepayment penalties in mid-2000, up from 50 percent in 1997, according to a Standard & Poor's survey. Specifically, the penalties often assess borrowers 5 percent of the loan amount outstanding if they pay the mortgage off within its first three to five years for any reason, whether to refinance, consolidate debts or sell the home. Why this differential treatment of fellow citizens? Lenders admit to these stricter provisions in the name of increased risk in lending to someone with a checkered credit record. Critics of this practice argue that such provisions are nothing more than banks practicing "predatory" lending aimed at low-income people who may not fully understand loan terms. Thus, for example, here is the summary of a newspaper account about what could happen to a subprime borrower. A couple with a sub-par credit history takes out two new home loans: A $102,000 loan at a 13.99 percent interest rate and a $10,000 line of credit at 21.9 percent. Apparently, they aren't planning to stay in their manufactured home for long. In fact, one reason they borrow the money is to fix it up so they can sell it and move to a bigger place. The work is finished in due time but by then, the couple find out they can't afford to move, because the bigger loan they got carries a prepayment penalty of about $7,000 if it is paid off within five years of loan inception. This little nugget of information might have been glossed over by the loan officer at the loan application stage. The couple did not know any better. They signed the paper that was put in front of them! Sadly, the people caught in this kind of a bind are the ones who can least afford to pay the prepayment penalty.

The bottom line is that prepayment penalties are no longer lurking in the dark alleyways of consumer lending but have waltzed their way into the borrowing mainstream. However, what the mainstream borrowers can afford is not necessarily what the cash-strapped families can bear, and extracting money (in the form of penalties) from those who already have financial issues may not be the best way to go. It is certainly not the American way!

What Are Your Rights As a Renter?

A 2003 poll conducted by the Independent Insurance Agents & Brokers of America found that 64 percent of respondents living in rental properties had no insurance. The most common misconception, the survey discovered, is that renters believe they are covered by their landlords' homeowner's policies. False!

In a perfect world, landlords and tenants would work together like a well-oiled machine, each generously doing their part to keep the other happy and not disturbing their neighbors' "peaceful enjoyment of the premises," as phrased in Mississippi's landlord-tenant law. While most tenant-landlord relationships fit this description, stories abound of landlord tyranny. And laws that protect both parties have become so complex that understanding your rights as a tenant can be like herding cats. Since landlord-tenant laws vary by state, the key is in knowing your rights—preferably even before you sign your rental agreement. Understanding your state law and the terms of your lease are your best guarantees against future problems.

Finally, to protect yourself from accidents occurring on rented property, get renter's insurance, which is quite affordable. Renter's insurance usually covers fire, lightning, windstorms, hail, explosions, vehicles, theft, and sudden or accidental damage from smoke. The average basic cost is about $100 per year for $10,000 coverage, depending on the facility's construction type.

The appendix to this chapter lists 15 common renters' rights. If any of your rights are violated, you should report your landlord to the appropriate authorities right away.

Auto Insurance

Automobiles also tend to be among people's most valuable possessions and, therefore, should also be insured against loss. And loss includes the vehicle being stolen. Every 25 seconds, a motor vehicle is stolen in the U.S. The overall odds of having a vehicle stolen is about 1:190 and the odds are considerably higher in urban areas as common sense would suggest. In terms of vehicle thefts reported per 100,000 people, Modesto, California, has the dubious distinction of being first in the country with 1,346; while Detroit, Michigan, ranks tenth with 905. Other well-known cities in the top ten include Phoenix, Las Vegas, Miami and San Diego. The latest publicly available data shows that thieves prefer to steal Honda Accords and Toyota Camrys. Maybe there are just so many of them on the roads that they are the easiest and the most convenient to steal. Among luxury cars, Cadillac Escalade is a popular choice of thieves. On average, insurance companies paid out about $167 per year in theft claims for every insured Escalade. The corresponding number for Corvettes is $75. At the bottom of the list is the Audi Quattro at $55. Keep these facts in mind the next time you are thinking of buying a car.

Auto insurance policies are comprised of four parts.[66] These parts, and their respective provisions, are:

Part A: Liability
- Required in most states.
- Pays injury and property damages to others when you are responsible for the loss.
- Covers costs of settling or defending claims for damages.

Policy Limits
- Insurance company will likely limit the total damages paid for any one accident.
- Typical single dollar limits are $50,000, $100,000, $300,000, and $500,000.
- Some insurers split the limits of liability coverage available.
- Example: Minimum Liability Requirements for Texas—20/40/15
- For Indiana, it is 25/50/10

- For Louisiana, it is a paltry 10/20/10
- For Illinois, 20/40/15.

So, in Illinois, if you have only the minimum, your insurer will cover at most:

- $20,000 bodily injury per person.
- $40,000 bodily injury per accident.
- $15,000 property damage per accident.

The question is: Who pays if the costs exceed these limits? You do, of course. Keep that in mind when you decide how much insurance to purchase. However, the higher the policy limits, the higher the premium. The general rule of thumb here is to start off with the minimum coverage limits when you are starting off in life and have little money to spare. Then, as you become more established in life, increase the coverage appropriately.

Part B: Medical Payments
- Reimburses for medical expenses resulting from an accident.
- Covers the insured, family members and passengers in covered autos.
- Covers injuries sustained as a pedestrian or while riding a bicycle.

Part C: Uninsured Motorists
- Pays when other driver has no insurance or in the case of a hit-and-run. Must meet the following criteria:
  —Other driver was at fault.
  —Other driver had no insurance and you know who they are.
  —Damages were incurred.
  —Additional coverage available for protection against under-insured motorists.

Part D: Damage to Your Car
Collision
- Pays the actual cash value of the damage (loss), minus any deductibles.
- Pays no matter who is at fault.
- Usually required for financed cars (lender wants to protect the investment).

Comprehensive
- Protects against loss to insured auto caused by any peril other than by collision.
- Examples: fire, theft, falling objects.

Then there are a number of factors that come into play in the determination of automobile insurance premiums. Some of these factors are:

- Where the car will be driven.
- Amount the vehicle will be driven.
- Personal characteristics of the driver.
- Type of automobile.
- Driving record of the insured.

To a great extent, your actions and your choice of vehicle options can influence your automobile insurance premiums. To hold these to a minimum,

- Take driver's education.
- Take defensive driving.
- Be a good student.
- Have airbags and a security system.
- Raise your deductibles.
- Raise your liability limits.

Other Types of Property and Liability Insurance

While homeowner's and automobile insurance are the most commonly needed types of property and liability insurance, people may have special needs for other related types of insurance. Some of these may include:

- Flood insurance—not included in standard homeowner's policies and is available as a separate policy.
- Earthquake insurance is available as an endorsement on homeowner's policies.
- Umbrella personal liability insurance—additional liability coverage.
- Insurance on other forms of transportation—mobile homes, RVs, boats, golf carts, motorcycles, etc.
- Professional liability insurance—lawsuit protection for professionals. This is especially important as you climb up the professional ladder. You need to be protected from lawsuits against you. Opposing counsel always looks at your financial means to decide whether it is worth her time to go after you in court.

Settling Claims

In the event a type of loss or accident that you are insured against occurs, it is important that you comply with the claims procedures established by your insurance

Anecdote: A Honking Issue

Collette is a young woman from South Africa. Let's just say that English is spoken a little differently there. Just how differently is illustrated in the following story.

Once she was riding in the passenger seat while a friend of hers, Susan, was driving her SUV through the busy streets full of end-of-workday traffic. Suddenly, another car swerves in front of them and cuts them off. Collette gets into a panic and starts screaming, "Susan, Susan, hoot the hooter, hoot the hooter . . ."

Susan starts laughing hysterically and grinds the car to a screaming halt while tears are rolling down her cheeks. "Honey, in this country, we say 'honk the horn' not 'hoot the hooter.' Hooting the hooter might get you free drinks though."

Thus, when driving, be a defensive driver and always remember to hoot that hooter!

company. The following are general recommendations that will help improve the likelihood your claim will be settled properly:

- After an accident, get names, addresses, phone numbers, driver's license numbers, insurance policy numbers, and description of vehicles of all parties involved.
- Take pictures or sketch the accident.
- Get names, addresses, and phone numbers of any witnesses.
- Contact the police immediately.
- Contact your insurance agent immediately.

In the event of an accident, your company will:

- Require timely notice of accident.
- Investigate the claim.
- Require you to prove your loss.

The claims adjustor will then:

- Evaluate the claim.
- Recommend settlement of the amount requested, or a lesser amount, or recommend denial of the claim.

A Bird's Eye View of the Insurance Industry

By Joe Gallo (BullishBankers, LLC)

The past year has truly been one of misery for many industries, most particularly the financial sector. The insurance industry has been one of the hardest hit in recent times. Many of the companies have lost a vast amount of share value in the past month, and conglomerate American International Group [AIG: 1.88, +0.07 (+3.87 percent)] is still reeling from its credit default swaps and loans from the U.S. Government. A global recession has hurt all aspects of their industry, with profits and revenues related to life insurance being the worst hit. The year 2009 will be a trying time for the industry, with a competitive race for survival among the incumbents. Below is a list of the primary competitors along with an assessment and predictions for future power in this changing industry.

MetLife

MetLife [MET: 32.46, +1.00 (+3.18 percent)] is the largest U.S. Life insurance company that primarily deals with customers in the U.S., Central America, Europe, and Asia. As I stated in an earlier article, Metlife appears to have encountered the worst of its problems and is now poised to expand. It was the first insurance company to raise an extensive amount of capital and is in a relatively stable financial condition. Most companies are taking a defensive capital stance, yet MET's solid financial positioning will offer the company the resources to be active as well as the opportunity to acquire assets to the detriment of its competitors. Management is also a crucial part to the strength of Metlife. They hold the key to one of the strongest investment portfolios, which is valued at approximately $322.5 billion. The company is considered to be in a very secure position, and the relatively conservative asset portfolio is a substantial benefit.

Metlife's management has stated that they would like to continue to develop their foreign market share. It is also very likely that they will get involved with the AIG asset off-loading that is predicted to happen in the near future. MET has the greatest potential to expand and is already seeing growth in revenues in the Chinese and Japanese markets.

MET's financials remain very strong. MET is in the top quartile of the industry in almost all major categories, with very respectable revenue growth of 14.6 percent. It also posted one of its highest EPS' last year, with annual earnings of $4.14 a share, despite some of the worst circumstances ever for insurance giants. Management believes that this growth and stability amid crisis only provides further credibility, proving that MET is better equipped to survive a recession and is positioned to emerge as the insurer of choice going forward.

AIG

American International Group [AIG: 1.88, +0.07 (+3.87 percent)] has plummeted in recent months following its risky credit default swap endeavors of 2008. It appears as though $150 billion of bailout funds may not suffice, as it is very likely that it will receive additional money from the government. This comes in light of news that AIG posted 4th quarter losses of -$61.7 billion, and over $100 billion in the past 5 quarters. Even scarier is the fact that this company has a present value market cap of only $1.4 billion dollars. AIG's original problems stemmed from selling credit default swaps, insurance contracts to back up collateralized debt obligations. When the value of these swaps plummeted, AIG was forced to cover the difference by paying more capital. AIG also took a major hit from its MBS (mortgage backed securities) exposure and was forced to take billions in write downs as the housing crisis escalated. The result was an original bridge loan received from the government for $85 billion which was later revised.

Already in an appalling situation with the government owning 79.9 percent of the company's equity, additional support would likely warrant adding AIG completely to the federal balance ledger. The equity value of AIG has become extremely diluted and is no longer a safe or a conservative investment. It also has lost the ability to pay its original bridge loans back to Uncle Sam unless a huge restructuring occurs. It is likely that the company will offer some of its assets as payment, but this will prove to be tricky as it will be very difficult to lock-in on a fair market assessment when everything is in such rapid decline. In addition, AIG also struggles because of the strict government oversight required as a result of taking significant aid. This has caused AIG to lose key management and employee talent to competitors and has formed a more rigid and regulated business environment.

I don't foresee AIG aiding any shareholders, but rather other insurance companies looking to expand their asset holdings at bottom prices. It is unlikely that this company will be able to independently move forward, and speculation is very high that the company will be split into three sub-sectors that will be controlled by the government. I anticipate the government taking either managerial control of these businesses or to take complete control of high valued assets to pay back the loan. I feel that this will lead to the eventual auctioning off of these valuable assets to other companies, because the government does not intend to be in the insurance business long-term.

Allianz

Allianz [AZ: 9.79, -0.02 (-0.20 percent)] is Europe's largest insurer, dealing primarily with insurance but also banking and asset management services. It is a German based company that appears to be in decent standing for the coming year. It posted larger than expected losses, but this comes in light of the sale of its Dresden Bank asset to Commerzbank. The losses realized from this sale comprised a large percentage of its $3.8 billion quarterly losses. Management, in their 2008 financial press conference, admitted that this was a mistake given the economic climate which has hurt the company since 2007.

It appears as though the worst is behind AZ, as the sale of Dresden has now given the company a solvency rate of 161 percent. In today's economy, this is a tremendous bonus that ranks it near the top of all its competitors. Worldwide, it also ranks #1 in property casualty insurance, #8 among all life insurers and #2 among all asset managers. It is the second largest insurance company in the world in terms of market capitalization.

The size of the asset management division would appear to be a weakness due to the problems created in the equity markets; however, 85 percent of the portfolio is in fixed income asset management, with the rest in equities and a mere 2 percent in the real estate market. The company is also extremely underweight in the variable annuities market, which provides yet another buffer from the market conditions. This has safeguarded AZ from the financial crisis, with Michael Diekmann, Allianz's CEO, stating that it had learned from the crisis in 2001–2002 and had prepared by having extra capital and a more efficient, less complicated structure of management.

AZ appears to have positioned itself well, and with an already expansive global presence, it should be able to remain a top competitor in the insurance industry. It is ranked as a top 5 competitor in 27 countries around the world. Due to size and financial positioning, I see the company staying relatively conservative in the near future, especially after being burned by the Dresden acquisition. However, that being said, it is still a good company that issues respectable dividends and appears to be a safe play.

Aflac

Aflac Incorporated is a health and life insurance provider through its subsidiary, American Family Life Assurance Company of Columbus [AFL: 36.17, +2.09 (+6.13 percent)]. While headquartered in Columbus, Georgia, and providing insurance throughout the United States, most of AFL revenues are earned in its Japanese market. Over the past 3 years, annuities from Aflac Japan have actually returned 72 percent of their annual revenues, while holding 87 percent of their total assets. Aflac Japan's greatest asset is their cancer policies which successfully funds a large percentage of the entire company.

Aflac has hurt itself by being over ambitious with its investment portfolio. It is one of the few companies who has not yet faced its stiffest challenges. It is still extremely susceptible to European bank troubles because of investments in subordinated financial instruments called "hybrid securities." These investments in hybrid securities total approximately $18.5 billion. This number is over one quarter of Aflac's total debt and perpetual securities as of their latest 10-K filing. Of this, $9.1 billion in securities has no maturity date which is very harmful because Aflac does not know for what period it is susceptible to losses. This safeguards the company in the short term with only $306 million due in 2009. In addition, they experienced losses due to CDO's.

The investment portfolio appears aggressive and laden with risk, and thus may come back to haunt Aflac in 2009. Also, Aflac posted nice returns in the fourth quarter, because 70 percent of the Japanese annuities market is denominated in Yen, as the significant currency appreciation of the yen inflates earnings. Yen also is the denomination of almost all of its securities, and it has been hurt with almost all investments in the Japanese economy in the last 2 years due to the poor interest rate environment.

Historically, Aflac has proven to be a fairly reliable company; however, with numerous obligations to European banks and a reliance on the Japanese economy, one may question its investment strategy. Aflac will have to await the end of the credit crisis and hope for a strong Japanese economy in order to achieve quality returns.

Prudential

Prudential [PRU: 43.68, +1.73 (+4.12 percent)] is the second largest life insurer in the United States. It has operations in the U.S, Europe, Asia, and Latin America. PRU has three main business components: Insurance, Investment, and Foreign Insurance and Investment. Like all other insurance companies, PRU has struggled to stay liquid as well as minimize investment losses.

PRU has gone through a number of downgrades from investors due to questions about its liquidity and ability to pay off debt. It faces a very high amount of operating debt relative to competitors, and this may force changes in the future. Analysts believe that all of 2009 debt should be payable because Prudential paused its stock buyback plan and froze dividends. However, this tight capital situation restricts its financial flexibility.

In addition to capital issues, PRU faces above average risk on variable life and annuities businesses, as well as equity markets pertaining to its asset management, both domestic and abroad. With volatile credit and investment markets, PRU must be extremely careful moving into the future.

Prudential has taken positive strides by both increasing its foreign market exposure by injecting $400 million into Japan and buying Yamato Life units, a Japanese insurance firm that recently declared bankruptcy. However, in a buyer's market, I don't foresee Prudential being capable of drastically improving its position relative to its competitors. I feel that Prudential has a lot of work to do; focusing internally on its own operations, straightening out its debt obligations, and minimizing investment losses.

Travelers

Travelers [TRV] is a company that provides various commercial and personal property and casualty insurance products and services. Its dominance of the commercial issuance market and strong financials places it above most of its peers. It has a strong financial position, courtesy of a large and strong balance sheet. Secure financials will allow it to be an active buyer in the auctioning of AIG non-core assets, which should take place in the near future.

TRV is especially solid in sales because of its diversified revenue stream. Its marketing of numerous products as well as a strong insurance based business model will allow it strong growth in the future. The company recently released a new model, CustomComps, which offers large businesses more options in choosing packages for their convenience. It is in these markets that TRV will continue to thrive and flourish in the future.

This past year, TRV posted a net income of $2.9 billion, which despite a decline, is encouraging considering the hurricane losses in the third quarter. It posted a very respectable return on equity of 12.8%. This solid year, despite facing natural disasters and financial crisis, speaks volumes about the management which has reaffirmed that they expect returns on equities to stay in the mid-teens.

In addition to the operating model, its investment portfolio has been one of a conservative nature. It has completely avoided CDO's and other security and credit swaps. This will prove a tremendous asset in the future, as insurance companies are primarily judged now on their investment portfolios' stability. Staying clear of these credit issues will allow TRV to focus on the basics and continue to post solid returns just like in the past year.

The Future

I don't believe that the Insurance Industry as a whole has completely reached bottom, with many companies' investment portfolios yet to incur all the losses that are anticipated. In the near future, the industry will once again present investment opportunities once all losses have been incurred. Once the dust from AIG settles, we will be able to see more clearly how this industry will move forward, as it is still murky. However, many companies are trading relatively cheap compared to their book value. While many are not in a solid financial position, several companies have set themselves up nicely for the long term. MetLife has clearly positioned itself to become the winner of the insurance race in the future. I feel that Travelers is a close second, and has proven itself to be a very stable company under quality leadership. The next 6 months will be a slow first leg of the race, but it should turn into an all out sprint after the turn.

Intuition from Insurance Research

Here, I will essentially summarize the work of four economists whose research forms the cornerstone of any work in insurance markets. Recall that asymmetric information is a common feature of market interactions.

That is, the seller of a product often knows more about its quality than the prospective buyer. Thus, for example, a job applicant will typically know more about his own ability than his potential employer. Similarly, the buyer of an insurance policy usually knows more about her individual risk than does the insurance company. What happens to prices and traded quantities if agents on one side of the market are better informed than those on the other? What can better informed agents do to improve their individual market outcome? What can the less informed agents do to improve their individual market outcome? These are some of the most intuitive questions on which the science of insurance is based.

George Akerlof was the first to explore the importance and implications of the fact that sellers in many markets are better informed about product quality than buyers. At any given price, a seller of high-quality units is less willing to sell than the seller of low-quality units.[67] Can you think of why?

> ## Auto Insurance Reality
>
> Auto insurance rule of thumb: The car that is moving at the time of the accident is the guilty party! In the world of auto insurance, it pays to stand still. For instance, if the car ahead of you brakes suddenly because the driver wants to admire a flock of flying geese, and you hit him, it is deemed to be your fault!

Rational buyers anticipate this, suspecting that the item they face is of low quality. This rational skepticism depresses prices, which further discourages sellers of high-quality units, who continue to leave the market until only low-quality items remain for sale. This is another manifestation of adverse selection. Adverse selection may thus hinder mutually beneficial transactions. And if every individual focuses on his or her own selfish betterment, then collectively society is better off. Akerlof's brilliance lay in suggesting that many market institutions we observe all around us may have arisen precisely to cope with the problem of adverse selection. This insight has led to a rich body of subsequent research.

Another economist by the name of Michael Spence asked under what conditions can the better informed sellers in the market truthfully and credibly transmit, or "signal," their information to the less informed (the buyers).[68] For such signaling to work, sellers of high-quality items must take observable measures that are too costly for low-quality sellers to mimic. So, for example, the "sellers" could be job applicants in a market where employers cannot observe the job candidates' ability directly, only indirectly through their educational record. If the less able students need to spend more effort and time than the smart students in order to obtain any given level of education, then the smart ones signal their ability by undertaking an education which is too costly for the less able students to mimic, given the prevailing wage difference.

In such circumstances, signaling overcomes the problem of adverse selection, albeit at a cost—the more able educate themselves more than the less able, even if education has no direct effect on their productivity. Spence pointed out the existence of a variety of situations and how these may entail different returns to education for men and women, or among the various races, even in the absence of innate productivity differences between these groups. Other examples of market signals are costly advertisements, guarantees, highly taxed dividends paid to shareholders, and a range of other observed phenomena.

Finally, two economists, Michael Rothschild and Joseph Stiglitz, provided a natural complement to Akerlof's and Spence's analyses.[69] They asked what less-informed consumers could do to improve their lot. They showed how, and when, less-informed consumers might extract information from their better informed counterparts on the other side of the market by offering a menu of contracts. A prime example can be found in insurance, where companies usually offer alternative contracts where higher deductibles may be traded off against lower premiums. In this way, their clients are, by their own choice of contract, effectively divided into distinct risk classes. Low-risk clients typically pay a lower premium, but have to accept a relatively high deductible, which is needed for high-risk clients to not mimic this option. Why is it not practical for high-risk clients to mimic the contract meant for low-risk clients?

Bringing It Together: Shop Around for the Right Policy

Here is a typical scenario. As a regular guy in your early twenties, you and your wife bought a new home and had your first child earlier this year. Based on the classes you took in college, you realize it may be wise to start thinking about buying some life insurance protection for your young family. So you scour the local billboards and watch TV commercials to find a local financial planner who will provide you with some direction. This is the professional with the message "I don't like people, I just love to sell insurance!" Not entirely trusting this guy, you do some research on your own on the Internet. You go to several Web sites with instant quotes and compare several of them. You find a promising policy from John Hancock Financial Services Inc. that provides more coverage for about $20 a month—less than half the cost of the policy your adviser (the guy who just loves to sell insurance) recommended, so you buy the John Hancock policy online.

Many consumers are embracing online insurance offerings from reputable companies to save both time and money. In the wake of the sweeping Gramm-Leach-Bliley legislation, enacted to law in 1999, which dismantled the Depression-era walls between insurers and banks, banks and other financial-services firms are moving into the business of selling insurance. At the same time, the number of Web sites offering insurance information and instant price quotes is on the rise. So consumers now have more choices than ever before. Sites like quotesmith. com have made consumers' searches a breeze. You can even compare across multiple policies. For any type of policy, you only need to fill in some basic information and out pops a bunch of insurance quotes, along with the insurance company ratings and other relevant information to help you come to a decision quickly and efficiently. After all, "when insurance companies compete, you win!"

Experts, however, argue that because there's so much information and so many options out there, it's very easy for consumers to be overwhelmed by their choices. The online insurance industry is in its infancy and only about 22 percent of property and casualty insurance sites offer online quotes. Further, only half that number allow users to purchase policies on the Internet. An even smaller number offer life insurance quotes and policy information. But, clearly, demand for these services is growing. One available statistic measured in 2005 shows that 13.6 percent of the U.S.-adult-active-online population, or 12.6 million consumers, purchased Term Life insurance using the Internet as part of the process.

Because so many factors are involved in deciding the right level of insurance coverage, some consumers are understandably leery about taking the do-it-yourself approach. But there are benefits to buying insurance on the Internet—most notably, you avoid the often intimidating initial consultation with an insurance agent who may be working for commission on behalf of certain insurance companies and may be a bit biased in his recommendations to you. Also, research evidence indicates that agents often "oversell" insurance and customers end up buying more than they need, all to line the agent's pockets with more commission dollars. In comparison, when you go to the appropriate Web sites, you're not paying exorbitant commissions for a straightforward product. Among the most popular insurance Web sites are InsWeb.com, an online insurance marketplace based in Gold River, California; Quotesmith.com, a Darien, Illinois, insurance price-comparison service; and Term4You.com, a site sponsored by Boston financial services giant John Hancock. Each provides users with a handful of policy quotes with terms that can be easily compared.

When getting started, financial planners suggest that the first step should be to determine how much coverage you need. The goal of life insurance is to replace the income of a family member should he or she die unexpectedly. The accepted rule of thumb is to purchase enough insurance to replace the income of the deceased for as long as surviving family members might need it. Sites like Mostchoice.com, an online financial planning and advisory service based in Atlanta, offers a needs analysis calculator that can help consumers determine how much they'll need in a life insurance policy. The site allows users to anonymously enter information about such factors as their annual income, assets, investments, and debts, and then estimates insurance needs. And while price is important, it's also necessary to carefully consider the reliability of the companies issuing the policies and the terms of the policies you're pricing in order to make a true apples-to-apples comparison. To learn more about a company's reliability and ability to pay out benefits, visit the site of insurance-news service Insure.com of West Hartford, Connecticut, which includes links to ratings information. Users can search by state, rating, or type of insurance to learn about a company's stability. The site also offers an explanation of how ratings are determined. Some insurance portals can help consumers sift through the confusing details and help answer some basic questions. Insurance.com, an affiliate of Fidelity Investments, the Boston financial-services firm, has an extensive glossary with words and terms to become familiar with when buying insurance. Understanding the myriad types of insurance policies available is also important. For example, experts suggest that you avoid buying "reentrant" term-life insurance, which means that at the end of a term, a policyholder must undergo a physical to get "reapproved" for that policy.

If the customer fails to pass the physical, she could end up paying a higher rate. And while the Internet has made shopping for insurance easier, consumers with complex financial situations, such as blended families or families with a special-needs child, would do well to consult a financial planner or insurance agent. In fact, a prudent approach might be to combine Internet research along with a conversation with a qualified agent. Doing some homework on the Internet before going into an insurance office can help put consumers at ease. The bottom line is to be educated and make decisions based on all the possible options you have. It is the same in trading. For easy trades, use a Web site that is cheap, like Scottrade, or a discount stock broker like Charles Schwab. For trades where you want some professional

Ten Insurance Dos and Don'ts

Neil Klemme, an agent with State Farm Insurance in West Lafayette, Indiana, wishes his clients and others would be mindful of the following:

1. Don't ever go without health insurance (even if you are a young college graduate and will be picking up coverage soon from an employer). Short-term health insurance is cheap and provides the coverage you need.

2. Buy high liability limits. It is not much more expensive and it's all that stands between your money/future earnings and the plaintiff's attorney.

3. Buy reasonable (i.e., higher) deductible policies (low deductibles are not always a good thing).

4. Don't buy insurance for the little things. Insurance is meant for catastrophic events in your life—not as warranty or maintenance issues for your property or appliances.

5. Use an insurance agent. The lay person knows little to nothing about insurance. Companies that have agents are not more expensive and you will get good advice at little or no extra cost.

6. Don't count on your life insurance at work. Many companies cut benefits, many people change jobs, and what they "give" you at work is usually not enough coverage. Take the time to figure out how much you might need (read this book again) and the type of policy you need.

7. Buy renters insurance. It is inexpensive, and your landlord's and/or parent's insurance does not cover you. Also, renter's insurance converts to homeowner's/condo insurance easily if/when you become a property owner.

8. Insure your recreational vehicles (i.e., boats, 4-wheelers, snowmobiles, etc). Your homeowner's and/or renter's policies do not extend to them. It is possible that your homeowner's policy would give you minimal coverage for theft on premises but you will not receive liability coverage or any off-premise coverage.

9. Motorcycles do not have a "grace period" for coverage. When you purchase an automobile, you have 14 days (every company is a little different) to call your agent and add the new vehicle. By contrast, you must call and add the motorcycle to your policy before you ever drive it.

10. You need disability insurance coverage. Your chances of becoming disabled at work are higher than outright death (as covered in this book) and you need to be adequately protected. Many companies offer it as part of your employment package. If they do, you should sign up.

input, consult a financial planner or use a full service broker like Merrill Lynch or Edward Jones.

Thought Questions

1. Do you think health care insurance has reached crisis levels in the U.S.?

2. Is there anything specific about health insurance vis-à-vis other insurance policies?

3. Why are some insurance policies a waste of your money?

4. Why is disability insurance a useful policy? Why do consumers overlook it?

5. Why do you think major health care insurers do not cover costs related to long-term medical and personal care?

6. Why is smoking looked upon so negatively by insurance companies relative to drug usage?

7. What is a common insurance mistake that is particularly applicable to health insurance policies?

8. In the Hurricane Katrina disaster, many residents with full homeowner's protection were told by the insurance companies they were not going to be reimbursed for the devastation of their homes. Do you know why?

9. How do you get classified as a subprime borrower?

10. What can you do if your landlord routinely violates your privacy rights by coming into your apartment unannounced?

11. What happens if you are hit from behind by an uninsured motorist and it is clearly his fault?

12. What are some actions you could take to lower your auto insurance premium?

13. With the rise of Web sites selling insurance policies and the growing popularity of the Internet overall, do you see the traditional insurance agent becoming extinct anytime soon? Why or why not?

14. What are two major problems that insurance companies have to deal with when deciding who to insure and what rate to charge them?

15. How can you as a consumer "signal" your quality to the insurance company so you can get the best rates?

16. Can you think of other areas in your life where you could apply the intuition developed by the four economists discussed in the section "Intuition from Insurance Research"?

17. What is special about Metlife and Travelers' insurance companies?

Notes

64. Examples of endorsements include earthquakes, back-up of sewer or drain, damage through hydrostatic pressure, mine subsistence insurance, nurses' professional liability, childcare liability, theft from a new construction, waterbed liability, building materials theft, and many more. Check with your insurance agent for a full list of endorsements that come with your homeowner's policy.

65. You can also buy additional coverage at extra cost.

66. Standard auto insurance policies have four broad classifications of autos: Normal, motorcycle, antique/classic, and commercial.

67. Akerlof, G., 1970. "The Market for 'Lemons': Qualitative Uncertainty and the Market Mechanism." *Quarterly Journal of Economics* 84: 488–500.

68. Spence, M., 1974. "Job Market Signaling." *Quarterly Journal of Economics* 87: 355–374.

69. Rothschild, M., and Stiglitz, J. 1976. "Equilibrium in Competitive Insurance Markets: An Essay on the Economics of Imperfect Information." *Quarterly Journal of Economics* 90: 629–650.

Appendix to Chapter 11

Important Insurance LinksINKS

- Insweb—http://www.insweb.com
- Quotesmith.com—http://www.quotesmith.com
- Term4You.com—http://www.term4you.com
- Mostchoice.com—http://www.mostchoice.com
- Insure.com—http://www.insure.com
- John Hancock Financial Services—http://www.johnhancock.com

Up Close: Fifteen Common Renters' Rights

1. The Fair Housing Act makes it illegal to deny housing to a tenant on the grounds of race, color, sex, religion, disability, family status, or national origin.

2. Residential rental units should be habitable and in compliance with housing and health codes—meaning they should be structurally safe, sanitary, weatherproofed, and include adequate water, electricity, and heat.

3. Many states limit the amount landlords can charge for security deposits. (See http://www.nolo.com/encyclopedia/ articles/lt/lt1.html to find out if yours is one of them.)

4. A landlord should make necessary repairs and perform maintenance tasks in a timely fashion, or include a provision in the lease stating that tenants can order repairs and deduct the cost from rent.

5. A landlord must give prior notice (typically twenty-four hours) before entering your premises and can normally only do so to make repairs or in the case of an emergency.

6. Illegal provisions in a rental agreement (provisions counter to state law) are usually nonenforceable in court.

7. If a landlord has violated important terms related to health, safety, or necessary repairs, you might have a legal right to break your lease.

8. If you have to break a long-term lease, in most states landlords are required to search for a new tenant as soon as possible rather than charge the tenant for the full duration of the lease.

9. Damage or security deposits are not deductible for "normal wear and tear." Some states require that a landlord give an itemized report of any deductions.

10. Most states require landlords to return refundable portions of a security deposit within fourteen to thirty days after the tenant has vacated the premises, even in the case of eviction.

11. Landlords usually can't legally seize a tenant's property for nonpayment of rent or any other reason, except in the case of abandonment as defined by law.

12. Landlords are legally prohibited from evicting tenants as retaliation for action a tenant takes related to a perceived landlord violation.

13. A landlord cannot legally change the locks, shut off (or cause to have shut off) your utilities, or evict you without notice; eviction requires a court order.

14. If a landlord makes life so miserable for you that you are forced to move, it may be considered "constructive eviction," which is usually grounds for legal action.

15. In many states, it's illegal for a lease to stipulate that the tenant is responsible for the landlord's attorney fees in the event of a court dispute.

Critical Info: Health Insurance Policy Provisions

In comparing health care coverage offered by different providers, you should examine the provisions of each type of plan. Provisions that are generally associated with health care coverage include:

Terms of Payment

How much your medical expense plan will pay is usually determined by the following four provisions:

- Deductible. The initial amount which is not covered and is determined on a calendar-year or per-incident basis.
- Participation (Co-insurance). Company pays only a portion of the medical expenses after the deductible. Plan may include a stop-loss provision to cap your out-of-pocket expenses.
- Internal limits. This limits the amount paid on certain items to usual, customary, and reasonable charges, even if the cost of the entire surgery or illness is within the norms.
- Coordination of benefits. This eliminates double payment when coverage is provided under more than one policy.

Terms of Coverage

Important provisions to consider in your health care policy:

- Persons and places covered. Who is covered and where are you covered?
- Cancellation. Obtain a policy that cannot be canceled unless premiums are not paid.
- Continuation of group coverage (COBRA). At your expense, you can continue your previous employer's coverage for up to eighteen months after you leave the job.
- Rehabilitation coverage. How much is provided?
- Pre-existing conditions. How are they covered?
- Pregnancy and abortion. What is the extent of the coverage provided?
- Mental illness. How restricted is the coverage?

SECTION C: ACTION PLAN

- Do a needs-analysis using some of the principles discussed here and compute an estimate of the amount your family might need if something happened to you. Do the same computations for your spouse. What discount rate would you use to compute an appropriate present value? Use the principles discussed in this book to justify your choice.

- Based on your needs-analysis, make sure you have adequate term insurance coverage.

- You should have some kind of health insurance protection as you graduate from college and before you start a job.

- Your property insurance coverages should have high deductibles in order to keep premiums reasonable.

- If you are in a line of work where disability is a concern, buy an adequate disability policy with a generous definition of what being disabled means.

- Avoid taking out insurance on small losses and instead focus on potentially large dollar losses with a small likelihood of occurrence.

Section D: Retirement

12

Retirement

The question isn't at what age I want to retire, it's at what income.
—George Foreman

When a man retires, his wife gets twice the husband but only half the income.
—Chi Chi Rodriguez

We Are All Potential Millionaires

Growing up, I was led to believe there was a God above who decided the station of life we were born in. Whether we were rich was simply a matter of winning the lottery of life by being born in the right family. And if we won the lottery of life, we would spend the rest of our lives not in working to earn money to feed our families but rather, in figuring out ingenious ways to spend it.

Contrarily, if we did not win the lottery of life, we would spend our lives figuring out ways to make a living and cutting corners to make ends meet. Never was it implied that we could be born a non-millionaire and then become one just by careful investing combined with the miracle of compounding and the time value of money (TVM).

My parents were educated people but this kind of thinking simply did not enter their consciousness. But, believe it or not, it is not only possible but an eminently reachable goal. To make my point, I will use some graphs and numerical examples depicting growth rates that are reasonable, based on the historic performance of the stock markets in the United States over the past seventy years or so. Remember that when we think long-term, as is the case with retirement, the day-to-day and short-term fluctuations of the markets get smoothed out over time and become increasingly investor friendly. And time is the one commodity that is firmly on the side of the relatively younger readers of this book.

The irony is that when we are young, retirement seems light-years away. And it is! We feel immortal. We *are* immortal! Nothing and nobody can touch us. We have little money to call our own but lots of energy and the feeling of "I-I-I" (invulnerability, invincibility and immortality). Investing for retirement seems like a waste of our money. Yet, ironically, we have all that is necessary to become a millionaire right there in our youth. We have little money (which is what we need to get started) and lots of time for time value of money (TVM) and compounding to work its magic on our little money to grow it into a million by the time we hit our golden years. How?

I will show you exactly how. Interestingly, we started our journey of Personal Finance by discussing TVM and we will end that journey discussing TVM. It's only fitting!

The bottom line is that just about anyone can retire as a millionaire with a little planning when they're young. It's amazing how relatively small deposits made when very young, then left to grow, can become a very large sum over time.

Let's consider a specific example.

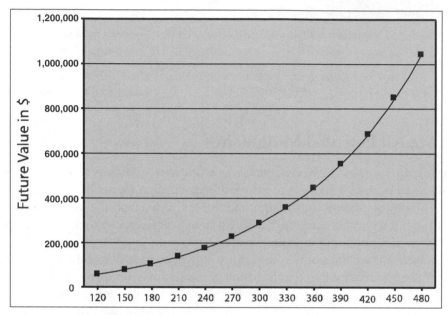

Figure 20: $300 Monthly Payments at 8 Percent Annual Interest

From the graph above, if we deposited $300 per month in an account paying an 8 percent annual rate, in forty years we will have over a million dollars in our account. The question is: Is it reasonable to expect an 8 percent interest rate in an investment account? To put this growth percentage in perspective, consider the following. According to Ibbotson Associates, the average annual return from the U.S. stock market between 1926 and 2003 was about 10 percent, while between 1990 and 1999 it was 18 percent. Based on these numbers, an 8 percent growth over a long horizon certainly appears more than reasonable. In fact, you could even use a higher return to do your computations and you would end up with a million dollars even sooner.

Now let's look at the numbers another way. Say you decide in your twenties to start a retirement account and you religiously put in a small amount every month for ten years straight. After that, just leave your money in the account and let it grow without any additional deposits. Simply set it and forget it! Here is a graph that illustrates the final value of your money.

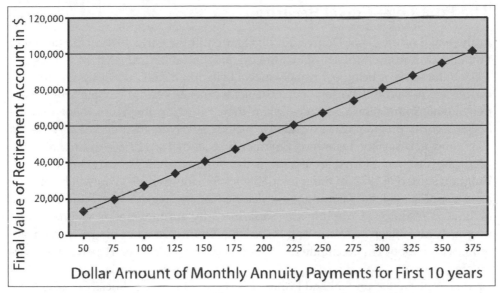

Figure 21: Monthly payments of the indicated amounts in the x-axis for 10 years and then do nothing for the next 35 years. Assume growth at 8% annually the entire period.

From this graph, we see that if a twenty-year-old started putting about $375 a month for ten years in an investment account paying an 8 percent annual rate (compounded monthly); then, after ten years, left the account alone without putting in any additional money, thirty-five years later (at 8 percent annual growth rate), he would have just over a million dollars in his account.

Thus, we are all paper millionaires—we just don't know it yet. So don't let anyone tell you that the only way to have lots of money is to be born rich! And while we wait for our retirement nest egg to grow in leaps and bounds over time, let's consider what our government has in mind for our retirement.

The Three-Legged Stool

Retirement plans play a crucial role in providing a source of income in our later years. We've all seen or heard about the "three-legged stool" that shows Social Security, our personal lifetime savings, and company retirement plans as the triad from which we will draw the funds to pay for our expenses after we retire. Let me provide you with an overview of each of those three legs.

The First Leg—Social Security

In the wake of the Great Depression that started in the early 1930s, U.S. President Franklin D. Roosevelt (FDR) signed the original Social Security Act on August 14, 1935. In those days, being old usually meant being poor. FDR, upon signing the historical act, is said to have opined: "Thanks to Social Security, people will have a dependable foundation of income when they retire." In the years following, the Social Security program was expanded to include Survivors Insurance that started in 1939, and a Disability Insurance Program that started in 1956. Additionally, the Medicare Program started in 1965 and the Supplemental Security Income (SSI) Program started in 1972. In order to qualify for SSI, for example, you will have to be age 65 or older, or blind (at any age), or disabled (at any age), or with limited income or limited resources. Currently, the Social Security Administration estimates that over forty-six million people receive SS benefits. Of these, a whopping 62 percent are retirees and about 11 percent are disabled workers, and another 11 percent are survivors.

It is important to understand is that FDR did not intend for Social Security to be the sole source of retirement income for retirees. As he himself stated, Social Security is meant to provide the "foundation" and nothing more. It was never intended to be a traditional pension plan. It was what is called a "pay-as-you-go" plan: each generation of active workers financing the benefits of the currently retired workers.

It would work perfectly as long as people did not live very long in retirement. And they didn't. In those early years, between the time one became eligible for full retirement benefits at 62 and one's demise, there was not a big time gap ensuring that each retiree did not tax the system too much, and the system hummed along beautifully. That is, until medical science got in the way. Advances in medicine, coupled with no major wars and relative prosperity over an extended period of time all worked together to ensure that Americans lived longer. That is precisely when the system started falling apart! According to the National Vital Statistics Report, the median survival age of Americans born between 1939 and 1941 was about 70. The median survival age of Americans born in 2002 is projected to be well over 80.

What does this do to the Social Security system? For one thing, more people are drawing longer from the system in retirement than ever before, and this was outside the calculus of Social Security's founding fathers. Not surprisingly, the ratio of the number of people contributing to the system for every person drawing from the system has declined dramatically over the years. For example, in 1960, there were about five people paying into the system for every beneficiary withdrawing money from the system. In 2000, there were only three people paying into the system for every beneficiary and the projected number is two people paying for every beneficiary in the year 2034. Also remember that of all the money coming to Social Security through payroll taxes, about 74.7 percent is paid out in benefits, about 24.6 percent is put in the Social Security Trust Fund, and about 0.7 percent is used in administration costs. It's this Trust Fund that in recent years has been the subject of intense debate as its levels dip lower causing concern that we may run through it in the next fifty years or so, and that future generations will have no Social Security to depend on.

We are simply living longer and thereby extracting from the system in greater amounts and over a greater number of years after retirement than could ever have been envisioned. Statistics show that by the year 2034 about seventy million people, or about 20 percent of the U.S. population, will be at least sixty-five years old. All of this paints a grim picture of what is going to happen to the Social Security Trust Fund by the time the current twenty year olds hit retirement age.

How Do We Tackle the Problem of the Shrinking Social Security Fund?

That's a loaded question. Of course, the easiest way to fix it is to raise Social Security taxes. We pay more in and there is more in the pot for everyone. So simple. But there is a catch!

Increasing any kind of taxes is not a popular course of action with a legislator who wishes to have a future in politics. Can you imagine someone proposing a hike in Social Security taxes as a campaign strategy and still expecting to be elected? So what can we do instead? Increase the retirement age, of course! Simply stated, the idea is to gradually increase the age at which we qualify for full benefits. That way, we artificially push back when retirees can start taking out of the system and help the SS fund to stay alive a while longer. Nobody has to raise those ugly taxes; we put a band-aid on the system and chug along blissfully. Everybody is happy and politicians can easily pass the buck along to the next administration. It is risky to take ownership of this gargantuan problem.

In **Figure 22**, we can see how the retirement age (the official age at which we qualify for SS benefits) changes. All of us born after 1960 will qualify for full retirement benefits only when we are sixty-seven years old. Stay tuned for more age-benefit adjustments!

Year of Birth	Full Retirement Age
1937	65
1938	65 & 2 months
1939	65 & 4 months
1940	65 & 6 months
1941	65 & 8 months
1942	65 & 10 months
1943–1954	66
1955	66 & 2 months
1956	66 & 4 months
1957	66 & 6 months
1958	66 & 8 months
1959	66 & 10 months
1960 & later	67

Figure 22: Year of birth and age for full retirement benefits.

The Bush Plan for Social Security

As we have identified above, the main problem with Social Security is longevity-related or demographic (if you want to use a fancy term). The SS Trust Fund is in a very fragile state and has to be nurtured along if it has any chance of surviving in the long term. Basically what the Trust Fund does is to take any surplus and invest it in U.S. Treasury Bonds (which, as we know, are very safe but also very limiting in returns) to be cashed in when the current generation retires. Following such a forward-looking strategy will allow the fund to stay in business until about 2042 (or 2052, depending on whose calculations you believe).

And then if changes are not made to the structure and the funding of the Trust Fund, benefits will have to be cut to ensure outflows do not exceed the revenues. That is basic Economics 101. While we can all quibble about the math and the projections made, everyone agrees that something needs to be done. The problem is that there is no universally painless solution and our threshold for accepting pain as a nation is very low. And, unfortunately, our elected officials tend to appease every demographic group—especially the very young and the very old—by telling each that any reform of the Social Security system is not going to hurt them, which is probably not accurate.

One quick solution that will never pass muster, is to raise the payroll tax from today's 12.4 percent to about 13.9 percent which would immediately stabilize the Social Security system for a good 75 years, according to the Social Security Trustees. Any delay in implementing an increase in taxes means that, to make the system stable for 75 more years will require an immediate and permanent reduction in benefits of about 13 percent. Time is of the essence with whatever course the government decides to adopt.

Retire Late, Make More

If you are a workaholic and hate the thought of retirement and don't even want to think about touching your retirement benefits, it turns out Uncle Sam may be looking for you. Specifically, if you choose to delay receiving benefits beyond your full retirement age, your benefit will be increased by a certain percentage tied to when you were born. The increase will be factored in automatically from the time you reach full retirement age until you start taking benefits, or reach age 70, whichever comes first. Further details are available on www.ssa.gov. The bottom line is that by delaying touching your benefits you are helping out Uncle Sam and the stretched Social Security system. This is their way of saying thanks to you.

Another way to reduce benefits and still keep the system going for a while is to increase the age of eligibility for full benefits (which will reach 67 for workers born in 1960 and later). Finally, benefits paid to upper income retirees could be reduced. As I said, none of these is painless to all and are merely band-aids for the actual problem.

But what exactly did our 43rd President propose? His idea was to allow younger Americans to put a portion of their taxes (about 4 percent of their payroll taxes was floated as a trial balloon) in a private account that will be there for them when they retire. Sort of like another 401(k) plan (which we will discuss later) but this one would be funded by your Social Security taxes.

While the idea of a federal government sponsored private retirement account for each citizen certainly sounds tempting at first blush, there are problems associated with setting them up. For one, in the short run, Social Security depends on taxes paid by today's workers to pay off today's retirees. If a significant chunk of those monies was diverted to private accounts, the government will have to come up with other means to fund the shortfall since the president has simultaneously promised older Americans that their Social Security withdrawals are safe.

This, in turn, implies that the president will have to sell Treasury bonds to cover the shortfall—some estimate to the tune of $1–2 trillion over the next ten years. And given that we are already in deficit spending mode as a nation, this promises to further burden our future citizens. For the moment, however, let us focus on the existing Social Security system that is in place and see what we have to do to qualify for benefits.

Who Qualifies for Retirement Benefits?

You qualify for full Social Security benefits by working a job and paying your Social Security (also known as FICA) taxes for at least a certain period of time and earning credits thereby. After you have accumulated a certain number of credits, you are done for the rest of your life. It's that simple. Thus, for example, to earn one credit you need to have earned about $700 dollars from your job and you can get a maximum of four credits (or, about $3,120 in employment earnings) per year. After you have accumulated forty credits, you are fully covered for retirement under Social Security.

Just about anybody can get retirement benefits. A worker who qualifies for reduced benefits around age sixty-two (must be insured; forty credits/ten years), qualifies for full benefits at age sixty-five (at age sixty-seven, if born after 1960). He could also qualify for increased benefits for retiring after the full retirement age. A wife or husband qualifies for benefits at her/his designated retirement age or at any age if caring for a child under sixteen, or if she/he were to be disabled. Divorced spouses may qualify under certain circumstances. Finally, an unmarried child qualifies if under eighteen (under nineteen if still in high school), or if disabled before age twenty-two.

And what do you have to do to qualify for Medicare coverage? You must be at least sixty-five years old and receiving Social Security disability benefits for at least twenty-four months or, if you have permanent kidney failure at any age. And, if you qualify for Medicare, it has two parts. Part A is called Hospital Insurance which covers most in-patient hospital expenses and has a reasonable deductible which is adjusted almost every year. Part B of Medicare, known as Supplementary Medical Insurance, has a

Benefits when Divorced

If you are divorced, your ex-spouse could qualify for benefits on your earnings under the following circumstances: Must have been married to you for at least 10 years; must have been divorced from you at least 2 years; be at least 62 years old; be unmarried currently; and must not be eligible for an equal or higher benefit from another source (including his or her own workplace).

reasonable monthly premium and is designed to cover about 80 percent of doctor bills and other out-patient medical expenses, applied after the first $100 in approved charges.

In order to apply for Social Security benefits, you need to provide your Social Security number, proof of age (birth certificate), latest W-2 or self-employment tax return, your earnings estimate, your bank information for direct deposit, any information you may have about your marriage and/or divorce, and any military or railroad service. Further information is available on the Social Security Administration's Web site (www.ssa.gov).

Disability Insurance under Social Security

The definition used by the federal government to determine if you are disabled is the following: A medical condition preventing substantial work for at least twelve months, or expected to result in death, based on age, education, and work experience.

The key here is the phrase "substantial work." You are an engineer by training (say). You have an accident which forces you to quit your engineering position and take a job at McDonald's flipping burgers at an hourly wage. You are not disabled according to the federal government. A better definition of disability from the consumer's standpoint is "the inability to perform your job due to a sickness or an injury." The government, however, uses a significantly more stringent standard for deciding whether you are disabled or not.

The Second Leg: Pension

Pension plans serve many purposes for employers and employees alike, and they come in many varieties. Yet few of us really understand the plans we have, despite the critical function they fulfill in our lives. To help increase that understanding, I begin by providing an overview of the most common retirement plans. I also provide a few definitions to help clarify some of the jargon commonly used by retirement professionals in discussing these plans.

Qualified versus Nonqualified Plans

A qualified retirement plan is one that meets the numerous requirements of the Internal Revenue Code (IRC) and the Employee Retirement Income Security Act of 1974 (ERISA). If you are wondering if a qualified retirement plan is like turning twenty-one and being able to walk into a bar legally, I am here to tell you, "more or less." Qualified plans meet the minimum standards set down by the government and, by extension, has its blessings, which come with important tax benefits. Also, a qualified retirement plan falls into one of three general categories: A defined benefit plan, a defined contribution plan, or a hybrid plan.

A non-qualified retirement plan, on the other hand, is one that does not meet the requirements of the IRC or the ERISA. To continue with our analogy from above, it's like being thrown out of a bar for being under-age! Essentially, these are non-standard retire-ment plans that do not have the government approval stamp but are used and funded by corporations to provide some form of a tax-deferred compensation to key officials. The downside is that these plans, while allowing broader flexibility for the employers, do not

> **Did You Know?**
>
> The complete Internal Revenue Code is more than 24 megabytes in length, and contains more than 3.4 million words. If printed 60 lines to a page, it would be more than 7,500 pages long.

receive the same favorable tax treatment as permitted for the qualified plans. Employers receive no tax deduction until the employee receives proceeds from the plan. The employees usually receive proceeds in the form of annuities and are taxed at ordinary income tax rates. The benefits can also be transferred into individual retirement accounts in order to defer taxes.

Defined Benefit versus Defined Contribution

A Defined Benefit Plan is really your grandfather's retirement plan. In the good old days when America reigned supreme in the world, its goods were in high demand and society was fresh from winning the Second World War, companies instituted plans whereby they vowed to take care of their retired workforce right to their deaths, based on a preset formula that factored in the employee's years of employment, pre-retirement wages, and/or age. "Till death do us part" really meant something then. These plans were funded entirely by the employer, and the responsibility for the payment of the benefit, and all the associated risk of coming up with the monies, rested with the employer. Put differently, the risk from these plans was shouldered entirely by the employers. The employee bore no risk! As you can imagine, it was a great system for employees and there was much joy and celebration among American workers. Life was great!

But over time, such retirement burdens started weighing heavily on employers' shoulders and soon there was a secret convention of employers (so secret that there exist no records of such a convention). After much soul searching, it was decided that they were fools for taking all the risk of funding their employees' retirement monies. So the companies decided to change course and offer a new kind of retirement plan—one where the risk of the plan would be borne entirely by the employee. The employer would pay its share in the pot and then let the employee decide how to invest the money. This was cheaper for the companies and the new plan was called a Defined Contribution Plan. Formally, we went from "ask what your company can do for you" to "tell us what you can do for your company."

Formally, a Defined Contribution Plan is a retirement plan in which the contribution is defined, but the ultimate benefit paid to the employee is not. Each employee has her personal account and the amount accumulating in this account at retirement depends on how much was contributed over the years and more importantly how the investment performed over the years. The investment risk rests solely with the employee due to her ability to choose from a number of investment options. The government sets a limit on how much can be contributed in our name each year no

Employer Contribution Limits

The total amount (over all defined contribution plans) that can be contributed by an employer in one employee's name for 2009 is the lesser of $49,000 and 100 percent of the employee's annual earnings.

matter how many different retirement plans we participate in. The total amount that can be contributed in one employee's name for 2009 is the lesser of $49,000 (it was $46,000 in 2008) and 100 percent of the employee's annual earnings. At retirement, benefits are typically paid in installments or as a lump sum; however, they may also be paid as an annuity.

The Most Popular Defined Contribution Plan: The 401(k)

Almost all of us will be dealing with a 401(k) plan in our working lives. The rest of us will have either a 403(b) plan (if you work for a non-profit like a foundation or a university) or a Keogh plan (if you have your own business). The name, 401(k), comes from the section of the Internal Revenue Code that defines this particular plan. The employer allows his employees to put in a part of their compensation (on a pre-tax basis) in this plan where it grows unfettered and untaxed until withdrawn at a certain age. But here is the beauty of the plan. In most cases, the employer matches his employees' contribution according to a set formula (the best is a dollar-for-dollar match-up to a pre-set maximum). Employers make their contributions even if the employee does not put in any contributions of her own. Sometimes such contributions can be tied to the underlying profits of the firm as part of some profit-sharing program.

A 401(k) plan generally offers participants an opportunity to direct their account contributions to a broad range of investment options ranging from low-risk bond mutual funds to high-risk growth mutual funds.

If you are completely disabled and cannot work, you can live off your 401(k) plan without being charged a 10 percent penalty regardless of how old you are. Before you get too excited, keep in mind that you will still owe ordinary income taxes on the money you withdraw. If you're disabled, you may also be able to take

Employee Contribution Limits

The employee's elective deferral to all 401(k) plans is limited to $16,500 in 2009 (it was $15,500 in 2008). Those who are age 50 and over in 2009, can contribute an additional $5,000 for the year. Generally, withdrawals from 401(k) plans are not permitted before age 59½ unless the employee retires, dies, becomes disabled, changes jobs, or suffers a financial hardship as defined by Internal Revenue Service regulations.

out any matching contributions your employer made even if you haven't completed the years of service normally required for full ownership. Most plans provide for full ownership whenever a participant becomes disabled. However, each plan does have its own definition of what's required to qualify for disability. Make sure you know what that definition is in order to qualify.

One oft-neglected benefit of making the maximum annual contribution to a 401(k) plan is that it can boost your children's chances of getting financial aid when they go to college. By increasing your 401(k) contributions to the maximum allowed you are shifting your assets around, improving your chances of qualifying for aid since such balances are excluded from most college-aid calculations and reduce your taxable income, which makes you look poorer.

Exempt from Bankruptcy?

Finally, a question on a lot of minds is whether the assets in your 401(k) are exempt from creditors in case you were to file for bankruptcy. And the short answer is, yes! Remember O. J. Simpson? He lost a civil lawsuit filed by his former in-laws to the tune of thirty plus million dollars. He had lost most of his assets by then and had almost nothing to pay the judgment with. However, to this day he collects a $25,000 a month retirement check that the opposing lawyers would love to get their hands on—but can't! More generally, the U.S. Supreme Court has held that savings in a qualified retirement plan, such as a 401(k) or IRA, are exempt from creditor claims in a bankruptcy. However, some courts have allowed the IRS to invade plan assets to recoup amounts owed by certain creditors.

Here is something to be careful about. If you're saving money that you plan to use before you retire, it is usually better to save it outside your 401(k) plan. While it is true that you can usually withdraw your after-tax 401(k) contributions at any time without taxes or penalty, remember that you'll owe taxes on any interest it earns, as well as a 10 percent early withdrawal penalty if you're under age 59½. The 10 percent penalty is an expense you wouldn't have if you had saved on an after-tax basis outside your 401(k) plan.[70]

Word of Warning about Borrowing from Your 401(k): Don't!

You should borrow from a 401(k) plan only as a last resort because you may change jobs before the loan is repaid. And, if you do, that loan is payable immediately with interest. If you are unable to come up with the necessary funds to repay the loan, things will turn ugly in a hurry! The unpaid debt will be labeled a "deemed distribution" from your 401(k). Translation—it will be taxed and, assuming you're younger than age 59½, penalized 10 percent in addition for an early withdrawal of the money. We are not done yet! Additionally, the interest you pay yourself on the loan comes from money on which you have already paid taxes. But for 401(k) purposes, it will count as untaxed earnings. That means you will pay taxes on that money again in retirement when you make withdrawals from your 401(k).

Historically, state and local governments were prohibited from offering 401(k) plans to their employees. This was once true of private, tax-exempt employers as well; however, as of January 1, 1997, the latter may now establish a 401(k) plan for their qualified employees.

Here's the Cliffs Notes version of the 401(k) plan:

- One of the best ways to save for your retirement. Few alternatives are better.
- Good chance that if you participate in one, your employer will just give you money for doing so.

- Start contributing at as early an age as you can and let time-value-of-money do its magic!
- Put all of the money into an equity index fund.

Other Types of Defined Contribution Plans

Here are some typical defined contribution plans. While this will suffice to familiarize you with the instruments, you will have to do some digging on your own if you want further details. The Web site maintained by the U.S. Government, http://firstgovsearch.gov, is a good retirement resource. One common feature with all of these plans is that contributions and earnings accumulate tax free. They have names like Profit Sharing plan, Money Purchase plan, Cash Balance plan, Target Benefit plan, Employer Stock Ownership plan (ESOP), 457 plan, Simplified Employee Pension (SEP) plan, and SIMPLE plan. Overall, these plans are variants of companies wanting to reward their employees with incentives designed to extract maximum effort out of them by aligning their personal interests with the interests of the firm. Economists call this minimizing the agency cost. Thus, for example, in a Cash Balance plan, the employer will credit an employee's account with a pre-set percentage of her annual compensation as well as interest charges. Basically, the plan provides benefits to employees in terms of a hypothetical account balance. Additionally, the hypothetical account is credited with interest based on an amount defined in the plan. A participant's benefit at retirement will equal the accumulation of such credits at retirement. ESOPs figured prominently in the news after the ENRON collapse when it came to light that hundreds of employees had invested their retirement monies in ENRON shares under ESOPs. When the company's shares fell to pennies in the wake of the accounting-related scandal, their nest eggs also vanished into thin air. One easy way to address potential problems with ESOPs is to limit the amount of your own company's stock in your retirement account. The problem with this is, what if you happen to work for a well-run and honest company like WalMart with real products and real profits? By not investing more than a certain amount in your own company shares, you may be unfairly handicapping yourself from maximizing your retirement portfolios.

Vesting—An Ancient Sport?

No, vesting is not an ancient sport or a variation of jousting! Very simply, vesting means ownership. When you are fully vested, you have full ownership. If you are 50 percent vested, you have ownership of only half of whatever it is. Get it? One of the best things about a 401(k) retirement plan is that it is mobile. You can take it with you when you leave a company after so many years. The question is, how much can you take with you or in other words, how vested are you in your own 401(k) plan? You are only entitled to all your money in your current 401(k) account if you are fully vested. Otherwise, you are only entitled to a part of it as determined by the vesting schedule of the company you are leaving. In fact, this is a question you

Types of Vesting

There are two types of vesting schedules available, "graded vesting" and "cliff vesting" schedules.

With a graded vesting schedule, your share of owning your employer's contribution increases proportionally with each year you stay in the company. For example, if your company had a five-year graded vesting schedule, you could be 20 percent vested after one year, 40 percent vested after two years, and so on. If you were wondering, by law, the longest graded vesting schedule a 401k plan can have, is six years.

With cliff vesting, your ownership of your employer's contributions goes from 0 to 100 percent after the preset period of time. Hence, if your cliff vesting period is three years, and you leave the company for greener pastures after two, you get zippo of your employer's contributions. The longest cliff vesting schedule currently allowed by law for contributions coming from employers is three years.

should ask your potential employers while they are wining and dining you and trying to get you to join their company. Ask how long it will take for you to be fully vested. The shorter the time for full vesting, the better it is for you. In most companies you are fully vested within five years. Make sure you factor that in before you decide to quit your job for another position elsewhere.

Vesting is an important concept in retirement because, if you leave a company after working a certain number of years, what do you do with the 401(k) plan of the company you are leaving? Do you have total control over it or just partial control? The answer depends on the vesting schedule of the company and how vested you are regarding that schedule.

The Third Leg: Do It on Your Own

An IRA, or Individual Retirement Arrangement, is a personal retirement savings plan available to most people receiving taxable compensation during the year. Compensation includes wages, salaries, fees, tips, bonuses, commissions, taxable alimony, and separate maintenance payments. Husbands and wives may each have an IRA even if one person in that marriage is not working. Except for an education IRA, annual individual contributions are limited to the lesser of total taxable compensation or the amount indicated in the handy-dandy table below depending on how old you are. According to **Figure 23**, your maximum contribution in 2009 is $5,000 if you are under age 50. Due to the tax benefits associated with an IRA you should max out your annual contributions. Also, the fact that you cannot carry over your contributions year-to-year dictates that you max out your contributions every year.

YEAR	AGE 49 & UNDER	AGE 50 & ABOVE
2005	$4,000	$4,500
2006, 2007	$4,000	$5,000
2008, 2009	$5,000	$6,000

Figure 23: IRA contribution limits

So much for the maximum contributions! There is no minimum or required IRA contribution, and all earnings within an IRA account are untaxed until withdrawn. Contributions may or may not be deductible in the tax year they were made depending on the type of IRA used and the owner's income tax filing status, Adjusted Gross Income (AGI), eligibility to participate in a tax-qualified retirement plan through employment, and whether or not the owner has any visible tattoos or piercings. Okay, that last part is not true! You can have a tattoo and still be eligible for tax deductions as long as you are not making too much money.

Money may be withdrawn from an IRA at any time, but withdrawals may be taxed at ordinary income tax rates. Withdrawals from an IRA other than a Roth or Education IRA prior to age 59½ will result in a 10 percent excise tax in addition to ordinary income tax. There are seven exceptions to the 10 percent penalty for withdrawals prior to your full retirement. The penalty does not apply to early withdrawals that:

- Occur because of the IRA owner's disability.

- Occur because of the IRA owner's death.

- Are a series of "substantially equal periodic payments" made over the life expectancy of the IRA owner.

- Are used to pay for unreimbursed medical expenses that exceed 7½ percent of AGI.

- Are used to pay medical insurance premiums after the IRA owner has received unemployment compensation for more than twelve weeks.

- Are used to pay the costs of a first-time home purchase (subject to a lifetime limit of $10,000).

- Are used to pay for the qualified expenses of higher education for the IRA owner and/or eligible family members.

Introduction of Senator Roth's Retirement Bill in March, 1999

Senators William Roth, Jr. (R-DE) and Max Baucus (D-MT) introduced the "Retirement Savings Opportunity Act of 1999." The bill proposed to significantly expand the IRA, Roth IRA, and 401(k) programs by:

- Significantly raising contribution limits to $15,000 for 401(k)s and $5,000 for IRAs.
- Permitting individuals age 50 and older to make additional "catch-up" contributions to IRAs and 401(k) plans.
- Eliminating the 25 percent of compensation limitation on contributions.
- Removing the income limits that currently apply to IRA programs.

The Most Important Form of IRA: The Roth IRA

Arguably, the most important IRA for young people is this one. It's named after Senator William V. Roth, Jr., who was the architect of the Retirement Savings Opportunity Act of 1999 in the Senate. The Roth IRA has the following features:

- Contributions to the account are not tax deductible.

- "Qualified" distributions (i.e., withdrawals) from the account are not taxable.

- Earnings on the account are taxable only when a withdrawal is not a "qualified" distribution.

No qualified withdrawals are allowed before a five-taxable-year period beginning with the year in which the taxpayer first contributed to a Roth IRA. In plain English, a qualified withdrawal is where you are allowed to take money out of your retirement account without the Federal government throwing the book and barking dogs at you.

> ## What Is a Qualified Distribution?
>
> In order to be called a "qualified" distribution, it has to meet one or more of the following conditions:
> - The withdrawal is made after the taxpayer attains age 59½.
> - The withdrawal is made by a beneficiary after the taxpayer's death.
> - The withdrawal is made because the taxpayer is disabled.
> - The withdrawal is made by a first-time homebuyer to acquire a principal residence.

The contribution limits are the same whether you do a traditional IRA or a Roth IRA. In 2009, the annual contributions to a Roth IRA are limited to $5,000 minus the taxpayer's deductible IRA contributions. However, and this is different from a traditional IRA, the contributions to a Roth IRA may be made even after the owner reaches age 70½. If you make too much money, however, you cannot enjoy the benefits of a Roth. The $5,000 limit is phased out as AGI increases from $166,000 to $176,000 (married filing jointly) or $105,000 to $120,000 (single filer). If you make too much money, you don't really need a Roth IRA and so, to be fair to the rest of us poor folks, the government gives us a Roth handicap.

For those of you thinking about transferring from a traditional IRA to a Roth IRA, here are the facts: You could transfer your traditional IRA into a Roth IRA only if your AGI (married or single) for the transfer year is $100,000 or less. The transferred amount must be included in that year's income, but the money transferred will be exempt from the 10 percent excise tax for a withdrawal

> ## A Glitch in the Roth Conversion Provision?
>
> In May 2006, President Bush signed a $70 billion tax cut provision that changed the eligibility rules for converting to a Roth from a traditional IRA. Namely, for one year only, 2010, taxpayers with a modified AGI of more than $100,000 will be allowed to convert a traditional IRA to a Roth IRA. Additionally, the income taxes due on conversions can be spread over two years. So the 2010 conversion amount may be included as taxable income in 2011 and 2012, thereby helping to spread out the tax burden. Word of caution, however! Removing the Roth IRA conversion cap does not imply that anyone can now fund a Roth IRA. It does, however, imply that anyone with an existing IRA will be able to convert to a Roth IRA.

prior to age 59½. Once again, no qualified withdrawals are possible within a five-year period. However, the income restriction for conversion is scheduled to be completely eliminated in 2010. That means, at least in 2010, everyone can convert their traditional IRAs to a Roth IRA.

> # Taking Advantage of 2010?
>
> One way to have taken advantage of the 2010 glitch in the IRA to Roth conversion was to have started funding a traditional IRA right in 2006. Even if you did not qualify to make a traditional IRA contribution on a before-tax basis, you could still have made an after-tax contribution to a traditional IRA. And then in 2010, you would be all set to convert to a Roth IRA!

The bottom line is that those of you starting a retirement fund should always select a Roth IRA over a traditional IRA. For those of you who have had a traditional IRA for a while that are thinking of switching to a Roth IRA, the answer is not so simple since the act of switching involves cost, including the payment of taxes and penalties on the pre-tax money you had growing in your regular IRA. For example, if you happen to use IRA money to pay the tax on a Roth conversion (and you are under age 59½), you'll probably have to pay a 10 percent (and, maybe even a 20 percent) penalty on the amount that's not rolled over into the Roth, or rolled into a Roth and then pulled out to pay the tax.

The relevant computation is whether, after those costs, the benefits of the Roth IRA stack up in your favor. The general rule of thumb is that if you have had your traditional IRA for 20 years or more, you are better off continuing with it. Further details on IRA provisions may be found in IRS Publication 590, Individual Retirement Arrangements. This publication may be obtained at no cost by calling 1-800-TAX FORM, or it may be downloaded online at www.irs.gov.

Other Types of IRAs

The chapter appendix provides a brief list of other types of IRAs available to consumers. If you need further details, this Web site has more information on all of these IRAs: http://www.open-ira. com/IRA_Center/Why start an IRA.htm.

Retirement FAQs

Following is a list of questions on retirement that I have been asked over the years by students in my personal finance class.

What's the best type of financial institution to use for an IRA?

You can establish an IRA just about anywhere you wish through a bank, a brokerage firm, a mutual fund company, or an insurance company. But while some of these institutions will allow you to invest the money any way you want, others may limit your selection or charge additional fees if you want to place money in something other than the types of investments offered through the financial institution itself.

Can I establish a Roth IRA regardless of how much I make?

While contributions to a Roth IRA are not tax deductible, penalty-free withdrawals can be made if you, the taxpayer, use the money for retirement after age 59½ or to purchase your first home.

The Roth IRA was created primarily to help low- and middle-income people save, and the law restricts the ability of upper-income taxpayers to open such an account. For example, a maximum of $5,000 a year can currently be contributed to an account by single tax filers with an adjusted gross income (AGI) of less than $105,000 and joint filers with combined income below $166,000. The maximum contribution phases out for single filers with adjusted gross income between $105,000 and $120,000; and for joint filers, the phase-out affects those with AGIs between $166,000 and $176,000. The bottom line is that if you earn enough money, you are out of luck as far as opening a Roth IRA goes. Sometimes making too much money has its drawbacks.

How do I convert my existing traditional IRA into a new Roth IRA?

The bottom line with these conversions is that when you opened your regular IRA, you did it with pre-tax money. Now when you want to convert it to a Roth, there are taxes that are due because Roth is about after-tax money, because you get the tax benefit at the end when you withdraw a large chunk of money with no taxes. The calculation then concerns whether the taxes you will have to incur in the conversion make it worthwhile to switch. The general rule of thumb is that the longer you have had a regular IRA the less sense it makes to switch to a Roth. To be specific, you must complete a Roth IRA Adoption Agreement and a Roth Conversion form. Also, you need to indicate on the Roth Conversion form whether taxes are to be withheld from the IRA funds or will be paid from another source. Once the Roth Conversion IRA has been established, assets in the ordinary IRA will be moved to the Roth Conversion IRA. If you do not wish to convert the entire amount, you must indicate on the conversion form the exact security description and the amount of cash that is to be moved from the ordinary IRA.

How do I use money saved in my Roth IRA to pay for college?

When Congress put the finishing touches on the Roth IRA, they allowed certain expenses for education to qualify as tax- and penalty-free distributions from a Roth IRA. Now, why is this important? Simply because the penalty for early distribution of a Roth IRA is 10 percent. Qualified expenses exempt from the penalty include college tuition, fees, books, supplies, and room and board. But there may be tax consequences from such an action. For example, if you had a Roth IRA with a value of $10,000, of which $7,000 are contributions and $3,000 are earnings, you could withdraw up to $7,000 (after the money has been invested for five years) without paying any taxes or penalties. If you withdraw the $3,000 in earnings, however, you'll have to pay taxes on that sum at your current rate.

What is a SEP? And can I invest both in a SEP and a traditional IRA?

SEP stands for simplified employee pension, a type of retirement plan that is popular among sole proprietors and owners of small businesses. A SEP is actually a special type of individual retirement account sometimes referred to as a SEP-IRA. Its purpose was to ensure that people working for very small businesses did not fall through the retirement cracks. If you are participating in a simplified employee pension (SEP) plan, the Internal Revenue Service will allow you to save even more money for retirement by allowing you to set up a separate IRA. The money you contribute to the IRA may or may not be tax deductible, depending on how much you earn and whether you're married or not. But even if you can't deduct the contribution on your income tax return, the investments inside the IRA will grow tax free until you begin making withdrawals.

What are the pros and cons of having large amounts of money in an IRA?

The simple answer is that you can't really do a whole heck of a lot with the money until you are almost 60 years old unless you are willing to pay a stiff penalty for putting your grubby hands on the money before then. But, I cannot see a downside to having a large retirement account. I remember a friend telling me that while money could not buy her happiness, she would rather have lots of money and be unhappy, than have no money and be unhappy over and above that.

Is my IRA subject to the claims of my creditors in a bankruptcy proceeding?

If you file for bankruptcy, your creditors may or may not be able to claim the assets of your IRA. It depends primarily on where you live. State law determines if IRAs are subject to the claims of creditors in a bankruptcy. Some states protect IRAs from the claims of creditors and others do not. But even in the same state, interpretation of bankruptcy law can vary from one court to another. As with most things in life, it is not exactly a black or white issue, but a shade of grey.

How is a 401(k) different from a regular pension like a defined benefit plan?

The biggest difference between a 401(k) and a regular pension is that a 401(k) gives you much more control over your retirement nest egg. A 401(k) is funded with your own money and, in some cases, by a contribution from your employer as well. You decide how much to save and how to invest. A traditional defined benefit pension is funded and controlled by your employer. It's often called a defined benefit plan because it promises to pay you a specific monthly income in retirement—in other words, a defined benefit. What you get when you retire will be based on your salary and the number of years you worked for the company. The company is supposed to put aside enough money to fulfill this promise but as some loyal workers have recently discovered, it's a promise that too many employers have been unable to keep. Most pension plans are covered by the Pension Benefit Guarantee Corp., which guarantees benefits to workers of qualified firms even if the firm is liquidated in bankruptcy.

How long do I have to wait after being hired to join the company's 401(k) plan?

Some companies allow workers to join their 401(k) plans immediately, but others utilize a federal law that allows a firm to wait until a worker has logged at least one year of service before joining the plan. The reason for that is that many employees quit before their first year is up and companies want to avoid the administrative costs involved in setting up a 401(k) for a worker who might not stay very long. A company is also allowed to exclude anyone under the age of 21 in part because younger employees often don't take advantage of the plans even when they are eligible. If younger workers are eligible to join the plan but don't, their lower participation rate can reduce the amount that other employees are permitted to contribute due to federal rules.

What happens to the money I put into a company's 401(k) plan?

The money is invested according to the choices you've made from a list of options offered by your employer. These options typically include stock and bond mutual funds, money market funds, a guaranteed investment contract (GIC) that pays a fixed interest rate, and your company's stock.

What information about my 401(k) plan am I legally entitled to have?

The federal government requires companies to provide only minimal information to workers who take part in a 401(k) plan. Technically, all you're entitled to is a summary of how the plan works, a summary annual report, and an annual statement. If the plan allows you to invest in the company's stock, you are also entitled to receive a prospectus or similar document. But that is only what is required by law. In today's Internet age, you can easily do your own research and find a lot more information than the minimum required.

What recourse do I have if my employer and I disagree about my 401(k) account?

Your employer is required by law to include a claims review process in which you can file a written claim with the plan administrator. That's the person or committee responsible for handling the day-to-day administration of the plan. The plan administrator must respond to questions from participants and give an explanation for any denial of benefits. If you don't find the explanation acceptable, you can request a review and if you're still not satisfied, you should find yourself a good lawyer.

How do I know how well (or poorly) my 401(k) investments are doing?

If you have invested in a 401(k) retirement plan, it is important to stay informed about your investment's performance. Fortunately, most plans now have all the relevant information on their Web sites that you can access with a simple login ID and password. For example, my money from the university is invested with TIAA-CREF and I can check on it whenever I want and even change the mix of assets my money is invested in. Very nifty, huh? But at a minimum, the company that administers your plan should be able to provide you with an annual statement that shows the amounts you have contributed and how those investments have performed.

Many plans report on a semiannual or quarterly basis and some even issue monthly updates.

Do employers guarantee 401(k) accounts?

Employers never guarantee 401(k) accounts. They are considered "fiduciaries" of 401(k) plans, which means they are legally responsible for supervising, not guaranteeing, the money you invest. And this supervisory relationship obligates the employer to protect your financial interests by choosing reputable and competent plan trustees, administrators, and investment managers and continuously monitor the performance of their duties. Well, at least that is true in theory. Furthermore, you must also be given the opportunity to move your money among the available investments at least quarterly, and sufficient information to help you make sensible, informed investment decisions. But your employer doesn't offer you protection against any investment losses you may suffer.

Does the government guarantee my 401(k) account?

This is a good question because you would think that the government should step in and provide assistance if your retirement fund failed for whatever reason. Sadly, there is no such guarantee for 401(k) accounts. While traditionally defined benefit pension plans are insured by the federal Pension Benefit Guaranty Corp., since the government wants to ensure that the payments a company promises its retirees will indeed be made, 401(k)s do not involve a promise of future benefits. The value of your account will rise and fall over the course of the years, and you could theoretically be wiped out if your investments perform badly. If it helps you sleep better, you may want to know that one of the duties of the federal Pension and Welfare Benefits Administration is to ensure that all employers and 401(k) trustees follow government requirements. That's not as good as a guarantee, but it's better than nothing.

What happens to my 401(k) account when I die?

One of the first things you are supposed to do when you join a 401(k) is to designate a beneficiary who will receive the money in your account when you die. If you somehow fail to designate a beneficiary, your estate will automatically become the beneficiary. If your beneficiary is your husband, he will have most of the same options with the money that you would have if you were leaving the company to take another job. Your husband could roll the money over into an IRA, or withdraw it all and pay income taxes on it.

Street Smarts: The Saga of Ganesh

From ancient Indian folklore, comes the story of Ganesh, a lovable god with an elephant's head and a human body. A long time ago, Lord Shiva, the ancient Hindu god of death and destruction, was waging war with his enemies. His wife was left behind (as was the custom in those days for wars were considered a man's domain) and wished to take a bath. Not having anyone to guard her royal chambers (everyone was presumably off at war), she summoned her son to stand guard at the doorway.

As luck would have it, Shiva chose that very time to return from his campaigns and found a strange man (not much father-son bonding here, obviously) guarding his wife's inner sanctum. Shiva, known for his temper, flew into one of his rages (anger management was not for the gods) and lopped off his head. Hearing the commotion, Shiva's wife came running out, only to discover that her son had been decapitated by his father.

Upon realizing what he had done, Shiva was very contrite (a typical husband at this point), and promised to make amends for his rash act by depriving the first living being he met of its head and replacing his son's missing head with it.

So, Shiva rushes out only to find a baby elephant, minding its own business. But Shiva, with almost no one to answer to, lops its head off (PETA did not exist then), rushes back home with it, places it on his son's shoulders, and brings him back to life. Thus, Ganesh was destined to spend the rest of his life (and live on in eternity) with an elephant's head. Because he lost his head (literally) guarding the entrance to his mother's chamber, he is considered to be the god of gateways, or the god who protects those who want to embark on a project or a new phase of their life—like starting a new business, getting married or maybe even retiring.

(Note: Other versions vary how Ganesh got his elephant head.)

Thought Questions

1. What is the intuition behind starting early with your retirement planning?

2. What is the one characteristic of compounding that helps those who start early?

3. Put yourself in the shoes of a 21-year-old college graduate who has $200 per month to put in a retirement account that averages about 6 percent in annual returns over the next ten years. If he were to contribute to his retirement account until he was 30 and then simply forget about the account until he was 65, how much would he have in his account?

4. What are some of the practical reasons why someone in their twenties may postpone starting with his or her retirement planning? Can you think of some other ways to prolong the life of the Social Security Trust Fund without raising Social Security taxes?

5. Why is raising Social Security taxes not a viable option for making the Social Security Trust Fund healthy again?

6. What are some of the benefits and costs of adopting the Bush plan to save Social Security?

7. Do you think Social Security should be saved? Is it possible it has outlived its useful life?

8. Why does the government limit the amount of money you can put in your retirement account and write it off from taxes?

9. When is it absolutely imperative for you to take advantage of a 401(k) plan at work?

10. What is one way to avoid the kind of disaster that ex-employees of ENRON encountered through their ESOPs?

11. Would you prefer a cliff vesting schedule or a graded vesting schedule? Why?

12. Do you think there is a chance the government will change the rules to delay full access to your 401(k) plans from the current 59½ to (maybe) around 62 years? Why or why not?

13. Do you think IRA contribution limits should be indexed to inflation? Why or why not?

14. Should there be a government mandated minimum contribution to your IRA account? Why or why not?

15. Under what kind of income profile over your lifetime would having a traditional IRA make more sense than having a Roth IRA?

Note

70. However, there are situations where it can make sense to use after-tax contributions for short term savings. For example, if your employer matches your after-tax contributions and if you're fully vested in the matching contributions by the time you withdraw the money, you may wind up with more money by saving in the 401(k) plan, even after taking the 10 percent early withdrawal penalty into account.

Appendix to Chapter 12

Other Types of IRAs

IRA	Brief Description
Simplified Employee Pension (SEP)	Set up by an employer for a firm's employees. An employer may contribute up to 25 percent of an employee's compensation annually to each employee's IRA, and as much as $49,000 in 2009.
A Savings Incentive Match Plan for Employees (SIMPLE)	Set up by a small employer for a firm's employees. Employees may contribute up to $11,500 per year to these IRAs and will receive some level of a matching percentage of pay from their employer. Specifically, the employer can choose either a 2 percent non-elective compensation or a dollar-for-dollar match of up to 3 percent of pay.
Spousal	Funded by a married taxpayer in the name of his or her spouse who has less than $2,000 in annual compensation. The couple must file a joint tax return in the year of contribution. The working spouse may contribute up to $5,000 per year to the Spousal IRA if spouse is under 50 years of age and up to $6,000 if 50 years or over.
Rollover	Set up by an individual to receive a distribution from a qualified retirement plan. Distributions transferred to a rollover IRA are not subject to any contribution limits. Additionally, the distribution may be eligible for subsequent transfer into a qualified retirement plan available through a new employer.
Inherited	A traditional or a Roth IRA acquired by a non-spousal beneficiary of a deceased IRA owner. Special rules apply to such inherited IRAs. A tax deduction is not allowed for contributions to this IRA. A rollover to or from another IRA owned by the heir is not permitted, and the proceeds must be distributed (and taxed) within a specific period as established by the Internal Revenue Code.
Education	Established after January 1, 1998, in order to provide funds that will allow a beneficiary to attend a program of higher education. This is the grandpa IRA designed for grandparents to set up an account for their grandchildren or a parent for their children. There are no tax deductions allowed for this contribution, but all deposits and earnings may be withdrawn free of tax and penalties as long as the proceeds are used to pay for the costs of higher education. Contributions are limited to a maximum of $2,000 per year, but are on top of the limits on any other IRA. They may be made regardless of the beneficiary's income, but cannot be made after the beneficiary reaches 18 years of age. If the distributions exceed the education expenses of the beneficiary, they are deemed as earnings and must be included in the beneficiary's gross income and subject to a 10 percent excise tax. Problem is, if you happen to make too much money, you can't start one of these! Contributions begin to phase out at $190K for joint filers and $95K for single filers.

Section D: Action Plan

- Start a Roth IRA as soon as possible and get into the habit of contributing something to it every month.

- Make sure you sign on to your work-related 401(k) and get your employer to contribute the maximum match.

- Go into your 401(k) and Roth IRA accounts from time to time and adjust the allocations to appropriate funds using the principles discussed in this book.

- Check your employer's vesting schedule and plan your career moves accordingly.

13

In Conclusion—The 50 Percent Rule

Life's a box of chocolates; you never know what you gonna get.
—Forrest Gump

At long last, we are near the end of our journey. But, in a metaphysical sense, the journey has only begun! We have studied the four core concepts on which the whole discipline of Personal Finance is based: Investments, Credit, Insurance, and Retirement. We may now be feeling a bit like all dressed up and nowhere to go. How do we put it all together in a way that makes sense? Are you guaranteed to do well if you follow the prescriptions laid out in the previous chapters?

Absolutely not!!

Here's why. It is the 50 percent rule. As my primary care physician is fond of telling me at annual physical time: "We only control 50 percent of our health under the best of circumstances." The other 50 percent are what we are born with which we have no control over—at least, not until medical science takes a major leap into DNA-based treatments. My best guess is that is a number of years off. So we can eat well, exercise, and take our vitamin supplements and control about 50 percent of what happens to us. It is the same way with Personal Finance—the 50 percent rule at work. We can take care of the 50 percent we have control over. We can do all the right things in life and still end up with problems with our retirement, credit cards, insurance or investment accounts. But here is the important lesson.

If you don't take care of the 50 percent that is within your control, you have absolutely no chance of success. Now that is a guarantee! They say success is nothing but preparation meeting opportunity. And if you are not prepared, you will miss your opportunities. It is as simple as that! So follow the rules and do the right things and chances are that the breaks will go your way. Now back to the doing-things-right part.

We need investments because we want to be able to grow our wealth. We can invest directly by buying (and selling) stocks, bonds, mutual funds, options, futures, or some combination of these or, we could invest indirectly through our pension funds—our 401(k)s and/or our IRAs. The same principles are at work here. We are trying to take the least amount of risk and make the most money: Maximizing returns while minimizing risk.

Where do credit and insurance fit into the big picture? Credit enables us to borrow beyond our means so we can afford the big ticket items without having to rob a bank. It transfers wealth from the future to the present so we can buy an expensive house (costing many times our current income) and/or a car and other important household appliances. The downside of this current infusion of cash is that we have an obligation to pay off the loan, along with its accumulated interest, over time. Therefore, credit used judiciously along with investments can give us a bump in our current affordability without creating too much of a dent in our future worth. This is important because we live in a world where things can go wrong, and worlds can turn upside down in an instant; i.e., if you were involved in a serious accident, or diagnosed with a serious ailment, or a tree falls on your house.

This is where insurance comes in. Insurance is a defensive strategy meant to protect our wealth from depletion through a severe incident which could wipe us out in a heartbeat. As in football, we need both offensive and defensive strategies in order to win the game of life. Investments, including retirement plans are offensive strategies designed to increase our wealth; credit is meant to artificially boost our current purchasing power in order to increase the quality of our lives. And insurance is a defensive strategy meant to protect our wealth from depletion and wipe out.

"Offense wins games; defense wins championships." The game of life is no different. Offense in the form of prudent investments both direct and indirect wins games and enables us to have a good life. But ultimately it's the defense we play (in the form of prudent insurance policies) that determines if we will win the championship of life. They are inexorably linked to help us succeed.

In many countries around the world, insurance is not a big factor at all. Health care is socialized, meaning that the government subsidizes its citizens' health care, so it is very affordable. Additionally, people do not sue each other if the coffee is too hot. Finally, labor is very cheap, so if you need to have your car repaired, you simply drive down to your neighborhood garage where your car is repaired without costing you an arm and a leg. Collectively, it means that insurance is not that big a deal and many families do not have insurance policies. They don't have to play any defense at all. It's all offense for them.

$2.9 Million Awarded for Hot Coffee

In 1994, a jury awarded $2.9 million to an 81-year-old woman scalded by hot coffee from McDonald's. Apparently McDonald's used to serve coffee really hot on advice from coffee consultants who claimed that brewing under super-high temperatures would make the coffee flavorful. Critics of this verdict have used it as another example of the litigious society we live in.

We live in the most advanced country in the world, but along with the tremendous benefits we enjoy in terms of material comforts and their affordability comes a heavy price. The price we pay is that we must continuously look over our shoulder to ensure we are not trampled by a frivolous lawsuit by fellow citizens intent upon a quick buck.

A Prescription for Living while at College

Have only one or two credit cards. Make sure you hold off on impulse big-ticket purchases and always pay off your charges quickly, if not totally, at the end of the month.

Life insurance policies are not necessary if you have no dependents to support. Make sure to have health insurance coverage either through your parents or through work. If you drive a car, make sure you have adequate auto insurance. If it is an old car, it probably does not make sense to have anything but liability insurance coverage. Liability insurance is usually the cheapest auto insurance coverage.

If you have some extra money, think about starting a Roth IRA. You can afford to take chances with your investments. Remember, you are investing for the long term (about a forty year time horizon). Buy a sector ETF that you think will outperform the market in the short run. Buy an index fund or an index ETF for the long term. Let TVM work for you in growing your retirement nest egg. Most importantly, try not to get into huge credit card debts and try not to mess up your credit history.

After Graduation—Invoke the 80–20 Rule

You have a job and are beginning to have a bit of discretionary wealth. Make sure to start paying off your student loans and any credit card debts you may have accumulated in college (in spite of my warnings above). Do this before putting your money anywhere else. You want to pay off, or at least pay down, your high interest loans before you start building your asset account.

If you just got married, you do have a dependent now: Each is the other's dependent. Consider getting a Term Life insurance policy which is cheap, but make sure that it is convertible to a cash value policy of your choice without any additional medical exams; that is, guaranteed renewable. Make sure you have adequate health and auto insurance protection. Regarding auto insurance, remember to have more than the minimum amount mandated in your state of residence. Also remember that, when you are no longer a student, you are liable to be sued more easily. Lawyers study your financial situation before deciding whether it is worth their while to sue you. The greater your perceived net worth, the more attractive a target you become.

Start budgeting your money and try to have some (even if it is $50 a month) to put into your Roth IRA. In addition, if your company has a 401(k) and your employer matches your contribution to it, this is free money. Make sure you take advantage by contributing your own money thereby getting the employer to put in the maximum amount possible.

If, after all this, there is any surplus, open a brokerage account and start investing outside your retirement account. Here, you will want to invoke my 80-20 principle which states that in your twenties, around 80 percent of your investment dollars should be in equity or equity-related investments—whether it be stocks, ETFs, equity mutual funds, options, etc., and about 20 percent in non-equity investments like a bond ETF and precious metal ETFs. The latter is to provide your investment portfolio with a floor to stabilize it in case of a short-to-intermediate term market turmoil.

In Your Thirties and Forties — Move to 70–30

This is where you are starting to bring in serious income BUT your expenses are also climbing as you have to cater to the needs of a growing family and your own upscale lifestyle.

It is advisable to have a compartmental approach towards investing—along with an overall 70–30 approach: 70 percent in equity and 30 percent in debt and precious metal, including gold, instruments. You may want to compartmentalize your investment account into a "serious" compartment and a "play" compartment. The money in your serious compartment might be earmarked for your children's college fund or a bigger home purchase, or a rainy-day fund. Investments should be in relatively low-risk, high-return assets. If you are in mutual funds or ETFs, they should be 4–5 star rated according to Morningstar or a comparable rating agency. In addition, you should have some bond ETFs or high grade bond mutual funds. Think about a precious metal ETF or even a gold index fund. Remember that gold and precious metal funds do well in a defensive, or depressed, economy and are good foils to bring some balance to your portfolio. Whatever you invest in, do not put more than 25–30 percent of your investing dollars in non-equity investments. You still need to grow your portfolio aggressively without sacrificing too much in downside risk.

In the play compartment, try to have some fun with your investments. Take some chances. If you think a particular company might take off in a few years, go ahead and buy some shares in it. Buy some high yield bonds. Buy some sectors you think have long-term potential. In other words, the sky's the limit in this compartment. If you read about a promising drug trial, find the parent company and buy some shares. A new technology in the offing? Track the parent company and invest. Just make sure that this money is not needed elsewhere by you or your family.

It might be time to trade in that Term Life policy for a fancier cash value policy like a Universal Life or, if you want to take some chances, maybe even a Variable Universal Life policy.

Make sure the charges on your credit cards don't get out of hand and that you are paying off all, or most, of your charges every month. In terms of retirement, make sure you feed the Roth IRA account and any 401(k) account that you may have through your employer, especially if your company is providing matching funds (translation, free money). Also, take advantage of the ESOPs if you have the opportunity, although you may want to make sure you do not put all your eggs in that one basket. Remember what happened to ENRON employees who did just that hoping for a golden retirement. They were left with nothing.

In Your Fifties: Think 50–50

More of the thirties but in a bigger and grander scale! Your children are becoming teenagers and college expenses are looming. Those college funds you set up in your late twenties or early thirties should be looking mighty attractive now.

Your house and cars are all, or mostly, paid off. Even though you are not getting the same kinds of tax breaks on your mortgage payment, you have the advantage of having significant equity in your house and other property. Start putting any surplus money into savings accounts with interest payments. Also start getting more conservative with your investments. Pull them out of risky ventures and consolidate them into blue chip stocks and high quality government and corporate bonds. The play compartment should get a revamping. You should still have play money but keep an eye out for some strategic profit-taking by selling some of your holdings at significant gains after a run-up in prices. You should start to get heavier on high-quality stocks and high-quality bonds and less on speculative/ high-risk assets.

Insurance needs decline as your children are growing up. Think in terms of scaling down the face value of the policy, which would also save you money in premiums. If you have significant cash value built up, you could reduce the face value of the policy and use the accumulated cash value to service the policy in order to combat the natural increase in death benefit costs in your policy.

Check your retirement accounts and follow the same approach there: Relatively less exposure to equities and more to high grade bonds; the equities themselves in high quality, proven stocks. At this stage of your life, you should have relatively more exposure to corporate bonds and less to treasuries. This way, there is still some risk being taken and returns earned, but the crucial downside is also protected.

In Your Sixties and Seventies: Think 35–65

They say sixties are the new fifties. People are living longer and healthier lives— well into their sixties, seventies and eighties. There is no need to hide behind the safety of bonds quite yet. Remember from earlier discussions that the high price of safety is the significantly reduced returns that bonds provide. You want your investment portfolio to keep generating decent returns and that means increased exposure to equities and maybe even some derivatives. While caution is clearly your watchword, you should not throw the baby out with the bathwater!

Regarding insurance, you can safely drop down the coverage to where it will cover your funeral arrangements and other final medical expenses. Your children are grown and have lives of their own. Your insurance needs should now be minimal.

In Your Eighties: Think 20–80

These days, people are leading long and healthy lives well into their seventies and eighties. This necessitates rethinking investment decisions well into our eighties. Traditional thinking stops at sixty. Then the assumption is that you start consuming your accumulated wealth till demise. Not anymore!

Given our extended longevity, our investment portfolio, including our retirement accounts, need to be in relatively aggressive growth mode well into our sixties, seventies and eighties. While the exposure to equities needs to ramp down to within 20 percent equity and 80 percent bonds by the end of our sixties, think high quality in both areas. You have to be careful about not taking large risks without sacrificing too much by way of returns. There is no one size fits all here—only your own awareness of how much risk you are comfortable taking. So the equities should be in high quality companies and certain sector ETFs, while the bonds should be in A-rated bonds, bond ETFs and treasuries. About 10 percent of your portfolio should be in precious metals and/or gold funds to provide you with an inflation buffer. The high quality bonds and bond ETFs along with the stocks will still provide some much needed growth while the precious metal and gold funds will provide some defense.

In sum, the way we live and think about our lives has changed dramatically over the last 15–20 years and will change further as medical science continues to advance and we are able to lead longer, healthier lives. Accordingly, our thinking about how to invest our money will also have to change to keep pace with our lives.

Big Picture

A young man hears that there is a Zen master living as a hermit in the forest. He decides to become his student. After much searching, he manages to stumble upon the hut of the old master (remember, teachers in those days lived the hard life). The awestruck student sees the elderly man in front of the hut, raking leaves. The young man rushes out and falls prone on the ground in front of the old man. Still in that respectful position, the young man introduces himself and expresses his desire to become the master's student. But there is no response from the elderly teacher. In fact, the old man continues with his raking and never even bothers to look up, or even acknowledge, the young man's presence (once again, recall we are in the days before teaching evaluations). Very disconcerted, the young man stands, scratches his head and ponders the situation. He decides to go over to another part of the forest and build his own hut. Ten years later, while raking leaves, he suddenly achieves enlightenment (satori). He immediately returns to the old Zen master (still raking leaves), bows, and says, "Thank you, Master!"

Go Forth and Prosper!

A Guide to
Understanding
Time Value of Money

TVM Awareness Quiz

1. Compounding refers to moving money from the present to the future.

2. Discounting refers to moving money from the future to the present

3. It will take approximately 12 years for your money to double at an interest rate of 6 percent.

4. If a bank charges a 13 percent nominal interest rate on a loan, the effective interest rate assuming monthly compounding is . . .

5. Time Value of Money calculations are determined by two values: principal and interest rate.

6. The process of determining the future value of a present amount is called discounting.

7. Interest rates associated with credit cards are significantly lower than if you were to get a mortgage loan.

8. If a bank charges a 13 percent nominal interest rate on a loan, is the effective interest rate assuming monthly compounding greater than 13 percent equal to 13 percent, or less than 13 percent?

9. Insurance premiums are computed on the basis of time value of money principles.

10. A stock or bond price is nothing but the discounted present value of all future cash flows attributed to the stock or bond.

If you missed a couple, you should pay closer attention. If you got them all right, you still need to listen because there is a lot of subtlety in these pesky little concepts that you need to absolutely understand in order to take full advantage of them in life.

Answers

(Don't peek till you have made a good faith attempt)

1. True

2. True

3. True

4. 13.8 percent

5. False: TVM is determined by three variables: Principal, interest rate and time period.

6. False

7. False

8. Greater than 13%

9. True

10. True

The Basics

Why Should I Learn Time Value of Money?

That's the most common question at the beginning of each semester. The reason is simple but you may not see it right away and some may never see it. The fact is that understanding time value of money (TVM) principles will help you make better decisions in your everyday personal life. It will help you understand how things like mortgages, car loans, home equity loans, retirement plans, insurance contracts, and credit card bills work. And, if you are in business, or into investing, it will most definitely help you make better business and/or investment decisions. Among other things, it will help you understand how to value basic financial securities like stocks and bonds and to do simple capital budgeting and related computations. Such knowledge will help you become a better employee and maybe even grant you the coveted "drop-by-unannounced" rights to your boss's house. Maybe you will even qualify for the employee-of-the-year trip to an exotic location where men wear flowered shirts and drinks are served with little umbrellas in them.

These days almost everybody (regardless of where you work and what your major is) is required to know the basics of discounting and compounding, i.e., TVM. But, unfortunately, while TVM is a relatively simple concept with far-reaching consequences, it is also the concept that provides students with the most trouble. It is not unusual to see university graduates in business and in engineering dissolve in a puddle of tears over TVM. Most have absolutely no clue about how to use the concepts to solve their own real world problems. The purpose of this guide is to make sure the same thing does not happen to you.

TVM has applications in all areas of our lives from investing to retirement (which is also investing), job contracts, insurance, credit, estate planning and a host of other issues. In fact, to fully appreciate any of the major financial decisions that you will soon have to be making, you need to really understand TVM and how it works. And by that I don't mean just being able to mechanically solve TVM problems in class but to be able to take the same concepts and apply them to your own personal situations appropriately.

TVM uses the time-tested concept of compounding to convert a sum of money from the present to some date in the future, and to discount a given sum of money from a given date in the future to the present. What makes the process of discounting or compounding interesting is that it is not a simple linear rule but an exponential rule. This will be illustrated later with a graph.

The Time Value of Money

Receiving $1,000 today is not the same as $1,000 received a year from now. We all seem to have an intuitive understanding of that fact even if we are not always able to articulate exactly why this is so. It's because money received sooner, rather than later, allows one to use the funds for investment or consumption purposes. Put differently, getting the money sooner allows you to invest it in an interest-bearing account whereby it grows in value. Or, if you received the money sooner and simply consumed it, it will give you pleasure right now which is better than delayed gratification. This concept is referred to as the TIME VALUE OF MONEY!

So, which would you rather have—$1,000 today or $1,000 in five years?

The corollary to the above is: If you had the choice of paying someone $5000 today versus $5000 five years from now, which would you choose?

The Intuition behind TVM

- The value of $100 received today is more than $100 received in the future, or

- The value of $100 received in the future is less than $100 received today.

Why TIME?

TIME allows us the opportunity to postpone consumption and earn INTEREST. And the fact that we use our money in one venture, say depositing it in a bank account, forces us to give up the opportunity of using the money for some other purpose. What our money could have earned in this alternative venture (that we are not allowed to use now) is called the OPPORTUNITY COST of our money.

So, for example, you have $500 that your grandmother gave you for Christmas and you decide to keep the money under your pillow for the next six months because you are afraid you will spend it otherwise. What is the opportunity cost of this action on your part? To answer this question, you will need to know what would be the best possible alternative for your money. You could open a bank account and earn (say) $10 interest over that period. So, the opportunity cost of your original action is $10, or 2 percent. Now, keep in mind that the opportunity cost is not the same for everybody. For example, your friend Sara, who is a genius in the stock market, could take the same amount of money, invest it in the market, and make a profit of $100 over a six-month period. So, Sara's opportunity cost is 20 percent. Get the picture?

Opportunity Cost

Determined by what you are giving up by investing your money in a particular venture. It is different for different people. In finance, opportunity cost is important because we do not want to give up the opportunity to make 10 percent on our money if we are using it only to make 7 percent currently.

How Can We Compare amounts in Different Time Periods?

The simple answer is: WE CANNOT! We can only compare monies at the same point in time. Otherwise, it is like comparing apples and oranges. If you are given money at two different points in time and asked to compare them, you can only do so after either compounding or discounting one of the cash amounts (using an appropriate compounding or discount rate) so they are both at the same point in time.

Simple Interest

Simple interest is the interest paid (or earned) on only the original amount, or the amount borrowed (or lent).

First, assume that you deposit $1,000 in an account earning 7 percent simple interest for 2 years. What is the accumulated interest at the end of the 2nd year?

Simple Interest (SI) = P_0 x i x n
Future Value (FV) = P_0 + SI

SI: Simple Interest

P_0: Deposit today (t=0)

i: Interest Rate per Period

n: Number of Time Periods

In the current case,
$$SI = P_0(i)(n)$$
$$= \$1,000(.07)(2)$$
$$= \$140$$

So what is the future value (FV) of the deposit?
$$FV = P_0 + SI$$
$$= \$1,000 + \$140$$
$$= \$1,140$$

Defining Present and Future Values

Future Value is the value at some future time of a present amount of money, or a series of payments, evaluated at a given interest rate.

And what is the Present Value (PV) of the previous problem?

The Present Value is simply the $1,000 you originally deposited. That is the value today.

Present Value is the current value of a future amount of money, or a series of payments, evaluated at a given interest rate.

Exponential Growth under Compounding

In contrast to simple interest, when interest is paid on not only the principal amount invested, *but also on any previous interest earned*, it is called compound interest.

Below is a graphic illustration of the growth of a single deposit of $1,000 at various interest rates—simple as well as compound. Notice the growth rate of money. Especially notice how, under the compound interest rate, there is an exponential growth of money towards the end.

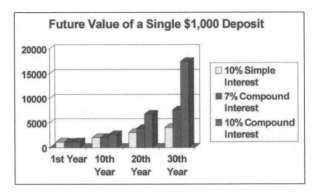

So, time is the crucial part of the growth here. If you were to take a 100-mile trip, for example, you would be halfway to your destination after 50 miles. Compound interest doesn't work the same way. If you're saving to retire in 40 years (say) you'll accumulate much less than half your financial goal after saving for 20 years. The majority of your contributions' growth occurs in later years, when time and compounding begin to work their magic.

For example, let us assume you contribute $200 a month to your retirement plan, and your contributions grow at 8 percent annually.

After 10 years, you'll have contributed $24,000 to the plan (unadjusted for time value of money) and with accumulated compound interest the total will be $36,589.

After 20 years, you'll have a total of $48,000 in contributions that will grow to $117,804.

After 30 years, you'll have contributed $72,000, but your retirement nest egg will increase to $298,072.

After 40 years, your $96,000 in total contributions will swell to an astounding $698,201.

Critical Factoid

Examine the numbers above to understand how time helps grow your savings, assuming $698,201 is the goal. After 10 years, you'll have accumulated only 5 percent of your eventual goal. After 20 years—halfway to retirement—your total will be only about 17 percent of your final goal. After 30 years—three-quarters into your retirement planning journey—you will only be at about 50 percent of your goal. So, over the last quarter of your time horizon, your savings grow an astounding 50 percent.

Single Sum Problems

Single sum problems involve a single dollar sum. Examples include situations where you might be promised (say, by your grandmother) $300 two years in the future and you would like to know its present value. Or, you may decide to open a bank account with $500 today and you would like to know how much it would grow into at the bank's stated interest rate. Notice that the defining characteristic of the above scenarios is moving a single sum of money either from the present to the future or moving a single sum of money from the future to the present.

These are called single sum problems. The formula to solve problems involving a single dollar sum is given by

$$FV_n = P_0 (1 + i)^n \qquad (1)$$

where,

FV_n = future value at time n

P_0 = present value at time 0 (i.e., right now)

i = interest rate per period

n = number of time periods

Future Value of a Single Sum

Let us now take equation (1) and rewrite it.

$$FV_n = P_0 \bullet FVF_{i,n} \qquad (1a)$$

By comparing equations (1) and (1a) we see that the term $(1+i)^n$ in (1) is represented by the term $FVF_{i,n}$ in (1a)—otherwise known as the Future Value Factor and is determined by two numbers—i and n. FVF is especially useful for those among you who want to use the tables (provided at the back of this guide).

The future value of single sum involves problems of computing the dollar value in the future of a single dollar sum in the present, at a certain growth rate. Typical examples include bank deposits and what they might grow to at a certain future date or a loan that you may have to repay in one lump sum in the future. In order to solve such problems, the FVF table will be supplied to you during exams and similar testing events. Following is a portion of a standard FVF table. Notice that the horizontal arm of the table contains the i's, or the interest rates, and the vertical arm of the table contains the time periods, n.

Now do you understand why the term $FVF_{i,n}$ is written with the i and n subscripts?

Period	6%	7%	8%
1	1.060	*1.070*	1.080
2	**1.124**	**1.145**	**1.166**
3	1.191	1.225	1.260
4	1.262	1.311	1.360
5	1.338	1.403	1.469

Important

Notice that the same formula (equation 1) can be used to solve both future and present value problems involving a single sum.

Examples

Here is an example of using the *FVF* tables to solve a problem.

1. Ali wants to know how large his deposit of $10,000 today will become at a compound annual interest rate of 10 percent for 5 years.

   Solution:
   $$FV_5 = \$10{,}000\ (FVF_{10\%,\,5})$$
   $$= \$10{,}000\ (1.611) = \$16{,}110$$

Here is another example.

2 . If you invested $2,000 today in an account that pays 6 percent interest, with interest compounded annually, how much will be in the account at the end of two years if there are no withdrawals?

   Solution:

   $$FV_2 = P_0\,(1 + i)^n$$
   $$= \$2{,}000\ (1.06)^2$$
   $$= \$2{,}247.20$$

Practice: Solve the same problem using the *FVF* table.

Present Value of a Single Sum

The present value of single sum involves problems of computing the present value of a single dollar sum somewhere in the future, at a given discount rate. Typical examples include estimating the present value of future promises or income. In order to solve such problems, we simply take equation (1) and rearrange it to get

$$PV_0 \quad = \quad \frac{FV_n}{(1+i)^n}$$

$$= FV_n \bullet \frac{1}{(1+i)^n} \tag{2}$$

$$= FV_n \bullet (PVF_{i,n})$$

Once again, we see that the term $\frac{1}{(1+i)^n}$ in equation (2) is represented by the term $PVF_{i,n}$ otherwise known as the **Present Value Factor** and it too is determined by two numbers—i and n. Hence, you can use PVF tables to solve the problem if you don't want to use the actual formula given by equation (2). A PVF table will be supplied to you during exams and similar events, and you can also find them at the back of almost all basic investment texts. Here is a portion of a standard PVF table. As with the FVF table before, the horizontal arm of the table contains the i's or interest rates, and the vertical arm of the table contains of the periods, n.

Period	6%	7%	8%
1	.943	.935	.926
2	**.890**	.873	.857
3	.840	.816	.794
4	.792	.763	.735
5	.747	.713	.681

Some Examples

Here is an example of using the PVF table.

1. What is the present value of $1000 received 2 years from now if the interest rate is 7 percent?

   Solution:

   $$PV_0 = \$1,000\ (PVF_{7\%,\,2})$$
   $$= \$1,000\ (0.873)$$
   $$= \$873$$

2. Assume that you need to have exactly $4,000 saved 10 years from now. How much must you deposit today in an account that pays 6% interest, compounded annually, so that you reach your goal of $4,000?

   Solution:

   $$PV_0 = FV_{10}/(1+i)^{10} = \$4,000\ /\ (1.06)^{10} = \$2,233.58$$

3. Joann needs to know how large of a deposit to make today so that the money will grow to $2,500 in 5 years. Assume today's deposit will grow to 4 percent compounded annually.

   Solution:

   $$PV_0 = FV_n/(1+i)^n$$
   $$PV_0 = \$2,500/(1.04)^5$$
   $$= \$2,054.81$$

Variations on the Above

We now know how to use the Single Sum formula to get either Present Values or Future Values. But what if I gave you both the *PV* and the *FV* and asked you to compute either *n* or *i*?

1. If one invests $2,000 today and has accumulated $2,676.45 after exactly five years, what rate of annual compound interest was earned?

   Hint: Use the appropriate single sum equation and solve for i.

2. If I invest $10,000 today in a savings account paying 6 percent interest (compounded annually), how long will it take for me to have $50,000 in my account?

   Hint: Solve for *n*.

Frequency of Compounding

Now we are going to learn another variation of single sum problems. So far, we have assumed that interest rate is compounded annually. But it does not always have to be that way. In fact, in most practical real world applications, it is not. Money is compounded more frequently than annually, such as every six months (twice a year), or every quarter (4 times a year) or monthly (12 times a year) and sometimes even daily. For practical purposes, the frequency of your payments (or receipts) also determines the compounding frequency. For example, credit card related loans are compounded monthly; cash advances on your credit cards are compounded daily, and so on. How do we solve TVM problems under those situations?

To see this, consider the Single Sum formula, equation (1), written in its most general form as

$$FV_{n,\,m} = P_0 \left[1 + \left[\frac{i}{m} \right] \right]^{m \bullet n} \tag{3}$$

Where

n: Number of Years

m: Compounding Periods per Year

i: Annual Interest Rate

$FV_{n,\,m}$: FV at the end of Year n (at compounding frequency m)

P_0: PV of the Cash Flow today

Notice that if we substitute $m = 1$ (or, annual compounding) in (3), we are back to equation (1).

Frequency of Compounding Example

Suppose you deposit $1,000 in an account that pays 12 percent interest, **compounded quarterly**. How much will be in the account after eight years if there are no withdrawals?

Solution: The way to solve this problem is to first recognize two things:

1. When you are given an annual interest rate of 12 percent compounded every quarter, that makes it an interest rate of $12/4 = 3$ percent every quarter. This is your i for the problem.

2. Eight years in quarters equals $8 \times 4 = 32$ quarters. This is your n for the problem.

Armed with this information, you are ready to do some serious problem solving.

$$PV_0 = \$1,000$$
$$i = 12\% \div 4 = 3\% \text{ per quarter}$$
$$n = 8 \times 4 = 32 \text{ quarters}$$

Solution based on formula:

$$FV_{32} = PV_0 (1 + i)^n$$
$$= 1,000(1.03)^{32}$$
$$= \$2575.10$$

Nominal Interest Rates

A real interest rate is one where the effects of inflation have been factored in. By contrast, a nominal interest rate is one where the effects of inflation have **not** been accounted for.

Here is an example illustrating the difference. Suppose I take out a $100 loan with the condition that I pay back $106 at the end of the year. Thus the loan has an interest rate of 6 percent. This 6 percent, however, is the nominal interest rate, because we have not accounted for inflation. So if the prices of goods and services increase by about 2 percent over the year, it is included in the interest you are paying on your loan and, therefore, it is easy to see that under such circumstances you are paying less (in real terms) for borrowing money—i.e., about 4 percent. Whenever people speak of the interest rate they're talking about the nominal interest rate, unless they state otherwise.

What does inflation do? It generally raises the price of everything in the economy or reduces the value of a dollar by that much—as with the 2 percent in the example above. Another way to see how this works is as follows. Suppose the inflation rate is 3 percent for that year. We can buy a basket of goods today and it will cost $100, or we can buy that same basket next year and it will cost $103. The Federal Reserve, America's Central Bank, is extremely vigilant about inflation by regulating the Federal Funds Flow rate (which is the rate the Federal Reserve charges on overnight loans between banks). How do they do that? They raise the Fed funds flow rate when inflation concerns are higher in order to deter borrowing by making it more expensive. Conversely, rates are lowered when the economy contracts in order to encourage consumer borrowing (and spending) by making borrowing costs cheaper.

Fed Funds Flow Rates

Very simply, it is the overnight lending rate between banks. Most recently, the Board of Governors of the Federal Reserve have held the Fed funds rate between zero and 0.25 percent in order to help banks get over the worst recession since the Great Depression. Analysts feel that, given the current economic climate, this rate will stay close to zero for the next couple of years at the very least. The implication for banks is that they can borrow money for free from the Federal Reserve which should help loosen credit and allow them to lend to consumers in order to get the economy moving.

Relationship between Mortgage Rate and Federal Funds Rate

There is a belief that when you are looking for a favorable mortgage rate, to either finance your home purchase or refinance an existing mortgage, the time to lock in a rate is when the federal funds rate is low. This implies that the two go in lock step and is actually not true. While there is some correlation between the two rates, as the chart below shows, any correlation is small. So don't let a low federal funds rate fool you where favorable mortgage rates are concerned. The current fed funds rate is near zero as discussed above, but home mortgage rates have been hovering in the 5.5–6.0 percent rate over this entire period and show no signs of going lower.

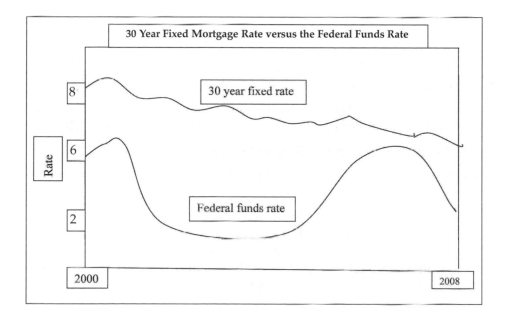

Effective Annual Interest Rate

The effective interest rate is the actual (or, real) rate of interest earned (or paid) after adjusting the *nominal rate* for factors such as the number of compounding periods per year.

$$i_{eff} = \left[1 + \left[\frac{i}{m}\right]\right]^m - 1 \tag{4}$$

where i is simply the given interest rate per period and m is the compounding frequency. Thus, $m = 4$ for quarterly compounding, $m = 12$ for monthly compounding, and $m = 365$ for daily compounding.

How does the effective interest rate relate to the nominal interest rate? As we have seen above, loans can be calculated with different compounding periods, i.e., monthly, quarterly, semi-annually, annually, etc. To protect the consumer, all loans should be stated in effective rate terms which factor in the compounding frequency

Caution

Note that with annual compounding, the nominal rate equals the effective rate.

on to the nominal rate. This makes it easier for the potential borrower to compare across loans and select the best rate when borrowing. These days, lenders are required by law to report the effective rate of interest on your loan in addition to the APR. So, you can easily infer the compounding frequency.

Example: What is the effective rate of a 12 percent APR loan that is compounded daily?

Solution: From the given formula, we can write

$$i_{eff} = \left[1 + \frac{.12}{365}\right]^{365} - 1$$

$$= 12.75\%$$

So, the effective rate of interest on your 12 percent loan is actually 12.75 percent.

Practice Problem: What is the effective annual rate of interest for a loan that has a 36 percent annual percentage rate, compounded monthly? **Answer: 42.58 percent**

More Examples of Single Sum Problems

1. How long does it take for an investment to quadruple in value if the investment yields 6 percent per year?

   Solution: Notice that we can take an investment of any value in this problem . . . so, for simplicity, let us assume an initial investment of $1 (i.e., PV=$1). However, keep in mind that the actual value of the initial investment does not matter. We will get the same answer regardless of the amount of initial investment chosen. In fact, you should all convince yourself of this by redoing the problem with different initial investments.

   - $PV = \$1$
   - $FV = \$4$
   - $i = 6\%$
   - **n = 24 years**
   - **Hint:** Use $1 as a PV; therefore the $FV = \$4$ if the value quadruples

2. What is the effective annual rate (EAR) of interest for a loan that has an 18 percent annual percentage rate, compounded monthly?

   Solution: Notice that if a loan has an annual 18 percent APR, the effective rate after monthly compounding will be considerably more than 18 percent. Can you articulate why? Talk it out!

   - $i = 0.18$
   - $m = 12$

- **EAR = 19.56%**
- **Hint:** Simply apply the information provided to the formula for i_{eff}.

3. The average price of a movie ticket at the end of 1988 was $5.50 and the average price of a movie ticket at the end of 1990 was $6.00. At what annual rate did ticket prices grow?

Solution:
- $PV = \$5.50$
- $FV = \$6.00$
- $t = 2$
- $i = 4.4466\%$

- **Hint:** There are two years over which the price has grown—from 1988 to 1989 (that's one year), and then from 1989 to 1990 (the second year).

4. If Abel invests $100 today in an account that earns 10 percent per year, compounded semi-annually, how much will he have in this account at the end of twenty years if he makes no withdrawals?

Solution:
- $PV = \$100$
- $i = 10\%/2 = 5\%$
- $n = 20 \times 2 = 40$
- $FV = \$704$

- **Hint:** transform the given values to a semi-annual basis (i.e., period = six months). What does that mean for adjusting n and i?

5. Suppose you are trying to borrow money from the bank to finance your business. And suppose you promise to repay the bank in two installments, one payment in two years for $5,000 and one payment in four years for $10,000. If the bank's opportunity cost of funds is 10 percent, how much is the bank willing to lend you?

Solution:
- PV of first payment = $4,132
- PV of second payment = $6,830
- Loan = sum of PVs = $10,962 (you can add cash flows at the same time)
- **Hint:** if you have a financial calculator, you can solve this in one step using the cash flow registers ($CF0 = 0$, $CF1 = 0$, $CF2 = 5000$, $CF3 = 0$, $CF4 = 10,000$) and solve for NPV.

6. Suppose Charlie borrows $100,000 today and must make monthly payments of $3,874.81 at the end of each month for thirty months. What is the annual percentage rate (APR) on Charlie's loan? What is the effective annual rate (EAR) on Charlie's loan?

   Solution:
   - $PV = \$100,000$
   - $CF = \$3,874.81$
   - $n = 30$
   - Solve for the monthly interest rate, i
   - $i = 1\%$ per month
   - APR $= 1\% \times 12 = 12\%$
   - EAR $= (1 + 0.01)^{12} - 1 = 12.68\%$

7. Calculate the effective annual rate (EAR) on a savings account with an annual percentage rate (APR) of 10 percent for the following compounding frequencies:

   a.   Semi-annual: $i = .05$ **EAR = 10.25%**
   b.   Quarterly: $i = .025$ **EAR = 10.3813%**
   c.   Monthly: $i = .008333$ **EAR = 10.4713%**
   d.   Daily: $i = .000274$ **EAR = 10.5156%**

8. Calculate the average annual interest rate on each of the following transactions:

   a.   You borrow $1,000 and repay $1,200 at the end of two years.
   b.   You borrow $1,000 and repay $1,350 at the end of four years.
   c.   You borrow $500 and repay $600 at the end of five years.
   d.   You borrow $250 and repay $500 at the end of eight years.
   Hint: identify PV, FV, and n.

   a. 9.54%, b. 7.79, c. 3.71%, d. 9.05%

Summary

Single sum problems involve a single dollar sum that you have to move either to the relative present (present value problem) or to the relative future (future value problem). The four possible variables are P_0, FV_t, i and n. You will be provided with information on any three and asked to find the fourth.

Annuities

The real fun begins now! Most of the interesting real world applications of TVM are where a series of (usually equal) cash flows are involved. Annuities are everywhere: student loan payments, car loan payments, insurance premium payments, mortgage payments, retirement savings—the list goes on and on. Therefore, it is essential that you understand how annuities work so you will know what you are doing when you undertake these transactions in your daily life.

Learn to Recognize Annuities

In order to solve for annuities, you have to first learn to recognize them. The problem is that real life applications will not scream annuities to you. They will come disguised in words and other terminology and you will need to infer them as annuities. So, how do you recognize annuities? Here are some examples.

- If one saves $1,000 a year at the end of every year for three years in an account earning 7 percent interest, compounded annually, how much will one have at the end of the third year?

Why is the above an annuity? Notice the wording of the problem. You want to save $1,000 every year for three years. Thus, there are multiple cash flows involved. That's your first and most important clue. In this case, you want to know the value of this annuity at the end of three years. So we can further say that this is a **FUTURE VALUE** of an annuity since the final date is in the future in relation to the cash flows involved. Three years in the future, to be exact. Here is another example of an annuity.

- If one agrees to repay a loan by paying $1,000 a year at the end of every year for three years and the discount rate is 7 percent, how much could one borrow today?

Why is this an annuity? Again, you are making multiple and equal payments toward a loan you take out today. Multiple (and equal) payments imply annuity. What kind of an annuity is it? Notice that you want to know how much you can borrow today, based on the future payments. The final destination is the present with respect to the cash flows involved. So, this is a PRESENT VALUE of an annuity.

> ## Emphasis
> Future value problems are where the cash flows have to be moved to some date in the future relative to the date of the cash flows. Thus, for example, cash flows may occur at times 1, 2, 3, 4, while you may want to know its value at time 5. Notice that 5 is in the relative future compared to times 1, 2, 3, and 4. So, this is an example of a future value problem.

- You make an $850 a month payment to your bank for a mortgage loan you have taken out.

Emphasis

Present value problems are where the cash flows have to be moved to some date in the present relative to the date of cash flows. Thus, for example, cash flows may occur at times 1, 2, 3, 4, while you may want to know its value at time 0 (i.e., at the present). Notice that 0 is in the relative present compared to times 1, 2, 3, and 4. Hence, this is an example of a present value problem.

Why is the above an annuity? Think of the equal and regular payments you are making to your bank.

Word of Warning

Don't get too caught up with the terms Present Value and Future Value. These are convenience terms only and not to be taken as the final word. The fact is that any time value problem can be solved using either the Present Value or the Future Value approach as we will see with examples.

How to Solve Annuity Problems

Let us assume you have a pretty good idea of how to spot annuities. The next step is to be able to value them in a way that is useful to you with regard to a financial decision you have to make.

You may wish to understand the present value of an annuity stream; for example, you may wish to know the present value of the $850 monthly mortgage payments. In that case, this is what you do.

Present Value of annuity stream = CF x [Present Value Factor for Annuity] (5)

where CF denotes a typical cash flow in the annuity stream. In the above examples, $850 is a cash flow (CF), or $1,000 is a CF. It is a representative cash flow in the annuity stream. What about the Present Value Annuity Factor? This is the number we need either from an appropriate table or computed directly from the appropriate formula.

Now, what if you had to estimate the value of a given stream of equal and regular cash flows at some date in the future? For example, you might like to know the value of your ($850) monthly mortgage payments 5 years from today. In TVM terminology, you would say

Future Value of annuity stream = CF x [Future Value Factor for Annuity]   (6)

Notice that the difference between the above two formulas is the replacement of the term "present" with "future". The basic formula remains the same—including the CF. The Future Value Factor for Annuity is either computed from a given formula or looked up directly from the appropriate table.

In sum, annuities are normally solved in two steps.

- The first step is to reduce the series of annuity payments to an equivalent single sum on the time line by using either equation (5) or (6), whichever is appropriate for the specific problem.
- The second step is to move that equivalent single sum to wherever the problem asks for on the time line.

The big question is what is the location, on the time line, of the equivalent single dollar sum you have computed using the formula in the last section. To determine this we will use the following rule.

- When using the Present Value Factor for Annuity (**PVFA**) to reduce an annuity stream to an equivalent single dollar sum on the time line, using equation (5), the resultant single sum is located **ONE PERIOD BEFORE THE START OF THE ANNUITY STREAM**
- When using the Future Value Factor for Annuity (**FVFA**) to reduce an annuity stream to an equivalent single dollar sum on the time line, using equation (6), the resultant single sum is located **ON THE DAY OF THE FINAL CASH FLOW IN THE ANNUITY STREAM**.

Annuity Formulas

Present Value Factor for Annuity

$$PVFA_{i,n} = \frac{1 - \frac{1}{(1 + i)^n}}{i}$$

where i denotes the interest rate per period
n denotes the NUMBER OF ANNUITY PAYMENTS.

Future Value Factor for Annuity

$$FVFA_{i,n} = \frac{(1 - i)^n - 1}{i}$$

where i denotes the interest rate per period
n denotes the NUMBER OF ANNUITY PAYMENTS.

> ## Caution
> - With annuities, n is determined by the number of annuity payments in the problem
> - In a single sum case, by contrast, n denotes the number of time periods.

Formulas or Tables?

The big question is, do you want to get used to solving TVM problems using tables or do you want to get in the habit of using the formulas from the get-go? As with everything else in life there are advantages and disadvantages to both. Also, understand that tables are nothing but the formulas computed for you over a range of i's and n's.

Advantage of Using Tables

Using the tables provides a mechanical approach to solving TVM problems. If you don't particularly want to get deep in the subject and want to know (or do) just enough to be able to solve problems, then this is the best approach for you. It provides a black box approach to solving TVM problems where you plug in the right combination of i and n and look up the value from the APPROPRIATE table. The operative word is APPROPRIATE.

Disadvantages of Using Tables

1. You have to know from which table to look up the values. Otherwise your problem will not work out correctly. So, you have to know what you are doing—to a degree.

2. Sometimes the rates and the periods that you need to solve a problem may not be available in the table. The tables are standardized and any non-standard problem like $n = 3.5$ or $i = 12.6$ percent may not have an entry in the tables. Then you have no choice but to use the formulas.

Advantage of Using Formulas

Provides the freedom to solve for any problem.

Disadvantage of Using Formulas

Sometimes the computations can be tedious. Looking up values from the tables is much easier.

Regardless of how you choose to solve your TVM problems, remember one thing. If you understand the above formulas, then using tables when the occasion calls for it will not be very difficult. But if you get dependent on tables, then switching to formulas might be more challenging. It's like learning to drive using a standard shift versus one with an automatic transmission. If you learn driving in a standard shift, you can always drive an automatic transmission. However, if you learn in an automatic , you are out of luck with a standard shift because you will have no idea how to work the clutch and manually shift gears. It's the same with formulas. They give you more flexibility.

Now it's time to get our hands dirty and solve an actual annuity problem using the principles we have learned.

Solving Annuity Problems

Problem 1: Using Present Value Factor for Annuity (PVFA)

Find the present value of the following annuity. (As always, assume the discount rate to be 5 percent).

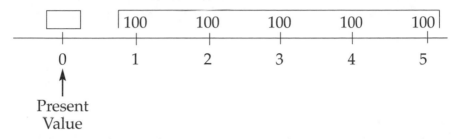

Solution: First notice the number of annuity payments in this stream. That would be $n = 5$. Also notice that the $CF = 100$. Finally, notice that this is a present value of annuity problem since the final destination is to the relative present with respect to the cash flows.

Armed with these observations, we are now ready to solve the problem. Accordingly, from equation (5),

$$PVA = CF \times PVFA_{n=5, i=5\%}$$

Substituting the values from the problem, we can say

$$PVA = 100 \times 4.3295 = \$432.95$$

where the PVFA number can either be looked up from the appropriate table or computed directly from the formula provided earlier.

The big question is: **where is this single sum located on the time line**? To see that, refer back to the rules for solving for annuities: when using equation (5) to reduce an annuity stream to an equivalent single dollar sum, the resultant single dollar sum is *located one period before the start of the annuity stream.*

Aha! Then the $432.95 is located at—time 0, right? And so $432.95 is also the Present Value (at time 0) of the annuity stream. The interpretation of $432.95 is the following: It is the present value of 5 payments of $100 each payable at the end of each of years 1 through 5.

> # Important
>
> Remember that once you compute the present value of annuity (*PVA*)—that would be $432.95 at $t = 0$—the single sum replaces the original annuity stream.

Problem 2: Using Future Value Factor for Annuity (FVFA)

Find the future value of the following annuity. (As always, assume the discount rate to be 5 percent).

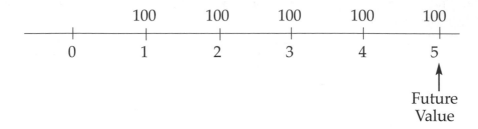

Solution: Notice the following right away: $CF = 100$ and $n = 5$, and $i = 5$ percent. Make sure you understand why this is so. Now using equation (6), we can write the future value of annuity (FVA) is given as:

$$FVA = CF \times FVFA_{n=5, i=5\%}$$

Substituting the values from the problem,

$$FVA = 100 \times 5.5256 = \$552.56$$

where the *FVFA* value can either be looked up from the future value of annuity table

Important

Remember that once you compute the future value of annuity (*FVA*)—that would be $552.56 at $t=5$—you can forget about the existence of the original annuity stream and work exclusively with the equivalent single sum located at $t=5$.

or computed directly from the *FVFA* formula provided earlier. The question is: Where is this single sum located on the timeline? To see that, refer back to the rule of solving for annuities: when using equation (6) to reduce an annuity stream to an equivalent single dollar sum, the resultant single dollar sum is *located on the day of the last payment in the annuity stream*.

This implies that $552.56 is located at—time 5, right? And $552.56 is also the Future Value (at time 5) of the annuity stream.

Problem 3

Assume you are going to receive payments of $500 in each of years 5, 6 and 7. What is the value of this annuity today (i.e., at $t = 0$)? Assume $i = 5$ percent.

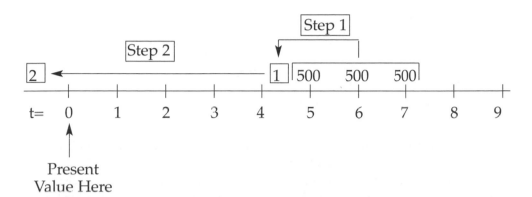

Solution: How many annuity payments are there? There are three annuity payments occurring at time 5, 6 and 7. So $n = 3$. Furthermore, CF = 500, $i = 5$ percent, and the final destination of the cash flows is at $t = 0$. So this is a present value of annuity problem. From equation 5,

$$PVA = CF \times PVFA_{n=3, i=5\%}$$

And from the present value of annuity factor table, corresponding to $n = 3$ and $i = 5$ percent, $PVFA = 2.7232$.

Hence, $PVA = 500 \times 2.7232 = \$1,361.60$—located at $t = 4$. WHY? We are, however, not done solving the problem because the problem asks us to move the cash flows to $t = 0$. So, we take the $1,361.60 located at $t = 4$ and move it to $t = 0$ as a single sum. To do so, we can use the tables as follows (or, we could compute the factor from the formula provided).

$$P_0 = 1361.60 \times (PVF_{n=4, i=5\%}) = 1120.19$$

Summary

To recap, notice how we solved the annuity problem in two steps. The first step consisted of reducing the annuity stream to an equivalent single sum and then in the second step we moved the resultant single sum to its desired destination (at time 0).

Problem 4

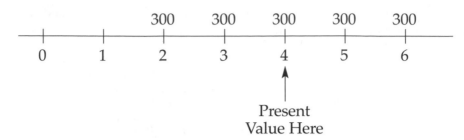

There are various ways of solving the above problem.

Approach 1

Treat the cash flows at t = 2, 3, 4 as a 3-payment annuity (annuity 1) and consider the cash flows at $t = 5$, 6 as another 2-payment annuity (annuity 2). The CF associated with both annuities is 300 and n_1 (the n associated with annuity 1) = 3, and n_2 (the n associated with annuity 2) = 2. Finally, notice that $t = 4$ is to the relative future relative to $t = 2$, 3 and to the relative present with respect to $t = 5$, 6. So the future value of annuity 1

$$FVA_1 = 300 \times FVFA_{n=3,\, i=5\%} = 945.75 \text{ (located at } t = 4)$$

and the present value of annuity 2

$$PVA_2 = 300 \times PVFA_{n=2,\, i=5\%} = 557.82 \text{ (located at } t = 4)$$

And the value of the cash flow stream at $t = 4$ is: \$1,503.57. Recall, we can add cash flows at the same point in time.

Approach 2

Treat the given set of cash flows as ONE annuity stream rather than TWO as in the previous approach. So, the present value of the annuity stream is given by

$$PVA = 300 \times PVFA_{n=5,\, i=5\%} = 1298.85 \text{ is located at } t = 1 \ldots \text{WHY?}$$

But we need to know the value of the cash flow steam at $t = 4$. To do so, we simply move the single sum, 1298.85, from $t = 1$ to $t = 4$.

So value of the cash flow stream at $t = 4$ is

$$1298.85 \times FVF_{n=3,\, i=5\%} = \$1,503.55$$

Approach 3

Once again treat the given set of cash flows as ONE annuity stream. The future value of this cash flow stream obtained by

$$FVA = 300 \times FVFA_{n=5,\, i=5\%} = \underline{\qquad} \text{ is located at } t = 6 \text{ (WHY?)}$$

Now move the resultant single sum from $t = 6$ to $t = 4$ using PVF (present value factor for a single sum). Make sense?

Note that all three approaches should give you the same answer.

Problem 5

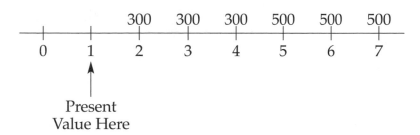

To solve this problem, first notice that we are dealing with two distinct annuity streams here.

The first one, annuity 1, is a 3-payment annuity with $CF_1 = \$300$ ($n_1 = 3$), while the second annuity, annuity 2, is a 3-payment annuity with $CF_2 = \$500$ ($n_2 = 3$). We are asked to find the value of the cash flow stream at t=1.

The most logical way to solve the above problem is to use present value of annuity factor.

$$PVA = 300 \times PVFA_{n=3,\ i=5\%} = 816.96 \text{ is located at } t = 1$$

$$PVA = 500 \times PVFA_{n=3,\ i=5\%} = \underline{\hspace{1cm}} \text{ is located at } t = 4. \text{ WHY?}$$

While one annuity stream has already been moved to the desired destination, one annuity is not. And that would be the equivalent single sum corresponding to the $500 annuity—which is located at $t = 4$. So we need to move this 3 periods back to $t = 1$. Make sure you understand this.

So, the present value of the $500 annuity at $t = 1$ is given by

$$[500 \times PVFA_{n=3,\ i=5\%}] \times PVF_{n=3,\ i=5\%} = 1176.15$$

Note that the $n = 3$ for the PVF above corresponds to moving the cash flow three periods from $t = 4$ to $t = 1$. And now that we have both annuities reduced to equivalent single sums at $t = 1$, we can simply add the two cash flows at $t = 1$ and we have our answer.

Answer: 1993.11.

Problem 6

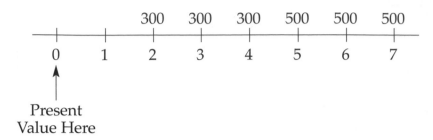

Present
Value Here

Once again, this is a two annuity problem identical to the one before, except now the final destination is at $t = 0$ rather than at $t = 1$.

So, the simplest way to solve the problem is to follow the exact same steps as in the previous problem with one additional step at the end.

Take the sum of cash flows at $t = 1$ and move that one period to $t = 0$. **Answer: 1898.20.**

Problem 7

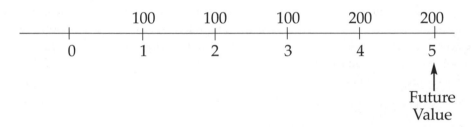

Future
Value

To solve this problem first notice that it involves two annuity streams: Annuity 1 is a 3-payment annuity ($CF = 100$, $n_1 = 3$), and annuity 2 is a 2-payment annuity ($CF = 200$, $n_2 = 2$). Also notice that the final point at which we want to know the value of the cash flow is to the relative future, given the cash flows. So we will use the future value of an annuity for this purpose. Make sense? But keep in mind that we can solve the same problem using the present value of an annuity too. More on that later.

$$FVA_1 = 100 \times FVFA_{n=3,\ i=5\%} = \underline{\qquad}$$

which puts the resultant single sum at t = 3. Next,

$$FVA_2 = 200 \times FVFA_{n=2,\ i=5\%} = \underline{\qquad}$$

which puts this single sum at $t = 5$.

Now we need to move FVA_1 located at $t = 3$ to $t = 5$. How do we do that?

And once we do that, we simply add it to the second single sum computed above. Why do we do this? After summing the two, you have your final answer. **Answer: 757.56**

Assignment

Can you solve the above problem using PVFA? Go ahead and try. The final answer would be the same.

Problem 8

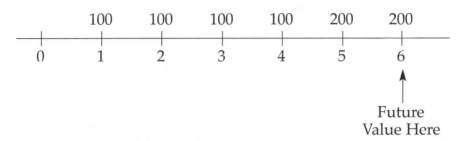

Notice that this is the same problem as the last one with one difference. The final cash flow is required at $t = 6$. So, we can do all the stuff we did for the previous problem and then move the final single sum (the answer to the last problem) from $t = 5$ to $t = 6$. How do we do that? **Answer: 795.44**

Solve the same problem using the present value of annuity factor.
To do so, notice that

$$PVA_1 = 100 \times PVFA_{n=3,\ i=5\%} = \underline{\hspace{2cm}} \text{ (located at } t = 0).$$

Now take the second annuity stream and do the following.

$$PVA_2 = 200 \times PVFA_{n=2,\ i=5\%} = \underline{\hspace{2cm}} \text{ (located at } t = 3).$$

Wait! We are not done yet. The two single sums need to be moved to their final destination: $t = 6$. How do we do that? After we move them, we need to sum them for the final answer. **Answer: 795.44**

Problem 9

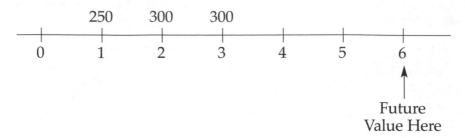

Here, notice that we have one single sum of $250 and one 2-payment annuity of $300 (i.e., $CF = 300$, $n = 2$).

First, lets take the single sum and move it 5 periods to $t = 6$.

Thus,

$$FV_6 = 250 \times (1.05)^5 = 319.07$$

which, if you wanted to use the tables, would look like

$$FV_6 = 250 \times FVF_{n=5,\, i=5\%} = \underline{\hspace{2cm}}.$$

Now let's take the 2-payment annuity and compute the future value of annuity as follows.

$$FVA = 300 \times FVFA_{n=2,\, i=5\%} = 615.00 \text{ (located at } t = 3)$$

Now we need to move this single sum to $t = 6$, the final destination. How do we do that? You should know this by now. **Answer: 1031**

Problem 10

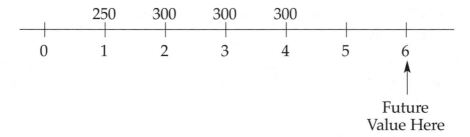

This is similar to problem 9 with a minor change. In this case, notice that we have one single sum of $250 and one 3-payment annuity of $300. The annuity is defined by $CF = 300$ and $n = 3$. Solve it as you would problem 9. **Answer: 1361.76**

Problem 11

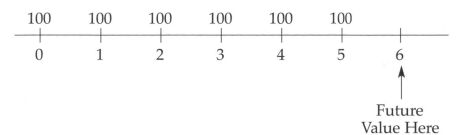

Notice that this is a 6-payment annuity with $CF = 100$ and $n = 6$. Since we are headed to the future with this problem

$$FVA = 100 \times FVFA_{n=6, \, i=5\%} = \underline{\hspace{2cm}} \text{ (located at } t = 5).$$

But we have to know the value of the annuity at $t = 6$. So that means that we have to move the equivalent single sum from $t = 5$ to $t = 6$. **Answer: 714.20.**

Solve the same problem using present value of annuity factor.
To do so, using equation (5), we can write

$$PVA = 100 \times PVFA_{n=6, \, i=5\%} = \underline{\hspace{3cm}} \text{(located at } t = -1)$$

Think about why PVA is located at $t = -1$. Ultimately, notice that $t = -1$ is just a relative number and you shouldn't get hung up with thoughts like $t = -1$ is meaningless, etc. For the moment, just run with it.

But we are not finished yet. This single sum needs to be moved to its final destination of $t = 6$. So we take the single sum and move it seven periods (from -1 to 6) to its final destination. How would you do that?

The moral of the story is that any problem can be solved using either Present Value or Future Value factors. Which one you use is up to you. The answer, however, would be the same regardless of how you get there.

SUMMARY
Steps to Solve Time Value of Money Problems

1. Read the problem thoroughly
2. Determine if it is a present value or a future value problem
3. Create a time line
4. Write down the cash flows and arrows on the time line
5. Determine if the solution involves a single cash flow, annuity stream(s), or a mixed flow involving both annuities and single sums
6. Solve the problem
7. Check with financial calculator (optional)

Some Quick Practice Problems Involving Annuities

Future Value of an Annuity

Problem	Periodic cash flow	Number of cash flows	Rate per period	Future value as of the date of the last cash flow
1	$1,000	5	4%	$5,416.32
2	$100	40	1%	$4,888.64
3	$2,000	20	2%	$48,594.74
4	$1,000	10	5%	$12,577.89
5	$1,000	12	1%	$12,682.50

Present Value of an Annuity

Problem	Periodic cash flow	Number of cash flows	Rate per period	Present Value at $t = 0$
1	$100	12	1%	$1,125.51
2	$1,000	30	1%	$25,807.71
3	$5,000	10	4%	$40,554.48
4	$10,000	12	3%	$99,540.04
5	$10,000	12	4%	$93,850.74

Some More ANNUITY Practice Problems

1. How much should you deposit in an account today so that you can withdraw $100 per year for four years, beginning two years from now, if your deposits earn 5 percent interest, compounded annually?
   - PV of annuity one year from today is $100 x (3.5460) = $354.60.
   - Value today of the $354.60 one year from today is $354.60 x 0.9524 = **$337.71**.

2. How much must I deposit in an account today so that I can withdraw $1,000 each year for four years, my deposits earn 4 percent interest (compounded annually), and my first withdrawal is ten years from today?
   - PV of annuity nine years from today is $1,000 x (3.6299) = $3,629.90
   - Value today of the $3,629.90 nine years from today is $3,629.90 x 0.7026 = **$2,550.32**

3. How much must I deposit in an account each year starting today so that I can withdraw $1,000 each year for four years, my deposits earn 4 percent interest (compounded annually), my first withdrawal is ten years from today, and my last deposit is nine years from today?
   - PV of annuity of $1,000 for four periods is $3,629.90
   - To solve for the payment, consider the $3,629.90 to be the future value (what you want in the account at the end of the ninth period) and solve for cash flows (deposits) that produce this future value.

- FV = $3,629.90; $n = 10$ (years 0 through 9); $i = 4\%$
- Annual deposit = **$302.34**

4. Suppose you want to save $8,000 for a new car. If you deposit $185.71 every month, beginning in one month, in an account that pays 12 percent interest per year, compounded monthly, how long will you be saving for your car? **Answer: 36 months.**

5. Congrats! You just won the $64 million Florida lottery. Now the You-Go-Guy Company is offering you $30 million in exchange for the 20 installments on your winnings. If your opportunity cost of funds is 8 percent, should you agree to this deal?

Given:

$CF = \$64,000,000/20 = \$3,200,000$

$n = 20$

$i = 8\%$

$PV = \$33,931,517.44$

Note that the annuity is worth almost $34 million to you, but Surely Company is offering only $30 million. So what should your decision be?

6. Roberta plans on retiring on her 60th birthday. She wants to put the same amount of funds aside each year for the next twenty years—starting next year—so that she will be able to withdraw $50,000 per year for twenty years once she retires, with the first withdrawal on her 61st birthday. Roberta is 20 years old today. How much must she set aside each year for her retirement if she can earn 10 percent on her funds?

Given:

$PV_{60} = \$50,000 \times (PVFA_{n=20, \, i=10\%})$

$PV_{60} = \$50,000 \times 8.5136$

$PV_{60} = \$425,678.19$

Because she will stop making payments on her 40th birthday (first is on her 21st birthday, last is on her 40th birthday), we must calculate the balance in the account on her 40th birthday:

$PV_{40} = PV_{60}/(1 + 0.10)^{20} = \$63,274.35$

Then, we need to calculate the deposits necessary to reach the goal:

$FV_{40} = PV_{40} = \$63,274.35$

$n = 20$

$i = 10\%$

$FV = CF \times FVFA_{n=20, \, i=10\%}$

$\$63,274.35 = CF \times FVFA_{n=20, \, i=10\%}$

$63,274.35 = CF \times 57.2750$

CF =payment = **$1,104.75 per year**

7. Have I got a deal for you! If you lend me $100,000 today, I promise to pay you back in twenty-five annual installments of $5,000, starting five years from today (that is, my first payment to you is five years from today). You can earn 6% on your investments. Will you lend me the money?

Given:

This is a deferred annuity problem

$CF = \$5,000$

$n = 25$

$i = 6\%$

$PV_4 = \$5,000 \times PVFA_{n=25,\ i=6\%}$

$PV_4 = \$5,000 \times (12.7834)$

$PV_4 = \$63,916.78$

$PV_0 = \$63,916.78/(1 + 0.06)^4 = \$50,628.08$

You probably shouldn't lend the money under these terms. If you lend me $100,000, I am repaying you using terms such that the present value of my repayment is only $50,628.08.

8. You have choices when subscribing to our magazine. You can

- pay $100 now for a four-year subscription, or

- pay $28 at the beginning of each year for four years, or

- pay $54 today and $54 again two years from today.

Which is the best deal for you, the subscriber, if your opportunity cost of funds is 10 percent?

Given:

(a) $PV = \$100$

(b) $PV = \$97.63$

(c) $PV = \$54 + \$54\ /(1+0.10)^2 = \$54 + 44.63 = \$98.63$

The best deal is to pay $28 at the beginning of each of the four years.

9. The Loans-R-Us loan company is willing to lend you $10,000 today if you promise to repay the loan in six monthly payments of $2,000 each, beginning today. What is the effective annual interest rate on Loans-R-Us's loan terms?

Given: If the company lends you $10,000 and you repay $2,000 immediately, you are really only borrowing $10,000 − 2,000 = $8,000. Therefore, you can use the regular annuity approach, modifying the PV and n:

$PV = \$8,000$

$CF = \$2,000$

$n = 5$

Solve for the i of the annuity:

$PV = CF \times PVFA_{n=5,\ i=?}$

$\$8,000 = \$2,000 \times PVFA_{n=5,\ i=?}$

or, $PVFA = 4$

Using the $PVFA$ table corresponding to the factor value nearest to 4 and $n = 5$ gives us $i = 8$ percent (corresponding to $PVFA = 3.9927$)

By directly using a financial calculator, we get $i = 7.9308$ percent (more precise).

10. You are considering the purchase of two different insurance annuities. Annuity A will pay you $18,000 at the beginning of each year for 8 years. Annuity B will pay you $14,000 at the end of each year for 15 years. Assuming your money is worth 7 peercent, and each costs you $70,000 today, which would you prefer?

   Answer: Annuity B

11. You deposit $15,000 each year for 10 years at 6 percent. Then you earn 8 percent after that. If you leave the money invested for another 3 years how much will you have in the 13th year?

   Answer: $249,045

Time Value, Annuity, Cash Flows, Present Value: A Real World Story

It appears that professional athletes are not getting the same attention from sportswear companies as they used to. This huge multibillion dollar shoe endorsement business has been soft as the soft economy has precluded kids (more specifically, parents buying for their kids) from buying expensive sneakers carrying the endorsement of their favorite NBA stars. Gone are the days of Michael Jordan when Air Jordans commanded a huge premium in the sneaker market and made Michael Jordan a wildly rich man. With those golden days behind them, shoe companies and athletes are now divorcing faster than celebrity marriages. A recent news story reported that Reebok International has cut its stable of athlete endorsers in half and recently terminated a $5 million per year contract with Shaquille O'Neal. OUCH! And those athletes that are still on the shoe company roster have signature shoes on store shelves—but are no longer benefiting from major marketing campaigns. Ouch again!

   The changing market in celebrity shoes might help explain why Vince Carter of the NBA's Toronto Raptors decided to walk away from his $800,000 per year, ten-year endorsement contract with shoemaker Puma. Carter was the 1999 NBA Rookie of the Year and has been compared to a young Michael Jordan. In the past, this kind of comparison and the accompanying publicity would have led to a marketing blitz from sportswear firms including shoe companies. Not anymore! The story from the frustrated Vince Carter camp maintains that Puma did not live up to its promotional obligations and the level of advertising was far lower than expected.

Thought Questions

1. How much money, in present value terms, is Vince Carter walking away from? Assume a 5 percent discount rate.

2. What would constitute an appropriate discount rate for a calculation such as this?

3. Consider the other side of the proverbial coin: The shoe companies. What kind of analysis should Puma or Reebok or Nike, or any other company, do before signing up the next celebrity endorser?

Specific Applications of Annuities in the Various Areas of Personal Finance

This section provides some directed applications of annuities in particular, and TVM principles in general, to examine specific issues within Personal Finance. It begins with a bond pricing example and then examine areas within credit, insurance and retirement.

Bond Pricing Example

From rational expectations we know that,

Price of a financial asset = Present Value of its future cash flows.

We apply this principle to price a bond. A bond is an example of a financial asset that is relatively easy to value. This is because its cash flow pattern is relatively certain and straightforward, unlike a stock which we will discuss next.

Let's start with an example. What price should we pay for a bond with an 8 percent semiannual coupon, a $1,000 face value and 10 years to maturity if we want a yield of 10 percent?

Answer: Mathematically, the value of a bond is given as the sum of its cash flows (*CF*):

$$\sum_{n=1}^{T} \frac{CF_n}{(1+i)^n} - \frac{CF_1}{(1+i)} + \frac{CF_2}{(1+i)^2} + \ldots + \frac{CF_t}{(1+i)^T}$$

But all of the cash flows are not even. The bond will pay semiannual coupon payments of $40 for 10 years followed by a return of the $1,000 principal at the end of the term. In order to put a value on these different payments, we need to perform further analysis.

Distilled to its essence, a bond with a fixed coupon consists of two components:
 1. A series of interest payments (an annuity); and

 2. The return of principal at maturity (a single sum).

Hence, in order to value the bond, all we need to do is value each piece separately and then add them all together. If we apply the present value of an annuity formula to the coupon payments, and the present value of a single sum formula to the return of principle at maturity, the math looks like this:

$$CF = \frac{\text{coupon rate x face value}}{\text{payment frequency}}$$

Present value of cash flows = $40 \times PVFA_{n=20, \, i=5\%} = \$498.49$

Present value of the principal repayment = $1000 \times PVF_{n=20, \, i=5\%} = \$376.90$

The price of the bond to yield 10% is then simply the sum of the two present values:

Bond Price = 498.49 + 376.90 = 875.39

Example 2

Today, at $t = 0$, a 3-year annual payment bond is priced at $973.757 to have a yield to maturity (YTM) = 7 percent. After that bond makes its date 1 interest payment, market rates are higher than date 0, so the bond will have a YTM = 8 percent. What will be the date $t = 1$ price of that bond? What will be the price of the bond after its date 2 coupon payment?
Answer: $964.34; $981.48

Solution:

$$973.757 = CF \times \underset{2.6243}{\underline{PVFA_{n=3, i=7\%}}} + \frac{1,000}{(1.07)^3}$$

$$CF = \$60$$

$$\textbf{Time 1 price} = P_1 = \frac{60}{1.08} + \frac{1,060}{(1.08)^2}$$

$$= \$964.34$$

$$\textbf{Time 2 price} = P_2 = \frac{1,060}{1.08} = 981.48$$

Practice Examples

1. What is today's value of a $1,000 face value bond with a 5 percent coupon rate (interest is paid semi-annually) which has three years remaining to maturity? The bond is priced to yield 8 percent. **Answer: $921.37**

2. An elderly neighbor asks you for investment advice. She has found an annuity that currently sells for $80,000. The annuity pays $800 per month (starting in one

month) for the next ten years. After a bit of research, you determine that annuities of similar risk earn annual percentage rates around 8.5 percent [Note: The monthly rate would be 8.5 percent/12]. She would like to know whether or not the annuity is a good deal. Is it? **Answer: No.**

A Stock Pricing Example

Unlike a bond, a stock is relatively difficult to value because there are more uncertainties with the cash flows associated with a stock than they are with a bond. As we have stated before, and in the main text, the price of a financial asset is the discounted present value of all future cash flows attributable to the asset. The problem is that the cash flows associated with a stock are relatively harder to pin down than they are with a bond. A stock may pay quarterly dividends, or it may not. It may pay a certain amount of dividends for a while and then, at the discretion of the corporate board, not pay any for a while. It may pay dividends and then increase its dividends or decrease them. All of this uncertainty plays havoc with the pricing of a stock. What do we do when a stock does not pay any dividends? Does it mean that we cannot value stocks? We can make certain assumptions about future cash flows and provide a value for the stock which changes with time.

Assuming that the future cash flows are in the form of dividends that go on into the indefinite future, we can express the present value of a stock (or, its current price) as

$$P_0 = \frac{D_1}{(1+r)} + \frac{D_2}{(1+r)^2} + \ldots + \frac{D_n}{(1+r)^n} + \ldots$$

$$\equiv \frac{D_1}{(1+r)} + \frac{D_2}{(1+r)^2} + \ldots + \frac{D_n}{(1+r)^n} + \ldots \frac{P_T}{(1+r)^T}$$

Where D_1 is the dollar dividend paid the next period (at time 1), D_2 is the dollar dividend paid two periods from now, and so on, r is the required rate of return, and P_T is the stock price at time T. Assume fur that $n < T$. Notice that we have simply expressed the stock price as the discounted present value of its future dividend cash flow stream. Since we do not know when the company will cease to exist in the future, if at all, we have to express the above as a continuous series of terms that go on in the future as implied by the dots. In mathematical jargon, we have written an infinite series. Can we find a nice and easy way to solve the above equation? It turns out we can—but only under very specific circumstances.

The first assumption is that the dividend rates have to grow at a constant rate g such that

$$D_t = D_0 (1+g)^t$$

The second assumption is that

$$r > g$$

If both of the above assumptions hold, we can express the above infinite series very simply as

$$P_0 = \frac{D_1}{r - g}$$

Note that the above simplified version of the current stock price is obtained as a limiting result assuming the stock can be treated as an asset that continues in the future with no finite ending date. That is a bit of a stretch but a workable assumption nevertheless for most companies that do exist for many years.

In general, the above expression can be written as:

$$P_t = \frac{D_{t+1}}{r - g}$$

where P_t is the stock price at any time t and D_{t+1} is the dollar dividend paid at period $t + 1$.

Practice Examples

1. HellNo, Inc. is expanding rapidly in the media industry. They paid a $2.75 dividend today that is expected to grow at a 20 percent annual rate over the next two years. The dividend is then expected to grow at a constant 8 percent annual rate. If the required rate of return on HellNo stock is 14 precent, what is the current price? **Answer: $60.79**

2. MakeMore, Inc. paid a $1.40 dividend today. If the dividend is expected to grow at a constant 5 percent rate and the required rate of return is 8 percent, what would you expect MakeMore's stock price to be 5 years from today? **Answer: $62.56**

Amortizing a Loan

Amortizing a loan simply refers to the process of paying off a loan—along with interest and the principal. Key to understanding the subject of amortizing a loan is to realize that every loan payment you make (usually at the beginning of every month) consists of two parts: One part consists of paying off a portion of the principal outstanding and the other part consists of servicing or paying the interest on the loan. The monthly payments are the same every month but a varying percentage of this constant sum goes into principal repayment and interest payment.

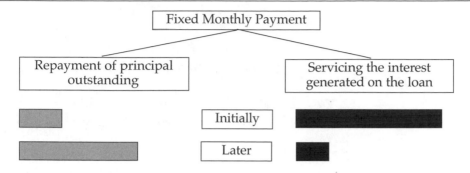

The diagram above elaborates on the above discussion. Thus, for example, in mortgage loans, the payments in the first few years of the loan go primarily toward payment of interest and little of the principal outstanding gets paid off. But towards the end of the loan, the situation reverses itself and relatively more of the payment goes toward paying off the principal and relatively less toward servicing the interest generated.

With that in mind, the formal steps toward amortizing a loan are as follows:

1. Calculate the payment per period.

2. Determine the interest in Period t. (Loan balance at $t-1$) x ($i\%/m$). Note that m is the payment frequency. So, $m = 12$ for monthly payments, and so on. Also, $i =$ the annual loan interest rate.

3. Compute principal payment in Period t. *(Payment – interest from Step 2)*

4. Determine ending balance in Period t. *(Balance – principal payment from Step 3)*

5. Start again at Step 2 and repeat.

Let us now apply the above steps in solving an actual loan amortizing example.

Example

Jorge Jo has borrowed $10,000 at a compound annual interest rate of 12 percent. Amortize the loan if annual payments are made for 5 years.

Step 1: Compute annual payments

$$P_0 \quad = CF \times PVFA_{i,n}$$
$$\$10,000 \quad = CF \times PVFA_{12\%,5}$$
$$\$10,000 \quad = CF \times 3.605$$
$$CF \quad = \$10,000/3.605 = \$2,774$$

So, Jorge's fixed annual payments for the duration of the loan are $2,774.

Step 2:

End of Year	Payment	Interest	Ending Principal	Balance
0				$10,000
1	$2,774	$1,200	$1,574	8,426
2	2,774	1,011	1,763	6,663
3	2,774	800	1,974	4,689
4	2,774	563	2,211	2,478
5	2,775	297	2,478	0
	$13,871	$3,871	$10,000	

The first payment of $2774 is split into $1,200 dollars of loan interest servicing and $1574 of principal repayment. The last payment of $2774 is split into $297 of loan interest servicing and $2,478 of principal repayment. After the final payment, the balance on the loan drops to zero and the loan is repaid in full.

Another example of loan amortization is provided in the table below. Consider a mortgage loan for $200,000. In the first example, it is a 30-year fixed rate mortgage at a 6 percent annual interest rate. The monthly payments are $1,199.10 which, as we have noted, goes partially to pay the principal outstanding and the rest to service the interest on the loan. Further, we see that over the course of the loan we will have paid about $232,000 in cumulative interest on a $200,000 loan.

Now let's introduce the following wrinkle. We decide that every month we are going to add in $100 with our payment with explicit instructions to apply it toward repayment of principal only. What happens? Watch the second row of the table below. If we meticulously followed our schedule of including that extra $100 every month along with our normal house payment (of $1,199.10) we would have paid off our entire loan within 24.6 years and would have made a cumulative interest payment of $182,537.97 (a 21 percent saving). What if we decided to add in an extra $200 per month toward the principal? Watch what happens to your loan in the third row of the table. The loan is paid off in 21 years (shaving off 9 years) with a cumulative interest payment of $151,875.87 (a saving in interest payment of over 34 percent). Finally, with a $300 per month additional payment toward principal, the entire loan is paid off in a little over 18 years incurring a total interest expense of $130,570.58.

What if you had a 15-year mortgage instead of a 30-year one? Assume all other terms of the loan are the same: a $200,000 loan at 6 percent annual interest. The second part of the table shows that if we are not making any extra payments, our monthly payments are $1,687.71. The payments are higher than in the 30-year mortgage which is to be expected since the loan horizon is half. After the loan is paid off in 15 years, we would have paid a cumulative interest of $103,788.46.

Loan Amount	Interest Rate	Loan Period (years)	Monthly Payments (dollars)	Optional Extra Payment per Month toward Principal (dollars)	Scheduled Number of Payments	Actual Number of Payments	Loan Paid off in (years)	Cumulative Interest Paid (dollars)
$200,000	6%	30	$1,199.10	$0	360	360	30	$231,676.38
$200,000	6%	30	$1,199.10	$100	360	295	24.6	$182,537.97
$200,000	6%	30	$1,199.10	$200	360	252	21	$151,875.87
$200,000	6%	30	$1,199.10	$300	360	221	18.4	$130,570.58
$200,000	6%	15	$1,687.71	$0	180	180	15	$103,788.46
$200,000	6%	15	$1,687.71	$100	180	165	13.75	$93,759.99
$200,000	6%	15	$1,687.71	$200	180	151	12.58	$85,558.04
$200,000	6%	15	$1,687.71	$300	180	141	11.75	$78,715.84

This is significantly less than the $231,676.38 we were paying in interest with a 30-year mortgage. So, an important lesson is that, for a given loan at a given interest rate, the shorter the mortgage period the less the interest payments that are incurred.

The most important lesson from the above table, in my opinion, is the fact that making a little extra payment toward principal each month can significantly reduce the loan repayment period as well as cost you less. The difference is more significant with longer maturity loans. Keep this in mind if/when you have a mortgage loan.

Practice Examples

1. A mortgage loan requires monthly payments of $1,000. You just made a payment yesterday and there are 20 remaining. The annual interest rate employed when the loan was initially made was 12 percent, while the appropriate market rate is now 9 percent. Compare the value of the remaining payments versus the principal balance outstanding. How much of the principal is still outstanding (the balance on the loan) after you make the first payment? **Answer: $462.40**

2. You take out a loan for $4,000 at an annual interest rate of 7 percent. You must pay back the loan in 5 annual installments. What is your annual payment? How much of the principal is still outstanding (the balance on the loan) after you make the first payment? **Answer: $975.56; $3304.44**

3. A 15-year mortgage loan requires monthly payments of $1,500. The APR on the loan is 6 percent. How much is the mortgage loan for? Assuming you let the loan run its course, what percentage of the last payment would go towards principal repayment and towards interest on the loan? What percentage of the first payment would go towards principal repayment and towards interest? What can you conclude from the two scenarios? **Answer: Mortgage loan = $177,755.27; Last payment: 99.5 percent towards principal, .5 percent towards interest; First payment: 40.7 percent towards principal, 59.3 percent towards interest.**

Conclusion: The amount that you pay in interest decreases over time and the amount that you pay towards principal increases over time.

4. Construct an amortization schedule for a 4-year loan of $25,000 if interest is 7 percent and you will make annual payments.

   Hint: First figure out the annual payments and then follow the usual recipe.

End of Year	Payment	Interest	Ending Principal	Balance
0				$25,000
1	$7,380.73	$1,750.00	$5,630.73	$19,369.27
2	$7,380.73	$1,355.85	$6,024.88	$13,344.39
3	$7,380.73	$934.11	$6,446.62	$6,897.77
4	$7,380.73	$482.84	$6,897.89	$0

5. Calculate the monthly payment of a 30-year (360 month) $250,000 mortgage. The annual interest rate is 7 percent. **Answer: $1,662.58**

Application of Loan Amortization to Automobile Refinancing

Suppose you borrowed $20,000 for 60 months on your new Honda Accord. Let's assume your credit was bad, you had no previous credit, or the dealer lied about your credit and charged you a greater APR than you should have paid. As Gordon Gekko said in *Wall Street*, "Greed is good." Suppose the dealer "got you approved when no one else would" at 21 percent APR for a 60-month car loan. Sound familiar? So you start paying off your car loan for 2 months, then refinance your car loan with another lender at 7 percent APR. Assume you have already made your second monthly payment under the old loan arrangement. What would have been your monthly payments under the original arrangement? What would they be under the new deal? How much total interest would you pay under each arrangement if you let them run the entire course?

In order to solve this problem, first figure out what your monthly loan payments would be under the original arrangement. First, your monthly interest rate is 1.75 percent under the original arrangement. So, invoking our annuity formula in terms of the present value of an annuity, we can write:

$$\$20{,}000 = CF \times PVFA_{i=1.75\%, n=60}$$

$$\Rightarrow CF = \$541.07$$

So, each monthly payment is $541.07. The question is, how much of this is principal repayment and how much is interest? To see that, consider the monthly interest charge on the loan.

Monthly interest charge = _____. Therefore, the principal repayment after the first payment is _____. So the principal outstanding after the first payment is _____. Similarly, when you make your second monthly payment of $541, the interest on the loan is: _____. Therefore, the principal repayment is: $541 – $348.41 = $192.59. o, after the second monthly payment, the principal outstanding is $19,909 – $192.59 = $19,716.41.

When you refinance your loan, you do so for $19,716.41 at the new APR of 7 percent.

So, your new monthly payments for the remaining 58 months of the loan are given by:

$$\$19,716.41 \quad = \quad CF \times PVFA_{i=0.58\%, n=58}$$

$$\Rightarrow CF \quad = \quad \$401.66$$

Total interest payments under the initial loan arrangement can be shown to be equal to: $12,464.[1]

By contrast, the total interest payment under the final loan arrangement can be shown to be equal to: $3,700 (approximately). So, by getting the better deal, you end up saving a lot of money in interest charges.

Credit Cards and TVM

If you happen to be a "revolver" in credit card parlance, you do not pay off your entire balance at the end of the month. Maybe you make a partial payment and carry the rest of it over to the next month and you make new purchases and things roll on. The credit card company loves you because they get to charge you finance charges and make a profit on their loan to you. Yes, the charges you make on the card are known as "unsecured loans." And they are expensive. Of course, if you are a "deadbeat" which, in credit card jargon, means you pay off your entire balance every month, and do not carry anything over, the credit card company gets minimal profits and calls you unflattering names.

So, if you are a revolver, I'll bet you are not exactly sure of how those finance charges, which tick you off, are calculated in the bill you get from your credit card company every month. You are not alone. Credit card companies are very smart. I have a mental picture of the banker in the NBC show *Deal or No Deal* calculating the finance charges and laughing heartily as you open your bill and gasp in shock.

---

[1]   The way to compute this would be to compute the fraction of each monthly payment that goes into servicing the interest generated on the loan and then summing those over the entire period of the loan.

There are actually two important ways credit card companies sock it to you. The first is whether they compute your charges based on a monthly periodic rate or a daily periodic rate. You see, the APR (annual percentage rate) that credit card companies are required to disclose by law is indeed the rate used to determine your finance charges. However, this is not really the true rate you are paying on your loan. That is determined by the effective interest rate which is higher than the stated APR. How much higher depends on the compounding frequency. Go back and review the effective interest rate formula provided earlier in the book. So, for example, if the stated APR on the card is 10 percent, then the effective interest rate the card carries is 10.47 percent assuming a monthly compounding frequency; if the stated APR is 20 percent then the effective interest rate is 21.94 percent, and so on. These effective rates would be even higher under daily compounding frequency. Try applying the effective interest rate formula to see this for yourself.

While most credit cards apply a monthly compounding frequency (since you are paying them every month), some might even apply a daily compounding frequency for cash advances. Make sure you read the *Important Disclosures* form that comes with your credit card when you first sign up. If you are not sure, don't hesitate to call the credit card company and verify the information before you use the card and get yourself into a world of trouble. "A stitch in time, saves nine!"

Once you have overcome the interest rate hurdle, there are other hurdles to worry about. The credit card companies can further get you by the way they compute your finance charges [average daily balance (ADB), and 2-cycle ADB are the most common]. If you don't know which method your favorite credit card uses, and don't plan accordingly, you could be in for a lot of money to the "banker". And he loves it! This will be in the *Important Disclosures* form too. By law, credit card companies have to declare it under "Methods of computing the balance of purchases".

Here is an example of the process for calculating the monthly finance charges under ADB and 2-cycle ADB.

	ADB		2-Cycle ADB	
APR	24%	24%	24%	24%
Monthly APR = $\frac{APR}{12}$	2%	2%	2%	2%
Previous Balance	$1000	$1000	$500	$1500
Current Balance	$1000	$1000	$1000	$1000
Average Balance	$1000	$1000	$750	$1250
Finance Charges = Monthly APR x Average Balance	$20	$20	$15	$25

Several important things can be concluded from the above table. If you are going to carry about the same balance month-to-month you are pretty much indifferent between a simple ADB and 2-cycle ADB. However, you would still prefer a card with a simple ADB. By contrast, if you think the balance on your card will increase over time, then a 2-Cycle ADB actually works in your favor relative to a card using simple ADB. Finally, if you are planning for your balances to decrease over time, then you are better off with a card using a simple ADB.

In sum, first figure out your behavior pattern with regard to carrying balances and get the right credit card for you. You will be much happier. I promise!

Application of TVM to Insurance

In order to under how insurance pricing is related to TVM, we have to be introduced to the mortality table. A mortality table documents how many men (or women) will die in a given year. Men and women have different death probabilities and are listed separately. Below is a typical mortality table classified by gender from age 1 through age 99. No mortality table goes beyond 100 and all life insurance contracts are designed to stop at 100. If you happen to live past 100 years of age, you are out of luck as far as life insurance coverage is concerned.

In the table below, if we started off with a sample of 1,000,000 men and 1,000,000 women, it is expected that 995,820 male children (997,110 female children) will make it to their first birthdays. Similarly, of 977,237 male 19-year-olds, only 975,416 are expected to make it to their 20th birthdays. Of 983,085 19-year-old girls, only about 982,082 are expected to make it to their 20th birthdays. So the probability of dying at any age is the number living at any age divided by the number dying at that age. Hence, the probability of a boy dying at 17 is $\frac{1,683}{980,614} = 0.0017$.

Mortality Table

	MALE			FEMALE		
Age	Number living	Number dying	Probability of dying	Number living	Number dying	Probability of dying
1	995,820	1,066	0.00107	997,110	867	0.00087
2	994,754	985	0.00099	996,234	807	0.00081
3	993,770	974	0.00098	995,436	787	0.00079
4	992,796	943	0.00095	994,649	766	0.00077
5	991,853	893	0.0009	993,883	755	0.00076
17	980,614	1,683	0.00167	984,985	936	0.00095
18	978,976	1,743	0.00178	984,049	964	0.00098
19	977,237	1,819	0.00186	983,085	1,003	0.00102
20	975,416	1,853	0.0019	982,082	1,031	0.00105
35	949,171	2,003	0.00211	963,712	1,590	0.00165
36	947,168	2,121	0.00244	962,122	1,693	0.00176
37	945,047	2,268	0.0024	960,429	1,815	0.00189
38	942,779	2,432	0.00258	958,614	1,956	0.00204
39	940,346	2,623	0.00279	956,658	2,124	0.00222
40	937,723	2,832	0.00302	954,534	2,310	0.00242
41	934,891	3,076	0.00329	952,224	2,514	0.00264
42	931,815	3,127	0.00356	949,710	2,725	0.00287
43	928,688	3,594	0.00387	946,985	2,926	0.00309
44	925,094	3,876	0.00419	944,059	3,135	0.00332
45	921,218	4,192	0.00455	940,924	3,349	0.00356
65	733,124	18,636	0.02542	813,402	11,867	0.01459
66	714,488	19,898	0.02785	801,535	12,825	0.016
67	694,590	21,144	0.03044	788,710	13,747	0.01743
68	673,446	22,351	0.03319	774,963	14,600	0.01884
69	651,095	22,550	0.03617	760,363	15,481	0.02036
70	627,545	24,795	0.03951	744,882	16,470	0.02211
71	602,750	26,099	0.0433	728,412	17,649	0.02423
72	576,651	27,477	0.04765	710,763	19,098	0.02687
73	549,174	28,909	0.05264	691,665	20,826	0.03011
74	520,265	30,274	0.05819	670,839	22,762	0.03393
75	489,991	31,452	0.06419	648,077	24,782	0.03824
96	9,833	3,781	0.38455	27,215	10,226	0.37574
97	6,052	2,906	0.4802	16,898	8,069	0.47497
98	3,145	2,069	0.65798	8,920	5,850	0.65585
99	1,076	1,076	1	3,070	3,070	1

Example

Suppose at the age of 40 Mr. Doordie decides to purchase a whole life policy with a face amount of $100,000. What is his premium?

Step 1: Calculate expected claim costs for Mr. Doordie (using a 5 percent interest rate)
Find the probability that a 40-year-old will die at each age between 40 and 99.

Age	Prob. of 40-year-old dying at specified age	Expected Claim Costs	PV of Expected Claim Costs
40	0.003020	$302	$302/1.05$
41	0.003280	328	$328/1.05^2$
42	0.003538	353.80	$353.80/1.05^3$
43	0.003832	383.20	$383.20/1.05^4$
44	0.004133	413.30	$413.30/1.05^5$
⋮			
96	0.004032	403.20	$403.20/1.05^{57}$
97	0.003098	309.80	$309.80/1.05^{58}$
98	0.002207	220.70	$220.70/1.05^{59}$
99	0.001147	114.70	$114.7/1.05^{60}$
Total			$22,373

So, for example, the probability of a 40-year-old dying before his 41st birthday =

$$\frac{\text{\# of 40-year-olds dying before 41st birthday}}{\text{\# of 40-year-olds alive}} = \frac{2,832}{937,723} = 0.00302$$

Probability of a 41 year old dying before his 42nd birthday =

$$\frac{\text{\# of 40-year-olds dying before 41st birthday}}{\text{\# of 40-year-olds alive}} = \frac{2,832}{937,723} = 0.00328$$

And so on . . .

Hence, from the above table, the present value of the expected claim costs for Mr. Doordie is = $22,373. This is his (one-shot) premium, which means he pays this amount once and he is covered for life.

Suppose, however, that Mr. Doordie does not have that kind of cash lying around. Does it mean he cannot have life insurance? Of course not! He can pay his insurance premium as a level annual premium which will be much more affordable. So, what is this level annual premium for Mr. D?

To solve this problem, first find the probability that Mr. D will be alive at each of the ages 41 through 99 for this will determine that he will be present to make the payments.

Age	Prob. of 40-year-old dying at specified age	Expected Claim Costs	PV of Expected Claim Costs
40	1.0	$302.00	$302/1.05$
41	0.996980	328.00	$328/1.05^2$
42	0.993700	353.80	$353.80/1.05^3$
43	0.990162	383.20	$383.20/1.05^4$
44	0.986330	413.30	$413.30/1.05^5$
⋮			
⋮			
96	0.004032	403.20	$403.20/1.05^{57}$
97	0.003098	309.80	$309.80/1.05^{58}$
98	0.002207	220.70	$220.70/1.05^{59}$
99	0.001147	114.70	$114.7/1.05^{60}$
Total			$22,373.00

- The probability that Mr. D will be alive at 41 to make his payment is the number of people alive at 41 divided by the number of people alive at 40 = 934891/937723 = 0.99698

- The probability that Mr. D will be alive at 42 to make his insurance payment is the number of people alive at 42 divided by the number of people alive at 40 = 931815/937723 = 0.993700

And so on . . .

Eventually, we can write the following in TVM terms:

$$\text{Lump Sum} = (1 \times P) + \frac{\text{prob. of living} \times P}{(1+i)^1} + \frac{\text{prob. of living} \times P}{(1+i)^2} + \ldots + \frac{\text{prob. of living} \times P}{(1+i)^n}$$

$$22{,}373 = (1 \times P) + \frac{0.996980 \times P}{(1.05)^1} + \frac{0.993700x\ P}{(1.05)^2} + \ldots + \frac{0.003354 \times P}{(1.05)^{58}} + \frac{0.001147 \times P}{(1.05)^{59}}$$

$$= \$16.30 \times P$$

Therefore, $P = \$1{,}372.58$—His annual premium.

Practice Example:

Consider the following mortality table.

Age	# People Living	# People Dying	Prob. of Dying
35	949,171	2,003	.00211
36	947,168	2,121	.00224
37	945,047	2,268	.00240
38	942,779	2,432	.00258
39	940,346	2,623	.00279

Assuming a 5 percent interest rate and you are currently 35 years old, how much would the one-time up-front payment be for a 5-year term policy with a $10,000 benefit? And what would an annual premium be for the same 5-year term policy with a $10,000 benefit? **Answer: $101.29; $22.78**

Application of TVM to Retirement

Applications of TVM to retirement involve problems of saving now and using the saved money later. These are nothing but simple variations on annuity problems that we have already seen in Part C. Here are some typical examples.

1. You decide that you want to save 2 million dollars for retirement. Assuming that you are 25 years old today, will retire at the age of 65, and can earn an 8 percent annual rate on your deposits, how much must you deposit each year to meet your goal? (Your first annual deposit will be one year from now). **Answer: $7720.52**

2. You believe that you will need $25,000 a year for 5 years in retirement. If you are 30 today how much must you save each year to meet your retirement goal if you plan to retire at 65? (Assume a 10 percent annual interest rate and that your first deposit will be 1 year from now and your first withdrawal will be 36 years from today). **Answer: $349.67**

3. Assume that you are 25 today and decide to save for retirement. If you save $800 a year and plan on withdrawing $40,000 a year for 10 years in retirement, will you have saved enough to meet your goal? (Assume a 9 percent annual interest rate and that your first deposit will be 1 year from now and your first withdrawal will be 41 years from now.) **Answer: YES**

4. You have been given the choice between two retirement policies:

   Policy A: You will receive annual payments of $26,000 beginning 35 years from now for 10 years

   Policy B: You will receive one lump sum of $200,000 in 40 years

   Which policy should you choose assuming an annual interest rate of 12 percent?

   Answer: Policy A

5. Beginning today, you save $1500 per year for 40 years (i.e., 40 payments). At t = 40 you begin withdrawing $17,000 per year for 10 years for your retirement (i.e., 10 withdrawals). You want to know how much of your savings is left at time 50. Assuming a 6 percent interest rate, how much is left in the account? (Your first deposit is today and your first withdrawal is at time 40). **Answer: $203,167.43**

6. You are 25 years old and decide to save $2,000 each year for retirement. You want to have $518,100 in your account when you turn 65. If your first deposit will be 1 year from now, what interest rate must you receive to meet your goal? **Answer: 8 percent**

General TVM Examples

Problem #1

You must decide between $25,000 in cash today or $30,000 in cash to be received two years from now. If you can earn 8 percent interest on your investments, which is the better deal?

Possible Answers:

A. $25,000 in cash today

B. $30,000 in cash to be received two years from now

C. Either option O.K.

Problem #2

What is the value of $100 per year for four years, with the first cash flow one year from today, if one is earning 5 percent interest, compounded annually? Find the value of these cash flows four years from today.

Possible Answers:

A. $400

B. $431.01

C. $452.56

The Ultimate TVM Challenge Problems

By now you must be foaming at the mouth wondering when this nightmare will end. Don't worry! The end is near. We will close with some real life problems you might encounter as you traipse through life. Try to solve these problems on your own before you look at the answers. If you can solve them with minimum help, you have mastered TVM and are well positioned to tackle life on your own financial terms. Good luck!

1. Beginning today, suppose you save $1000 per year for 40 years (i.e., 40 deposits). At t = 40 you begin withdrawing $20,000 per year for 10 years for your retirement. Since you might live longer than you think, you want to know the amount X of savings you will have left at date t = 50 if you follow the preceding plan. If the interest rate is 7 percent, what is X? **Answer: $124,550**

   Hint: Draw the timeline and put down all the payments on it. The savings (inflow) is positive and withdrawals (outflow) are negative. This is a future value of annuity (FVFA) problem and you have to determine the net future value of inflows and outflows at t = 50.

0	1	...	39	40	...	49	50
1,000	1,000		1,000	20,000		20,000	X

   FV_{50} (1000's) $= 1000x \, (FVFA_{n=40, \, i=7\%}) \times (1.07)^{11}$

                         $= \$420,212$

   FV_{50} (20000s) $= 20000 \times (FVFA_{n=10, \, i=7\%}) \times (1.07)$

                         $= \$295,662$

   X $= FV(\text{deposits}) - FV \, (\text{withdrawals})$

                         $= 420,212 - 295,662$

                         $= \$124,550$

2. You have found the used car you want, and it lists for $4,000. The dealer will allow you to choose the payment method. You may choose "zero percent" 1 year financing and make 12 equal monthly payments beginning in 1 month. Or you may take a $248.32 discount and pay cash. What is the EAR that is implicit in the "zero percent financing" given the alternative cash method.

   Hint: First figure out what the true "value" of the car is. Next figure out what the equal monthly payments have to be so that the present value of such monthly payments equals the true value.

   $$\text{Payments } 333.33 = \frac{4,000}{12}$$

   With monthly payments you need to know the monthly rate r_m, which is the rate that causes the PV_0 (payments) to equal the true cost of $3,751.68 which is (4,000 − 248.32)

   $3751.68 = 333.33 \times PVFA_{n=12, \, i = i_m}$

   $r_m = 0.01$ (this is the monthly rate)

   i_{eff} (the effective annual rate) $= (1.01)^{12} - 1 = 12.68\%$

3. You borrow $10,000 for six years, $r = 10$ percent, and you must repay in 6 equal installments. After your second payment at $t = 2$, what is the remaining balance on the loan?

   Hint: First figure out what your equal monthly payments have to be such that you can pay off (principal and interest) a loan in six years. Now break down each monthly payment into the amount that is used to pay off the principal outstanding and the amount that is the interest accrued on the loan. Start from the first payment and then go to the second payment.

$$10,000 = C \times PVFA_{n=6,\ i=10\%}$$
$$\Rightarrow \quad \text{payment, } C = 2296.00$$

At $t = 1$, you owe interest $= 1000 = 0.10\,(10,000)$
$\Rightarrow \quad$ Principal repaid $= 2,296 - 1,000 = 1,296$
$\quad \therefore$ ending balance $= 8,704$

At $t = 2$, you owe interest $= \$870.40$
$\Rightarrow \quad$ Principal repaid $= 2296 - 870.40 = \$1425.6$
$\quad \therefore$ ending balance $= 8704 - 1425.6 = \$7278.40$

4. Mr. Rogers goes to the bank to borrow $100,000 for five years. To obtain the loan, Mr. Rogers must pay 12 percent annually plus 3 points (3 percent). The points are paid up front, while all interest is paid when the loan matures. If Mr. Rogers accepts the loan, what is the true interest rate?

   Answer: 12.68%

   Hint: Remember that points are taken off the face value of the loan at inception. First pretend that there are no points and solve for the future value of a loan with PV = 100,000 and the interest, etc., given. Now imagine that you actually have in hand the promised value less the points BUT the future value of the loan is still the same as before. Solve for the interest rate.

   In five years, Mr. Rogers must repay $100,000 \times (1.12)^5 = \$176,234$

   Points $= 0.03 \times (100,000) = \$3,000$

   Rogers' net borrowing $= \$97,000$

   $\therefore 97,000 \times (1 + i)^5 = 176,234$

   $i = 12.68\%$

5. You want to deposit $X at t = 1, 2, 3 and 4, so that you can withdraw $500 at t = 5, 6 and 7. What is X if the discount rate is 8 percent?

Hint: Draw a time line and express all cash flows as they occur in the time line. Remember that AT ANY GIVEN POINT IN TIME, the

$$FV(\text{deposits}) = PV(\text{withdrawals}).$$

0	1	2	3	4	5	6	7
	X	X	X	X	500	500	500

There are 2 annuity streams here. The first one (the deposit annuity) is a 4-payment annuity stream with cash flows occurring at 1, 2, 3, and 4. The second one is a 3-payment annuity stream with the cash flows occurring at 5, 6, and 7.

The FVA of the deposit annuity = $X \times FVFA_{n=4,\ i=8\%}$ = 4.5061X (located at $t = 4$)

The PVA of the withdrawal annuity = $500 \times PVFA_{n=3,\ i=8\%}$ = 1288.55 (located at $t = 4$)

Therefore, using the idea [at $t = 4$]

$FV(\text{deposits}) = PV(\text{withdrawals})$

$4.5061X = 1288.55$

Or, $X = \$285.96$

TVM Is Everywhere

You have to be able to spot TVM concepts directly or indirectly in matters you come across in everyday life. Here is an excerpt from a news item reporting that new home sales have tumbled over the past month.

A separate report Tuesday showed that existing home sales—by far the lion's share of the nation's housing market—rose to near record levels last month, bucking forecasts of a modest decline.

But the new home sales are closely watched by economists because they have a far greater economic impact. They create jobs in construction, and new home buyers are likely to spend more money on new appliances and furnishings than existing home purchasers.

How do we interpret this? When home sales drop, the present value of home ownership declines. How about new homes? New homes are watched by economists because they signify demand of home construction-related products and services—including new employment. Thus, when new home construction increases, the present value of home ownership also increases. Realtors keep track of these figures to gauge whether the value of existing homes will increase, decrease or stay the same. When new home construction goes up, prices of home-construction–related products like vinyl siding, lumber, brick, etc., also go up and in turn, the value of homes also goes up (a direct impact of an increasing present value placed on home ownership). The opposite is true when new home construction goes down. The value of home ownership declines and that, in turn, signals a buyers' market or a market where homes can be purchased at a discount from their present values.

Here is an article on a different topic.

As the third season of Fox's hugely popular talent search gears up for its finale, millions of fans wonder who will emerge as the next "American Idol" and receive a recording contract.

But winning isn't everything. Some of the show's past contestants have signed record deals and released chart-topping albums without winning the competition. Clay Aiken, who finished a controversial second to Ruben Studdard last season, has sold more than 2.5 million copies of his debut album, "Measure of a Man."

Think of the winner of the Idol contest as one whose present value (of all future earnings) is considered to be the highest by the judges and the voting body. That is not to say that those who don't win don't have as high a present value. So far, a lot of near winners have managed to release successful CDs and received significant publicity after their *Idol* days. They can be thought of as undervalued commodities who since have emerged as shining stars and taken their "stock" upwards. Then there are *Idol* stars whose stars have dimmed. Recall Justin Guarini who started with a bang but has since fizzled out. His present value has declined considerably.

At the other extreme is the 21-year-old engineering student, William Hung, famous for his off-key singing, comic performance of Ricky Martin's "She Bangs" during the first round of the third season's *Idol* auditions that won him a record contract with Koch Entertainment. His debut album, "Inspiration," sold nearly 120,000 copies, broke into the Billboard Top 40 Chart in the first week, and debuted at No. 1 on Billboard's Independent Chart. Talk about an undervalued commodity! Here is someone whose present value was initially considered almost zero in the entertainment field, and who has since capitalized on his notoriety and silliness, to propel his present value of future cash flows sky-high.

In summary, TVM concepts are everywhere. Learn to recognize them when you read articles or books (even those that seem unrelated to finance) and understand the implication of the information you are receiving. Doing so will open up a whole new vista for you.

Table 1—Future Value of $1 at the End of n Periods (FVF)

Number of Periods	1%	2%	3%	4%	5%	6%	7%	8%	9%	10%	12%	14%	15%	16%	18%	20%	24%	28%	32%	36%
1	1.0100	1.0200	1.0300	1.0400	1.0500	1.0600	1.0700	1.0800	1.0900	1.1000	1.1200	1.1400	1.1500	1.1600	1.1800	1.2000	1.2400	1.2800	1.3200	1.3600
2	1.0201	1.0404	1.0609	1.0816	1.1025	1.1236	1.1449	1.1664	1.1881	1.2100	1.2544	1.2996	1.3225	1.3456	1.3924	1.4400	1.5376	1.6384	1.7424	1.8496
3	1.0303	1.0612	1.0927	1.1249	1.1576	1.1910	1.2250	1.2597	1.2950	1.3310	1.4049	1.4815	1.5209	1.5609	1.6430	1.7280	1.9066	2.0972	2.3000	2.5155
4	1.0406	1.0824	1.1255	1.1699	1.2155	1.2625	1.3108	1.3605	1.4116	1.4641	1.5735	1.6890	1.7490	1.8106	1.9388	2.0736	2.3642	2.6844	3.0360	3.4210
5	1.0510	1.1041	1.1593	1.2167	1.2763	1.3382	1.4026	1.4693	1.5386	1.6105	1.7623	1.9254	2.0114	2.1003	2.2878	2.4883	2.9316	3.4360	4.0075	4.6526
6	1.0615	1.1262	1.1941	1.2653	1.3401	1.4185	1.5007	1.5869	1.6771	1.7716	1.9738	2.1950	2.3131	2.4364	2.6996	2.9860	3.6352	4.3980	5.2899	6.3275
7	1.0721	1.1487	1.2299	1.3159	1.4071	1.5036	1.6058	1.7138	1.8280	1.9487	2.2107	2.5023	2.6600	2.8262	3.1855	3.5832	4.5077	5.6295	6.9826	8.6054
8	1.0829	1.1717	1.2668	1.3686	1.4775	1.5938	1.7182	1.8509	1.9926	2.1436	2.4760	2.8526	3.0590	3.2784	3.7589	4.2998	5.5895	7.2058	9.2170	11.703
9	1.0937	1.1951	1.3048	1.4233	1.5513	1.6895	1.8385	1.9990	2.1719	2.3579	2.7731	3.2519	3.5179	3.8030	4.4355	5.1598	6.9310	9.2234	12.166	15
10	1.1046	1.2190	1.3439	1.4802	1.6289	1.7908	1.9672	2.1589	2.3674	2.5937	3.1058	3.7072	4.0456	4.4114	5.2338	6.1917	8.5944	11.805	16.059	21.646
11	1.1157	1.2434	1.3842	1.5395	1.7103	1.8983	2.1049	2.3316	2.5804	2.8531	3.4785	4.2262	4.6524	5.1173	6.1759	7.4301	10.657	15.111	21.198	29.439
12	1.1268	1.2682	1.4258	1.6010	1.7959	2.0122	2.2522	2.5182	2.8127	3.1384	3.8960	4.8179	5.3502	5.9360	7.2876	8.9161	13.214	19.342	27.982	40.037
13	1.1381	1.2936	1.4685	1.6651	1.8856	2.1329	2.4098	2.7196	3.0658	3.4523	4.3635	5.4924	6.1528	6.8858	8.5994	10.699	16.386	24.758	36.937	54.451
14	1.1495	1.3195	1.5126	1.7317	1.9799	2.2609	2.5785	2.9372	3.3417	3.7975	4.8871	6.2613	7.0757	7.9875	10.147	12.839	20.319	31.691	48.756	74.053
15	1.1610	1.3459	1.5580	1.8009	2.0789	2.3966	2.7590	3.1722	3.6425	4.1772	5.4736	7.1379	8.1371	9.2655	11.973	15.407	25.195	40.564	64.358	100.71
16	1.1726	1.3728	1.6047	1.8730	2.1829	2.5404	2.9522	3.4259	3.9703	4.5950	6.1304	8.1372	9.3576	10.748	14.129	18.488	31.242	51.923	84.953	136.96
17	1.1843	1.4002	1.6528	1.9479	2.2920	2.6928	3.1588	3.7000	4.3276	5.0545	6.8660	9.2765	10.761	12.467	16.672	22.186	38.740	66.461	112.13	186.27
18	1.1961	1.4282	1.7024	2.0258	2.4066	2.8543	3.3799	3.9960	4.7171	5.5599	7.6900	10.575	12.375	14.462	19.673	26.623	48.038	85.070	148.02	253.33
19	1.2081	1.4568	1.7535	2.1068	2.5270	3.0256	3.6165	4.3157	5.1417	6.159	8.6128	12.055	14.231	16.776	23.214	31.948	59.567	108.89	195.39	344.53
20	1.2202	1.4859	1.8061	2.1911	2.6533	3.2071	3.8697	4.6610	5.6044	6.7275	9.6463	13.743	16.366	19.460	27.393	38.337	73.864	139.37	257.91	468.57
21	1.2324	1.5157	1.8603	2.2788	2.7860	3.3996	4.1406	5.0338	6.1088	7.4002	10.803	15.667	18.821	22.574	32.323	46.005	91.591	178.40	340.44	637.26
22	1.2447	1.5460	1.9161	2.3699	2.9253	3.6035	4.4304	5.4365	6.6586	8.1403	12.100	17.861	21.644	26.186	38.142	55.206	113.57	228.35	449.39	866.67
23	1.2572	1.5769	1.9736	2.4647	3.0715	3.8197	4.7405	5.8715	7.2579	8.9543	13.552	20.361	24.891	30.376	45.007	66.247	140.83	292.30	593.19	1178.6
24	1.2697	1.6084	2.0328	2.5633	3.2251	4.0489	5.0724	6.3412	7.9111	9.8497	15.178	23.212	28.625	35.236	53.108	79.496	174.63	374.14	783.02	1602.9
25	1.2824	1.6406	2.0938	2.6658	3.3864	4.2919	5.4274	6.8485	8.6231	10.834	17.000	26.461	32.918	40.874	62.668	95.396	216.54	478.90	1033.5	2180.0
26	1.2953	1.6734	2.1566	2.7725	3.5557	4.5494	5.8074	7.3964	9.3992	11.918	19.040	30.166	37.856	47.414	73.948	114.47	268.51	612.99	1364.3	2964.9
27	1.3082	1.7069	2.2213	2.8834	3.7335	4.8223	6.2139	7.9881	10.245	13.110	21.324	34.389	43.535	55.000	87.259	137.37	332.95	784.63	1800.9	4032.2
28	1.3213	1.7410	2.2879	2.9987	3.9201	5.1117	6.6488	8.6271	11.167	14.421	23.883	39.204	50.065	63.800	102.96	164.84	412.86	1004.3	2377.2	5483.8
29	1.3345	1.7758	2.3566	3.1187	4.1161	5.4184	7.1143	9.3173	12.172	15.863	26.749	44.693	57.575	74.008	121.50	197.81	511.95	1285.5	3137.9	7458.0
30	1.3478	1.8114	2.4273	3.2434	4.3219	5.7435	7.6123	10.062	13.267	17.449	29.959	50.950	66.211	85.849	143.37	237.37	634.81	1645.5	4142.0	10143.
40	1.4889	2.2080	3.2620	4.8010	7.0400	10.285	14.974	21.724	31.409	45.259	93.050	188.88	267.86	378.72	750.37	1469.7	5455.9	19426.	66520.	*
* 50	1.6446	2.6916	4.3839	7.1067	11.467	18.420	29.457	46.901	74.357	117.39	289.00	700.23	1083.6	1670.7	3927.3	9100.4	46890.	*	*	*
60	1.8167	3.2810	5.8916	10.519	18.679	32.987	57.946	101.25	176.03	304.48	897.59	2595.9	4383.9	7370.1	20555.	56347.	*	*	*	*

Note: n = number of periods, i = interest rate per period.

Table 2—Future Value of a *n*-Payment Annuity of $1 (*FVFA*)

Number of Periods	1%	2%	3%	4%	5%	6%	7%	8%	9%	10%	12%	14%	15%	16%	18%	20%	24%	28%	32%	36%
1	1.0000	1.0000	1.000	1.0000	1.0000	1.0000	1.0000	1.0000	1.0000	1.0000	1.0000	1.0000	1.0000	1.0000	1.0000	1.0000	1.0000	1.0000	1.0000	1.0000
2	2.0100	2.0200	2.0300	2.0400	2.0500	2.0600	2.0700	2.0800	2.0900	2.1000	2.1200	2.1400	2.1500	2.1600	2.1800	2.2000	2.2400	2.2800	2.3200	2.3600
3	3.0301	3.0604	3.0909	3.1216	3.1525	3.1836	3.2149	3.2464	3.2781	3.3100	3.3744	3.4396	3.4725	3.5056	3.5724	3.6400	3.7776	3.9184	4.0624	4.2096
4	4.0604	4.1216	4.1836	4.2465	4.3101	4.3746	4.4399	4.5061	4.5731	4.6410	4.7793	4.9211	4.9934	5.0665	5.2154	5.3680	5.6842	6.0156	6.3624	6.7251
5	5.1010	5.2040	5.3091	5.4163	5.5256	5.6371	5.7507	5.8666	5.9847	6.1051	6.3528	6.6101	6.7424	6.8771	7.1542	7.4416	8.0484	8.6999	9.3983	10.146
6	6.1520	6.3081	6.4684	6.6330	6.8019	6.9753	7.1533	7.3359	7.5233	7.7156	8.1152	8.5355	8.7537	8.9775	9.4420	9.9299	10.980	12.135	13.405	14.79
7	7.2135	7.4343	7.6625	7.8983	8.1420	8.3938	8.6540	8.9228	9.2004	9.4872	10.089	10.730	11.066	11.413	12.141	12.915	14.615	16.533	18.695	21.126
8	8.2857	8.5830	8.8923	9.2142	9.5491	9.8975	10.259	10.636	11.028	11.435	12.299	13.232	13.726	14.240	15.327	16.499	19.122	22.163	25.678	29.731
9	9.3685	9.7546	10.159	10.582	11.026	11.491	11.978	12.487	13.021	13.579	14.775	16.085	16.785	17.518	19.085	20.798	24.712	29.369	34.895	41.435
10	10.462	10.949	11.463	12.006	12.577	13.180	13.816	14.486	15.192	15.937	17.548	19.337	20.303	21.321	23.521	25.958	31.643	38.692	47.061	57.351
11	11.566	12.168	12.807	13.486	14.206	14.971	15.783	16.645	17.560	18.531	20.654	23.044	24.349	25.732	28.755	32.150	40.237	50.398	63.121	78.998
12	12.682	13.412	14.192	15.025	15.917	16.869	17.888	18.977	20.140	21.384	24.133	27.270	29.001	30.850	34.931	39.580	50.894	65.510	84.320	108.43
13	13.809	14.680	15.617	16.626	17.713	18.882	20.140	21.495	22.953	24.522	28.029	32.088	34.351	36.786	42.218	48.496	64.109	84.852	112.30	148.47
14	14.947	15.973	17.086	18.291	19.598	21.015	22.550	24.214	26.019	27.975	32.392	37.581	40.504	43.672	50.818	59.195	80.496	109.61	149.23	202.92
15	16.096	17.293	18.598	20.023	21.578	23.276	25.129	27.152	29.360	31.772	37.279	43.842	47.580	51.659	60.695	72.035	100.81	141.30	197.99	276.97
16	17.257	18.639	20.156	21.824	23.657	25.672	27.888	30.324	33.003	35.949	42.753	50.980	55.717	60.925	72.939	87.442	126.01	181.86	262.35	377.69
17	18.430	20.012	21.761	23.697	25.840	28.212	30.840	33.750	36.973	40.544	48.883	59.117	65.075	71.673	87.068	105.93	157.25	233.79	347.30	514.66
18	19.614	21.412	23.414	25.645	28.132	30.905	33.999	37.450	41.301	45.599	55.749	68.394	75.836	84.140	103.74	128.11	195.99	300.25	459.44	700.93
19	20.810	22.840	25.116	27.671	30.539	33.760	37.379	41.446	46.018	51.159	63.439	78.969	88.211	98.603	123.41	154.74	244.03	385.32	607.47	954.27
20	22.019	24.297	26.870	29.778	33.066	36.785	40.995	45.762	51.160	57.275	72.052	91.024	102.44	115.37	146.62	186.68	303.60	494.21	802.86	1298.8
21	23.239	25.783	28.676	31.969	35.719	39.992	44.865	50.422	56.764	64.002	81.698	104.76	118.81	134.84	174.02	225.02	377.46	633.59	1060.7	1767.3
22	24.471	27.299	30.536	34.248	38.505	43.392	49.005	55.456	62.873	71.402	92.502	120.43	137.63	157.41	206.34	271.03	469.05	811.99	1401.2	2404.6
23	25.716	28.845	32.452	36.617	41.430	46.995	53.436	60.893	69.531	79.543	104.60	138.29	159.27	183.60	244.48	326.23	582.62	1040.3	1850.6	3271.3
24	26.973	30.421	34.426	39.082	44.502	50.815	58.176	66.764	76.789	88.497	118.15	158.65	184.16	213.97	289.49	392.48	723.46	1332.6	2443.8	4449.9
25	28.243	32.030	36.459	41.645	47.727	54.864	63.249	73.105	84.700	98.347	133.33	181.87	212.79	249.21	342.60	471.98	898.09	1706.8	3226.8	6052.9
26	29.525	33.670	38.553	44.311	51.113	59.156	68.676	79.954	93.323	109.18	150.33	208.33	245.71	290.08	405.27	567.37	1114.6	2185.7	4260.4	8223.0
27	30.820	35.344	40.709	47.084	54.669	63.705	74.483	87.350	102.72	121.09	169.37	238.49	283.56	337.50	479.22	681.85	1383.1	2798.7	5627.7	11197.9
28	32.129	37.051	42.930	49.967	58.402	68.528	80.697	95.338	112.96	134.20	190.69	272.88	327.10	392.50	566.48	819.22	1716.0	3583.3	7425.6	15230.2
29	33.450	38.792	45.218	52.966	62.322	73.639	87.346	103.96	124.13	148.63	214.58	312.09	377.16	456.30	669.44	984.06	2128.9	4587.6	9802.9	20714.1
30	34.784	40.568	47.575	56.084	66.438	79.058	94.460	113.28	136.30	164.49	241.33	356.78	434.74	530.31	790.94	1181.8	2640.9	5873.2	12940.	28172.2
40	48.886	60.402	75.401	95.025	120.79	154.76	199.63	259.05	337.88	442.59	767.09	1342.0	1779.0	2360.7	4163.2	7343.8	22728.	69377.	*	*
50	64.463	84.579	112.79	152.66	209.34	290.33	406.52	573.76	815.08	1163.9	2400.0	4994.5	7217.7.	10435.	21813.	45497.	*	*	*	*
60	81.669	114.05	163.05	237.99	353.58	533.12	813.52	1253.2	1944.7	3034.8	7471.6	18535.	29219.	46057.	*	*	*	*	*	*

Note: *n* = number of periods, *i* = interest rate per period.

Table 3—Present Value of $1 at the End of n Periods (PVF)

Number of Periods	1%	2%	3%	4%	5%	6%	7%	8%	9%	10%	12%	14%	15%	16%	18%	20%	24%	28%	32%	36%
1	.9901	.9804	.9709	.9615	.9524	.9434	.9346	.9259	.9174	.9091	.8929	.8772	.8696	.8621	.8475	.8333	.8065	.7813	.7576	.7353
2	.9803	.9612	.9426	.9246	.9070	.8900	.8734	.8573	.8417	.8264	.7972	.7695	.7561	.7432	.7182	.6944	.6504	.6104	.5739	.5407
3	.9706	.9423	.9151	.8890	.8638	.8396	.8163	.7938	.7722	.7513	.7118	.6750	.6575	.6407	.6086	.5787	.5245	.4768	.4348	.3975
4	.9610	.9238	.8885	.8548	.8227	.7921	.7629	.7350	.7084	.6830	.6355	.5921	.5718	.5523	.5158	.4823	.4230	.3725	.3294	.2923
5	.9515	.9057	.8626	.8219	.7835	.7473	.7130	.6806	.6499	.6209	.5674	.5194	.4972	.4761	.4371	.4019	.3411	.2910	.2495	.2149
6	.9420	.8880	.8375	.7903	.7462	.7050	.6663	.6302	.5963	.5645	.5066	.4556	.4323	.4104	.3704	.3349	.2751	.2274	.1890	.1580
7	.9327	.8706	.8131	.7599	.7107	.6651	.6227	.5835	.5470	.5132	.4523	.3996	.3759	.3538	.3139	.2791	.2218	.1776	.1432	.1162
8	.9235	.8535	.7894	.7307	.6768	.6274	.5820	.5403	.5019	.4665	.4039	.3506	.3269	.3050	.2660	.2326	.1789	.1388	.1085	.0854
9	.9143	.8368	.7664	.7026	.6446	.5919	.5439	.5002	.4604	.4241	.3606	.3075	.2843	.2630	.2255	.1938	.1443	.1084	.0822	.0628
10	.9053	.8203	.7441	.6756	.6139	.5584	.5083	.4632	.4224	.3855	.3220	.2697	.2472	.2267	.1911	.1615	.1164	.0847	.0623	.0462
11	.8963	.8043	.7224	.6496	.5847	.5268	.4751	.4289	.3875	.3505	.2875	.2366	.2149	.1954	.1619	.1346	.0938	.0662	.0472	.0340
12	.8874	.7885	.7014	.6246	.5568	.4970	.4440	.3971	.3555	.3186	.2567	.2076	.1869	.1685	.1372	.1122	.0757	.0517	.0357	.0250
13	.8787	.7730	.6810	.6006	.5303	.4688	.4150	.3677	.3262	.2897	.2292	.1821	.1625	.1452	.1163	.0935	.0610	.0404	.0271	.0184
14	.8700	.7579	.6611	.5775	.5051	.4423	.3878	.3405	.2992	.2633	.2046	.1597	.1413	.1252	.0985	.0779	.0492	.0316	.0205	.0135
15	.8613	.7430	.6419	.5553	.4810	.4173	.3624	.3152	.2745	.2394	.1827	.1401	.1229	.1079	.0835	.0649	.0397	.0247	.0155	.0099
16	.8528	.7284	.6232	.5339	.4581	.3936	.3387	.2919	.2519	.2176	.1631	.1229	.1069	.0930	.0708	.0541	.0320	.0193	.0118	.0073
17	.8444	.7142	.6050	.5134	.4363	.3714	.3166	.2703	.2311	.1978	.1456	.1078	.0929	.0802	.0600	.0451	.0258	.0150	.0089	.0054
18	.8360	.7002	.5874	.4936	.4155	.3503	.2959	.2502	.2120	.1799	.1300	.0946	.0808	.0691	.0508	.0376	.0208	.0118	.0068	.0039
19	.8277	.6864	.5703	.4746	.3957	.3305	.2765	.2317	.1945	.1635	.1161	.0829	.0703	.0596	.0431	.0313	.0168	.0092	.0051	.0029
20	.8195	.6730	.5537	.4564	.3769	.3118	.2584	.2145	.1784	.1486	.1037	.0728	.0611	.0514	.0365	.0261	.0135	.0072	.0039	.0021
21	.8114	.6598	.5375	.4388	.3589	.2942	.2415	.1987	.1637	.1351	.0926	.0638	.0531	.0443	.0309	.0217	.0109	.0056	.0029	.0016
22	.8034	.6468	.5219	.4220	.3418	.2775	.2257	.1839	.1502	.1228	.0826	.0560	.0462	.0382	.0262	.0181	.0088	.0044	.0022	.0012
23	.7965	.6342	.5067	.4057	.3256	.2618	.2109	.1703	.1378	.1117	.0738	.0491	.0402	.0329	.0222	.0151	.0071	.0034	.0017	.0008
24	.7876	.6217	.4919	.3901	.3101	.2470	.1971	.1577	.1264	.1015	.0659	.0431	.0349	.0284	.0188	.0126	.0057	.0027	.0013	.0006
25	.7798	.6095	.4776	.3751	.2953	.2330	.1842	.1460	.1160	.0923	.0588	.0378	.0304	.0245	.0160	.0105	.0046	.0021	.0010	.0005
26	.7720	.5976	.4637	.3607	.2812	.2198	.1722	.1352	.1064	.0839	.0525	.0331	.0264	.0211	.0135	.0087	.0037	.0016	.0007	.0003
27	.7644	.5859	.4502	.3468	.2678	.2074	.1609	.1252	.0976	.0763	.0469	.0291	.0230	.0182	.0115	.0073	.0030	.0013	.0006	.0002
28	.7568	.5744	.4371	.3335	.2551	.1956	.1504	.1159	.0895	.0693	.0419	.0255	.0200	.0158	.0097	.0061	.0024	.0010	.0004	.0002
29	.7493	.5631	.4243	.3207	.2429	.1846	.1406	.1073	.0822	.0630	.0374	.0224	.0174	.0135	.0082	.0051	.0020	.0008	.0003	.0001
30	.7419	.5521	.4120	.3083	.2314	.1741	.1314	.0994	.0754	.0573	.0334	.0196	.0151	.0116	.0070	.0042	.0016	.0006	.0002	.0001
40	.6717	.4529	.3066	.2083	.1420	.0972	.0668	.0460	.0318	.0221	.0107	.0053	.0037	.0026	.0013	.0007	.0002	.0001	*	*
50	.6080	.3715	.2281	.1407	.0872	.0543	.0339	.0213	.0134	.0085	.0035	.0014	.0009	.0006	.0003	.0001	*	*	*	*
60	.5504	.3048	.1697	.0951	.0535	.0303	.0173	.0099	.0057	.0033	.0011	.0004	.0002	.0001	*	*	*	*	*	*

Note: n = number of periods, i = interest rate per period.

Table 4—Present Value of a n-Payment Annuity of $1 (PVEA)

Number of Periods	1%	2%	3%	4%	5%	6%	7%	8%	9%	10%	12%	14%	15%	16%	18%	20%	24%	28%	32%
1	0.9901	0.9804	0.9709	0.9615	0.9524	0.9434	0.9346	0.9259	0.9174	0.9091	0.8929	0.8772	0.8696	0.8621	0.8475	0.8333	0.8065	0.7813	0.7576
2	1.9704	1.9416	1.9135	1.8861	1.8594	1.8334	1.8080	1.7833	1.7591	1.7355	1.6901	1.6467	1.6257	1.6052	1.5656	1.5278	1.4568	1.3916	1.3315
3	2.9410	2.8839	2.8286	2.7751	2.7232	2.6730	2.6243	2.5771	2.5313	2.4869	2.4018	2.3216	2.2832	2.2459	2.1743	2.1065	1.9813	1.8684	1.7663
4	3.9020	3.8077	3.7171	3.6299	3.5460	3.4651	3.3872	3.3121	3.2397	3.1699	3.0373	2.9137	2.8550	2.7982	2.6901	2.5887	2.4043	2.2410	2.0957
5	4.8534	4.7135	4.5797	4.4518	4.3295	4.2124	4.1002	3.9927	3.8897	3.7908	3.6048	3.4331	3.3522	3.2743	3.1272	2.9906	2.7454	2.5320	2.3452
6	5.7955	5.6014	5.4172	5.2421	5.0757	4.9173	4.7665	4.6229	4.4859	4.3553	4.1114	3.8887	3.7845	3.6847	3.4976	3.3255	3.0205	2.7594	2.5342
7	6.7282	6.4720	6.2303	6.0021	5.7864	5.5824	5.3893	5.2064	5.0330	4.8684	4.5638	4.2883	4.1604	4.0386	3.8115	3.6046	3.2423	2.9370	2.6775
8	7.6517	7.3255	7.0197	6.7327	6.4632	6.2098	5.9713	5.7466	5.5348	5.3349	4.9676	4.6389	4.4873	4.3436	4.0776	3.8372	3.4212	3.0758	2.7860
9	8.5660	8.1622	7.7861	7.4353	7.1078	6.8017	6.5152	6.2469	5.9952	5.7590	5.3282	4.9464	4.7716	4.6065	4.3030	4.0310	3.5655	3.1842	2.8681
10	9.4713	8.9826	8.5302	8.1109	7.7217	7.3601	7.0236	6.7101	6.4177	6.1446	5.6502	5.2161	5.0188	4.8332	4.4941	4.1925	3.6819	3.2689	2.9304
11	10.3676	9.7868	9.2526	8.7605	8.3064	7.8869	7.4987	7.1390	6.8052	6.4951	5.9377	5.4527	5.2337	5.0286	4.6560	4.3271	3.7757	3.3351	2.9776
12	11.2551	10.5753	9.9540	9.3851	8.8633	8.3838	7.9427	7.5361	7.1607	6.8137	6.1944	5.6603	5.4206	5.1971	4.7932	4.4392	3.8514	3.3868	3.0133
13	12.1337	11.3484	10.6350	9.9856	9.3936	8.8527	8.3577	7.9038	7.4869	7.1034	6.4235	5.8424	5.5831	5.3423	4.9095	4.5327	3.9124	3.4272	3.0404
14	13.0037	12.1062	11.2961	10.5631	9.8986	9.2950	8.7455	8.2442	7.7862	7.3667	6.6282	6.0021	5.7245	5.4675	5.0081	4.6106	3.9616	3.4587	3.0609
15	13.8651	12.8493	11.9379	11.1184	10.3797	9.7122	9.1079	8.5595	8.0607	7.6061	6.8109	6.1422	5.8474	5.5755	5.0916	4.6755	4.0013	3.4834	3.0764
16	14.7179	13.5777	12.5611	11.6523	10.8378	10.1059	9.4466	8.8514	8.3126	7.8237	6.9740	6.2651	5.9542	5.6685	5.1624	4.7296	4.0333	3.5026	3.0882
17	15.5623	14.2919	13.1661	12.1657	11.2741	10.4773	9.7632	9.1216	8.5436	8.0216	7.1196	6.3729	6.0472	5.7487	5.2223	4.7746	4.0591	3.5177	3.0971
18	16.3983	14.9920	13.7535	12.6593	11.6896	10.8276	10.0591	9.3719	8.7556	8.2014	7.2497	6.4674	6.1280	5.8178	5.2732	4.8122	4.0799	3.5294	3.1039
19	17.2260	15.6785	14.3238	13.1339	12.0853	11.1581	10.3356	9.6036	8.9501	8.3649	7.3658	6.5504	6.1982	5.8775	5.3162	4.8435	4.0967	3.5386	3.1090
20	18.0456	16.3514	14.8775	13.5903	12.4622	11.4699	10.5940	9.8181	9.1285	8.5136	7.4694	6.6231	6.2593	5.9288	5.3527	4.8696	4.1103	3.5458	3.1129
21	18.8570	17.0112	15.4150	14.0292	12.8212	11.7641	10.8355	10.0168	9.2922	8.6487	7.5620	6.6870	6.3125	5.9731	5.3837	4.8913	4.1212	3.5514	3.1158
22	19.6604	17.6580	15.9369	14.4511	13.1630	12.0416	11.0612	10.2007	9.4424	8.7715	7.6446	6.7429	6.3587	6.0113	5.4099	4.9094	4.1300	3.5558	3.1180
23	20.4558	18.2922	16.4436	14.8568	13.4886	12.3034	11.2722	10.3711	9.5802	8.8832	7.7184	6.7921	6.3988	6.0442	5.4321	4.9245	4.1371	3.5592	3.1197
24	21.2434	18.9139	16.9355	15.2470	13.7986	12.5504	11.4693	10.5288	9.7066	8.9847	7.7843	6.8351	6.4338	6.0726	5.4509	4.9371	4.1428	3.5619	3.1210
25	22.0232	19.5235	17.4131	15.6221	14.0939	12.7834	11.6536	10.6748	9.8226	9.0770	7.8431	6.8729	6.4641	6.0971	5.4669	4.9476	4.1474	3.5640	3.1220
26	22.7952	20.1210	17.8768	15.9828	14.3752	13.0032	11.8258	10.8100	9.9290	9.1609	7.8957	6.9061	6.4906	6.1182	5.4804	4.9563	4.1511	3.5656	3.1227
27	23.5596	20.7069	18.3270	16.3296	14.6430	13.2105	11.9867	10.9352	10.0266	9.2372	7.9426	6.9352	6.5135	6.1364	5.4919	4.9636	4.1542	3.5669	3.1233
28	24.3164	21.2813	18.7641	16.6631	14.8981	13.4062	12.1371	11.0511	10.1161	9.3066	7.9844	6.9607	6.5335	6.1520	5.5016	4.9697	4.1566	3.5679	3.1237
29	25.0658	21.8444	19.1885	16.9837	15.1411	13.5907	12.2777	11.1584	10.1983	9.3696	8.0218	6.9830	6.5509	6.1656	5.5098	4.9747	4.1585	3.5687	3.1240
30	25.8077	22.3965	19.6004	17.2920	15.3725	13.7648	12.4090	11.2578	10.2737	9.4269	8.0552	7.0027	6.5660	6.1772	5.5168	4.9789	4.1601	3.5693	3.1242
40	32.8347	27.3555	23.1148	19.7928	17.1591	15.0463	13.3317	11.9246	10.7574	9.7791	8.2438	7.1050	6.6418	6.2335	5.5482	4.9966	4.1659	3.5712	3.1250
50	39.1961	31.4236	25.7298	21.4822	18.2559	15.7619	13.8007	12.2335	10.9617	9.9148	8.3045	7.1327	6.6605	6.2463	5.5541	4.9995	4.1666	3.5714	3.1250
60	44.9550	34.7609	27.6756	22.6235	18.9293	16.1614	14.0392	12.3766	11.0480	9.9672	8.3240	7.1401	6.6651	6.2492	5.5553	4.9999	4.1667	3.5714	3.1250

Note: n = number of periods; i = interest rate per period.

About the Author

Sugato Chakravarty is a professor and the head of the Department of Consumer Sciences and Retailing at Purdue University. He received his B.S. in chemical engineering from Jadavpur University (India), his M.S. in mechanical engineering from the University of Kentucky, and his Ph.D. in finance from the Kelley School of Business at Indiana University.

Over his career, Sugato has worn many hats. He has taught and researched in interdisciplinary fields of psychology, marketing, finance and mathematics. His primary research areas include market microstructure, banking and asset pricing involving stock, options and fixed income securities, and spans both domestic and foreign markets. Dr. Chakravarty's research has appeared in leading academic journals, including the *Journal of Finance, Journal of Financial Economics, Journal of Business, Journal of Financial and Quantitative Analysis, Journal of Empirical Finance*, and the *Journal of Financial Markets*. His work has been cited in leading newspapers like the *Wall Street Journal, Barron's, Investor's Business Daily* and others. His research has also been used as evidence in hearings by the U.S. Congress. He serves as Associate Editor of the *Journal of Financial Markets*. Dr. Chakravarty has won research awards including the Barclay's Global Investors Research Award for the best paper on Australasian Markets (with P. Kalev and L. Pham) and the Best Paper Award (with B. Van Ness and R. Van Ness) at the Eastern Finance Annual Conference. He has also won a Q-group Research award and is listed in the *Marquis Who's Who in American Education*. He is probably best known for his work on the decimalization of stock prices, insider trading and stealth trading. According to Harzing's *Publish or Perish* citation tracking software, Dr. Chakravarty's research has been cited well over 1,000 times. At Purdue, he is best known for popularizing a Personal Finance course that teaches undergraduates the basic skills of money management, credit, insurance, and retirement. The course also covers popular and current topics relating them to the basic principles. The class is structured around the football cliche: "*Offense wins games but defense wins championships.*" Dr. Chakravarty argues that in order to win the game of life one needs to have solid offensive and defensive strategies. Investments (including those for retirement) is an offensive strategy while insurance is a defensive strategy. Credit plays the role of good special teams in that a judicious use of credit can move the line of scrimmage from one's 20-yard line to the 45 or 50 yard line making it easier to score a personal finance touchdown. The class boasts enrollments of over 400 students every semester and is an elective in almost all majors across the West Lafayette campus. Dr. Chakravarty loves to spend time with his family including his wife, two dogs, three cats, and lots of colorful tropical fish. He plays his guitar, piano, and mouth harp whenever the mood hits him.

Index

Post-course Questionnaire

Post-course Questionnaire

Name: _____

1. I believe investing is only for those with lots of money.
   a. Strongly disagree
   b. Disagree
   c. Could go either way
   d. Agree
   e. Strongly agree

2. Time value of money (TVM) concepts are a total waste of my time. I know I will never use them in my life.
   a. Strongly disagree
   b. Disagree
   c. Could go either way
   d. Agree
   e. Strongly agree

3. I know how to pick stocks/mutual funds.
   a. Strongly disagree
   b. Disagree
   c. Could go either way
   d. Agree
   e. Strongly agree

4. I believe that mutual funds are the only way to invest—individual stocks are for the   professional investors only.
   a. Strongly disagree
   b. Disagree
   c. Could go either way
   d. Agree
   e. Strongly agree

5. I know what an ETF is.
   a. Strongly disagree
   b. Disagree
   c. Could go either way
   d. Agree
   e. Strongly agree

6. I am not in favor of making investment decisions myself. In the future, I plan to hire professional financial planners to make those decisions on my behalf.
   a. Strongly disagree
   b. Disagree
   c. Could go either way
   d. Agree
   e. Strongly agree

7. Only qualified professionals should be making investment decisions—not individuals like me.
   a. Strongly disagree
   b. Disagree
   c. Could go either way
   d. Agree
   e. Strongly agree

8. Credit cards are wonderful things. I wish I had more of them.
   a. Strongly disagree
   b. Disagree
   c. Could go either way
   d. Agree
   e. Strongly agree

9. Checking my credit report is a waste of my time.
   a. Strongly disagree
   b. Disagree
   c. Could go either way
   d. Agree
   e. Strongly agree

10. I know all there is to know about insurance. The class cannot teach me anything new.
    a. Strongly disagree
    b. Disagree
    c. Could go either way
    d. Agree
    e. Strongly agree

11. I know what a Roth IRA is.
    a. Strongly disagree
    b. Disagree
    c. Could go either way
    d. Agree
    e. Strongly agree

12. I believe that I am too young to think about planning for retirement. I will consider it when I am older and have money to spare.
    a. Strongly disagree
    b. Disagree
    c. Could go either way
    d. Agree
    e. Strongly agree